FUNDAMENTALS OF REAL ESTATE INVESTMENT
second edition

AUSTIN J. JAFFE
Pennsylvania State University

C. F. SIRMANS
Louisiana State University

PRENTICE HALL, Englewood Cliffs, New Jersey 07632

Library of Congress Cataloging-in-Publication Data

Jaffe, Austin J.
   Fundamentals of real estate investment/Austin J. Jaffe, C. F.
Sirmans.—2nd ed.
     p. cm.
   Includes bibliographies and index.
   ISBN 0-13-343476-1
   1. Real estate investment. I. Sirmans, C. F. II. Title.
HD1382.5.J32 1989
332.63'24—dc19   88-7981
                               CIP

Editorial/production supervision: *Lisa Schulz Garboski*
Cover design: *Lundgren Graphics, Ltd.*
Manufacturing buyer: *Margaret Rizzi*

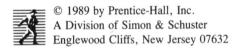 © 1989 by Prentice-Hall, Inc.
A Division of Simon & Schuster
Englewood Cliffs, New Jersey 07632

Printed in the United States of America

10 9 8 7 6 5 4 3 2 1

ISBN   0-13-343476-1

Prentice-Hall International (UK) Limited, *London*
Prentice-Hall of Australia Pty. Limited, *Sydney*
Prentice-Hall Canada Inc., *Toronto*
Prentice-Hall Hispanoamericana, S.A., *Mexico*
Prentice-Hall of India Private Limited, *New Delhi*
Prentice-Hall of Japan, Inc., *Tokyo*
Simon & Schuster Asia Pte. Ltd., *Singapore*
Editora Prentice-Hall do Brasil, Ltda., *Rio de Janeiro*

CONTENTS

Part II   The Investment Environment

Part III   Financial Analysis

Part V Conclusion

PREFACE

This second edition of *Fundamentals of Real Estate Investment* is intended to provide an introduction to the real estate investment process. This process is a series of organized and coordinated steps that investors may follow to systematically analyze potential real estate investments in the real world. Several topical areas are treated within the discussion, including the investment decision, the environment for investing, the development of cash flow statements, and the analysis of investment criteria. In the end, the investor must make a choice between various alternatives. This is what real estate investment analysis is all about. By following the investment process developed in this book, we believe that the choice can be made much easier and that the results will be more consistent with expectations.

The basis for the book is the equity valuation model. This approach was developed in the late 1960s and early 1970s and effectively serves as a historical turning point in the analysis of real estate investments. The use of discounted cash flow models permitted the explicit modeling of many factors relevant to the investment that previously had been neglected or grossly approximated. Using the equity valuation model, investors may estimate several parameter values and, more importantly, alter their estimates repeatedly to see what the various impacts are on the outputs of the analysis.

There have been many developments in the field over the past thirty years. One of the most noticeable changes is in the area of tax law. Major changes in the law governing the treatment of depreciation, capital gains, minimum taxes, recapture, and other items have occurred with tax legislation in 1976, 1981, 1984, and 1986. *Fundamentals of Real Estate Investment* provides the latest tax treatment of real estate investments. In addition, there have been major developments in the areas of real estate finance, land use law, financial theory, and risk analysis. This book surveys many of these developments to provide an overview of these topics.

Those students interested in a more detailed analysis are referred to the predecessor of this book, *Real Estate Investment Decision Making* (Prentice-Hall, Inc., 1982). In our earlier book, more extensive treatment is provided of market, legal, financial, and tax analyses. In addition, a broader discussion is provided of the history of real estate investment analysis, the real estate investment criteria, risk analysis, and several of the advanced tools for investment analysis.

Fundamentals of Real Estate Investment is divided into five parts. Part I provides a discussion of some basic concepts, including an overview of the real estate investment process, risk analysis, and the time value of money. The real estate investment process using the equity valuation model forms the foundation for the book. Part II describes the investment environment. Separate chapters are provided for each of the major environments: market analysis, legal analysis, financing analysis, and tax analysis.

Part III outlines the financial analysis requirements for real estate investors and is the core of the book. There are three types of decisions the investor confronts: operating decisions, financing decisions, and reversion decisions. While some of these decisions are made prior to the acquisition of the investment, several are required subsequent to purchase. Part IV is devoted to investment criteria and the production of financial output to assist in making the investment decision. Several criteria are presented, including the traditional rules of thumb, ratios, and appraisal techniques. In addition, the well-known discounted cash flow models called "net present value" and "internal rate of return" are provided. A discussion of the importance of risk analysis is also included and several techniques are illustrated. Finally, an extensive case study in Chapter 14 provides a real world example of how this analysis may be directly applied to making investment decisions. Part V provides a brief conclusion, emphasizing several important points in the book and raising questions and issues that hopefully may be answered in the future.

Throughout the book, there are numerous examples and illustrations. In addition to the case study in Chapter 14, each chapter contains several illustrations within the text as well as numerous questions and problems at the end. Real estate investing is a numbers game in some respects, and students must "get their hands dirty" by doing the basic calculations. References are also included for students who seek additional reading material and a broader exposure to the field.

In addition to the end-of-chapter material, this book is supported with an Instructor's Manual containing a variety of resources to assist in the teaching of this material. Suggested answers to the questions and problems are provided, as well as overheads and sample test questions.

Students should have had an introduction to economics, if possible, before enrolling in this course. In addition, it is helpful if students have had a course in financial management, although this is not required. Some math is used but only basic algebra. Also, experience using calculators is expected since some of the problems are extensive.

The authors wish to thank colleagues at various schools and in various real estate businesses for their suggestions and criticisms on this and earlier versions of the manuscript.

It is especially gratifying when others offer compliments based upon portions that were helpful in actual real estate practice. The authors are also indebted to scores of classes over the past ten years at five national universities where our students have demanded high quality treatment of these issues. This process has led to a better manuscript.

The authors also wish to thank Jean Campbell, Krisandra Guidry, and Mary Fabre for their help with the computational material in the book, including the testing and verification of the solutions to the problems. Additionally, a special thanks to Jill Szymanski for her valuable assistance in this revision process. We also wish to thank the the secretarial staffs, especially Bessie Aveva, at our respective schools as well as the editors and staff at Prentice Hall. Thanks also to our wives, who put up with our late nights and weekends at the office so that we might complete this project.

While every effort has been made to make this manuscript error-free, inevitably, some errors go undetected. The authors wish to thank reviewers and other readers without indictment; remaining errors are the sole responsibility of the authors. Finders are encouraged to send their troves to the authors with our sincere thanks.

Austin J. Jaffe
C. F. Sirmans

1

THE INVESTMENT DECISION

Value is at the heart of the real estate investment decision. The main question to be answered in this text is: *How do real estate investors determine the price they are willing to pay for a property they want to buy and how is the investment decision made?* The *value* of an investment can be broadly defined as the present worth of the future benefits from owning an investment. Thus value represents the present worth of the income that an investment is expected to generate.

We must analyze the real estate project to determine the present worth of the benefits in view of our objectives, goals, and constraints. This is called the *investment value* of property. We compare this investment value with the *market value* of the investment, the price that participants in the marketplace are willing to pay for the investment, in order to make the investment decision.

This chapter gives an overview of the real estate investment decision. The *real estate investment process* provides the real estate investor with a systematic method for considering the many contingencies on which the value and thus the investment decision in income-producing property depend. This investment process applies to *all* types of income-producing real estate, including, for example, apartment complexes, office buildings, income-producing single-family projects, shopping centers, industrial properties, and vacant land. This process takes the investor through the acquisition phase, the operations phase, and the disposition phase. Within each of these various stages, decisions that have an impact on the overall investment decision must be made.

SOME BASIC INVESTMENT CONCEPTS

This section introduces some basic investment concepts: the definition of investing, the risk-return trade-off underlying investment decisions, the investor objectives, and the concept of value.

Investing: A Definition

The investment decision is essentially a choice between consumption in the present and consumption at a future time. Investment is, in essence, present sacrifice for expected future benefit. Because the present is relatively well known and the future is uncertain, investment decisions represent *certain sacrifice* for *uncertain benefits*. In the case of income-producing real estate, these benefits take the form of future cash flows or increases in property values or both. As will be demonstrated later, the possibility of maximizing wealth motivates the purchase of property rights in an income-producing asset.

Real estate valuation involves the problem of evaluating alternative future cash flows and converting these flows into value estimates. The investment decision is based on expectations regarding

1. The timing of the expected cash outflows and inflows
2. The magnitude of the expected cash outflows and inflows
3. The riskiness of the expected cash outflows and inflows

Timing is important because the inflows or outflows that occur affect the investment value and thus the wealth position of the owner, who trades present money for future money. To induce this trade, however, there must be compensation for the "time value of money." Of course, the rate of compensation varies from investor to investor. The mechanics of compound interest demonstrate the precise effects that cash flows have on value as a result of differences in timing. The time element for investment decisions is thus easily captured through the "discounting" of the expected future inflows.

The Risk-Return Trade-Off

Another key factor influencing the investment decision is risk. Real estate investment decisions involve many complex, dynamic, and uncertain elements. The degree of uncertainty can range from the deterministic situation where all variables are known to highly probabilistic situations where little information is available about many variables. The time dimension can range from static to dynamic, with complexity measured in terms of the number of variables to be analyzed in the investment decision.

**Exhibit 1-1   Examples of Alternative
                Investors' Objectives**

Some investors may have personal or rather unusual investment objectives in addition to those mentioned in the text. For example, consider the investor who purchases real estate because he or she obtains pleasure from driving by the apartment building and showing it off to friends. Or the investor who purchases property because in the local business community, owners of large parcels tend to be highly regarded. Finally, consider the investor who is only interested in certain types of property such as small apartment buildings, and only if they are located on a specific street.

While these objectives may seem strange to some individuals, they may be the basic reasons that motivate investors. To the extent that *utility* or satisfaction is perceived by the investor at the time of the real estate acquisition, these objectives make as much sense as do any of the more conventional and more typical financial objectives. In such cases, the benefits from these factors may aid in the decision as to whether an investment should be made.

There are two basic sources of financial returns from owning income-producing real estate: the annual cash flow from operations and the cash flow from the disposition of the investment at the end of ownership (typically, sale). Estimates of both the annual income and the receipts from disposition are necessary in order to determine the value of the asset. Both are seldom precisely known. Future operating cash flows are uncertain and a real estate investment has no fixed future price.

The model of real estate investment decision making presented in this text rests on the assumption that *cash flow*—the dollars remaining after all prior claims are met—serves as the basis for investment decisions. Claims include operating expenses, financing costs, and taxes. This after-tax cash flow is the one valued by investors in the market.

The investor tries to (1) evaluate the circumstances that affect a real estate investment's cash flows and (2) enumerate the key events on which such cash flows are contingent. For example, the cash flow from an apartment project depends on the rents that can be charged, which in turn is related to supply and demand conditions in the apartment rental market. These contingencies must be taken into account in order to value an investment project properly.

Obviously, many potentially relevant events may affect an investment. Since the analyst must focus on the most relevant, three problems arise, including how to

1. Identify the contingencies on which cash flows are dependent
2. Estimate the cash flow from a real estate project once the contingencies have been identified
3. Convert the cash flow estimates into a value

Investor Objectives

Every investor should have an overall financial plan based on current financial resources and on reasonable expectations of future financial position and income. It is important to prepare an investment plan that correlates with the other segments of the investor's financial plan and incorporates strategies, goals, and objectives to meet potential requirements and any legal restrictions.

Real estate investing that can satisfy objectives includes one, all, or any combination of the following:

1. Means of building an estate
2. Pride of ownership
3. Hedge against inflation
4. Desired rate of return on equity invested

Investment opportunities in real estate vary enough in size and character to meet almost every financial constraint and investment objective.

The identification of the appropriate objective or objectives is crucial to effective decision making. It is clear that all investment opportunities will not appeal to all investors. A major downfall is the failure to understand and specify objectives prior to the commitment of funds to an investment. As we will see in Chapter 2, *we assume that the basic investor objective is wealth maximization.*

Often the investor sees only the rewards associated with a real estate investment and ignores the risks. However, because the risk-return trade-off is faced in all investment decisions, the following basic definitions are important:

Risk is the variation in the expected future benefits.

Return is the amount of inflow generated by an investment each year. There are numerous levels of return. The most important from the equity investor's viewpoint is the after-tax cash flows.

Rate of return is the relationship between the cash flows and the amount invested, typically measured in a percentage per year on the equity.

Risk analysis is the orderly process of identifying the contingencies on which the success of an investment depends.

There are several general categories of risk associated with a real estate investment, as we will see. In addition, there is a positive relationship between the amount of risk and the expected return. It is difficult to determine the level of risk to assume. However, a general principle applies to investment decision making: *Risk and expected return are directly related to each other.* The primary task of the real estate investor is to identify and evaluate the major factors contributing to expected risk and return.

Value

Value is defined as the present worth of rights to future benefits arising from ownership. This definition implies the necessity to express the future benefits in dollars and then discount them to a present amount at the appropriate rate, a capitalization process most commonly known as the income approach to value. To apply this technique correctly, two elements are imperative: (1) an accurate forecast of the future benefits expressed in terms of dollars and (2) the selection of the appropriate rate at which to discount the benefits.

There are two major value concepts of concern: market value and investment value.

Market value represents the present value of the anticipated benefits from the market's perspective. The various investors in the marketplace view the risk-return trade-off and arrive at expectations of the returns and the risks associated with an investment. The expectations are then converted into a value.

Since value depends on the discounted future benefits, it is affected by expectations. So value can be defined in terms of the present worth of the rights to the income stream. It is therefore assumed that the property is bought for the right to the income stream that will be generated.

Since this text is particularly concerned with *investment value,* we must determine the maximum price for a particular interest that an investor is willing to pay. Turvey called investment value the "ceiling price" and asked:

> What determines a purchaser's ceiling price for a particular interest? In the case of a purchaser who is an investor and buys the interest for the income he expects to receive from it, his ceiling price will equal the present value to him of the anticipated net income discounted at a rate of interest equal to the yield obtainable on alternative investments with similar characteristics. This rate of interest will thus reflect not only the riskiness of the investment, the expected duration of the income and so on, but also the price at which alternative investment interests can be acquired. The present value of the interest to the purchaser consequently reflects the attraction of investment in alternative properties.[1]

To summarize the basic investment principles, we have defined *investing* as the sacrifice of certain outflows for expected, but risky, inflows. Obviously there is particular concern with the expected after-tax inflow in relation to

---

[1] Ralph Turvey, *The Economics of Real Property* (London: Allen & Unwin, 1957), pp. 8–9.

the amount of outflow (equity). Risk and return tend to go hand in hand, as investments with high expected returns typically have high expected risks. So it is wise to evaluate the expected risk-return trade-off for an investment according to subjective preferences and arrive at an investment value. This investment value is then compared with the market value of the investment.

THE REAL ESTATE INVESTMENT PROCESS

Any successful real estate investment requires careful analysis of the many contingencies on which the decision depends. Figure 1-1 outlines the *real estate investment process*. The five basic steps that lead to the final investment decision can be summarized as follows:

1. Identify the goals, objectives, and constraints of the various participants in the investment process which an investment must satisfy in order to be acceptable.
2. Analyze the overall investment environment—market, legal, financing, and tax— in which the investment decision must be made.
3. Forecast the expected future benefits and costs (cash flows) arising from the ownership of the investment.
4. Apply appropriate decision-making criteria to compare the benefits with the costs of the investment. An analysis must be carefully developed to be relatively certain of the investment's ability to meet the constraints and objectives of *all* the participants in the investment process.
5. Accept or reject the investment under the assumptions of the input variables.

The purpose of the investment process is to discover whether a specific investment is feasible. A real estate investment is feasible when the investor determines that there is a reasonable likelihood of satisfying explicit investment objectives which must be tested against a specific set of constraints.[2]

Thus the investment process is simply a structure whereby the expected risks and expected returns can be analyzed.

Step 1: Identifying Investor Objectives

The *first step* in the investment process is to identify the goals, objectives, and constraints of the four major participants in a real estate investment: the equity investor, the mortgage lender, the user of the real estate (the tenant), and the government (federal, state, and local). Figure 1-2 outlines some of the relationships between them.

Each participant has different, and often conflicting, objectives for entering into the investment. And each participant places constraints and restric-

---

[2] James A. Graaskamp, *A Guide to Feasibility Analysis* (Chicago: Society of Real Estate Appraisers, 1980).

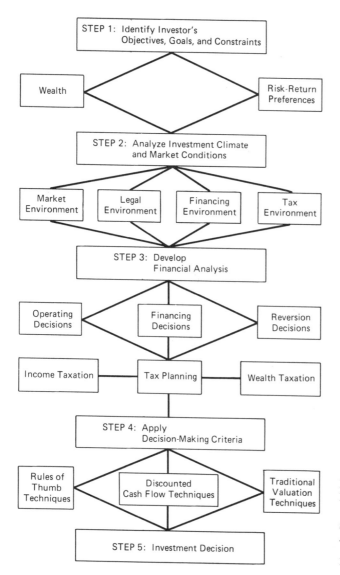

Figure 1-1   Real Estate Investment Process.

Source: Austin J. Jaffe and C. F. Sirmans, *Real Estate Investment Decision Making*, 1982, p. 8. Reprinted by permission of Prentice-Hall, Inc., Englewood Cliffs, N.J.

tions on the feasibility (the probability of financial success) of a real estate investment. All the constraints must be carefully analyzed when considering a real estate investment because failure to do so will be potentially disastrous.

The equity investor.   The equity investor is the decision maker who chooses the specific form of business entity appropriate for the ownership of an investment. These forms include ownership as an individual, a partnership (limited or general), a corporation, a real estate investment trust, a syndication,

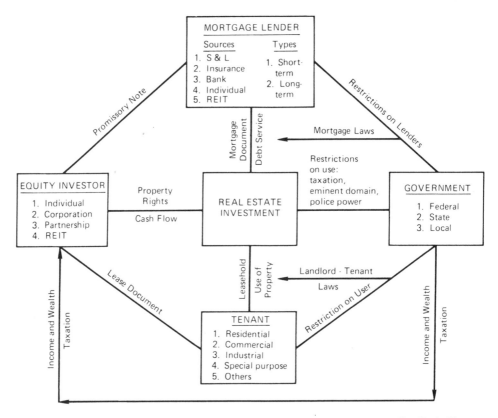

Source: C. F. Sirmans and Austin J. Jaffe, *The Complete Real Estate Investment Handbook, 2/e,*
1984, p. 6. Reprinted by permission of Prentice-Hall, Inc., Englewood Cliffs, N.J.

Figure 1-2   Participants in The Real Estate Investment Process.

and so forth. All of these business entities have various advantages and disadvantages, which we will examine later.

The equity investor is interested in the amount of cash flow from an
investment and must be certain of having the legal right to the cash flow.
The legal viewpoints related to ownership of real estate rights are extremely
important in investment decision making.

The mortgage lender.   The second major participant in the real estate
investment process is the mortgage lender. Most real estate investments use
a substantial amount of borrowed funds. In order to borrow a substantial
amount of funds, the borrower (equity investor) typically has to pledge the
real estate as security for the debt. The mortgage lender is obviously interested
in the recovery of the amount lent as well as in earning a rate of return on
the loan. To the mortgage lender, the mortgage is an investment.

The tenant.   The third major participant is the user of the real estate—the tenant who buys the immediate right of possession from the landlord (equity investor) in exchange for the payment of consideration (rent). The tenant's requirements must be carefully analyzed, for without the tenant, there is no income from the real estate investment.

The *lease* is the document that links the equity investor, the investment, and the tenant. The laws governing leases differ substantially between states, and therefore no legal decision should be made without specific counsel in the jurisdiction in which the property is located.

The government.   The fourth major participant in a real estate investment is the government. All levels—federal, state, and local—have an impact on the real estate investment decision-making process. The government not only influences the relationships between the equity investor, the mortgage lender, and the tenant but also places restrictions on the use of the real estate investment.

Step 2: Environment for Decision Making

The *second step* in the investment process involves analysis of the overall climate affecting the investment. This step encompasses four distinct areas of analysis: the market environment, legal environment, financing environment, and tax environment.

More specifically, this step is concerned with the examination of business risk for a specific investment. As one of the major categories of risk to which a real estate investor is exposed, *business risk* is defined as the variability of the expected net income from a real estate investment. An investment produces two potential sources of net income: the annual flow from operations and the flow from the reversion (typically, sale). Market analysis is aimed at identifying the factors, and the probability of their occurrence, that influence net income. The key factors are rents, vacancies, operating expenses, and expected future selling price at the end of the holding period.

The market environment.   An understanding of the supply and demand forces that influence the feasibility of a particular investment is extremely important. Market analysis must take into account these forces at the national, state, and local levels.

The demand for real estate is derived from the demand for the goods and services that it provides. For example, the demand for residential properties is derived from the demand for housing services; the demand for shopping centers is derived from the demand for retail goods, such as clothes and shoes that the stores will provide; the demand for office buildings is derived from the demand for professional services, such as medical and dental care.

Real estate investors often believe that the real estate itself has an intrinsic value. However, value comes from the services that a real estate investment provides. Therefore the lesson is to analyze the correct source of demand. If the investor knows six dentists who demand an office building, the task is much easier. All that is necessary is to determine the specific characteristics that they require in their offices. If tenants are not known, the analyst might infer that there is a demand for office buildings because of increases in aggregate statistics, such as population, income, and employment. Obviously, the latter situation entails substantially more uncertainty than the former. All too often *secondary data* are used to infer demand conditions.

The real estate market is divided into numerous submarkets, such as the residential, industrial, commercial, and vacant land markets. Obviously, even these groups can be subdivided further. The market can also be divided by size of project, by location, or by type of structure. All of these constitute the market environment and should not be overlooked.

Another common error that the analyst makes is the failure to consider *both* sides of the market. Often the analyst will consider only the demand side while ignoring the supply side. *The analyst must identify the appropriate submarket in which a real estate investment is competing or will compete (as in the case of a proposed development) and identify the supply and demand influences operating in that market.*

Market analysis is frequently concerned with a reduction of aggregate data such as population, employment, and income to factors that are more relevant to a particular project. To a great extent, however, it deals with factors beyond the investor's control.

One of the purposes of market analysis is to identify the user of the services provided by the investment. The characteristics and preferences of potential tenants must be carefully analyzed to identify the demand for any given real estate project appropriately. Other factors to be considered are the physical and structural characteristics of the site, the condition of improvements, transportation access, and personal-response factors such as security. All of these attributes are part of the "service" that the project supplies to meet the potential demand.

The legal environment. The legal environment plays a major role in investment analysis. Whereas market analysis is concerned with the economic constraints on an investment, analysis of the legal environment examines the legal constraints. From a legal perspective, real estate is a complex commodity. As Figure 1-2 indicates, the real estate investment process involves many legal relationships between the various participants. Legal constraints are imposed on the real estate, the equity investor, the mortgage lender, and the tenant. All levels of government impose different legal constraints on the investment.

One of the major legal decisions concerns the choice of business entity for undertaking the investment. The most popular forms are individual ownership, the partnership, and the corporation. Since most real estate investments involve large sums of capital, investors typically form a business entity. Each entity has advantages and disadvantages, and factors such as liability, management, ease of transferability, and taxation greatly influence the decision.

The ownership of real estate provides certain property rights. Examples are the right to use and the right to sell the property. The quality and quantity of property rights associated with the ownership of real estate are of great concern because these rights are valued in the real estate market. Any limitation on these rights reduces the investment's value.

Limitations on property rights may stem from public and private sources. Public influences on property rights are the result of some governmental action. At the federal government level, the greatest impact consists of income and wealth taxation. At the local government level, the greatest impact consists of various forms of land-use controls. Private sources may curtail property rights by placing deed restrictions to limit the use of the real estate.

The property rights in real estate can be "sold" separately. In the case of income-producing real estate, the owner "sells" the right of use to the tenant. In return, the tenant pays the owner a price (rent). A potential investment should be carefully investigated as to limitations on the property rights in order to preclude eventual losses.

Another major area of concern is the relationship with the user of the real estate—the tenant. This relationship is specified in the *lease document*. Here the investor must be aware that the lease covers a great deal more than simply the amount of rent due each month. To be feasible, an investment must satisfy the constraints of the legal environment.

One of the most difficult areas in real estate investing is the analysis of the sociopolitical aspects of the legal environment. Any real estate investment (particularly a large-scale development) can affect the well-being of society as a whole. While there may be a demand for a particular project and while the project may be "legal," public sentiment against the project may be a complicating factor.

The relationship of real estate investment to the community as well as the environment within the realm of the community's own interests should be carefully analyzed, as these values must be dealt with in the decision-making process. In many cases, the investor must be prepared to comment on the compatibility of an investment with community standards and expectations. What is technically legal at any given time may not be politically permissible. Such considerations can place constraints on the total feasibility of a particular real estate investment.

The financing environment.   Every real estate investment involves the use of money. There are two sources: debt and equity. A real estate investor could use all equity or all debt or some combination of the two. This last situation is the typical case.

To be feasible, a real estate investment must provide enough income to cover the cost of debt and equity. The cost of borrowing is generally referred to as the interest rate. The cost of equity is the required rate of return on the equity position. This *equity yield* could be measured on a before- or after-tax basis. We will argue for the after-tax rate as being the most appropriate.

On the debt side, the mortgage investor (lender) has traditionally accepted a fixed rate of interest and a sinking fund payback of the amount lent over the mortgage maturity—i.e., fixed-rate, amortizing loans. In recent years there have been numerous variations in mortgage-lending practices, such as variable rate loans and equity participation loans. The changes have been prompted, for the most part, by unexpected inflation in the economy.

On the equity side, investors have used a wide variety of techniques to obtain the necessary equity funds. The equity position in a real estate investment is expected to have more risk exposure than the mortgage position because the equity claim is, in essence, the "residual" claim associated with the investment. The equity position could receive cash inflow in the form of either periodic cash flow or an expected capital gain (or some combination).

Both debt and equity capital tend to flow into those sources that have the highest expected rate of return for a given level of risk. For example, if the return on capital increases in some segment of the financial market, lenders (or equity) investors may move funds out of real estate into this other segment. As a result of these shifts in financial markets, we see movements upward and downward in the amount of funds (both debt and equity) invested in the real estate market.

The tax environment. One of the most important governmental influences in investment decisions is the power of taxation. Taxation of the incomes of individuals and businesses by the federal government was not permitted under the U.S. Constitution until the passage of the Sixteenth Amendment in 1913. The Congress enacts the tax laws that specify how the tax is to be determined. The Internal Revenue Service (IRS) administrates the laws, collects taxes, and issues regulations implementing and interpreting the tax laws. There exists a special court, the Tax Court, in which taxpayers may contest the rules and decisions of the IRS.

The influence of taxes is important in making the investment decision, since taxes influence the amount of cash flow from an investment. Recall that we defined *investing* as the outflow of cash (equity from the investor's perspective) in return for expected cash inflow. The important cash inflow is the amount left after taxes have been paid.

The government is interested in the amount of taxable income (and thus taxes), whereas the investor is interested in the after-tax cash flow. These are not measured in the same way. An investor must carefully analyze the tax environment in order to make correct investment decisions.

**TABLE 1-1 Expected Cash Flow from Operation
for Each Year**

	Potential gross income (PGI)
minus	Vacancy and bad debt allowance (VBD)
plus	Miscellaneous income (MI)
equals	Effective gross income (EGI)
minus	Operating expenses (OE)
equals	Net operating income (NOI)
minus	Debt service (DS)
equals	Before-tax cash flow (BTCF)
minus	**Taxes (tax savings) from operation (T)**[*]
equals	After-tax cash flow (ATCF)

[*] See Table 1-2.

Step 3: Cash Flow Forecasting

As outlined in Figure 1-1, the *third step* in the real estate investment process
is to forecast the expected cash flows from an investment. The cash flows
must be forecast for the period of time during which the investment is expected
to be held. Because cash flows from the investment are not known, the investment decision is based on reasonable expectations.

There are two major sources of cash flows from a real estate investment—
the annual cash flow from rental collections and *the cash flow from the disposition (typically, sale) of the investment.* The cash flow that is of greater interest
is the amount left after all costs of operating and selling the investment have
been paid. These include operating expenses, payments on mortgage debt,
and income taxes.

Cash flow from operation.   Table 1-1 measures the *expected annual
cash flow* from the operation of a real estate investment. Table 1-2 measures

**TABLE 1-2 Expected Taxes from Operation
for Each Year**

	Effective gross income (EGI)
minus	Operating expenses (OE)
equals	Net operating income (NOI)
minus	Interest on debt (I)
minus	Depreciation deduction (D)
minus	Amortized financing costs (AFC)
plus	Replacement reserves (RR)
equals	Ordinary taxable income (OTI)
times	Investor's marginal tax rate (τ)
equals	**Taxes (tax savings) from operation (T)**

the expected *taxable income* from operation. *The equity investor is interested in the cash flow, whereas the government is interested in the taxable income.* The two income streams are related by the taxes due from operation. They are *not* the same.

   Potential Gross Income.   The starting point in calculating the cash flow from operation each year is the *potential gross income (PGI)*. PGI is the estimated rent per unit for each year multiplied by the number of units available for rent. For example, if a shopping center has 100,000 square feet of rentable area on which the expected rent is $8 per square foot per year, the PGI would be $800,000 for that year.

   Effective Gross Income.   Since it is unlikely that an investment will be completely occupied all year round or that all rents will be collected, an allowance for vacancy and bad debt must be deducted. There may also be miscellaneous income from other types of operation, such as parking space rentals. This miscellaneous income would be added to PGI. The net effect of these items results in *effective gross income (EGI)*.

   Net Operating Income.   From the EGI, the operating expenses are deducted to result in *net operating income (NOI)*. Operating expenses include those items associated with operating the investment, such as repairs, management fees, property taxes, insurance, advertising fees, and utilities.

   Before-Tax Cash Flow.   The debt service (payment on mortgage debt) is subtracted from net operating income to yield *before-tax cash flow (BTCF)*. The final step in the calculation of the *after-tax cash flow (ATCF)* is the subtraction of the income taxes due on operation from the BTCF. The ATCF is what concerns the equity investor.

   After-Tax Cash Flow.   Table 1-2 calculates the *ordinary taxable income (OTI)* and *taxes from operation (T)*.[3] The calculation of taxable income differs in several ways from the calculation of cash flow. For tax purposes, the investor is allowed to deduct the operating expenses from the gross income. While interest on mortgage debts is tax deductible, the principal portion of any debt service is not. A deduction for depreciation of the investment is also permitted. This is not a cash outlay, however, it is simply an allowance for tax purposes.

   The next item in the calculation of taxable income is the amortized financing costs, or the costs associated with placing a mortgage against an investment. Although these costs cannot be deducted in the year incurred, they can be amortized (written off) over the life of the mortgage debt. The final adjustment is the replacement reserves. These represent an allowance for the replacing

----

   [3] A real estate investment can also generate other types of taxes from operation. These will be examined in Chapter 7.

TABLE 1-3   **Expected Cash Flow from Sale of an Investment**

	Expected selling price (SP)
minus	Selling expenses (SE)
equals	Net sale proceeds (NSP)
minus	Unpaid mortgage balance (UM)
equals	Before-tax equity reversion (BTER)
minus	Taxes due on sale (T')*
equals	After-tax equity reversion (ATER)

* See Table 1-4.

of personal property. While these reserves may represent cash flow items, they are not deductible for tax purposes.

The taxes from operation are estimated by multiplying the taxable income by the marginal tax rate. In addition to these ordinary income taxes, there may be some minimum tax due on what is known as tax-preference income. These concepts will be examined in other chapters.

Cash flow from reversion.   The second source of cash flow comes from the disposition (typically, sale) of the investment. Since real estate is usually held for a limited period, this cash flow must be forecast in addition to the cash flow from operation. Table 1-3 measures the cash flow from the sale. Table 1-4 measures the taxable income and taxes due on the sale.

As we will discuss in upcoming chapters, there are other methods of disposition (such as tax-deferred exchanges), but the primary method is that of sale. These other methods of disposition simply complicate the investment model. However, we will outline these other methods and demonstrate their impact on the investment decision.

TABLE 1-4   **Expected Taxes Due on Sale of an Investment**

TAXABLE INCOME	
	Expected selling price (SP)
minus	Selling expenses (SE)
equals	Amount realized (AR)
minus	Adjusted basis (AB)
equals	Total gain on sale (TG)

TAXES DUE ON SALE	
	Total gain (TG)
times	Investor's marginal tax rate (τ)
equals	Taxes due on sale (T')

Selling Price. The starting point in the calculation of both cash flow and taxable income is the expected future selling price. Remember that because the investment decision is being made now, it is based on the expected inflows. So we forecast the expected change in value to determine the anticipated selling price at the end of the holding period.

Net Sales Proceeds. Selling expenses associated with the disposition of the investment are deducted from the expected selling price. Selling expenses include brokerage fees, legal fees, and other costs associated with the disposition (sale) of the property. The result is the net sales proceeds (NSP).

Before-Tax Equity Reversion. The before-tax equity reversion (BTER) is the net sale proceeds minus the unpaid mortgage (UM) balance. Most mortgage loans call for the repayment of the loan when an investment is sold. So if the investment is sold prior to the mortgage maturity, the outstanding balance must be paid.

After-Tax Equity Reversion. The final step in calculating the cash flows from sale is the deduction of any taxes that are due.

Table 1-4 shows how to calculate taxes due on the sale of an investment. To begin, we deduct expected selling expenses from the selling price to obtain the amount realized. Then we deduct the adjusted basis from the amount realized to arrive at the total gain on sale. The adjusted basis is the original cost plus the cost of capital improvements minus the total cumulative depreciation deductions.

The taxable income from sale is the amount of the total gain. This taxable income is then multiplied by the investor's marginal tax rate to result in the taxes due on sale.

Referring again to Table 1-3, we see that the taxes due on sale are then subtracted from the before-tax equity reversion to result in the after-tax cash flow from the sale (ATER) of the investment.

Using these estimates of the expected cash flow from operation and the cash flow from sale, the investor is now prepared to apply various criteria to examine the relationship between cash inflows and cash outflows.

Step 4: Criteria for Decision Making

The *fourth step* in the investment process is to apply the decision-making criteria. Compare the benefits with the costs and ask: *How much should be paid?* Alternatively, if a certain price is paid, what is the expected rate of return from the investment? Does the expected rate of return compensate for the risks?

The decision-making criteria fall into three broad categories: rules-of-thumb techniques, traditional appraisal methods, and discounted cash flow (DCF) models. Each of these methods has advantages and disadvantages.

Rules-of-thumb techniques. Many investors employ rules of thumb in making decisions. These techniques are fairly simple and have a number of limitations which make them, at least from a theoretical viewpoint, less desirable as decision-making criteria. We will deal more fully with these limitations in Chapter 11.

Some of the more popular rules of thumb are the gross income multiplier, the overall capitalization rate, and the equity dividend rate. The *gross income multiplier* simply measures the relationship between value (selling price) and gross income from operations. The *overall capitalization rate* (or its reciprocal, the *net income multiplier*) is the ratio of net operating income to value. The *equity dividend rate* is the ratio of before-tax cash flow (typically for the first year) to the amount of equity invested. All of these are useful criteria for the initial screening of prospective investments.

Traditional appraisal methods. The second major set of techniques for estimating value consists of the traditional appraisal models: direct sales comparison approach, cost approach, and income approach.

Using the *direct sales comparison approach*, we estimate the value of an investment by comparing it with similar properties that have recently been sold. The pertinent question is, How much would the comparable property have sold for if it were similar to the investment under consideration? Then, by adjusting for differences, an indicated value for the investment can be obtained.

Another traditional appraisal method is the *cost approach*, where an estimate of the value of an investment is made based on the cost of reproducing the property using the current construction costs and considering the condition and location of the property. If the investment involved is an existing building, for example, the investor would compare this estimated value with the selling price to make the investment decision.

A third appraisal method is the *traditional income approach*, where *value* is defined as the present worth of the expected income stream. Using this method, the value is estimated by "discounting" the net income from operations and revisions at an appropriate "capitalization" rate.

Discounted cash flow (DCF) models. The third and final major set of decision-making criteria for real estate investment analysis consists of discounted cash flow (DCF) models. These are based on the concept that the value of a real estate investment is equal to the present worth of the future cash flows.[4] To use DCF models, we first forecast the expected cash flows

---

[4] To be technically correct, the income approach is also a type of DCF model.

and then discount future cash flows at the required rate of return. Discounted cash flow models recognize that a dollar today is worth more than a dollar tomorrow: the essence of present value and the time value of money.

There are two basic DCF models: net present value and internal rate of return. To use the *net present value method*, we discount the expected cash flows using the required rate of return for the perceived risks. If the present value of the cash inflows exceeds the present value of the cash outflows, the investment is accepted. If the present value of the cash inflows is less than the present value of the outflows, the investment is not accepted.

With the *internal rate of return method*, we compare the inflows with the costs and calculate the rate of return. The internal rate of return (IRR) is the rate that equates the present value of the cash flows with the present value costs of investing. Once the IRR has been calculated, it is compared with the required or hurdle rate of return. If the calculated rate of return is greater than or equal to the desired rate of return, the investment is made. If it is less than the desired rate, the investment is not made.

The discounted cash flow models can be used with either before-tax or after-tax inflows in relation to the cost (equity) of investing. The DCF models may also be used to test the sensitivity of the rate of return, and hence the investment decision, to the various assumptions that must be made in forecasting the cash flows for a real estate investment.

Step 5: The Investment Decision

Now that all of the considerations have been analyzed, a decision must be made. The various assumptions and estimates have been reviewed and checked for accuracy, and potential white elephants have been discarded. Therefore we are ready to make a wealth-maximizing investment in real estate.

SUMMARY

This chapter introduced some basic investment concepts. Because real estate investing requires the outflow of a *certain* amount of money in return for an expected, but *uncertain*, cash flow, we are concerned with determining the value.

In Chapter 1 the real estate investment process was outlined as a step-by-step framework for decision making. Each step was discussed in the light of its importance to the total process. The following chapters focus on the more intricate details of each of these steps. Chapter 2 examines the investor's objectives.

QUESTIONS

1-1. What is investing?

1-2. What is the relationship between risk and return?

1-3. Why is the risk-return relationship important for investors?

1-4. *Value* is a slippery term. How is value defined for real estate investment analysis?

1-5. What is the relationship between market value and investment value? How are they distinguished?

1-6. Describe the real estate investment process. What is its purpose?

1-7. Who are the major real estate investment participants?

1-8. There are four major environments in which the investor is situated. Describe each of these and discuss how each environment might have an important impact on the investment.

1-9. How is *after-tax cash flow* defined? What is its relationship to taxable income?

1-10. What are the two basic discounted cash flow models?

PROBLEMS

1-1. A real estate investment has the following inputs:
   a. Asking price: $900,000
   b. Rentable area: 10,000 square feet
   c. Rent per square foot: $15 per year
   d. Vacancy losses: 7 percent per year
   e. Operating expenses: $42,000
   f. Debt service: $85,300, of which $81,000 is interest
   g. Depreciation deduction: $42,500
   h. Investor's marginal tax rate: 28 percent
   Compute the expected after-tax cash flow (ATCF) from operation for year 1.

1-2. You have recently sold your apartment building for $500,000. It was purchased for $400,000 five years ago. You have taken depreciation deductions of $18,000 per year. The unpaid mortgage balance is $325,000. Your marginal tax rate on ordinary income is 28 percent. Compute your after-tax equity reversion (ATER).

1-3. Using the information in Problem 1-1, compute the following:
   a. Gross income multiplier
   b. Net income multiplier
   c. Overall capitalization rate
   d. Operating expense ratio
   e. Equity dividend rate
   f. Loan-to-value ratio

1-4. Using the facts from Problem 1-1, suppose the appropriate overall capitalization rate was 10.5 percent. What is the indicated value of the property using the estimated net operating income?

SELECTED REFERENCES

BROWN, ROBERT K., "The Investment Counselor's Role in the Development Process," *Appraisal Journal*, 39 (July 1971), 225–36.

JAFFE, AUSTIN J., and C. F. SIRMANS, "Improving Real Estate Investment Analysis," *Appraisal Journal*, 49 (January 1981), 85–94.

LANDAUER, JAMES D., "Real Estate as an Investment," *Appraisal Journal*, 28 (October 1960), 426–34.

MONTGOMERY, J. THOMAS, "Real Estate Investment Risk: Basic Concepts," *Appraisal Journal*, 44 (January 1976), 9–22.

TURVEY, RALPH, *The Economics of Real Property*. London: Allen & Unwin, 1957.

2

RISK, RETURN, AND DECISION MAKING

In Chapter 1 we outlined the real estate investment process. The initial step in the process required an analysis of the investor's objectives regarding risk, return, and other dimensions. In this chapter we introduce some additional principles about real estate as an investment and discuss some popular reasons why real estate continues to be an attractive investment vehicle.

This chapter builds on the framework developed in Chapter 1 in a number of ways. First, some basic principles are examined in addition to those introduced in Chapter 1. We discuss the difference between speculation and investment, the special attributes of real estate as an investment, and the expected relationship between risk and return. We also discuss some of the reasons why investors are attracted to real estate and the extent to which these reasons are likely to result in financial gain for the investors.

Although there are several possible objectives for real estate investors, this book argues that with the exception of special cases, the presumed objective of real estate investors is to become as wealthy as possible through investment acquisition, operation, and disposition decisions. Therefore the goal of wealth maximization is assumed to be the investment objective of the typical investor.

The concept of market efficiency is introduced and is shown to be one of the more useful notions for modern real estate investment analysis. With these concepts, it is then possible to define a "good investment" and to introduce a model that can be used to identify such investments. The final section discusses the reasons why the model is useful for solving the problem of choosing real estate investments.

SOME CHARACTERISTICS OF REAL ESTATE INVESTMENTS

In Chapter 1, *investment* was defined as the present sacrifice of resources for the expected future benefits of resources. Typically, the resources involved refer to cash of the equity investors as well as debt financing of the lender. However, since equity investors reap the benefits of financing success, the risk of loss is also borne by them even if mortgage or other debt financing is employed.

Since the definition of investing is quite broad, it is useful to further refine the concept of investing to illustrate the following items: (1) the relationship between investment and speculation, (2) the main parts of real estate as an investment, and (3) the relationship between risk and return. This discussion will lead us to the investment model used throughout this book: the *equity valuation model*. This technique will permit a systematic analysis of potential real estate investment projects, taking into account, in an orderly and logical way, all the considerations indicated in the real estate investment process in Chapter 1.

This method will also provide clear but general decision rules so that an investor can decide which, if any, investments should be acquired of those available and which should be avoided. Clearly, unlike some approaches, this analysis implies that some real estate projects are unattractive as investment vehicles, especially for certain investors, whereas others provide opportunities to increase investors' wealth positions. The analysis and techniques discussed in this book provide tested methods of achieving financial success as a real estate investor.

Speculation versus Investment

Some individuals like to distinguish between two types of economic activity: speculation and investment. To these individuals, *speculation* involves the acceptance of large risks and unsecured gambles with borrowed funds for the sole purpose of fast returns in ventures of dubious activity. This line of thinking has also associated "speculators" with such epithets as sneaky, immoral, corrupt, and nonproductive. On the other hand, individuals who saved their own funds and who, over time, without as much risk and with less fanfare, slowly acquired interests in real estate were said to engage in the process of *investment*. These investors were the "good guys" and were thought to provide economic benefits to society. Speculators supposedly harmed society and thus became known as the "bad guys."

It is surprising that this distinction continues to be shared by many people today. In many ways, it is difficult if not impossible to distinguish between investors and speculators. Furthermore, even if such a distinction can be made, it is doubtful whether it is useful for any productive purpose. For example, if an individual acquires a parcel of real estate, whether his or

**Exhibit 2-1   Why Are Speculators
Unpopular?**

The history of capitalism is filled with stories about the cunning and perverse speculator. This culprit is frequently identified as an immoral and greedy character who seeks profits at the expense of others and whose self-interest is distasteful to everyone. It is little wonder that speculators have developed a bad reputation.

The important question in this matter is whether this unpopularity is warranted. The text attempts to convince the reader that, economically speaking, a "speculator" does not materially differ from an "investor" and that the activity of speculation *helps* society by ensuring more accurate prices. Buyers, sellers, consumers, governments, and others all benefit from improved information from market transactions.

It seems that some members of society are offended by the economic success of such speculators. This success comes with the accompanying amount of risk, of course, and therefore, in the long run, speculators are likely to earn only normal rates of return when adjusted for risk, like most classes of investors. Since their activities provide benefits to society, speculators should be encouraged rather than discouraged in most markets, including real estate markets. However, it seems likely that they will continue to be unpopular for some time to come.

her intentions are to develop the land and live there for forty years or to hold the land undeveloped for two years and then resell it should make little difference to society. In both cases, the real estate is acquired by the highest bidder and is used in the manner the investor chooses. If, subsequently, another investor would like to use the real estate in a more productive manner, the second investor could outbid the "speculator" and redevelop the property. In any case, with each subsequent purchase, the real estate is used as productively as possible by everyone involved.

Does it make any difference to society if the investor has a long planning horizon or a short one? Does it matter if all cash is used to finance the investment or if a lender willingly agrees to lend the investor money to help finance the investment? Does the reason why an individual buys property make any difference? If the answer to any of these questions is yes, then it follows that an individual or a group of individuals would be interested in acquiring the real estate from the investor or speculator and using the property in a way they would prefer. If so, society in general benefits, as each transaction helps to ensure that the property goes to the user who values it the highest.

Therefore, not only is the historical distinction between investment and speculation immaterial, it can also be argued that "speculators" *aid* society by helping to make markets clear at *better* (and often higher) prices. Without such activity, it would become more difficult to transact real estate, and market prices would be less representative of the value placed on the property by society at that point in time.

The Uniqueness of Real Estate as an Investment

Real estate as an investment consists of several parts. Each part provides a separate reason why real estate continues to be attractive as an investment. Each part, when added to the others, gives investors an opportunity that is unique across a wide spectrum of investments available. Therefore it is important to be able to identify the major parts of real estate investments and to be able to account for each part systematically when doing a financial analysis.

The benefits of owning real estate as an investment can be divided into seven parts.

Rental income is one of the principal benefits for many types of projects. The payment made by users of the land to the owner of the land is called "economic rent." Whether or not the land is rented to a tenant, an economic rent accrues to the owner. If the owner chooses to rent the land, the contract rent that is agreed upon is a function of the economic rent the market is willing to pay for the space. Therefore the investor benefits from owning the real estate by collecting the rental income if the economic rent on the property is high relative to that of other properties in the area.

Appreciation refers to changes in the value of the real estate over time. Some of the change in the property's value may be due to inflation; some may result from changes in the supply and demand forces in the market for the real estate. As will be shown in Chapter 4, changes in value due to inflation do not affect the wealth of the investor. Only changes in the relative value of the land are of interest to the investor. These relative price changes may occur for a variety of reasons including growth in the community, specific improvements on the land, restrictions on the supply of competing properties, shifts in the tastes and preferences of consumers, and changes in the needs of society regarding property and the use of land.

Financial leverage is often considered to be one of the principal benefits of real estate investing. It is said that investors benefit by using debt financing if the cost of financing is less than the rate of return earned by owning the real estate. Since interest payments are tax deductible, the appropriate comparison should be the after-tax cost of borrowing relative to the after-tax rate of return on the investment. Many investors feel that since a large percentage of the typical real estate investment is financed with debt, the opportunities for gains from leverage are greater in real estate than in other areas of investment.

Control of the investment is another reason why real estate is an attractive area for investing. Many investors are interested in the managerial aspects of the investment. Rather than desiring a passive investment where managerial decisions are made for the investor, such as in common stocks or corporate bonds with publicly traded firms, some investors want to manage their own investments directly. For such investors, the opportunity to develop, modify, manage, and change real estate is precisely what they are seeking.

Inflation hedge is a concept that has become increasingly popular since the early 1970s. It has frequently been alleged that real estate is as fine an inflation hedge as any other vehicle available to investors. An *inflation hedge* is an investment whose return equals or exceeds the rate of inflation over long periods of time. Such an investment is of interest to investors to the extent that some investments fail to keep pace with inflation and, over time, the real wealth of investors falls due to the reduction in the purchasing power of the dollar. It has often been alleged that real estate as an inflation hedge is superior to other investments.

Security is another reason why investors seek real estate. Land is fundamental to modern living, not because urban society requires the soil for crop yield but because the city remains the center of modern economic life. As such, land situated in prime locations will retain its importance in years to come. For investors seeking security in their investments, land may be an attractive option.

Real estate may also provide benefits to investors who seek real estate as a *portfolio asset*. It is well known that the risk of loss can be reduced by diversification into investments with different financial characteristics than those currently in an investor's portfolio. Increasingly, real estate projects are being evaluated as a portfolio asset by life insurance companies, pension funds, bank holding companies, and other large firms. With real estate's other attributes, the potential as a diversification asset has attracted a host of new investors in recent years.

The Relationship Between Risk and Return

The relationship between risk and return is one of the most important relationships for the real estate investor. It is important for two reasons. First, if the relationship is maintained, the investor knows that expected high rates of return are likely to be accompanied by an equivalent high level of risk. Second, if the relationship is weakened, the investor knows that in some cases high rates of return are possible with low amounts of risk. Therefore, a basic understanding of risk and return is essential.

In market economies, some investors prefer safe investments while others prefer riskier ones. In order for investors to accept riskier investments, however, they must be promised a higher expected rate of return. If not, no rational

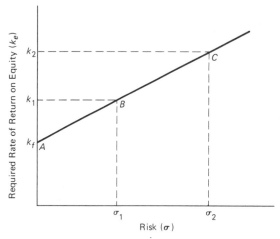

The Relationship Between Risk and Return

Figure 2-1 The Relationship Between Risk and Return.

Source: Austin J. Jaffe and C. F. Sirmans, *Real Estate Investment Decision Making*, 1982, p. 25. Reprinted by permission of Prentice-Hall, Inc., Englewood Cliffs, N.J.

investor would accept the riskier investment; the investor would be better off with the safer investment earning the same level of return.

Therefore, it is likely that a positive relationship would exist between expected (or required) rates of return and risk. Figure 2-1 illustrates the relationship between risk and return. The figure indicates that the higher the level of risk (σ), the higher the required rate of return on equity (k_e). When there is no risk associated with the investment, it is reasonable to expect to earn the risk-free rate (k_f). At point A there is no risk to the investment and the risk-free rate is expected to be earned.

However, if a rate of return is desired that is greater than the risk-free rate (the lowest rate of return available), then the investor necessarily has to take on some risk. This amounts to moving up the risk-return trade-off. Note that Figure 2-1 indicates two combinations of risk and return. Points B and C indicate two levels of risk and return possibilities. Also note that at point B, the investor requires a lower rate of return than at point C, since the risk is much less at point B than at point C.

There are several types of risk in the world of real estate investment analysis. These include *financial risk*, or the risk of defaulting on borrowed funds; *business risk*, or the risk of income losses resulting from changes in economic conditions; *inflation* (or *purchasing power*) *risk*, or the risk of losses in real value due to changes in the nominal prices of goods and services; and others. Each type of risk can be represented, conceptually, as a premium that must be added to the risk-free rate to compare it with the required rate of return by the investor.

The important point here is that the analysis of return necessitates the analysis of risk. The two are inseparable and, as a result, it is essential that investors study both when making investment decisions.

INVESTOR OBJECTIVES

To enable the investor to choose projects among several alternatives, one of the first steps in the investment process is the choice of investment objective. Although there are likely to be differences between investors regarding interests, risk preferences, and tastes, it is argued that the objective of most investors is *wealth maximization*. This objective is broad and general, but it provides a conceptual framework for real estate investment analysis.

The Choice of Investor Objectives

Investors often say that they have several different reasons for investing in real estate. Some of the more frequently cited reasons are listed in Table 2-

**Exhibit 2-2 Pension Funds "Discover"
Real Estate**

Although financial institutions such as life insurance firms and savings and loan associations have long been institutional forces in real estate investment markets, other institutional investors have recently entered real estate markets seeking the types of benefits that are uniquely available in real estate. Pension funds in particular have dramatically increased their holdings of income-producing real estate in response to changes in the regulatory and tax environment of the early 1980s.

More than ever, pension funds are seeking real estate as a portfolio asset because it is widely believed to be an excellent complement to common stocks and corporate bonds for diversification purposes. The main idea is that the overall risk of the pension fund's portfolio can be substantially reduced with the inclusion of high-quality real estate. This is because the performance of real estate investments is unlikely to directly mirror the performance of these types of securities. Although no one can predict the future, building a well-diversified portfolio can help to ensure that the risk of the portfolio is kept as low as possible for each level of return.

The idea of "not putting all your eggs in one basket" is an old one. With such new financial instruments as mortgage-backed securities affecting the real estate market, the concept of diversification has taken on additional importance for many institutional real estate investors. It seems that there will eventually be even more investment in real estate by pension funds and other types of financial institutions. Many observers feel that the recent surge in investment activity is just the beginning of a long relationship between real estate and pension funds.

TABLE 2-1   Possible Investor Objectives

1. Maximization of gross income
2. Maximization of net income
3. Maximization of taxable income
4. Maximization of before-tax cash flow
5. Maximization of after-tax cash flow
6. Maximization of income after taxes
7. Maximization of leverage gains
8. Maximization of depreciation write-offs
9. Maximization of interest deductions
10. Maximization of appreciation
11. Minimization of operating expenses
12. Minimization of negative before-tax cash flow
13. Minimization of negative after-tax cash flow
14. Minimization of income taxation
15. Minimization of management expenses
16. Minimization of financing expenses
17. Minimization of required equity down payment
18. Achievement of an "acceptable rate of return"
19. Achievement of "sufficient returns to pyramid"
20. Achievement of "satisfactory" results
21. Maximization of profits
22. Maximization of rate of return
23. Maximization of social benefits
24. Maximization of wealth

1. Some investors seek income; some seek appreciation. Others purchase real estate as an inflation hedge; others purchase it to gain from leverage. Still others have nonfinancial objectives, such as control over tangible assets and power to build structures on the site. Some investors may purchase real estate in an attempt to avoid paying rent to a third party. All of these reasons may be part of the same story. And all of them are consistent with the fact that real estate provides a host of opportunities for various types of investors.

Another issue deals with the behavior of investors. Traditionally, it has been assumed that investors are interested in maximizing some type of combination of benefits. For example, an investor may be interested in choosing the project with the greatest amount of after-tax cash flow.

Some analysts, however, may not use a maximization objective; they may be "satisfied" with a certain level of cash flow. These investors would be interested in securing projects that meet certain criteria. Once such projects had been found, they would be deemed acceptable and the searching for other projects would cease.

Finally, there may also be investors who are interested in a different type of objective. These investors seek to minimize some cost. For example, an investor interested in minimizing tax liability or minimizing required equity contributions might choose a different project than an investor who follows a different objective. In these cases, the investor's specific circumstances may dictate the choice of investment project.

The Goal of Wealth Maximization

It is argued in this book that the appropriate goal for most investors is to maximize investor wealth. As will be shown in Chapter 12, this goal is not the same as maximization of rate of return. However, the goal *is* consistent with choosing projects using the net present value of equity technique.

There are several attractive features of the goal of wealth maximization. It is general and can therefore be applied to a wide range of investors and types of investments. It is broad and can therefore take into account several of the attributes that go into real estate as an investment. It is consistent with the well-being of investors in that the project that increases the wealth of the investor the most is the project that makes the investor best off.

Suppose an investor wanted cash flow and inflation hedge from an investment. The investor might consider a number of projects that are expected to yield these benefits. If the investor were to select a project based on only those two characteristics, he or she might neglect such considerations as appreciation, management concerns, and leverage choices. Even though the investor was primarily concerned with only two of the aspects of real estate as an investment, it is reasonable to presume, for example, that he or she would prefer more appreciation to less, fewer management problems to more, and greater leverage gains to less, for the same amount of cash flow, inflation hedge, and risk. Therefore it is important that the investor's objective take all those things into account.

The objective of wealth maximization does precisely that if the measurement of additions to wealth is robust enough. As will be shown later in this chapter, the net present value of equity is a model that indicates how much wealth the investor receives as a result of purchasing the investment. Therefore, with a model such as the net present value of equity, the investor can feel confident that choosing projects according to the results of the model will make him or her as rich as possible, on an expected basis, taking into account cash flow, appreciation, leverage, managerial expenses, inflation, and other concerns. In addition, the model can also take into account risk preferences of different investors as well as various risk levels of different projects. Therefore the model is well suited for investors seeking to maximize their wealth positions through investment in real estate.

THE STORY OF REAL ESTATE: A PARABLE

Once upon a time, in a land not so far away, there was a unique asset called real estate. It was widely heralded as being the very best investment in the world. It promised the highest income for its owner, and the highest rates of appreciation, throughout the land. It also kept up with or exceeded the rate of inflation in most years, could be financed with "other people's money" to a large extent, and provided opportunities for direct management and control. And it also came in several sizes and shapes for investors with different preferences, expectations, and budgets.

With such credentials, it did not take very long for real estate to become the most active and most talked about investment in the land. Fewer and fewer investors looked elsewhere; everyone became interested in owning real estate. Indeed books were written at a rapid pace in those days. Advertisements appeared in all newspapers and bulletins. People gave up their full-time jobs to become investors. Few members of the town were unaware of these developments.

But in a matter of weeks, it seemed, trouble began. Despite all the interest in real estate, it became increasingly difficult to find property for sale. At the time, this seemed illogical. In retrospect, however, this development occurred for two reasons. First, with everyone wanting to buy and few individuals wanting to sell real estate, it is not surprising that it was difficult to find real estate for sale. Second, when someone did want to sell (generally, that person didn't "want" to sell—he or she "had" to sell for some reason unrelated to the attractiveness of the property), the property was only on the market for a very short period of time. (This was often as little as a few days in the beginning, but by the end of this period it had dropped to only a few hours! It had been rumored that if this kept up, property would be sold within minutes!)

Everyone thought the world was doomed because unless you knew someone with "too much" real estate (an unlikely prospect for most people), you were likely to, as it was said, "never get your hands on some." However, it didn't take very long before a new development took place which led to a new complaint that was heard throughout the land. Not only was it difficult to find property for sale—and if you were so lucky, you had to buy it immediately before someone else bought it—but one day the leaders of the town observed that real estate was beginning to sell for increasingly higher prices. This was thought to be a terrible development in the overall scheme of things, since real estate was so very important to the people of this town. It had become the focus of their lives.

Indeed, as more parcels were sold, it became clear to everyone that the price of real estate was steadily rising. This development was generally condemned by all, but the real estate buying continued at a rapid pace. Landowners were accused of being greedy and sinful. Investors were threatened by governmental officials and their jealous neighbors. Potential investors were also mad, but this was probably because they were too late to get in on the action.

It didn't take long before the price of real estate was quite high. Real estate became known as a great thing to own but something that was impossible to buy. Investors began to return to stocks, bonds, and other types of investments. People began to think about other things once again.

Something else happened as well. The rate of return from holding real estate began to fall. The income and appreciation that was expected now became increasingly a matter of concern because without them the investors would lose money. The most recent investors made the most noise because they seemed to accept the facts the hardest: They weren't going to get rich by owning real estate. In addition, lenders saw that they could make a lot more money by charging increasingly higher and higher rates on their loans, especially on long-term mortgages. Some lenders even invested in real estate themselves. The tax law hadn't changed, but it seemed that new investors couldn't benefit as much as in the old days.

In the end, some investors never quite recovered from these developments. They seemed to spend the rest of their lives telling stories about the "good old days" when real estate was "selling for a song." Other investors could never understand what had happened to the real estate market. They often blamed the "developers from the East" and the "greed of the bankers" for ruining the opportunities for investors.

And there was another group who never really said much about the changes except that one could tell that they had changed as well; they were never quite as interested in real estate again. Some became interested in oil and gas technology; others invested in computer firms and microcomputer software. They seemed happy enough and they seemed to make just as much money, but they never talked about real estate again.

Simply because real estate possesses several investment attributes does not mean real estate is a good investment. In the beginning of time it may have been true, but in modern times there is a different story to tell.

The Concept of Market Efficiency

The attractiveness of real estate as an investment vehicle is well known. The special features of the asset, such as a fixed supply, longevity, and the heterogeneity of each parcel, suggest that real estate would be of special interest to numerous investors. In addition, governmental policies have traditionally been favorable to real estate since the founding of our nation and especially during the present century. Finally, several institutions have emerged to deal with real estate. These institutions not only finance complex investments but offer very specialized and highly professional management services. There are also highly specialized brokerage firms that facilitate the buying and selling details in the real estate business. As a result, there is an extraordinary amount of interest in real estate markets.

The concept of *market efficiency* refers to the extent to which market prices reflect available information about buyer and seller behavior. This notion of efficiency does not refer to how well the market works in terms of enabling investors, for example, to sell as quickly and as cheaply as possible, or how long it takes or how difficult it is for a local banker to approve a borrower's application for a thirty-year mortgage. This definition of market efficiency refers to how rapidly public information about the attractiveness (or unattractiveness) of market investments affects the market's price. If the market price quickly and accurately reflects the information, the market is said to be *efficient*. If the market price does not reflect the information (i.e., the price is slow or very slow to adjust to the new information), the market is said to be *inefficient*.

Whether or not the market meets the efficiency test is an important determination. If the market is found to be relatively efficient, then it is unlikely that investors, using market information, will be able to consistently earn high rates of return with low levels of risk (sometimes called "abnormal returns"). The reason is that in such a market, the attractive attributes about the investment are likely to be reflected in the price prior to the investor's purchase.

If the market is not so efficient, some investors may be able to use favorable (unfavorable) information to buy (sell) real estate before others know about the information and adjust their expectations upward (downward). If so, trading in an inefficient market suggests the possibility of such abnormal returns for investors. All one has to do is find such a market and obtain new information

Exhibit 2-3   Why the "Efficient Market Hypothesis" Is Important

The concept of market efficiency is often referred to as the "efficient market hypothesis," or EMH. Based on the research in financial markets in the 1960s, this name was given to a method of approaching the analysis of assets and prices in various types of markets. The text briefly describes the central idea of the concept of market efficiency. Interested readers are referred to any modern corporate finance or investment text for additional discussion.

The EMH is important for real estate as well as other analyses because it provides a basis for the analysis of market prices and investor behavior. If this approach is adopted, investors can assume that when, for example, a real estate investment is sold, both the buyer and the seller, using market and perhaps other kinds of information, come to an agreement (a "meeting of the minds"). As a result, unless there is evidence to the contrary, it may be presumed that the value of the property is the sale price as of the date of the transaction. The EMH tells us that available information affecting the value of the asset now and in the future is likely to be used by market participants when making actual transactions.

Note that the EMH does not require that investors predict the future. Nor does it presume that all investors earn the same rate of return. In fact, the EMH may be useful even if the particular real estate market is sometimes slow to adjust to new information that subsequently affects actual prices. The EMH permits the analysis of market behavior under the belief (and, it is hoped, evidence) that, in general, available information is used by market participants such that eventual sale prices will reflect available information *before* the sale takes place. If so, the EMH will serve as a valuable framework for understanding market activities and as a conceptual basis for making real-world, normative investment decisions.

before others do and process this information in a useful way so as to make better investment decisions as a result.

This approach becomes an important part of the method in this book. The real estate investment process can be used to ensure that real estate parcels are selling for their "correct" (i.e., efficient) prices. If a parcel of real estate is available for a different price than the investor believes is the efficient one, the investor may be in a position to buy it and earn an abnormal return on the investment.

WHAT IS A GOOD INVESTMENT?

It is now quite easy to define a good investment. A *good investment* is *one that promises an abnormally high rate of return*. Stated another way, a good investment is one that is "worth" more than it "costs." Such an investment expects to yield a high rate of return relative to an expected small amount of risk. Clearly, every investor would be interested in investments with a weak and favorable relationship between the expected rate of return and the expected level of risk.

Unfortunately, in many markets in the real world, it is difficult to find investments that promise high returns and low risks. (After all, if they were readily available, who wouldn't buy them!) Indeed, it is unlikely that available information would not affect prices of real estate. The only question is, How rapidly are such prices affected?

In real estate markets, researchers know very little about the extent to which markets meet the efficiency test. There is some evidence that in the long run, risk and return are closely related. There is also some evidence that the returns from investing in real estate and in unimproved land approximate the returns from investing in other areas, once risk is adjusted for. This is precisely what would be expected in a market economy with numerous participants, considerable interest, and a healthy flow of market information.

Can We Measure a Good Investment?

There is an excellent way of testing to see if real estate is a good investment or not, using the definition above. A well-known investment model called the equity valuation model can be used to identify potentially good investments. The equity investment model has two forms: the net present value of equity (NPV_e) and the internal rate of return on equity (IRR_e). Both can be used to select good investments. However, as will be shown in Chapter 12, these models are not interchangeable, and care should be used when selecting between the two.

The *net present value of equity* is defined as the difference between the investment value of equity and the required equity outlay. Mathematically, this model can be represented as follows:

$$\text{NPV}_e = \sum_{t=1}^{n} \frac{\text{ATCF}_t}{(1 + k_e)^t} + \frac{\text{ATER}_n}{(1 + k_e)^n} - (\text{MV} - \text{MD}) \qquad (2\text{-}1)$$

where

NPV_e = net present value of equity
ATCF_t = after-tax cash flow in the tth period
ATER_n = after-tax equity reversion in the nth period
n = expected holding period
k_e = required rate of return on equity
MV = current market value of the property
MD = mortgage debt used to finance the investment

If the net present value of equity is greater than zero, this tells the investor that the present value of equity (the present value of the after-tax cash flows each tth period plus the present value of the after-tax equity reversion at the end of the nth period, discounted by the required rate of return on equity) is greater than the required equity outlay (the difference between the market value of the property at the time of acquisition and the mortgage used to finance the purchase, or the equity down payment). In such cases, the investor should buy the property.

If the net present value of equity is less than zero, the investor should avoid the property because the investor would be buying a parcel of real estate where the cost of the investment (i.e., the down payment) is expected to be worth more than the present value of the benefits (i.e., the investment value of equity). If so, the investor would be worse off by purchasing the investment.

There is also a similar rate-of-return calculation. This approach is called the *internal rate of return on equity*. This measure is defined as the rate, IRR, such that Equation (2-2) holds true:

$$0 = \sum_{t=1}^{n} \frac{\text{ATER}_t}{(1 + \text{IRR}_e)^t} + \frac{\text{ATER}_n}{(1 + \text{IRR}_e)^n} - (\text{MV} - \text{MD}) \qquad (2\text{-}2)$$

where

IRR_e = internal rate of return on equity

In this case, a comparison is required between the internal rate of return on equity and the required rate of return on equity. If the internal rate exceeds the required rate, the investment is an attractive one for the investor.

Why the Equity Valuation Model Works

The equity valuation model is an extremely useful tool for real estate investors because it identifies for each investor, at any point in time, those investments that are expected to make the investor wealthier and those investments that are expected to make the investor poorer. A frequently accepted goal for investors is to increase their wealth as much as possible by investing in real estate. If this is accepted as a goal, the equity valuation model shows clearly whether potential investments are acceptable or not. However, if the question is which of several investments should be chosen, the investor *cannot* use either the net present value or the internal rate of return versions of the equity valuation model. (This issue is addressed at length in Chapter 12.)

The equity valuation model provides answers for the central question in real estate investment analysis, Will the acquisition of the parcel of real estate under consideration be likely to make the investor richer or poorer in a world of risk and uncertainty? This model enables the investor to identify in a systematic fashion the parameters that affect the answer to the question and quantify several of the important parts of the question. While good judgment is always required, the model enables the investor to come to terms with the central issue and make a decision of critical importance to the success of the venture.

SUMMARY

Real estate investment analysis involves the analysis of several things. First, many attributes of real estate make it a potential investment for many people. Second, in well-functioning markets, it is reasonable to expect a close relationship between risk and return. Third, the concept of market efficiency is important in that the degree of efficiency is likely to affect the potential opportunities for real estate investors. Fourth, a good investment is one that increases the wealth of the investor on a risk-adjusted basis. Fifth, the equity valuation model can be used to identify potential investments that are expected to add to the wealth of specific investors. Finally, the equity valuation model has two formats: the net present value of equity and the internal rate of return on equity. Both can be used to identify good investments, but there are some critical differences between the models.

QUESTIONS

2-1. Is there a difference between *speculation* and *investment*? Explain.

2-2. What characteristics of real estate help to distinguish it from other investments?

2-3. Do you think there is a precise trade-off between risk and return in real estate markets? What are the implications of your answer?

2-4. The text provides a list of several investor objectives. Is the goal of wealth maximization superior to many of these objectives? Why or why not?

2-5. What does the concept of market efficiency mean for real estate investors?

2-6. The text defines a *good investment* as one with an expected abnormally high rate of return. Do you think real estate markets frequently provide these types of opportunities? Why or why not?

2-7. Demonstrate how the use of the equity investment model can be used by real-world investors.

PROBLEMS

2-1. Suppose you had the following choices:

a.

INVESTMENT	EXPECTED RATE OF RETURN	STANDARD DEVIATION
A	15%	2%
B	15%	3%

Which investment would you prefer?

b.

INVESTMENT	EXPECTED RATE OF RETURN	STANDARD DEVIATION
C	15%	3%
D	16%	3%

Which investment would you prefer?

c.

INVESTMENT	EXPECTED RATE OF RETURN	STANDARD DEVIATION
E	15%	3%
F	16%	4%

Which investment would you prefer?

2-2. An investment has a total value of $200,000. The investor can borrow $150,000. The present value of the expected after-tax cash flow (from operation and reversion) is $40,000. Is this a good investment?

2-3. Suppose you have the following information:

INVESTMENT	NPV
A	$5,000
B	8,000

Which investment would you prefer?

2-4. A particular real estate investment was purchased for $500,000 (all cash). It was sold one year later for $525,000. It also generated $50,000 in income during that year. What was the investor's actual rate of return?

2-5. You have been given the opportunity to invest in a parcel of vacant land. The price is $100,000. You expect to sell the land for $120,000 one year from now.

Given the riskiness of this type of investment, you feel that the required rate of return should be 25 percent. Is this a good investment?

2-6. Using Equation (2-1) in the chapter, compute the net present value of equity given the following:

YEAR	MARKET VALUE	MORTGAGE DEBT	ATCF	ATER
0	$500,000	$400,000		
1			$10,000	
2			12,000	
3			18,000	
4			13,000	
5			8,000	$100,000

The investor's required rate of return is 15 percent.

2-7. Illustrate that as the required rate of return on equity increases, the NPV of equity decreases.

2-8. Using the facts in Problem 2-6 and Equation (2-2) in the chapter, compute the internal rate of return on equity.

2-9. Using Figure 2-1, what happens to the risk-return trade-off if
   a. Expected inflation suddenly increases?
   b. There is an increase in the risk premium?

SELECTED REFERENCES

BEDFORD, E. W., "Why Buy Real Estate?" *Appraisal Journal*, 13 (April 1945), 135–37.

BREALEY, RICHARD, and STEWART MYERS, *Principles of Corporate Finance* (2nd ed.). New York: McGraw-Hill, 1984.

ROULAC, STEPHEN E., "Can Real Estate Returns Outperform Common Stocks?" *Journal of Portfolio Management*, 2 (Winter 1976), 26–43.

SIRMANS, C. F., and JAMES R. WEBB, "Investment Yields in the Money, Capital, and Real Estate Markets: A Comparative Analysis for 1951–1976," *Real Estate Appraiser*, 44 (November–December 1978), 47–51.

WENDT, PAUL F., and SUI N. WONG, "Investment Performance—Common Stocks versus Apartment Houses," *Journal of Finance*, 20 (December 1965), 633–46.

ZERBST, ROBERT H., and BARBARA R. CAMBON, "Real Estate: Historical Returns and Risks," *Journal of Portfolio Management*, 10 (Spring 1984), 5–20.

3

REAL ESTATE
INVESTMENT
MATHEMATICS

In this chapter we review some of the basic mathematical mechanics for making real estate investment decisions. Specifically, we discuss how to do the following:

1. Calculate the present value of a lump-sum future amount.
2. Calculate the present value of a series of unequal future amounts.
3. Calculate the rate of return on an investment. This rate is generally referred to as the *internal rate of return*.
4. Calculate the mechanics of a mortgage (both monthly and annual payments), including
   a. Calculation of *debt service* (payment)
   b. Calculation of the amount outstanding at any point of mortgage life
   c. Calculation of the amortization schedule (interest and principal for each payment)

The compound interest tables in the Appendix are used in making real estate investment decisions. There are three sets of tables:

Table 1—Present Value of $1.00 Factors
Table 2—Mortgage Constant (Monthly Payments)
Table 3—Proportion of Mortgage Outstanding

Table 1 provides the factors for finding the present value of a payment to be made in the future at various rates of discount. Table 2 provides the mortgage constant factors for monthly payments. The mortgage constant, when multiplied by the amount borrowed, tells the investor the payment necessary to fully amortize (pay off) the loan. Table 3 provides the proportions outstanding on mortgages. These are useful in determining the interest-principal amounts on mortgages.

HOW TO CALCULATE PRESENT VALUE

The present value of $1.00 factors in Table 1 of the Appendix are constructed using the following equation:

$$\text{PVF}_{i,n} = \frac{1}{(1 + i)^n} \qquad (3\text{-}1)$$

where

$\text{PVF}_{i,n}$ = present value of $1.00 factor at rate i for n periods
i = rate of discount
n = number of periods

The present value of any future amount is calculated by multiplying the present value factor by the future amount. In equation form:

$$\text{PV} = (\text{PVF}_{i,n})\text{FV} \qquad (3\text{-}2)$$

where

PV = present value
$\text{PVF}_{i,n}$ = present value of $1.00 factor at rate i for n periods
FV = future value

Example 3-1: Present value of a future amount.   What is the present value of $1.00 to be received six years in the future, discounted at 12 percent per year?

$$\text{Present value} = \text{PVF}_{i,n} \text{ (future value)}$$

$$= \frac{1}{(1 + .12)^6} (\$1.00)$$

$$= .50663 \ (\$1.00)$$

$$= \$.50663$$

Thus, $1.00 to be received six years from now is worth about 51 cents today, at a discount rate of 12 percent. The factor, .50663, for 12 percent interest for six years, can be found in Table 1 of the Appendix (pages 380–386) by using the column labeled 12 percent for six years.

Stated differently, an investor could pay 51 cents today for an investment that would sell for $1.00 six years in the future and earn a rate of return of 12 percent.

Example 3-2: Present value of a lump sum.   Suppose a real estate investor is considering purchasing a parcel of vacant land. The investor expects to sell the parcel for $25,000 five years from now. How much could be paid today for the investment if the investor wants to earn a return of 15 percent per year?

The present value of $25,000 five years from now at a rate of 15 percent is

$$\text{Present value} = \text{Future value } (\text{PVF}_{i,n})$$

$$\text{Present value} = (\$25,000) \frac{1}{(1.15)^5}$$

$$= \$25,000 \, (.49718)$$

$$= \$12,430$$

The present value factor, .49718, can be found in Table 1 of the Appendix by using the column labeled 15 percent for five years. Multiplying this factor by the expected $25,000 results in a price of $12,430. Thus if the investor paid $12,430 for the investment and sold it for $25,000 in five years, the rate of return would be 15 percent per year.

Example 3-3: Rate of return.   Suppose the investor in Example 3-2 paid $13,570 for the parcel of land and sold it five years later for $25,000. What would be the rate of return on the investment?

In this type of situation, we know the present value ($13,570) and the future value ($25,000). What we do not know is the rate that will make the two values equal after a five-year period of time. The answer can be found as follows:

$$\text{Present value} = \text{Future value } (\text{PVF}_{i,n})$$

$$\$13,570 = \$25,000 \, (\text{PVF}_{i,5})$$

$$.5428 = (\text{PVF}_{i,5})$$

The question is, What rate (i) will make this equation true?

One solution is to simply choose an i and solve the equation. Suppose, for example, we were to "guess" 12 percent. Solving the equation yields:

$$.5428 = \frac{1}{(1.12)^5}$$

$$.5428 \neq .5674$$

Obviously the equation does not hold at 12 percent. Thus we must pick another rate. Should it be larger or smaller than 12 percent. It should be larger. Why? Because the larger the rate, the smaller the number yielded by the right-hand side of the equation. (The reciprocal of 1.12 raised to the fifth power is larger than, for example, the reciprocal of 1.15 raised to the fifth power. Try it and see.)

Thus, suppose we select 13 percent. Solving the equation:

$$.5428 = \frac{1}{(1.13)^5}$$

$$.5428 = .5428$$

Thus the correct rate is 13 percent. If the investor paid $13,570 for an investment and sold it five years later for $25,000, the rate of return would be 13 percent per year.

Another solution is to take the equation

$$.5428 = \frac{1}{(1 + i)^5} = \text{PVF}_{i,5}$$

and look through the factors in Table 1 of the Appendix for five years until the factor .5428 is found. This factor is found in the 13 percent column for five years.

Example 3-4: Present value of an unequal series.   A real estate investment is expected to produce the after-tax cash flows (ATCFs) shown in Table 3-1. What is the present value of these cash flows at a rate of 12 percent? The present value factors (PVF) from Table 1 at 12 percent are shown in column 3. Multiplying these factors by the yearly ATCF yields the present value of each cash flow. Adding the present values results in a total present value of $85,498.68. What does this mean to the investor? It means that the investor can pay up to $85,498.68 for the investment and, assuming the invest-

TABLE 3-1   Example of Present Value of an Unequal Series

(1)	(2)	(3)	(4)
		PRESENT VALUE	
YEAR	ATCF	FACTOR @ 12%	PRESENT VALUE
1	$20,000	.89286	$17,857.20
2	20,400	.79719	16,262.68
3	30,000	.71178	21,353.40
4	20,600	.63552	13,091.71
5	20,200	.56743	11,462.09
6	10,800	.50663	5,471.60
		Total Present Value =	$85,498.68

ment generates the expected ATCF, earn a rate of return of 12 percent per year.

Suppose the investor pays more than $85,498.68 for the investment. What would happen to the rate of return? It would be lower. For example, if the investor paid $90,289.55, the rate of return would be 10 percent. Should the opposite occur and the investor pays $79,032.51, the rate of return rises to 15 percent. Thus the lower the price, the higher the rate of return for a given set of cash flows. Note, however, that these changes are based on the assumption that the estimated ATCFs are correct. The *actual* (realized) rate of return may be different from the *expected* if the actual cash flows are different from the expected. The actual return cannot be calculated until an investment is bought, operated, and sold. The actual income streams would then be known with certainty. *Investing, however, requires the investor to commit the outflow in the present in return for the expected (but risky) inflows in the future.*

HOW TO FIND NET PRESENT VALUE

Example 3-5: Net present value of an investment.   The net present value (NPV) of an investment is equal to the present value of the inflows minus the present value of the outflows. Suppose an investor pays $97,175 in equity for an investment. The expected cash flows from operations are shown in Table 3-2. What is the *net present value* of the investment? The concept behind NPV is very simple: If an investment is "worth" more than it "costs," then accept it. If not, reject it.

Assuming that the investor requires a 12 percent after-tax rate of return, the net present value is $3,016. The decision rules are:

$$\text{Accept if NPV} \geqslant 0$$
$$\text{Reject if NPV} < 0 \tag{3-3}$$

At a rate of return of 12 percent, the present value of the cash inflows exceeds the present value of the outflows by $3,016. Thus the decision would be to

TABLE 3-2   Net Present Value of an Investment at 12%

YEAR	EQUITY	ATCF	ATER	PVF @ 12%	PRESENT VALUE
0	−$97,175	—		1.00000	−$97,175
1		$20,000		.89286	17,857
2		20,400		.79719	16,263
3		30,000		.71178	21,353
4		20,600		.63552	13,092
5		20,200		.56743	11,462
6		10,800	$29,000	.50663	20,164
				Net Present Value =	$ 3,016

TABLE 3-3 Net Present Value of an Investment at 14%

YEAR	EQUITY	ATCF	ATER	PVF @ 14%	PRESENT VALUE
0	−$97,175	—		1.00000	−$97,175
1		$20,000		.87720	17,544
2		20,400		.76947	15,697
3		30,000		.67497	20,249
4		20,600		.59208	12,197
5		20,200		.51937	10,491
6		10,800	$29,000	.45559	18,132
				Net Present Value = − $ 2,865	

invest. In this example, the cash inflows are "worth" $100,191, but they only "cost" $97,175.

Suppose, however, that the investor requires a higher rate of return. Will the decision still be to invest if the required rate is 14 percent? To find the NPV at 14 percent (PV of cash inflows minus PV of cash outflows), we discount all the cash flows at 14 percent (see Table 3-3).

The NPV of −$2,865 indicates that an investor requiring a 14 percent rate of return should not invest in this project. As the required rate of return goes up for a given set of cash flows, the NPV decreases.

It seems intuitive that there must be a rate at which the present value of the inflows is equal to the present value of the outflows. This rate is called the *internal rate of return (IRR)* and is illustrated in Example 3-6.

HOW TO CALCULATE THE RATE OF RETURN

Example 3-6: Rate of return on an investment.   Continuing with the numbers developed in Examples 3-4 and 3-5, what is the expected rate of return? The *IRR* is defined as the rate that will make the present value of the cash inflows equivalent to the present value of the outflows. Another way to define the IRR is the rate that will make the NPV of an investment equal to zero. There is no simple way to directly compute the IRR without a calculator that performs the function. The alternative is a trial-and-error (or iterative) approach. When a rate of return is tried and the resulting NPV is positive, the rate should be raised. If the NPV is negative, the rate should be lowered.

Returning to Example 3-5, the foregoing analysis indicates that 12 percent is too low a rate, since the NPV was a positive $3,016, and that 14 percent is too high, since the NPV was a negative $2,865. Therefore let us try 13 percent (see Table 3-4).

The resulting NPV is a positive $7.00, indicating that the IRR is very close to 13 percent; in fact, it is just above 13 percent (13.0022 percent).

TABLE 3-4 Example of Calculating the Internal Rate of Return (IRR)

YEAR	EQUITY	ATCF	ATER	PVF @ 13%	PRESENT VALUE
0	−$97,174	——		1.00000	−$97,175
1		$20,000		88496	17,699
2		20,400		.78315	15,976
3		30,000		.69305	20,792
4		20,600		.61332	12,634
5		20,200		.54276	10,964
6		10,800	$29,000	.48032	19,117
				Net Present Value = $	7

This rate, 13.0022 percent, will make the present value of the cash inflows equal to the cash outflows. Therefore the expected rate of return on the investment of $97,175, assuming the expected cash flows will be realized, is approximately 13 percent. Under these assumptions, the IRR on this investment is 13 percent.

THE MECHANICS OF MORTGAGES

The Mortgage Constant

Table 2 of the Appendix gives the "mortgage constant." The mortgage constant, when multiplied by the amount borrowed, results in the amount of debt service (payment) to be made each period. In equation form:

$$\text{Payment} = \text{Amount borrowed } (MC_{i,n}) \qquad (3\text{-}4)$$

where

MC is the mortgage constant at interest rate i for a maturity of n periods.

Table 2 relates to payments made monthly.

Example 3-7: Calculating payments on monthly mortgage. Mr. B borrows $75,000 from the City Bank. The loan is at 12 percent interest with payments to be made *monthly* over a period of twenty years (240 monthly payments). What is the monthly debt service?

Table 2 gives the mortgage constant under monthly payments. At 12 percent interest for twenty years, the monthly mortgage constant is .01101. The monthly payment is thus:

$$\text{Payment} = \text{Amount borrowed (mortgage constant)}$$
$$= \$75,000 \ (.01101)$$
$$= \$825.75$$

The annual payment is twelve times the monthly payment:

$$\text{Annual payment} = \$825.75\ (12)$$
$$= \$9,909$$

Mr. B must make a payment of $9,909 each month for 240 months (or twenty years). At the end of twenty years, he will have amortized (paid off) the entire loan.

Example 3-8: Determining the outstanding balance (monthly payments). What amount of the $75,000 would be outstanding after six years of monthly payments?

There are two procedures that can be used to determine the proportion outstanding.

Under the first approach, the numbers would be calculated as follows. The original amount outstanding is $75,000. The debt service is a constant amount of $825.75 each month. Since the interest rate is 12 percent annually (or 1 percent monthly), the amount of interest in month 1 is $750 ($75,000 × .01). The total payment is $825.75 and the interest payment is $750; thus the principal amount is $75.75 ($825.75 − $750.00). At the end of month 1, the amount outstanding is $74,924.25. This is the original balance, $75,000, minus the principal payment in month 1, $75.75. Using this new balance, the interest payment in the second month is $749.24 ($74,924.25 × .01). The principal payment in the second year is $76.51 ($825.75 minus $749.24). The amount outstanding at the end of the second month is $74,847.74. This process is continued each month.

Note that at the end of six years (72 months), the amount outstanding is $67,061. The original amount was $75,000. This is a proportion of:

$$\text{Proportion outstanding after 6 years} = \frac{\$67,061}{\$75,000}$$
$$= .89415$$

The second approach would use the mortgage constant tables to calculate the proportion outstanding.

$$\text{Proportion outstanding} = \frac{\text{Mortgage constant total term}}{\text{Mortgage constant for remaining term}}$$

Using the 12 percent, monthly Table 2:

$$\text{Proportion outstanding} = \frac{.01101}{.01231}$$
$$= .89439$$

The proportion outstanding after six years is found by dividing .01101, the mortgage constant for the total term (12 percent for twenty years, monthly payments), by .01231, the mortgage constant for the remaining term (12 percent for fourteen years, monthly payments).

Multiplying the proportion outstanding, .89439, by the original amount, $75,000, yields the amount outstanding after six years:

$$\text{Amount outstanding} = \$75,000 \, (.89439)$$
$$= \$67,079.25$$

Table 3 of the Appendix gives the proportion outstanding on mortgages at various interest rates, maturities, and holding periods. These proportions *assume monthly compounding* and are very helpful in setting up the mortgage amortization schedule when monthly payments are made.

Example 3-9: Calculating the amortization schedule (monthly payments). Allocate the payment in Example 3-7 between interest and principal for years 1 through 6.

If a mortgage calls for monthly amortization, the first approach in Example 3-8 for allocating between interest and principal payments each month is a tedious task. The allocation has to be made for each month. Using the proportion outstanding (in Table 3 of the Appendix), the investor can easily allocate between interest and principal as shown in Table 3–5.

The numbers were calculated as follows. The proportion outstanding at the end of each year is found by using Table 3 under 12 percent, twenty-year (240 months) maturity. The amount outstanding at the end of each year is found by multiplying the amount borrowed ($75,000) by the proportion outstanding at the end of each year (column 2). The amount of principal each year is found by subtracting the amounts outstanding at the end of each year. For example, the principal payment in year 1 ($961) was calculated by taking the difference between the $75,000 and the amount outstanding at the end of year 1 ($74,039). The difference between the debt service each

TABLE 3-5 Amortization Schedule for $75,000 Mortgage at 12% Rate for 20 Years, Monthly Payments

(1) YEAR	(2) PROPORTION OUTSTANDING*	(3) AMOUNT OUTSTANDING	(4) ANNUAL DEBT SERVICE	(5) INTEREST	(6) PRINCIPAL
0	1.00000	$75,000			
1	.98718	74,039	$9,909	$8,948	$ 961
2	.97273	72,955	9,909	8,825	1,084
3	.95646	71,735	9,909	8,689	1,221
4	.93811	70,358	9,909	8,532	1,377
5	.91744	68,808	9,909	8,359	1,550
6	.89415	67,061	9,909	8,162	1,747

* From Table 3 of the Appendix.

year ($9,909) and the principal payment ($961) results in the amount of interest paid in year 1 ($8,948). This process is continued for each year.

SUMMARY

A thorough understanding of the methods discussed in this chapter can make them a useful tool for real estate investors. Our discussion has centered on the key areas for real estate investment decision making. These include how to (1) calculate the present value of future cash inflows, (2) calculate the net present value, and (3) calculate the internal rate of return. It is also important that the investor understand the mechanics of mortgages. The basic elements are how to calculate the debt service and the mortgage amortization schedule. The amortization schedule is necessary in order to determine the amount of interest deductible for tax purposes.

QUESTIONS

3-1. Why are the mathematical techniques described and illustrated in this chapter important for real estate investors?

3-2. There are three sets of tables in the Appendix to this book. Describe how each type is calculated.

3-3. How do present and future values differ?

3-4. "The calculation of the rate of return is actually similar to the present value calculation." True or false? Explain.

3-5. What is an amortization schedule and how is it derived?

3-6. Why is the calculation of the proportion of loan outstanding a useful result?

PROBLEMS

3-1. A real estate investor is considering the purchase of a parcel of vacant land that is expected to have a value of $500,000 five years from now. The investor's required rate of return is 15 percent per year. How much should the investor pay for the land?

3-2. An apartment building has a current market value of $750,000. If the value of the property is expected to increase by 5 percent per year, how much will the property be worth in three years?

3-3. You promise to pay a lender $631.93 per month for twenty-five years. The lender wants to earn 12 percent per year. How much will the lender loan you today?

3-4. Using the facts in Problem 3-3, how much will you owe at the end of five years? Ten years?

3-5. Using the facts in Problem 3-3, suppose you wanted to borrow $65,000. What is the lender's net present value? What is the lender's internal rate of return? Would the lender make the loan?

3-6. A real estate investment was purchased for $1,000,000 and sold six years later for $1,340,000. What was the percentage increase in the property's value per year?

3-7. A mortgage loan of $1,000,000 was made at an interest rate of 12.5 percent with monthly payments for twenty years.
   a. What is the monthly payment?
   b. What is the annual payment?
   c. Allocate the payments for years 1 through 5 between interest and principal.
   d. What is the amount outstanding at the end of eight years?

3-8. A mortgage loan of $450,000 was made with payments of $5,417 per month for twenty-five years. What is the interest rate on the loan?

3-9. A real estate investment has the following cash flows:

YEAR	CASH FLOW
0	−$100,000
1	15,000
2	20,000
3	18,000
4	12,000
5	85,000

If the investor's required rate of return is 15 percent, what is the net present value?

3-10. Using the facts in Problem 3-9, compute the internal rate of return.

SELECTED REFERENCES

ELLWOOD, L. W., *Ellwood Tables for Real Estate Appraising and Financing* (3rd ed.). Chicago: American Institute of Real Estate Appraisers, 1970.

GOEBEL, PAUL R., and NORMAN G. MILLER, *Handbook of Mortgage Mathematics and Financial Tables*. Englewood Cliffs, N.J.: Prentice-Hall, Inc., 1981.

JAFFE, AUSTIN J., and C. F. SIRMANS, *Real Estate Investment Decision Making*. Englewood Cliffs, N.J.: Prentice-Hall, Inc., 1982.

4

THE MARKET ENVIRONMENT

In this chapter we begin our analysis of the second step in the investment process—analyzing the environment in which the investment decision is being made. One of the most important aspects is market analysis. The real estate market represents the interaction between the demand for and the supply of real estate. The market determines the price (rent) to be charged on various types of real estate in different locations. The locational aspect is very important in market analysis.

The market environment is also concerned with analyzing the demand for ownership and the way the value of an investment is determined. Obviously, the economic factors create risks that must be considered in the decision-making process. This chapter examines the market environment and describes how the investor uses this information to make investment decisions.

PURPOSE OF MARKET ANALYSIS

We have defined *real estate investing* as the sacrifice of certain outflows for uncertain inflows. Forecasting the future inflows from an investment is risky. The investor must examine the factors influencing the inflows and formulate expectations from this analysis. To begin, the investor must carefully analyze the market forces influencing the investment decision. This analysis is critical: A mistake in the identification of present or future market forces can be costly or result in project failure.

The critical elements of an investment include the quantity and certainty of gross income, operating expenses (operating ratio), and resultant net income over some future time period. Value is a reflection of future income expectations (benefits), and such estimates are risky. The only insurance against risk—and the only clarification (to a limited degree) of uncertainty—is an in-depth market study with a principal thrust concerning supply and demand. Perhaps the most neglected area of real estate investment theory and practice is the requisite market study as a first step in value estimation.

What is the purpose of the market analysis? The answer is simply, To reduce the risk associated with investing. One of the major risks is economic or business risk. Business risk is related to such factors as

1. National economic trends, such as unemployment or recession
2. A deteriorating economic base
3. Economic obsolescence, perhaps due to a changing neighborhood
4. Flood, fire, and other natural or man-made disasters
5. Functional obsolescence, lack of quality construction, or age
6. Properties having high operating expense ratios and requiring very specialized kinds of management (i.e., nursing homes, hotels)
7. Legal restrictions, such as zoning changes
8. Population and sociodemographic trends
9. Changes in income levels, tastes, and preferences of tenants

These are only some of the factors that influence the business risk to which an investment is exposed. Obviously some types of real estate investment are subject to more business risk than others. All involve risk, however, and the purpose of market analysis is to analyze this category of risk.

Business risk is a function of general economic conditions and characteristics of the investment and is not related to the financial structure (debt-equity mix). Therefore the variability of net income is generally the most appropriate measure of this type of risk.

A real estate investment produces two potential sources of net income: the annual net operating income and the net income from the future disposition (typically, sale). Because market analysis identifies the variability of net income from these two sources, the investor should know which factors influence the variability. There are several factors, including rent per unit, vacancy level, operating expenses, estimated selling price at the end of the holding period, and selling expenses.

An Illustration

To illustrate the sensitivity of value estimates to changes in rents, suppose an investor is considering a building with 100 units. Market analysis indicates a range in rents from $175 to $200 per month per unit. Therefore the potential gross income will vary between \$210,000 to \$240,000 per year, a considerable difference.

An analysis of competing properties indicates a value estimate of five times the potential gross income (PGI). This is referred to as the gross income multiplier (GIM). The investor would thus obtain an estimated value between \$1,050,000 and \$1,200,000:

$$Value = PGI \ (GIM) \tag{4-1}$$

$$Value = \$210,000 \ (5) = \$1,050,000$$

$$Value = \$240,000 \ (5) = \$1,200,000$$

This is a range in value of \$150,000, which is a sizable difference in value for only a \$25 range in rents. Therefore investment values are very sensitive to errors or bad estimates.

Market analysis helps narrow the range in the key factors influencing net income—rents, operating expenses, vacancies, and future selling price. Small changes in these inputs to the investment process can make a difference in the estimated value for an investment and in the expected rate of return.

THE REAL ESTATE MARKET

The real estate investor must focus considerable attention on the real estate market. The *real estate market* can be defined as a mechanism by which real estate goods and services are exchanged—a mechanism influenced by the wants of the participants in the market as well as by political and governmental intervention in the marketplace.

The purpose of the real estate market is to allocate a scarce commodity. This scarce commodity is real estate, which includes both land and improvements to the land and the property rights associated with the ownership. The real estate market, like any market, allocates this scarce resource by using the price mechanism. Generally we find that the person willing to pay the most for the real estate acquires the rights associated with that ownership. In some instances, the public has decided that the scarce resource should be allocated by the government. The implementation of land use controls such as zoning ordinances can be viewed as an example of this type of allocation.

The real estate market links the supply and the demand for real estate. There are two types or categories of supply and demand with which the investor must be concerned. The first is the supply and demand for the use of the real estate. This involves the tenant's perspective. The second is the supply and demand for the ownership of an investment, or the equity investor's perspective. The equity investor must consider both of these.

The Tenant's Perspective

The demand for a real estate investment is based on the flow of services that it produces. For example, the demand for an apartment from the tenant's perspective is based on the housing services provided. Some of these services are shelter, comfort, prestige, access to work or shopping, safety, and social opportunities. Thus the tenant is buying a set of services, not merely a physical living unit.

For these services, the tenant pays a "price" called rent. The greater the demand for the services, the greater the rent. Generally we do not observe the rent per unit of services but rather the rent per physical unit—for example, the rent per apartment or the rent per square foot of retail space. Remember, however, that the tenant is really buying the services. So the investor must be certain that the investment provides the level of services demanded.

The Equity Investor's Perspective

The second type of supply and demand analysis involves the buying and selling of the ownership of the investment. For example, suppose that fifty apartment buildings were bought in a particular real estate market during a given period. We would conclude that there had been a total demand for fifty apartment buildings. This buying and selling involves placing a value (or selling price) on the expected future income (from rental and future disposition).

The value represents the present worth of the expected future income. To illustrate, suppose an investment is expected to produce $10,000 in net income per year for ten years. In addition, the investment has an expected selling price of $100,000 at the end of the ten years. The investor requires a 12 percent return per year on the investment. What is the value of the investment?

To find the value, take the forecasts of income from operation and sale and discount them at the appropriate rate. However, this valuation process raises several questions. How is the expected income determined? What is the risk associated with future income, that is, how certain are we that the investment will generate the expected cash flows? How is the appropriate rate of discount determined?

All of these questions (and others) must be answered from the equity investor's perspective. This is what market analysis is all about. Viewing the investment from the tenant's perspective helps the investor determine the expected net income and variations over the holding period. Market analysis from the equity investor's perspective helps determine the relationship between value, risk, and cash flow from the investment.

Therefore market analysis identifies supply and demand factors from

Exhibit 4-1   Where Is the Real Estate Market?

Despite the considerable attention that most real estate texts devote to "the real estate market," students may be surprised to learn that the market is difficult to find. Most markets have a central location and a formal, physical site, but real estate markets rarely do. Such characteristics assist market participants in buying, selling, or collecting information about the economic qualities of the assets and rights traded.

In the case of real estate, there is no central market. There is no building such as the New York Stock Exchange for trading real estate investments. (For some, this means that real estate investing is more fun!) Although real estate is often sold at security markets as a financial claim, there are several reasons why real estate investments lack a central clearinghouse.

For example, since real estate investments are tied to a particular site, it is difficult to interest buyers who are unfamiliar with the locale of the investment. The locale is not only critical to the success of the investment, but each locale may exert a different influence on real estate investment returns. These factors retard the ability of market makers to extend the scope of the market beyond the local investment community. In addition, the uniqueness of the parcels precludes easy property descriptions for those parcels that come "on the market." If a national real estate market is ever to exist, it is essential that a standard information form be developed in order to facilitate the conveyance of information for trading. With the wide variety of real estate and the difficulties involved in adequately describing it, the prospects for a fully developed national real estate market are not great. Finally, the thinness of most real estate markets suggests that it would be difficult to maintain active trading, since most parcels come on the market so infrequently that it makes more sense to "make a market" when the asset needs to be sold.

It should be noted, however, that recent developments in some financial markets have increased the marketability of some forms of real estate investments. These include such investments as mortgage-backed bonds, REITs, and mutual funds secured by mortgages. They are helping to make a type of national real estate market. In the future, it may be easier for someone in Pennsylvania to buy real estate interests in California, and it will probably be in the form of a financial claim such as a bond or a mutual fund share.

both the tenant's and the landlord's (equity investor's) perspective. It also helps to consider market conditions from the seller's and the equity investor's perspective. Changes in factors that influence the number of tenants and the rents tenants are willing to pay will also affect the expected income from an investment. These changes can have an impact on the value of the investment from the equity investor's perspective. Likewise, various factors can influence the equity investor's behavior in the marketplace. For example, if equity investors perceive a particular real estate investment as becoming more risky because of international, urban, or neighborhood trends, this increased risk would be reflected in the valuation of the investment.

DECISIONS FROM THE MARKET STUDY

The market study analyzes the likely present and future demand for an investment and the existing and likely future supply of closely competitive facilities. From this, the investor formulates four conclusions:

1. The various prices and their probabilities at which the particular investment (existing or proposed) might be rented and expected future changes in rents
2. An estimate of the quantity (occupancy ratio or, conversely, vacancy ratio), such as apartment units or square feet of office space, likely to be sold or rented per year at those prices
3. A discussion of the specific conditions such as financing terms, sales techniques, or certain amenities, which are required for sale or rental
4. An estimate of the probable future trends in selling price for the type of investment under consideration in its market environment

It is obvious that the market study determines the first inputs to the cash flow statement. Remember that cash flow from a real estate investment can arise from two sources: the annual cash flow from operating the investment and the cash flow from the future disposition (usually sale) of the investment.

The market study also shows future trends in the expected market value (or selling price) of the investment. Increases (or decreases) in market value are caused by relative price changes or inflation. It is also possible to have both simultaneously. *Inflation* is defined as increases in all prices at the same rate of change. A *relative price change* is one in which the price or value of an investment rises (or falls) relative to prices of the other goods (investments) in the economy.

However, the investor must understand that the present investment value is not influenced by inflation. Although inflation affects the future value, it does not affect the present value of an investment. On the other hand, expected relative price changes affect both the future and the present value of an investment.

Risk versus Uncertainty

A distinction is sometimes made between risk and uncertainty. *Risk* is associated with situations in which a probability distribution of the returns from investment can be estimated. *Uncertainty*, on the other hand, is associated with situations in which estimates of probability distribution are impossible. This distinction is not made in our discussion: Risk and uncertainty are used synonymously.

However, we realize that probability distributions of expected returns can be estimated with some precision. Some investments may have distributions that can be estimated objectively with statistical techniques. When such methods are used, risk is said to be measured by objective probability distributions.

On the other hand, there are many investment situations in which statistical data cannot be used. The investor may have few or no historical data to use, particularly when the investment is a new project. However, the investor may rely heavily on historical data for similar projects and personal judgment. This is called *subjective probability distributions*. Thus *risk* (or uncertainty) refers to an investment whose return cannot be predicted with certainty but for which an array of alternative outcomes and their probabilities can be estimated. This is a major purpose of market analysis.

Risk Over Time

How does the risk for an income stream change over time? Figure 4-1 shows the distribution of expected cash flow from an investment for years 1, 5, and 10. The distribution becomes flatter over time, indicating that there is more uncertainty about expected cash flows in later years. The dashed lines show the standard deviation, a well-known measure of risk, attached to the cash flow each year. The lines diverge from the expected cash flow over time, which indicates that the riskiness is increasing. If the cash flow in later years could be estimated equally as well as the cash flow in earlier years, that is, if risk were constant through time, the standard deviation would be constant and the dashed line would not diverge from the expected value.

In setting up the expected cash flow each year, some factors are probably the key to riskiness over time. For example, it is relatively easy to forecast the depreciation deduction and debt service with a fixed-rate mortgage in later years, but much harder to forecast the expected rents, vacancies, or selling price. The market forces that cause these factors to vary are difficult to forecast as time increases.

This fact makes the investor base judgments on short-term holding period forecasts of cash flows. It has been argued that, on the average, income-producing properties typically are sold or refinanced within ten years or less of

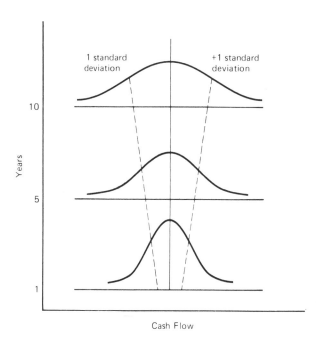

Years

10

5

1

Cash Flow

1 standard deviation

+1 standard deviation

Figure 4-1 Risk as a Function of Time.

Source: Austin J. Jaffe and C. F. Sirmans, *Real Estate Investment Decision Making*, 1982, p. 72. Reprinted by permission of Prentice-Hall, Inc., Englewood Cliffs, N.J.

purchase. Longer-term forecasts of the expected cash flows should generally be used only in such cases as long-term leases.

Inflation, Relative Price Changes, and Market Analysis

Market analysis is particularly aimed at identifying potential relative price changes in an investment. These price changes are caused by shifts in supply or demand or both for a particular investment, including real income changes, population growth (or decline), changes in neighborhood characteristics, or changes in tax laws.

It is important to understand the impact of relative price changes. The price of a particular investment can increase or decrease relative to other goods. Unexpected relative price declines have a negative impact on the rate of return for a particular investment. Likewise, unexpected relative price increases have positive effects on rates of return.

To illustrate relative price changes, consider the following simple example. An investor purchases a parcel of land for $10,000. One year later the land is sold for $12,000 (ignoring all holding costs and assuming no inflation). The investor has thus earned a 20 percent return.

$$\$10,000 = \frac{\$12,000}{(1 + R)^1}$$

$$R = 20\%$$

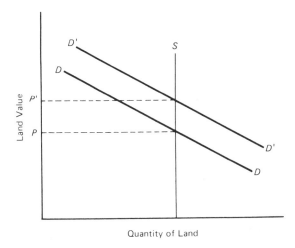

Figure 4-2   A Shift in the Demand for Land.

Source: Austin J. Jaffe and C. F. Sirmans, *Real Estate Investment Decision Making*, 1982, p. 74. Reprinted by permission of Prentice-Hall, Inc., Englewood Cliffs, N.J.

But how is the investor able to sell the investment for a higher price? Figure 4-2 illustrates this for the simple case. The curves S and D represent the supply and demand curves for land. Suppose that population growth shifts the demand curve for land to D'. The price then rises from P to P' in real terms.

The present value of an investment depends on two factors: the estimated future value and the rate of return. Obviously, if the rate of return is held constant and the estimated future value is increased, the present value will be higher. In the simple example, the present value would be $12,000 instead of $10,000 if the expected future value is increased to $15,000 because of a relative price change. If the price is higher because of neutral inflation (or an equal percentage change in all prices), the present value would not be higher because the required rate of return must be increased to compensate for the purchasing power risk to which the investor is exposed.

If we view the required rate of return, k, as the sum of the risk-free rate, k_f, the market risk premium, k_m, and the inflation premium, k_p, then

$$k = k_f + k_m + k_p \qquad (4\text{-}2)$$

If there is no inflation, $k_p = 0$. In the example above, if the risk-free rate is 5 percent and the market risk is 15 percent, the required rate of return is 20 percent.

$$k = k_f + k_m + k_p \qquad (4\text{-}3)$$

$$k = .05 + .15 + .00$$

$$k = .20$$

Assume that inflation now increases from 0 percent annually to 5 percent annually. In our example, the land that sold for $10,000 a year ago would sell for $12,000 without inflation. With inflation, however, it sells for an additional $500, or $12,500. The question is whether the investor is any better off due to this inflationary effect. The answer is no.

If inflation is 5 percent, then $k_p = .05$. The required rate of return, k, becomes

$$k = k_f + k_m + k_p$$

$$k = .05 + .15 + .05$$

$$k = .25$$

The present value of the investment is

$$PV = \frac{\$12,500}{(1 + .25)^1}$$

$$PV = \$10,000$$

This may seem surprising, since inflation increases the future rather than the present value of the land. However, the important point is that it also increases the required rate of return to keep the real value constant.

Because financial markets anticipate inflation, inflation premiums, k_p, are incorporated into market interest rates. Therefore, since inflation affects all assets in nominal dollars equally, a higher required rate of return means that the real value (and return) stays constant.

Obviously, some changes in the value of real estate have occurred due to increasing demand for, or perhaps supply restrictions of, property during recent years. Although accumulated wealth is largely attributed to inflation, it is actually due to changes in demand or supply or both in the real estate market and to changes in the value of indebtedness assumed by borrowers prior to rising interest rates. Market analysis is aimed at trying to uncover these potential relative price changes. To understand the investment process, one must understand the impact of inflation and relative price changes on present values and required rates of return.

MEASURING RISK AND RETURN

Modern real estate investment analysis defines *risk* as the dispersion of an investment's returns—the positive and negative deviations from the expected return. The most widely used method of risk analysis utilizes the expected (mean) rate of return as an indication of an investment's profitability, and the variance (or standard deviation) as an indication of its risk.

Business risk, broadly defined, is the risk inherent in investing in real estate, as measured by the variability in the rate of return for an all-equity-financed investment. A general way of viewing the rate of return, k, that should be required on an investment is

$$k = k_f + k_m$$

The term k_f is the risk-free rate, and k_m is the premium for business risk. The risk-free rate applies to an investment where there is no chance that the realized rate of return will be less than the expected rate of return. The risk-free rate is simply compensation for postponing current consumption plans. The risk premium is the additional return necessary to compensate investors for bearing the risk that the realized rate could be lower than expected. Thus k is the required rate of return and reflects compensation for both waiting and risk.

Expected Rate of Return

A simple measure of the overall rate of return from an investment is calculated as follows:

$$R = \frac{\text{NOI}}{\text{Value}} \tag{4-4}$$

where

R = overall rate of return (sometimes called the overall capitalization rate)
NOI = expected net operating income
Value = value of the investment

For example, an investment under consideration is expected to generate $100,000 per year. The value is $1 million. The overall rate, R, is thus 10 percent ($100,000 divided by $1,000,000).

There is the possibility, however, that the net operating income will not be as expected. Suppose an investor decides that there are six chances out of ten that the actual net operating income will be $100,000. The investor also feels that there is a .25 probability that the investment will generate $80,000 and a .15 probability that $110,000 will be realized. These outcomes are summarized in Table 4-1.

$E(R)$ denotes the expected rate of return, which is the weighted average

TABLE 4-1 Illustration of Expected Rate of Return for Investment A

VALUE	NET OPERATING INCOME (NOI)	PROBABILITY (p_i)	OVERALL RATE (R)
$1,000,000	$ 80,000	.25	.08
1,000,000	100,000	.60	.10
1,000,000	110,000	.15	.11

of possible rates of return using the probabilities (p_i) as the weights. Thus $E(R)$ can be written as follows:

$$E(R) = R_1 \times p_1 + R_2 \times p_2 + R_3 \times p_3 + \ldots + R_m \times p_m \qquad (4\text{-}5)$$

$$= \sum_{i=1}^{m} R_i \times p_i$$

where R_i represents the overall return from the ith "state of the world," m is the number of "states of the world," and p_i represents the probability of the ith "state of the world."

For investment A, the expected rate of return is

$$E(R_A) = .08(.25) + .10(.60) + .11(.15)$$

$$= .0965, \text{ or } 9.65\%$$

Measuring Risk

To measure risk, investment analysis uses *variance* or *standard deviation*. These measure the dispersion of the expected return around the mean (expected) value and provide information on the extent of possible deviations of the actual return from the expected return. The greater the variance in expected return, the greater the risk.

The variance (σ^2) of the mean is given by

$$\sigma^2 = \sum_{i=1}^{m} [R_i - E(R)]^2 p_i \qquad (4\text{-}6)$$

(σ is the Greek letter sigma. The variance is thus read "sigma squared.")

To calculate the variance:

1. Calculate the deviation of each possible outcome from the expected value $[R_i - E(R)]$
2. Raise this deviation to the second power $[R_i - E(R)]^2$
3. Multiply this term by the probability of getting R_i (that is, p_i) $[R_i - E(R)]^2 \times p_i$
4. Sum these products, $\sum_{i=1}^{m} [R_i - E(R)]^2 \times p_i$

Note that the distribution of returns is measured in percentages. The dimension of σ^2 is in "percentages squared," which, of course, is economically meaningless. Thus we take the square root of the variance, which results in the standard deviation (σ) in "percentages":

$$\sigma = \sqrt{\sigma^2} \qquad (4\text{-}7)$$

Because standard deviation also measures the variability of the distribution, it is stated in percentages. For ranking investment proposals, however, either the variance or the standard deviation can be used, since both are always greater than or equal to zero.

The standard deviation for investment A is

$$\sigma_A = \sqrt{.00010275}$$

$$= .01014$$

Thus, for investment A, the expected overall return $E(R_A)$ is 9.65 percent with a standard deviation, σ_A, of 1.014 percent.

The Decision Rules for Mean-Variance Analysis

To evaluate investments using the expected return and variance (or standard deviation), apply the following decision rules:

Investment A is preferred to investment B if one of the following two conditions holds:

1. The expected return of A exceeds (or is equal to) the expected return of B *and* the standard deviation of A is less than the standard deviation of B.

or

2. The expected return of A exceeds that of B *and* the standard deviation of A is less than (or equal to) that of B.

In equation form, these decision rules can be written as follows:

$$E(R_A) \geq E(R_B)$$

$$\sigma_A < \sigma_B$$

or

$$E(R_A) > E(R_B)$$

$$\sigma_A \geq \sigma_B$$

In the example, the expected return, variance, and standard deviation for investment A are

Expected return: $E(R_A) = .0965$

Variance: $\sigma_A^2 = .00010275$

Standard deviation: $\sigma_A = .01014$

Suppose the expected return, variance, and standard deviation for investment B are

Expected return: $E(R_B) = .0965$

Variance: $\sigma_B^2 = .00015$

Standard deviation: $\sigma_B = .01225$

TABLE 4-2   Illustration of Risk and Return

INVESTMENT	RETURN $E(R)$	RISK (σ)
C	.11	.02
D	.13	.02
E	.11	.03

Note that both investments have the same expected return of 9.65 percent. However, investment A is preferable to B under condition 1. The expected return from both investments is the same, but investment A has a smaller variance (or standard deviation). Investment B is thus more risky in terms of variance from the expected return.

Further Examples

The mean-variance decision rules help the investor select and, more importantly, understand the relationship between expected returns from an investment and the risks. To further illustrate these decision rules, suppose an investor has the investment opportunities shown in Table 4-2.

Which of these should the investor select? Using the decision rules, compare investments C and E. Both have the same expected return, but C has less risk because the standard deviation is smaller. Thus C is preferred to E. Now compare investments C and D. These have the same risk, but D has a higher expected return. Therefore D is preferred to C. Since D is preferred to C and C is preferred to E, investment D is preferred to E. Now, if the investor were to choose among the three, investment D would be selected.

However, sometimes there are problems with the mean-variance decision rules. Suppose an investor has the choices shown in Table 4-3. Which should the investor select? We cannot use the mean-variance rules because, in this case, the expected risk and expected return are greater for investment G than for investment F. The question that the investor must answer is, Does the increase in return "compensate" for the increase in risk? If it does, then choose G over F. If it does not, the investor would prefer investment F. This is a major reason why the investor must identify his or her particular preference on the risk-return trade-off.

TABLE 4-3   Another Illustration of Risk and Return

INVESTMENT	RETURN $E(R)$	RISK (σ)
F	.11	.02
G	.13	.03

TABLE 4-4   Common Errors in Analyzing Markets

TYPE OF ERROR	PERCENTAGE OF REPORTS
1. Unspecified research direction	73%
2. Statistics without explanation	82
3. Misspecification of supply and demand	67
4. Failure to correlate supply and demand	60
5. Inattention to economic indicators	76
6. Omission of primary data	49

COMMON ERRORS IN ANALYZING MARKETS

A recent survey of real estate market analyses examined the question, What have been the deficiencies of real estate market and investment analyses that have been prepared, and what can be done to improve them? This survey examined forty-five feasibility reports prepared by consultants, appraisers, and market analysts with established national or regional reputations.[1] It found that the caliber of market analysis reports was substantially below the "state of the art." Six of the most common errors made in analyzing real estate markets are summarized in Table 4-4.

Unspecified research direction.   The appropriateness of any investment decision can only be evaluated when the investor's goal or objective is known. As noted previously, the analyst must determine what decision the investor is trying to make.

Statistics without explanation.   Nearly all market analysis reports contain large amounts of statistics on such factors as population growth, employment levels, income levels, and transportation facilities. The purpose of the market analysis is not to describe but to explain. How do these relate to the problem at hand?

Misspecification of supply and demand.   As noted previously, market analysis centers on understanding supply and demand for a given investment. What is the market for the investment under consideration? What segment of the market is being served by the project? How does this project compare with competing projects?

Failure to correlate supply and demand.   The investor must carefully analyze supply and demand to determine expected vacancy rates for the invest-

---

[1] Gary W. Eldred and Robert H. Zerbst, "A Critique of Real Estate Market and Investment Analysis," *Appraisal Journal*, 46 (July 1978), 443–52.

ment under consideration. From this the investor must make quantitative decisions regarding the ability to rent the investment.

Inattention to economic indicators.   The investor must also analyze the possible effects of the regional and national economic climate on local economies and decide how possible downturns will affect the investment. Leading economic indicators may be used in investment decision making.

Omission of primary data.   Data can be classified as primary or secondary. *Secondary data* are collected for some purpose other than the study at hand. This type of data is available from such sources as the U.S. Bureau of Census, trade associations, and planning agencies. While typically cost-free, these frequently do not fit the investment process very precisely.

Primary data, on the other hand, are gathered specifically for the investment decision. Primary data help determine the tastes and preferences of the particular segment of the real estate market to which an investment is aimed. Types of data include vacancy surveys, rental rates, and operating expense levels of competing investments.

FACTORS TO CONSIDER IN ANALYZING MARKETS

The general factors influencing real estate investments can be broadly classified as those influencing demand and those influencing supply.

Income.   Because the demand for real estate is dependent on income, and real estate is used to produce products and services, the investor must carefully consider the demand for the products or services produced using the real estate. For example, the demand for residential units is derived from the demand for housing.

The level of income determines the demand for real estate and indicates the ability to obtain financing.

Demographic factors.   Demographics, or population characteristics, are one of the major determinants of the long-term direction of real estate markets. Profiles of age, rates of family formation, fertility, mortality, and migration are extremely important. Migration trends are probably the most difficult to forecast but have the most impact on real estate markets.

Supply factors.   The existing supply of real estate includes structures that have been built over a long period of time. New structures added in any one year may exceed the old structures torn down, but seldom is the net increase a very large proportion of the total supply. Thus the supply of real estate at any point in time is relatively fixed. The characteristics of existing and new supply such as age, location, and physical conditions should be compared with the investment under consideration. These give the investor some idea of how his or her investment would compete in the market.

Economic trends.   The real estate investor should monitor the important indicators of economic activity that forecast recessions or growth. Some good indicators are interest rates, construction activity, and unemployment levels.

Table 4-5 lists the factors to be considered before investing. These include delineation of the market area, demographic analysis, discussion of the economy of the market area, construction and real estate activity, and the political and legal aspects. The key factor for successful analysis is not what the investor can find out about the market, but which of all these factors will have a significant impact on the investment decision.

Physical Characteristics

The physical attributes of land and improvements play a crucial role in the overall feasibility of an investment. These attributes may limit utility or provide opportunities to create competition.

The physical attributes include

1. Size and shape of the site
2. Topography
3. Storm water drainage
4. Watersheds, springs, or other water factors
5. Soil and subsoil characteristics
6. Utilities
7. Functional layout of the improvements
8. Personal-response factors, such as security
9. Transportation access
10. Physical condition of improvements

The investor is obviously concerned with matching the demands in the marketplace to the supply. The key question is whether the investment under consideration provides the services demanded by prospective users.

Sociopolitical Environment

As we have stated, the purpose of market analysis is to help the investor identify the degree of business risk for an investment. All real estate investments are subject to business risk, since the net income is not known with certainty.

TABLE 4-5   Real Estate Market Analysis for an Investment

I. Delineation of the market area
    A. Metropolitan area
        1. Name of standard metropolitan statistical area (SMSA)
        2. Identification of entire area
            a. County or counties
            b. Principal incorporated and unincorporated urbanized areas (10,000 or more population)
        3. Geography
            a. Size (land area)
            b. Major topographical features
        4. Climate
            a. Rainfall
            b. Temperature changes (monthly, seasonal)
            c. Relative humidity
        5. General urban structure; location of facilities
            a. Significant geographic submarkets in SMSA
            b. Employment areas
            c. Shopping areas (central-business-district, regional, and community shopping centers)
            d. Principal transportation facilities (air, highway, rail, water)
            e. Educational facilities
            f. Community facilities (religious, cultural, recreational)
        6. Direction of city growth
        7. Commuting patterns (journey to work)
        8. Any major community developments and/or special features or characteristics germane to the market analysis

II. Demographic analysis
    A. Population
        1. Most recent estimate for total population
        2. Past trends in population growth
        3. Estimated future population
            a. 1990, 1995, 2000 totals and average annual rate of growth
            b. Changes in population due to
                (1) Net natural increase
                (2) Migration
        4. Distribution by age groups
            a. 1980 census
            b. Most recent estimates
    B. Households
        1. Most recent estimates for household formations
        2. Past trends in household formations
        3. Estimated future total households and average annual rate of growth
        4. Current trends in household size (increasing, decreasing)

III. Economy of the market area (Demand Side Analysis)
    A. Economic history and characteristics
        1. General description
        2. Major economic activities and developments
            a. Before 1980
            b. Recent and present

TABLE 4-5 (CONT.)   Real Estate Market Analysis for an Investment

    B. Employment, total and nonagricultural
        1. Current estimates
        2. Past trends
        3. Distribution by industry groups
            a. For each period, past and present
            b. Numerical and as percent of all employment
        4. Estimated future employment
            a. Total
            b. By industry groups
        5. Trends in labor participation rate
        6. Trends in female employment
    C. Unemployment
        1. Current level
        2. Past trends
    D. Economic-base analysis
        1. Metropolitan area compared with national and state employment data
        2. Discussion of principal employers
            a. Primary industries (manufacturing, construction, mining)
            b. Secondary industries (TCU), trade, FIRE, services, governments)
            c. Location and accessibility
        3. Payroll data (census of manufacturers, trade, services, governments)
    E. Income data
        1. Personal income by major sources
            a. By type: wage and salary, proprietors
            b. By industry: farm, nonfarm, government
        2. Per capita personal income
        3. Family-income distribution
            a. All families
            b. Owner households
            c. Renter households
            d. Households with female heads
        4. Projections for growth in personal income
IV. Construction and real estate activity (Supply Side Analysis)
    A. Building and construction industry
        1. Residential building by type (single family, multifamily, rental, or sales)
            a. Historical and recent trends (past 10 years)
            b. Building permits: monthly for current and previous year
            c. Conversions and demolitions
        2. Nonresidential construction
            a. Commercial
            b. Industrial
            c. Institutional
        3. High-rise building activity (minimum height of five stories above ground)
            a. Residential
            b. Commercial (offices, stores, hotels and motels, multiple-use)
            c. Other (governmental, schools, hospitals)
        4. Heavy engineering construction
    B. Demand-and-supply analysis for properties other than residential
        1. General demand factors in metropolitan area
            a. Number of potential new employees
            b. Number of potential new tenants or owner users

TABLE 4-5 (CONT.)   Real Estate Market Analysis for an Investment

    c. Movement of firms in and out of the area
    d. Recent trends in replacement ratios
  2. Existing inventory, by property type
    a. Price: sale or rental rates
    b. Quantity: net leasable square footage
    c. Year built: before 1980, 1980–present, new
    d. Competitive status
    e. Vacancy factors
  3. Projected production, by property type
    a. Price: sale or rental rates
    b. Quantity: net leasable space
    c. Probable conditions (financing, marketing, absorption rates)
C. Housing inventory, by type (single-family, multifamily)
  1. Most recent estimates
  2. Past trends including 1980 census
    a. Index of housing values and rents
  3. Principal characteristics
    a. Tenure of occupancy
    b. Value of houses and monthly contract rent
    c. Type of structure
    d. Year built
    e. Vacancy ratios: percent of total units (total, homeowner, rental)
D. Residential sales and rental markets
  1. General market conditions
  2. Major subdivision activity
    a. Current
    b. Past trends
  3. Trends in sales prices or monthly rentals
    a. Existing units
    b. New units
    c. Sales prices or monthly rentals adjusted to square-foot basis
  4. Unsold inventory of new sales housing
    a. Price ranges
    b. Number of months unsold
    c. Absorption rates
    d. Environmental ratings
    e. Competitive status with other sales properties
  5. New rental housing
    a. Date of completion
    b. Type of units and rental ranges
    c. Marketing experience to date
    d. Absorption rates
    e. Environmental ratings
    f. Competitive status with existing rental housing
  6. Residential units under construction
    a. Volume
    b. Types of units
    c. Probable environmental ratings
    d. Probable marketing schedules

TABLE 4-5 (CONT.)   Real Estate Market Analysis for an Investment

    E. Other housing markets
        1. Public and governmental subsidized housing
           a. Identification and location
           b. Existing and planned
        2. Specialized submarkets for housing demand and supply
           a. College or university housing
           b. Housing for the elderly
           c. Military housing
    F. Real estate loans and mortgage markets
        1. Sources and availability of funds
        2. FHA, VA, FNMA, GNMA
        3. Interest rates and terms of mortgages
        4. Recordings of mortgages and/or deeds of trust
        5. Foreclosures
           a. Overall trend
           b. Conventional, FHA, other

  V. Political and legal aspects (Legal Environment Analysis)
    A. Land-use planning
        1. Regional
        2. County (counties)
        3. Incorporated cities in SMSA
    B. Zoning
        1. Review of present zoning ordinances for county (counties) and cities
        2. Zoning history and present attitudes of zoning authority
        3. Identify raw land presently zoned for land use of subject property
    C. Ordinances, codes, regulations
        1. Subdivisions
           a. Submission procedures
           b. Requirements for improvements
        2. Building codes
        3. Health and public safety
        4. Allocation of land for schools, recreational areas, open space
    D. Municipal services
        1. Public safety
           a. Fire
           b. Police
        2. Hospitals and health care
        3. Utilities
    E. Ecological
        1. Environmental impact studies
        2. Limited growth policies
        3. Floodplains and flood control
        4. Solid-waste disposal
    F. Property taxation
        1. Tax rate per $1,000 valuation
        2. Assessment ratio as percent of market value
        3. Special assessment districts

TABLE 4-5 (CONT.)   Real Estate Market Analysis for an Investment

VI. Sources of information
   A. Types of data
      1. Population
      2. Employment
      3. Personal income
      4. Planning
      5. Building
      6. Zoning
      7. Other pertinent
   B. Sources of data
      1. Secondary data sources
         a. Census of population
         b. Census of construction
         c. Census of housing
         d. Bureau of Labor Statistics
         e. National Planning Association
         f. Local planning agencies
      2. Primary data sources
         a. Real estate brokers
         b. Appraisers
         c. Construction firms
         d. Mail questionnaires

Source: U.S. Dept. of Housing and Urban Development, *FHA Techniques of Housing Market Analysis.*
(Washington, D.C.: August, 1970).

Another important set of factors that influences the decision-making process is referred to as the sociopolitical environment. Whereas market analysis is aimed at identifying the demand and supply factors, the sociopolitical environment is concerned with the relationship between an investment and the neighborhood (or community).

While an investment may be legal (say, in terms of zoning), it may not be perceived as "good" by a given neighborhood or community. All real estate investments, and particularly large-scale projects such as shopping centers, create "external" influences on a neighborhood. These externalities—increased property values, increased traffic, noise—must be dealt with by the investor. External effects can be both positive and negative, and a neighborhood may perceive that an investment imposes more negative influences than it does positive. The investor may have to face these questions (and other constraints) in the decision-making framework.

Adverse public reaction to potential investments is as serious a constraint as the possibility of lack of demand or competition. Business risk should thus be viewed in a much larger framework than just supply and demand (economics). The sociopolitical environment is as important, though often much more difficult, to identify. A cursory review of any newspaper will reveal articles related to this environment.

**Exhibit 4-2 Leading Issues in the
              Sociopolitical Environment**

During the past several years, the public has continued to take an active role in the redefinition and reregulation of real property rights. In many ways, the sociopolitical environment is often the most important area for real estate investors, especially real estate developers.

For example, although land-use controls through zoning date back to the beginning of the twentieth century in the United States, modern local governments have often gone far beyond the adoption of a comprehensive zoning plan for the primary purpose of separating inharmonious land uses. Some cities have regulations on the size and shape of commercial signs, on the types of advertisements, and on the nature of permitted activities on the property. In addition, local ordinances frequently require investors to obtain numerous permits before building additions, making alterations, extracting tree stumps, and even excavating swimming pools. Some cities require that builders refrain from casting shadows on their neighbors; others forbid any new construction at all. Some cities, in fact, now possess a bundle of property rights that resemble the private bundle of the property owner of only a few years ago.

While it is important to identify the leading sociopolitical issues of the local community *before* large amounts of resources are committed, it is essential that the investor develop a high level of political acumen regarding land-use issues in communities with active state and local governments. The specialists in this area are usually attorneys and, sometimes, former political officials. It may be worthwhile to employ the services of these experts for certain real estate investments, since this area is a growing aspect of real estate investment decision making.

A Sample Market Analysis

Table 4-5 illustrates the various types of factors that should be considered in analyzing the real estate market. First, delineate the market area. Second, analyze its demographic characteristics, including population growth, estimated future population growth, age distribution, and number of households. Third, consider those factors influencing the demand for a real estate investment, including employment trends, income data, and the economic base of the neighborhood.

Fourth, analyze the supply side of the market. This includes examining the building and construction industry, analyzing housing market and mortgage market trends, and inventorying existing competition. Fifth, analyze the political and legal areas. These include land-use planning, zoning, building

TABLE 4-6 Market Analysis of a Potential Apartment Investment

APARTMENT PROJECT	NO. OF UNITS	TYPE	APARTMENT MIX				ESTIMATED OCCUPANCY	COMMENTS
			SQ. FT. FLOOR AREA	RENT PER MONTH	SQ. FT. RENT PER MONTH	RENT PER ROOM		
1. Oakbrook Village	52	1BR, 1BA, ST	453	$260	$.57	$ 86.67	98%	Student oriented, well landscaped, two miles from university on student bus route, drapes and carpets, completely furnished, quiet
	55	2BR, 2BA, F	939	400	.43	100.00	99%	
	49	1BR, 1.5BA, TH	729	325	.45	108.33	97%	
2. Tiger Plaza	68	1BR, 1BA, F	709	294	.41	98.00	97%	Large complex, student oriented, drapes and carpets, completely furnished, tennis court and pool, one mile from university, on student bus route
	79	2BR, 1BA, F	893	354	.40	88.50	99%	
	73	3BR, 1.5BA, F	1,044	468	.45	93.60	98%	
3. Plantation Trace	23	1BR, 1BA, 2nd Fl, F	676	295	.44	98.33	97%	Student oriented, drapes and carpets, large closets, washer-dryer connections, pool, tennis court, clubhouse site needs additional landscaping
	24	1BR, 1BA, 1st Fl, F	742	318	.43	106.00	97%	
	24	1BR, 1BA, TH	796	319	.40	106.33	97%	
	25	1BR, 1BA, 1st Fl, F	796	337	.42	112.33	98%	
	27	2BR, 2BA, F	931	397	.43	99.25	99%	
	25	2BR, 1BA, F	864	367	.42	91.75	99%	
	21	2BR, 1.5BA, TH	890	377	.42	94.25	98%	
	21	3BR, 2BA, F	1,168	477	.41	95.40	98%	

APARTMENT MIX

APARTMENT PROJECT	NO. OF UNITS	TYPE	SQ. FT. FLOOR AREA	RENT PER MONTH	SQ. FT. RENT PER MONTH	RENT PER ROOM	ESTIMATED OCCUPANCY	COMMENTS
4. Place du Plantier	28	1BR, 1.5BA, TH	633	280	.44	93.33	98%	Student oriented, well-maintained landscape, pets allowed, tennis court, clubhouse, well lighted, drapes and carpets, completely furnished, on student bus route
	31	1BR, 1BA, F	633	295	.47	98.33	97%	
	30	2BR, 1BA, F	873	350	.40	87.50	99%	
	30	2BR, 1.5BA, TH	963	360	.37	90.00	99%	
	29	2BR, 2BA, F	962	375	.39	93.75	98%	
	32	3BR, 2BA, F	1,136	440	.39	88.00	98%	
5. Embassy	40	1BR, 1BA, F	735	320	.44	106.67	97%	Student oriented, half mile from university, site needs additional landscaping, very small kitchen space, drapes and carpets, completely furnished
	44	1BR, 1BA, F	595	290	.49	96.67	97%	
	47	2BR, 1.5BA, F	935	400	.43	100.00	99%	
	44	2BR, 1BA, F	727	335	.46	83.75	98%	
6. Sharlo/Sharlo Terrace II	78	1BR, 1BA, F	614	280	.46	93.33	97%	Large complex, student oriented, drapes and carpet need replacing, large closets, pool
	74	2BR, 2BA, F	838	370	.44	92.50	99%	
	73	3BR, 2BA, F	980	440	.45	88.00	98%	

DEFINITIONS: BA = Bathroom
BR = Bedroom
F = Flat
FL = Floor
ST = Studio
TH = Townhouse

codes, municipal services, property taxation, and other aspects of the legal environment.

Finally, identify the types and sources of data for market analysis.

Rental and Vacancy Forecasts: An Illustration

One of the key purposes of market analysis is to determine the expected rental for the investment under consideration. The major technique for determining expected rents and vacancies is to compare similar properties. Using an apartment investment as the subject property, Table 4-6 shows how this is done by listing the data on six comparable properties.

In the analysis, the investor first determines the current rental income of the comparable properties. The rent is given per apartment unit, per square foot, and per room. Note that although the rent per apartment varies from $260.00 to $477.00 per month, and the variation per room is from $83.75 to $112.33, in terms of square footage, the variation is much lower. The mean rent per square foot is $0.43, with only a $0.06 deviation in either direction (excluding the 1BR, 1BA studio in Oakbrook, which is not typical of market rent). The mean rent per room is $95.95, with a deviation of approximately $12.00 in either direction. This points out the necessity of measuring rent in various units and of comparing rent on a basis most similar to the market.

In the analysis, it is also important to determine who the tenants are and what special services or amenities are necessary to secure this rent. Obviously, in a student market, proximity to the university and the availability of public transportation are necessary. Although the apartments usually have identical layouts or floor plans, are there additional features in the subject property such as an extra bath that will make it more appealing? Or are there missing features that will make it less appealing?

Table 4-6 also gives the occupancy rates for the various comparables. This is important in establishing the expectations regarding vacancies for the investment under consideration. The same process is used to forecast rent and vacancies for other types of investments. If the subject property is 100 percent occupied when other similar properties have vacancies, the rent may be underpriced or vice versa if the subject property is underoccupied.

QUESTIONS

4-1. What is the purpose of market analysis?

4-2. What is business risk? How is it measured?

4-3. What is the relationship between *risk* and *time*?

4-4. "Inflation has no effect on equity values; only relative price changes do." True or false? Explain.

4-5. Can real estate investors benefit from expected inflation? Unexpected inflation?

4-6. How is the expected rate of return measured? How is the variance of the expected return measured?

4-7. Illustrate how the decision rules for mean-variance analysis can be used when an investor tries to decide between two alternative investments.

4-8. What are the most common errors found in real estate market studies?

PROBLEMS

4-1. An investment with a value of $500,000 has the following expected NOI:

STATE OF WORLD	NOI	PROBABILITY
1	$50,000	.05
2	55,000	.80
3	65,000	.15

a. Calculate the expected overall rate of return.
b. Calculate the variance and standard deviation.

4-2. An investor is considering the purchase of a parcel of land.

a. Suppose there was no expected inflation and the required rate of return was 10 percent. Suppose also that the investor expected to sell the parcel for $100,000 after a three-year holding period. How much should be paid now?

b. Suppose the investor paid $75,132 for the investment and sold it for $110,000. Relative to the required rate of return of 10 percent, would the earned rate of return be higher or lower?

c. Suppose there was inflation at a rate of 5 percent and the investor expected to sell the land for $114,266. How much should be paid today?

4-3. Under what situations would an investor be able to benefit from the following?
a. Expected relative price increase
b. Expected relative price decrease
c. Expected inflation (neutral; all prices increasing)
d. Expected deflation
e. Unexpected relative price increase
f. Unexpected relative price decrease
g. Unexpected inflation
h. Unexpected deflation

4-4. Suppose an investor faces the following choices:

INVESTMENT	EXPECTED RETURN $E(R)$	RISK (σ)
A	.15	.02
B	.15	.03
C	.15	.03
D	.14	.03
E	.15	.02
F	.16	.03

Which should the investor select between
a. Investments A and B?
b. Investments C and D?
c. Investments E and F?

SELECTED REFERENCES

BARRETT, G. VINCENT, and JOHN P. BLAIR, *How to Conduct and Analyze Real Estate Market and Feasibility Studies*. New York: Van Nostrand Reinhold, 1982.

BOWES, W. A., "What Is Market Analysis?" *Real Estate Appraiser*, 34 (July-August 1968), 11–14.

ELDRED, GARY W., and ROBERT H. ZERBST, "A Critique of Real Estate Market and Investment Analysis," *Appraisal Journal*, 46 (July 1978), 443–52.

GRAASKAMP, JAMES A., *A Guide to Feasibility Analysis*. Chicago: Society of Real Estate Appraisers, 1970.

JAFFE, AUSTIN J., and ROBERT G. BUSSA, "Using a Simple Model to Estimate Market Rents: A Case Study," *Appraisal Journal*, 45 (January 1977), 7–13.

MESSNER, STEPHEN C., BYRL N. BOYCE, HAROLD G. TRIMBLE, and ROBERT L. WARD, *Analyzing Real Estate Opportunities—Market and Feasibility Studies*. Chicago: Realtors National Marketing Institute of the National Association of Realtors, 1982.

REDMAN, ARNOLD L., and C. F. SIRMANS, "Regional/Local Economic Analysis: A Discussion of Data Sources," *Appraisal Journal*, 45 (April 1977), 261–72.

VERNOR, JAMES D., *Readings in Market Research for Real Estate*. Chicago: American Institute of Real Estate Appraisers, 1985.

5

THE LEGAL
ENVIRONMENT

In the real world, there is a certain amount of risk associated with the legal environment. As a result, an investor must pay attention to the local, state, and federal laws that affect the environment. *Legal risk* is the possibility that the government will alter the laws that affect the real estate investment.

There are many effects of legal risk. For example, if a property owner is interested in converting his or her property to a condominium in the near future, this action will affect several groups of people. For instance, current tenants will be affected by the change because their leaseholds will not be available in the future. In addition, tenants in other buildings may be affected because the supply of rental space will be less than in the past. Prospective purchases of condominium units may also be affected by the new project. Mortgage lenders who have creditor interests in the apartment building have an interest in the outcome of the conversion because the mortgage note must be satisfied before the conversion is complete. Finally, various units of government are interested in the outcome. In every case, each participant has an economic interest in the "property rights" that have been developed and are protected by the legal system. Therefore a complete real estate investment analysis requires a basic understanding of the modern legal environment. Note, however, that this chapter is not intended to be an all-inclusive summary or substitute for legal counsel.

SOME BASIC DEFINITIONS

In order to study the legal environment in real estate, it is necessary to learn a number of basic definitions. These include the doctrine of property as a "bundle of rights," real estate, realty, real property, personalty, personal property, and fixtures.

It is sometimes said that real estate consists of a set of rights. These rights may be linked together by size, shape, nature, or duration. They may be vast and all-inclusive or few and limited. The complete set of rights is often referred to as the entire bundle of rights. In Anglo-American law, this bundle is called "fee simple absolute." In actuality, the study of real estate is the study of the bundle of rights.

In order to apply the doctrine of the bundle of rights, it is necessary to distinguish between real estate and real property. Although these terms are often used synonymously, there are distinctions between them. *Real estate* refers to the (a) physical object (land and its improvements), (b) the profession of brokers, appraisers, counselors, and others concerned with the land and

**Exhibit 5-1   Why an Analysis of the Legal
                Environment Is Fundamental**

Investors should treat the legal environment as another arena for analytical decision making. This is because, as in the market, financing, and taxation environments, the legal environment often permits a wide variety of choices for investors. These choices can have sizable impacts on the success or failure of most real estate investments.

Some investors seem to treat the legal environment relating to real estate investments as a constraint. While this approach may be satisfactory in some instances, with state and local governments taking an increasingly active role in property right determinations and redefinitions, those investors who choose to learn about the nature of the legal environment *before* making the investment decision are likely to have more tools available to them than those investors who do not concern themselves with the legal issues.

It is sometimes said that "real estate investing is 97 percent law." While this is obviously an exaggeration, the investor who is aware of local ordinances and their impacts on property and its value is the one who is far ahead of others with respect to knowledge about the conditions in which the property is located. Since the law of real estate is unique, it seems only natural that investors should try to understand as much of the legal environment as possible before making the investment decision.

its usage, and (c) the academic field of study interested in the process and institutions dealing with land usage and alteration among several interested parties in society. *Real property* refers to the rights associated with the *realty*, or the physical real estate. Therefore *realty* and *real estate* are synonymous terms. It is apparent, then, that the rights in the assets and not merely the assets are of particular interest in examining these resources for investment purposes.

A similar distinction is made between personalty and personal property. *Personalty* is defined as movable objects. Since land and permanently attached structures are fixed, personalty can be viewed as any other objects except realty. On the other hand, *personal property* consists of the rights associated with the personalty. Although these distinctions are not as general as real property rights, they are basic to our legal system. For example, the right of possession exists for both realty and personalty.

It is also possible for an object to become permanently attached to the real estate. Such an object is then called a *fixture*. Although the law provides some guidelines in these cases, it is sometimes difficult to determine whether an object that formerly was personalty is now a permanent attachment to the real estate and thus a fixture. It is important to recognize that fixtures become a part of the real estate and are therefore valued with the real estate for nearly every economic purpose.

THE REAL ESTATE INVESTMENT PARTICIPANTS

There are four major real estate participants in the real estate investment process: the equity investor, the mortgage lender, the tenant, and the government. Each has a particular interest and specific legal environment in which to operate. (The relationships between these participants were outlined in Figure 1-2, "Participants in the Real Estate Investment Process.")

The equity investor must decide on the appropriate organization form. The mortgage lender will be one of several types, using various types of instruments. The tenant is likely to vary with the type of property. The government may be at the federal, state, or local level.

The Equity Investor

The equity investor is faced with several choices regarding the type of business organization. The decision is to choose the one that is best for the investor, given the specific objectives of the owner. In the typical case, the equity investor is usually concerned with taxation, liability, marketability, method of creation, and expected duration of the organization. After considering all of these, the investor decides on the best organization form for each investment. Table 5-1 illustrates the various forms of ownership.

TABLE 5-1 Selected Alternative Forms of Ownership

Individual (Proprietorship)
General partnership
Limited partnership
Ordinary corporation
Subchapter S corporation
Land trust
Real estate investment trust (REIT)
Joint venture
Syndication

Individual (proprietorship).   Individual ownership is very simple to form and operate for a small enterprise. The transferability of assets is easy and inexpensive, and management of the company remains a personal responsibility. For some types of operation, this form is suitable. However, for many small operations, it may not be the most advantageous ownership form. The taxation treatment is according to regular, individual tax rates. Proprietorships have unlimited liability, which permits suitors seeking damages to have access to personal, nonbusiness assets. The aspects of unlimited liability and sole responsibility for decisions may be an incentive to use one of the other forms.

General partnership.   This is very similar to proprietorship. General partnerships are created by agreement of the parties. In general, partnerships offer individual proprietors the advantages of joint decision making and risk sharing with the disadvantage of potential management disagreements and differences of opinion. Tax treatment is according to individual rates, but each partner applies the investor's individual tax rate. Potential liability remains unlimited. Although marketability and disposition can be complicated, it is fairly simple in most cases.[1]

Limited partnership.   Limited partnership is a relatively new, and extremely popular, type of business entity. It attempts to secure the best of both worlds: limited liability on the part of limited partners and taxation at personal rates.

This form also requires a general partner (or partners) to serve as managing agent for the entire operation. In addition, termination provisions are typically provided in the agreement. However, marketability is somewhat difficult due to problems with transfer of ownership, and withdrawal of the general partner can terminate the partnership agreement. Therefore this form would be attractive to investors who seek a passive investment, free of management problems and obligations, and one in which liability is limited to the amount

---

[1] However, there are a number of concurrent estates available which can result in significant differences at the time of disposition.

invested, tax losses offset ordinary income, and where marketability is not the most important consideration.

Ordinary corporation. The well-known corporate form is often viewed as "the only realistic business form" by many investors. There are, of course, advantages such as limited liability, ease of marketability of ownership "shares," generally centralized and constant management, and a perpetual life for the business. However, other factors are less favorable. Income earned by the corporation is taxed twice, once at the corporate rate and again when dividends distributed to shareholders are taxed at ordinary rates after the initial tax-free levels.[2] In addition, tax losses can only offset previous tax payments at the corporate rate. Finally, for some small companies, it may be more expensive and time consuming to form a corporation or to dissolve one than for the partnership forms.

Subchapter S corporation. The Subchapter S corporation is a special form allowed by the 1958 Technical Amendments Act to the Internal Revenue Code. It was designed to avoid the double taxation provision of corporate income and retain the other provisions of corporate treatment. Subchapter S corporations may now have up to fifteen shareholders (up from ten prior to the Tax Reform Act of 1976) if it operated as a tax corporation for the preceding five years. In addition, all shareholders must be individuals (partnerships and their corporations are specifically excluded) and residents of the United States. There are some additional income requirements, but the basis of this form permits limited liability with tax treatment preferable to the double taxation of corporations. Management considerations depend on the specific organizations, and marketability is somewhat affected by the additional requirements and the upper limit on partners. Recent changes in the tax law are likely to make Subchapter S elections a more viable option.

Land trust. The land trust is only available in a few states. It was created in Illinois and enjoys its widest usage there. Under this arrangement, title passes to a trustee who holds the title to property only for the purpose of carrying out the wishes of the owners or beneficiaries. Therefore the trustee does not take over the operations of the property without the written permission of the beneficiaries.

The land trust has been criticized by tenant groups as being a form that serves no particular purpose except to hide the true ownership of property. If a dispute arises between a tenant and the owner, the land trust becomes a shield between the often angry tenant and the true owner. The trustee, of course, may not be able to make many operating decisions without the permission of the owner.

---

[2] Current law permits the first $100 in dividends ($200 if married and filing jointly) to be tax-free.

TABLE 5-2 Summary of Characteristics of Business Organizations

	TAXATION STATUS	INVESTOR'S LIABILITY	TRANSFERABILITY	MANAGEMENT	METHOD OF CREATION	DURATION
Individual	Flow through (single)	Unlimited	Transferable	Personal	Individual	Terminated by death or agreement; deceased interest becomes part of the estate
General partnership	Flow through (single)	Unlimited	Not transferable	All partners in absence of agreement have equal voice	Created by agreement of the parties	Terminated by death, bankruptcy, or withdrawal of a partner
Limited partnership	Flow through (single)	Limited	Transferable	General partners have equal voice; limited partners have no voice	Created by agreement of the parties	Termination provided in the agreement
Corporation	Non-flow through (double)	Limited	Transferable	Shareholders elect directors who set policy	Charter issued by state	Perpetual
Subchapter S corporation	Non-flow through (single)	Limited	Limited by maximum number of shareholders	Varies with specific organization	Charter issued by federal tax authority	Terminated by actions of shareholders
Land trust	Flow through (single)	Limited	Very transferable	Beneficiaries	Created by trust document if permitted by state law	Terminated by trustees, beneficiaries, or terms of agreement
Real Estate Investment Trust (REIT)	Modified flow through (tax losses cannot exceed cash distribution)	Limited	Modified	Trustees	Created by agreement of the parties and charter issued by state	Perpetual

On the other hand, proponents have argued that there is more substance to a land trust. This form permits limited liability on the part of the owners, enables tax treatment at ordinary rates, and offers considerably more ease in marketability than partnerships or Subchapter S corporations. There are other advantages also. Thus the land trust remains an attractive option in some states despite legal struggles to prohibit its usage.

Real estate investment trust (REIT).   The REIT is a special version of an equity trust. It is governed by specific rules and regulations that permit limited liability, tax treatment based on ordinary income, and good marketability. Management is typically handled by an advisory board, since an REIT must have at least 100 shareholders. However, tax losses may not be "passed through" to shareholders as in partnership forms. In addition, poor performance in the late 1960s and 1970s has soured many individuals on REIT ventures. It remains, however, a viable form, given the limitations of small investors seeking passive interests in real estate. There has been renewed interest in REITs in recent years.

Joint venture.   This form is a special arrangement that, unlike most of the previous forms, is not expected to be an ongoing concern. Two or more parties are needed to create a joint venture, which can take on any legal ownership form. Real estate development is a good example, since the developer may need to offer additional incentive to equity holders in order to interest them in somewhat risky ventures. Therefore joint ventures are the legal arrangement for some real estate investments.

Syndication.   Syndication, like the joint venture, is not truly an ownership form, but rather a technique to raise capital for investment purposes. The organizer or syndicator is frequently the general partner in a limited partnership and often benefits from management fees and an active role in the operation. Syndicates are really associations for conducting business and thus differ from legal forms of ownership. However, a potential investor may wish to organize a syndicate for investment in larger projects or to attract capital for limited partnerships.

Table 5-2 summarizes the major characteristics of the business organizations discussed in this chapter. It should be emphasized that each investor will have different objectives in selecting the appropriate business organization. Therefore no single organization is "best" for real estate investing.

The Mortgage Lender

The second participant in the real estate investment process is the mortgage lender. An investor seeking sources of funds for investment has a growing number of financial institutions from which to choose. Table 5-3 presents

TABLE 5-3 Total Mortgage Originations by Major Type of Lender (in Millions of Dollars)

LENDER	1–4 FAMILY ($)	(%)	MULTIFAMILY ($)	(%)	NONRESIDENTIAL ($)	(%)	FARM ($)	(%)	TOTAL ($)	(%)
Savings & Loan Associations	61,902	84.6	5,113	6.9	5,570	7.6	583	0.8	73,168	100
Commercial Banks	21,681	54.2	3,028	7.6	12,901	32.2	2,395	6.0	40,005	100
Mortgage Companies	15,409	90.0	661	3.9	1,057	6.2	—	—	17,127	100
Life Insurance Companies	361	3.6	768	7.7	7,466	74.5	1,431	14.3	10,026	100
Mutual Savings Banks	6,297	67.4	1,369	14.6	1,678	17.6	3	—	9,347	100
Federal Credit Agencies	2,652	28.4	1,114	11.9	335	3.6	5,224	56.0	9,325	100
State and Local Credit Agencies	1,522	55.8	829	30.4	201	7.4	179	6.6	2,731	100
All Others	205	16.2	398	31.5	659	52.2	—	—	1,262	100
Total	110,027	67.5	13,279	8.1	29,866	18.3	9,816	6.0	162,988	100

Note: Amounts may not add to total due to rounding.
SOURCE: U.S. Department of Housing and Urban Development.

the breakdown of mortgage originations by institution. As indicated, two-thirds of all mortgages were on small (one-to-four-family) residential units. This indicates the predominance of mortgage finance for residential property. While savings and loan associations originated 44.9 percent of all mortgages, commercial banks were a distant second with 24.5 percent of the originations. Most savings and loan association mortgages consisted of single-family residences and small income-producing buildings (84.6 percent). Mortgage companies, although a much smaller institution, placed 90 percent of their mortgages in this category. On the other hand, life insurance companies placed a majority of their funds in mortgages on nonresidential property such as shopping centers and office buildings. Federal credit agencies such as the Veterans Administration, Small Business Administration, and Farm Credit Administration appeared as the sixth largest supplier of mortgage funds to the market. Finally, state and local credit agencies, although small in size, have become one of the largest sources of mortgage funds. In general, mortgages tend to be concentrated in savings and loans and commercial banks with a majority financing single-family and small income-producing property.

The following discussion highlights the major financial institutions and the prospect of each institution as a source of funds for the real estate investor.

Savings and loan associations.   Savings and loan associations, often called "thrift institutions," specialize in making single-family loans based on time and passbook deposits at their institutions. However, the investor in income-producing real estate may also view savings and loans as a source of funds, since many small income-producing properties are financed with loans from these institutions. In recent years, savings and loans have taken a much more active role in the financing of multifamily and commercial mortgages. The savings and loan association of the future may be much less specialized than in the past due to the changing legal environment of financial institutions.

Commercial banks.   Historically, commercial banks have been more diversified than savings and loan associations, mutual savings banks, or mortgage companies. In recent years, commercial banks have expanded their operations to include more multifamily and commercial mortgages. They have also been active in short-term construction loans for multifamily housing. The investor in income-producing real estate may use a commercial bank as a source of long-term credit and particular short-term credit such as construction funds.

Mortgage companies.   Mortgage companies are specialized firms that are usually privately owned and that deal mostly with construction and development loans. They also service loans as well as originate loans for governmental agencies in the secondary mortgage market. The real estate investor seeking short-term construction loans may find private mortgage companies to be sources of capital, although these are smaller institutions compared with the others previously mentioned.

Life insurance companies.   Life insurance companies are well-established real estate lenders, although this does not appear to be true to the casual observer. Despite the fact that these companies have declined in importance in terms of residential loans in recent years, they continue to be a major source of capital for multifamily property and large commercial projects. A real estate developer may find life insurance companies a sound source of long-term permanent financing.

Federal credit agencies.   Federal credit agencies play an important role in the market for single-family loans, multifamily loans, and farm credit. Since most of their assets are held in the form of mortgages, some of the agencies may assist in supplying funds. The available federally subsidized programs are numerous and frequently very detailed regarding qualifications and program changes. However, for some investors in multifamily housing, the federal agencies may be a viable credit source.

Other institutions.   There are, of course, other institutions such as mutual savings banks, state and local credit agencies, pension funds, and REITs. Each has particular interests and legal requirements. Many may provide funding for certain types of investment projects for a particular investor. All have invested in the real estate market due to its recent history of stable growth and asset protection.

Individuals.   The final category is those few individuals with enough liquid money willing to lend it to a real estate investor in the form of a mortgage over a long-term period. A common example is the seller who takes back a purchase-money mortgage or one who accepts a second or junior mortgage in lieu of cash at the time of sale. Such occurrences are not as rare today as they once were due to rapidly rising property values.

The Tenant

The third participant is the immediate user of the real estate—the tenant. The tenant in feudal times had very few rights for the duration of the leasehold. However, the development of landlord-tenant law is evidence of the shift toward protection and existence of the rights of tenants. A brief overview of this law will be presented later in this chapter.

There may be different legal ramifications for each type of tenant. One classification divides various leaseholds according to expected duration of the estate. In nearly every case, the legal differences between the tenancies will be directly related to the rights associated with the document (lease) between the equity investor (or agent) and the tenant (or agent).

Residential users. This is the most commonly encountered type of tenant for most small income-producing real estate. Residential users consist of tenants in single-family dwellings, small apartment buildings, six-flat apartment buildings, garden-type apartments, large complexes, and others. Residential tenants are primarily interested in suitable living conditions. Depending on the geographical area of the country and on local market conditions, the typical lease for a residential property will extend from a monthly leasehold up to two years or longer. Compared with long-term commercial leases, these are quite short.

Compared with other types of tenants, residential tenants are more concerned with the physical amenities within the building. In most agreements, maintenance is expected to be performed by the lessor on a regular basis and, for serious problems, at the notice of the tenant. Failure to provide these services often results in management problems, tenant turnover, and landlord-tenant disputes. In fact, most of the new landlord-tenant laws enacted during the past fifteen years are a result of problems encountered with residential property.

In addition, items such as groundskeeping, snow removal, and the overall maintenance of the property's grounds are important to residential tenants. Since residential tenants view their leaseholds as their "homes," management should treat the property accordingly. Effective property management is essential in assisting the investor to maintain a good rapport with tenants.

The problems of management are well known to many investors in residential real estate. However, these problems can be minimized if prudent management techniques are followed. The residential tenant may be one of the most difficult management problems for the unsuspecting investor, but without the property manager, income-producing apartment buildings would be valueless.

Commercial users. There are several types of commercial tenants, or users, involved in a commercial or business activity. These include wholesale and retail stores, office buildings, and shopping centers. Commercial tenants tend to be larger, more sophisticated, and often more financially secure. In addition, leases for commercial use frequently involve *percentage leases*. These leases allow for the remittance of a percentage of sales or income for the rental payment. In some cases, this percentage is in addition to a minimum guaranteed rent.

Although some commercial leases are not percentage leases, most are long term. It is possible to find commercial leases for thirty or forty years for large firms or *anchors* in some shopping centers. Commercial leases are also frequently quoted on a square foot (or sometimes front footage) basis. This unit of measurement enables quick comparisons in what are often highly competitive markets.

Commercial leases may also have specific clauses that are characteristic of this type of lease. There may be restrictions and requirements regarding the number of hours the firm must be open for business. This is especially common if the percentage lease is in use and gross income is applied as a measure of volume sales. In addition, there may be some specific requirement regarding business records and audit procedures, another frequent provision in commercial leases. Finally, the commercial tenant may be limited to only performing certain activities while on the lessor's premises.

Industrial users.   Industrial tenants are generally users of property in which the interior of the buildings is unfinished. Warehouses, plants, utilities, and factories are typical examples. Since this type of property tends to be quite large, industrial leases tend to be quite extensive and are often specially designed for the user. The growth of industrial parks has led to much more careful analysis of the economics of leasing industrial space versus an outright purchase of the property.

Industrial tenants are concerned with access, production efficiency, and safety conditions in the facility. Their leases tend to be long term and are typically net of maintenance, utilities, and other operating expenses. Because industrial real estate is very competitive, leases must be negotiated very carefully. Since many of the facilities are large, a small error in negotiation may result in a very expensive leasing obligation.

Special-purpose users.   There are a number of other tenants that lease space for other specific purposes. Some examples of special-purpose users are theaters, assembly halls, and sports arenas. Leasing arrangements and terms vary with each specific use. The requirements of the lessor (landlord) to the lessee (tenant) depend on the value of the economic activity to be performed on the property. Each industry tends to have its own institutional standards regarding leasing terms. For example, a lease for a movie theater may specify a percentage rate with a minimum per-seat guarantee. In addition, the revenue from the concessions may also be included in the lease.

Special-purpose buildings require a much more critical analysis of the activity performed on the premises. Furthermore, more information may be needed to ascertain the riskiness of the tenant and the tenant's ability to make the rental payments. In some cases, however, the profitability of a successful enterprise may result in a very successful real estate investment for the building's owner.

The Government

The final primary participant in the real estate investment process is the government. Generally, the impact of government regulation and influence is felt by all the other participants. Typically, government influence is divided into three categories: federal, state, and local governments. Together these three "public sectors" greatly affect real estate investment decisions.

Federal. The most visible impact that federal government has on a real estate investment is its ability to tax the income from real estate. Chapter 7 is devoted to an analysis of taxation and tax planning to assist the investor in legally avoiding unnecessary tax payments. However, other federal regulations on the use of real estate can be equally important. For example, the right of eminent domain rests with the federal as well as state governments. This right, discussed later in this chapter, permits the taking of private real estate for public purposes as long as "just compensation" is paid. Therefore, if the government decides that your property is needed for a public purpose, it may be obtained through this right, or limitation of your rights of eminent domain.

Federal land-use regulations have resulted from a growing public awareness of conservation and environmental impacts that occur during some uses of land. The federal government has taken an active stance in this area, and the future appears to hold an even greater participation by federal authorities.

Finally, the federal government also retains the right of *escheat*, or the taking of property when no heirs or will can be found after the death of the owner(s). Further, estate taxes can dramatically affect the returns and worth of property at the time of death.

State. Property law varies from state to state. Although modern property law comes from early English common law and is generally followed throughout the United States,[3] differences occur as courts and legislatures attempt to deal with various issues. Therefore, most of property law comes from state law.

Various states have defined different estates and interests. Some states have adopted the title theory of mortgages. Others have followed the lien theory. Certain states have created new laws to meet changing conditions in the area of consumer protection of urban tenants in landlord-tenant law or, in some of the western states, in dealing with water rights. Finally, each state has various income, property, and estate tax laws which can significantly affect the value and return of real estate. In general, there are many areas where real estate is affected by state government and its law. Many of these considerations are treated below.

Local. Local government may be the municipality, county, or other political boundary. It is characterized by smaller and more-detailed concerns. Examples of local government action include building codes, zoning ordinances, and set-back requirements.

The local government can have a significant influence. Recent moves

---

[3] This is not true of Louisiana, which follows the French or Napoleonic legal system. Also, certain elements of Spanish law are found throughout the state laws in the southwestern portion of the United States.

toward rent control ordinances have been controversial in many communities. Some local governments have also attempted to deal with growth and expansion by limiting (or in some cases forbidding) the issuance of new housing permits. Another example is the recent interest in condominium conversions. Although many real estate developers and investors view local government as an obstacle to their objectives, it is becoming an ever-increasing political force.

RELATIONSHIP BETWEEN THE REAL ESTATE INVESTMENT AND THE PARTICIPANTS

We have described some of the legal aspects of the primary participants in the real estate investment process. Now let us focus on the relationship between the participants and the investment vehicle: the land, improvements, and the property rights associated with the realty.

Property Rights of the Equity Investor

The equity investor, as we have already said, acquires a bundle of rights as an investor in real estate. These entitle the investor to a cash flow. The magnitude and safety of the cash flow is directly related to the magnitude and quality of the bundle of rights and interests that the investor acquires in taking title to the property. Sometimes the rights are present interests; other times they involve future interests. Some rights are concurrent interests; others are rights in the land of others. All interests that entitle rights to valuable property are presumed to have value. It is important that the investor understand the basic differences between the many forms of property interests or *estates*.

Freehold estates.   Freehold estate interests are widely held and represent the most complete interests available in many cases. With the exception of life estates, freehold estates are potentially infinite in duration. The name *freehold* comes from the common law where it referred to the interests in land that were associated with free men. Because they were the only estates that were given full protection of law, they are large and powerful interests today. There are basically four types of freehold estates: fee simple absolute, defeasible fees, fee tail, and life estates.

The largest and most complete estate available is called *fee simple absolute*, or *fee simple*. Potentially infinite as long as heirs can be found, it can be passed on to future heirs without restriction or limitation. A fee simple estate is the complete bundle of rights (subject to the traditional government limitations).

The second category of fee estates consists of *defeasible fees*. These are identical with fee simple estates except they are defeasible depending on the occurrence of some event. An example would be a grant of property to "Mr.

Jones and his heirs as long as the property would be used for the benefit of the children in the community." This is called a *fee simple determinable* or a *qualified fee*, since the existence of the fee estate is determined by the event that the property is used "for the benefit of the children in the community." Another example would be if Mr. Brown grants to "Mr. Smith and his heirs but if smoking is permitted on the premises, then Mr. Brown has the right to reenter and repossess the property." Such a grant creates a *fee simple subject to condition subsequent* for Mr. Smith. Clearly, if the specific condition (i.e., smoking) occurs (with "permission"), then the grant dictates that Mr. Smith may lose his interest and the estate may "revert" to Mr. Brown if he elects to take the property.

A final example is a *fee simple subject to executory limitation* or *devise*. This is really either of two estates. If it is subject to limitation, it is created by deed. If it is subject to devise, it is a creation by last will and testament. As an example, assume Mr. White by deed conveys his property to "Mr. Black and his heirs but if Mrs. Black remarries, then the property goes to Mr. Green and his heirs." In this case, Mr. Black is said to have a *fee simple subject to executory limitation*. The limitation, of course, is that if Mrs. Black remarries, then Mr. Green will take title to the property in fee simple.

A third category of freehold estate, which in modern law is unenforceable or viewed as a modified fee simple estate, is called the *fee tail*. This estate specifies that the property would pass according to the "heirs of his body." If the holder of the fee tail produced a male[4] heir, then at the time of his death,[5] the property would pass to the lineal heir. If the line were to be stopped, the property would, by design, revert to the original grantor (or his heirs). As one can imagine, there were so many problems with this estate that modern law has attempted to eliminate its usage and, in most cases, states will not enforce a fee tail conveyance. Though rarely seen today, it is a reminder of the common law heritage.

The final freehold estate is a *life estate*. There are basically two types of life estates: *conventional life estates* and *legal life estates*. The first is characterized by the words in the deed "for the term of his natural life." The grantee in this case would have a conventional life estate that would entitle him or her to use the property (but not damage it), take "fruits" from it, and even sell the interest to other parties. However, at the time of the life tenant's death, the grantor (or heirs) would get back the interest in the property.

It is also possible for the life estate to be measured by the life of someone other than the recipient of the grant. In this case, the life estate is called *pur autre vie* ("for another's life").[6] For example, assume Mrs. Howard grants her property to Mrs. Roberts for the life of Mr. Howard. When Mr. Howard

---

[4] In medieval times, only males could hold title to property at the sufferance of the king. Later the estate known as *fee tail female* was introduced to specify a line of female descendants.

[5] It was assumed that only males could hold property interests.

[6] The name of this estate is taken from Old French.

dies, Mrs. Roberts's interest is extinguished and the property reverts to Mrs. Howard.

A common form of *legal life estates* refers to wives' interests in their husbands' property called *dower rights* and husbands' interests in their wives' property called *curtesy rights*. These rights are in disfavor with courts and in many states are no longer enforceable. However, in the states where they are, these estates refer to rights that may result in surprises at the time of the spouse's death if the grantee is not careful. In many cases, title assurance methods have eliminated much of the risk of "legal life estate surprises."

Clearly, the analysis of freehold estates is complex and intricate. This review exposes the reader to some of the terminology and concepts of estates in land. It is not intended to be a substitute for legal counsel. It should be apparent, however, that there are many kinds of estates available for interests in property.

Concurrent estates.   Concurrent estate interests are used when more than one person desires joint ownership of property. There are four types of concurrent estates: joint tenancy, tenancy in common, tenancy by the entirety, and tenancy in coparcenary. It is important to distinguish between these estates.

Joint tenancy is an estate that specifies that the surviving tenants will divide the property of the deceased cotenant equally, immediately upon the death of the cotenant, and without entering the estate of the deceased cotenant. All tenants are said to own the entire property as joint owners. The right of survivorship (by the surviving cotenants) is a characteristic of this estate. Finally, in order to create a joint tenancy, one must meet the "four unity tests." This requires that all the cotenants enter the agreement at the same time (unity of time), all acquire their interests by a single conveyance (unity of title), all interests are of the same type and duration (unity of interest), and all have an undivided right to use the property (unity of possession). If one or more of these unities cannot be met or are broken over time, the property is not a joint tenancy but a tenancy in common.

A *tenancy in common* is a concurrent ownership form where each tenant owns an undivided portion of the property but not necessarily in equal amounts. Further, a tenant may sell his or her interest at will and not disturb the estate. Finally, a tenancy in common permits the passage of property to heirs rather than automatically to cotenants, as in joint tenancy. For several reasons, tenancy in common is preferred by courts and state lawmakers over joint tenancy. The opposite was true in common law, but in modern courts the complications that arise through the use of joint tenancies (and concurrent tenancy in common) have led some states to abolish joint tenancies and still others to apply a very strict interpretation of the four unities test.

For some husbands and wives the joint tenancy may seem to be the preferred concurrent estate. However, the estate known as tenancy by the entirety was specifically designed for husbands and wives. A *tenancy by the entirety* is very similar to a joint tenancy except it requires an additional fifth unity: unity of person. This means that the husband and wife during marriage are viewed as one legal person in this estate. If one dies, the property automatically goes to the survivor. In addition, neither spouse can voluntarily dispose of an interest in the property without the permission of the other. In a joint tenancy, any tenant can act and be held responsible for the whole tenancy. Finally, in the event of a divorce, the tenancy by the entirety is destroyed and a tenancy in common remains.

The final tenancy is the *tenancy in coparcenary*. It is really an extinct estate which, if found, is typically viewed as a tenancy in common. It was the estate left without male heirs but with at least two female heirs. The female heirs are said to be tenants in coparcenary. Thus this estate was created by the law of inheritance and receives virtually no legal usage today.

Future interests. These estates are interests in existing property which will not begin until some future date. These acknowledge that the holder of the future interest has an estate presently: the right to use and enjoy property at some time in the future. In addition, some future interests may never become possessory interests if certain events do not occur. These are called *contingent estates*. These may be contrasted with future interests that are known to occur at some definite point in time, or *vested estates*.

All future estates can be classified as one of five types: reversions, possibilities of reverter, rights of reentry, remainders, and executory interests. *Reversions* are future interests that entitle the holder to recover a possessory interest at a future time. An example is the interest at the time of the death of the life tenant. Since all life tenants will die, reversions are said to be vested interests. *Possibilities of reverter* are future interests associated with a determinable fee. Recall that in a determinable fee, the owner of the fee may retain the interest for life and pass it to his or her heirs and they to theirs, "as long as" the event specified occurs (or does not occur). Because the future interest may never become a possessory estate, it is classed as a "possibility of a reverter."

A *right of reentry* is also the future interest associated with a determinable fee but specifically with a fee simple subject to condition subsequent. The right of reentry gives the original grantor the "right to reenter" the property if certain conditions occur (or do not occur). As noted earlier, the grantee has the right to take back the property. In the case of nearly all of the other future estates, they become possessory estates automatically.

Remainders are the granting away of the reversionary interests. Remainders typically follow life estates but may also follow some fees, fee tails, or terms for years. Remainder interests must become possessory interests. Finally, *executory interests* are technical future interests that may be created by deed or will and that permit transfer of property rights after the death of the grantor. It is an interest that may become a possessory interest at some future date or due to the occurrence of some event. Courts tend to prefer remainders, contingent on some event occurring, rather than executory interests for the reason of freer alienation of land.

Interests and rights in the land of others.   The final area of property rights of the equity investor consists of a set of related rights of nonpossessory interests. There are four main types: easements, profits, licenses, and covenants.

An *easement* is interest in someone else's land that entitles the holder to use and enjoy the land in some manner. A common example is a utility easement for running underground water pipes over a portion of another property owner's land. For investors in real estate, it is important to identify any easements that may stop the usage of land in some way and thereby have an adverse effect on the value of the property.

A *profit* is very similar to an easement, but in addition to permitting the use of another's land, it grants the holder of the profit the right to take away the soil or raw materials from the land. Clearly, a profit implies an easement, since it encompasses all the interests of an easement and more. A profit may also be a valuable property right depending on the type of property and the value of the soil and natural resources.

A *license* is a personal privilege granted to the holder to go on another's land without being a trespasser. A license is not an interest in land, nor is it a possessory estate. As a mere permission, it is limited in the extent of its rights. Frequently, a license may be revoked by the licensor at his or her discretion.

Finally, a *covenant* is a promise to do or not do a specific thing. In terms of real estate, a covenant may restrict the building of auxiliary buildings in a certain subdivision. Conceptually, covenants are restrictions that stop the owner from using his or her land as he or she pleases. In some cases, this might be a critical factor in the valuation of property. In that event, the existence of a covenant is an important factor for the real estate investor.

The Mortgage Lender and the Mortgage Document

The relationship between the mortgage lender and the real estate investment is spelled out in the mortgage document. Although there is a brief discussion regarding the use of mortgages for real estate finance in Chapter 6, the discussion in this section centers on two main parts. The first part reviews the concept of the mortgage instrument as security and the second part highlights the requirements for a valid mortgage.

Nature of the mortgage instrument.   The mortgage process technically contains a *mortgage*, or the written instrument that pledges real property as security for an obligation, and a *promissory note*, or the written promise of one person to repay an amount of money according to agreed terms and conditions. It is important to recognize that the financing process involves both a mortgage and a note. If the note were to be written without a mortgage, it would be, in effect, unsecured. Therefore both are essential ingredients for the functioning of the mortgage as a secured instrument. Once the note is repaid, a *release* is sought from the lender in order to free the property that was held as security.

The concept of the mortgage instrument has a long history in common law. Over time, however, two "theories" of mortgage law developed: the *title theory* and the *lien theory*.[7] Basically, since states that have adopted the title theory view the adoption of a mortgage as a change in possession and a conveyance of title, the use of a mortgage in a title state is paramount to a conveyance of property rights between the equity holder (mortgagor) and the mortgage lender (mortgagee). In states that have adopted the lien theory, by far the majority, different results occur. In lien theory states, the existence of a mortgage implies that the mortgagee merely has a claim against the property in the event of a default. Therefore there is no conveyance of title and fewer property rights have been transferred.

Finally, in some states, a device that is quite similar to a mortgage is used for security. This device is called a *deed of trust* (or *trust deed*). Unlike the ordinary mortgage, the deed of trust involves a third person. In using it, the borrower (or *trustor*) transfers the title to the real estate to a *trustee* who holds it in trust for the lender (or *beneficiary*) for performance of the obligation owed by the borrower to the lender. When the obligation is fulfilled, the title is reconveyed to the trustor by the trustee.

Requirements for a valid mortgage.   A number of elements are necessary for a mortgage to be free of defects. However, in some cases, the law may hold that certain defects in the mortgage document can result in the mortgage remaining as a so-called equitable mortgage. A valid mortgage must name the mortgagor and the mortgagee. It must contain the words of conveyance to clearly indicate that a mortgage is being agreed upon. It must specify the debt to be secured, and it must be recorded.

The mortgage must adequately describe the realty being mortgaged. In title states, the mortgage must clearly state the conditions upon which the title will be "defeated." This is called the *defeasance clause*. The mortgage must be signed by the mortgagor and in some states must be sealed and witnessed. The document must also be delivered and accepted.

Finally, mortgage law has specified other requirements regarding satisfaction of the mortgage, acceleration of the note, possible extensions of the mortgage, assignment of the mortgage, and release of the mortgage. A full discussion

---

[7] These "theories" are related to the discussion of mortgages in Chapter 6.

of these clauses is beyond the scope of this book, but in many cases, the advice of experienced counsel is very helpful. These instruments are the only way the mortgage lender can specify his or her legal rights to the real estate.

The Tenant and Leaseholds

The tenant also acquires a set of legal rights that include more than the use of the property for the period of the lease. The tenant has a legal interest in the real estate called a *nonfreehold* or *leasehold estate*. Each is frequently classified according to its expected duration.

Nonfreehold (leasehold) estates.   Generally there are four types of tenancy: tenancy for years, tenancy from period to period, tenancy at will, and tenancy at sufferance. With the exception of the last one, all are estates because they represent interests and rights in land.

A *tenancy for years* is a leasehold estate in which the beginning and end of the estate are clearly specified. For instance, if you have an estate for twenty years, at the end of that period, the property would automatically revert to the lessor.

A *tenancy from period to period* may last as long as a tenancy for years but implies that the tenant may stay on the premises for consideration of rent according to the terms stated in the original tenancy. This implied tenancy may be terminated with sufficient notice given by either party. Sufficient notice may be defined within the document or measured by local law or tradition. A typical period of notice is six months.

A *tenancy at will* is the least structured. In this leasehold, the lessor offers the lessee (tenant) to continue the estate "for as long as the lessee wishes." Thus a tenancy at will is an estate of indeterminate duration and involves fewer restrictions on either party than any of the other leasehold estates. The notice period for termination is typically stated in the lease or is determined by state statute or state court precedent.

Tenancy at sufferance is the legal term for the tenant who remains after the expiration of a previous lease. The tenant who continues without the consent of the lessor is "at the sufferance" of the lessor. Thus it is not an estate but a possession without legal right. It is said that a tenancy at sufferance differs from a trespasser only because the original entry was legal. Although tenants at sufferance possess civil and human rights, they have no real property rights.

Lease analysis.   The lease is the legal document that conveys a legal interest (leasehold) in real property. However, as we will see, the lease also represents a contract between landlord and tenant that contains a set of express and implicit conditions that bind the parties.

It should be pointed out that the major legal difference between a leasehold and other interests where the owner conveys rights (such as licenses, easements, or profits) is that the lease conveys the right of exclusive possession. Interests in the land of others convey the right to *use* the land but do not convey the right of possession. The legal test to determine if a conveyance is a leasehold is whether or not the transaction of rights results in a transfer of possession. If so, then a leasehold state has been created.

The essential elements of a lease include identification of landlord and tenant, both of whom must be of legal age and otherwise capable of entering the agreement; identification of the leased premises with sufficient precision to avoid ambiguity; specification of the amount of rent to be paid and the time and method of payment; and an indication of the term or length of the leasehold to which the parties have agreed. In some leaseholds the term is not specifically agreed upon at the time of signing.

In addition, and depending on the legal requirements of the state, other clauses are also found in most leases. A frequently used covenant describes the permissible uses allowed under the lease. For commercial property, this clause specifies what types of activities will be permitted by the lessor. In the case of a shopping center, this clause is critical because the selection of tenants is made according to economic function as well as risk and safety of the lessee. In residential leases, this clause ensures a minimum amount of conflict between tenants, since all are presumed to want peaceful and quiet usage of their rental space.

Another important covenant specifies the maintenance and repair responsibilities of the landlord. However, consistent with recent changes in landlord-tenant law, landlords are held responsible for physical maintenance and repair of appliances and urban services even if these promises are not expressly provided.

Leases also have provisions for assignment and subleasing, specifying the rights of the lessee should he or she wish to convey the rights of the leasehold before the end of the lease.

Finally, leases frequently include clauses concerning the status of the leasehold in the event of condemnation, casualty loss, or destruction. Although the outcomes may vary according to express covenants and state laws, the typical result is that the lessee is freed from rental obligation if the physical premises are "uninhabitable."

Other considerations. The development of landlord-tenant law during the past two decades is one of the major changes in property law. As a result, the landlord is now required to deliver possession to the tenant at the beginning of the lease.[8] In a famous New Jersey case, the court ruled that the "covenant

---

[8] Whether this consists of "actual" or "legal" possession varies according to state. According to the majority view, the English rule is followed, which requires actual possession to be delivered to the tenant.

of quiet enjoyment" was implied by all leases and if the landlord failed to provide this provision, the tenant could argue that he or she could not enjoy the premises and, in effect, that the leasehold was being terminated by "constructive eviction."[9]

Additional responsibilities of the landlord include the landlord's duty to deliver habitable premises. This shift from common law was based on the doctrine held by the court for all urban dwellings of "the implied warranty of habitability."[10] Courts also shifted the burden of repair and maintenance more squarely on the shoulders of the landlord. Now landlords have a larger responsibility than ever for repairing "defects that interfere with basic habitability."

Governmental Limitations on Property Rights

Government laws and regulations can have a dramatic impact on real estate investments. Much of this area remains controversial and deals with politically sensitive issues. Resolution of conflicting land uses and protection of public interests by land-use control[11] are two areas that merit discussion.

Conflicting land uses. The law attempts to resolve matters where a conflict of usage creates a problem. Four common types of conflicts concern nuisance, lateral support, water rights, and air rights.

The law of *nuisance* requires that a user of property operate in such a way that the use does not interfere with neighboring usage or with the public's right to use the property. Public nuisances are of particular concern, since such an activity can cause "injury to the public health, morals, safety or general welfare of the community." Nuisance doctrine is much less specific, and often the rulings are based on a case-specific analysis. In general, it protects holders of property interests from injury due to interference from others.

Lateral support is a property right that entitles the owner of property to have his or her land supported by adjoining land.[12] For example, the owner of an apartment building that begins to lean due to a weakening of the lateral support from the adjacent land is entitled to seek legal remedies. Although the property holder does not own the adjacent land, his or her right to receive lateral support is "an absolute right inherent in the land itself."

---

[9] See *Reste Realty* v. *Cooper* (1968).

[10] See *Javins* et al. v. *First National Reality Corp.* (1970).

[11] Many potential conflicting land uses involve private property rights exclusively and thus no government activity is necessary. However, many of these disputes seek governmental authority to rectify the issue, often by taxing the wrongdoer based on a measure of the damages to the plaintiff. Economists have shown that governmental action may not be needed in many of these disputes, since the conflicting parties can negotiate the damages between themselves.

[12] A similar notion is the doctrine of subjacent support that gives property holders the right to expect support from beneath the surface of the land once a structure is erected.

Water rights and *air rights* are two of the most visible areas in which interests may conflict. However, each area has developed a body of case law regarding the central question, Who owns what? Water rights refer to the title of lands under water and the rights of the water itself. This is clearly an important area in some of the arid states, and also where two adjoining land owners share a water supply or rely on a common water source for their livelihood. Many of the problems regarding water rights arise from the differences between two conflicting theories of water usage: the *riparian rights theory* and the *prior appropriation doctrine*. The riparian rights theory holds that the water rights belong to the adjacent landowner and no one can use water at the deprivation of others with an equal opportunity to use it. This theory has been rejected by many western states in favor of the prior appropriation doctrine that establishes a priority schedule for users. Those there first have the best claim to use of the water.

Air rights also involve conflicts of usage. Traditionally this was an area of torts, but with the development of technology, these property rights are becoming more important. Formerly, planes had free access to the "paths in the sky," since the sky was considered to belong to the public. However, if damage is done to property on earth, modern property law holds that this is a taking of property and that compensation must be paid to the property owner. This area is also controversial, and the courts will probably provide more rulings and precedent in the next few years.

Land-use control.   For the urban property holder, land-use control has become one of the most important legal areas of interest. As noted earlier, some of the limitations result from local governmental action, while others are due to state or local law. In many urban areas land-use control has been a hotly contested issue and one that will be important for years to come.

Some of the main techniques and methods that the public sector uses for land-use control include (but are not limited to) zoning laws, regulation of land development, urban land-use planning, eminent domain takings, environmental controls, and aesthetics as a land-use goal.

Zoning laws have been passed by most municipalities throughout the United States. These local ordinances typically provide a "master plan" by which the urban and nearby rural land will be utilized in a systematic and organized fashion. The issues of the value of zoning ordinances, their implementation, the costs of their usage, and the changes in property rights associated with the adoption of zoning ordinances have become well known to economists, city planners, and politicians and to many potential investors in real estate. The issues are far too complex for a cursory treatment here, but it is apparent that zoning and other land-use planning programs are becoming an increasingly important consideration for real estate development and investment.

Other *regulations of land development* have also emerged in recent years. Some cities hope to limit the extent of urban growth by refusing to issue

Figure 5-1 Property Rights in Land.

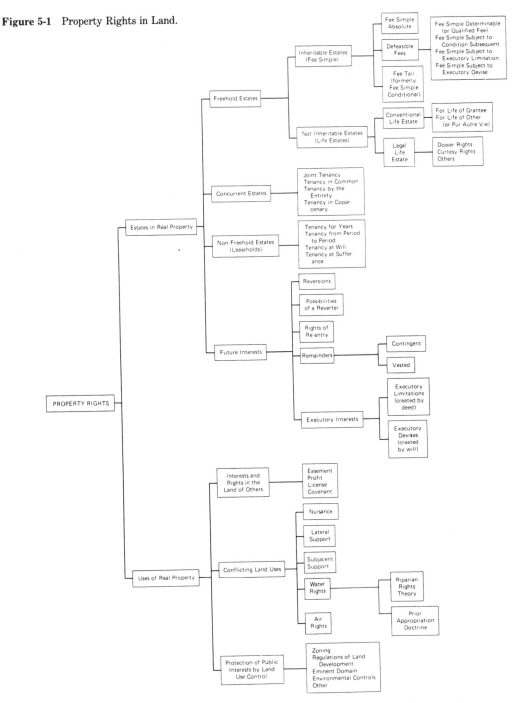

Source: C. F. Sirmans and Austin J. Jaffe, *The Complete Real Estate Investment Handbook, 2/e*, 1984, p. 92. Reprinted by permission of Prentice-Hall, Inc., Englewood Cliffs, N.J.

building permits or by limiting the number to be issued each year. Another method is to limit the "urban service boundary" outside of which police, fire, water, and other local services will not be extended. Once again, the issues can become complex and often raise the emotional levels of those involved. To some, this activity is called economic (or legal) extortion, since builders and developers are frequently asked by the local municipalities to pay "development fees" to help offset the additional costs to the city of having to provide extra urban services. To others, this type of regulation appears to be the only hope for rationing growth in urban areas among potential users.

The government may also take property by condemning it and using it for public purposes. This power, called *eminent domain*, requires that *just compensation*, or an amount in dollars equal to the market value of the loss, be paid to the former holder of the real property. Frequently, eminent domain proceedings are controversial and make headlines. However, empirical studies have shown that just compensation is not always equal to the owner's loss in market value.

Environmental controls are also becoming a relevant issue for much real estate development. Many municipalities now require environmental impact statements prior to the approval of large developments. These concerns have become more prevalent as cities pay more attention to growing problems in areas of energy, resource demands, and urban structure.

Finally, a new movement has argued for *aesthetics as a land-use goal*. Although traditionally the law of nuisance failed to uphold "unsightliness" as a legal nuisance, recent municipal ordinances have sought, in the interest of society's welfare, to limit the use of billboards, signs, and other "visual pollution." This is a relatively new and highly controversial area for government intervention and indicates the extent to which the investor must examine the role of governmental influence before investing in real estate.

Figure 5-1 classifies the major property rights of real estate participants. Nearly all the property rights that appear in the figure were discussed in this chapter.

RELATIONSHIPS BETWEEN PARTICIPANTS

Each of the four primary participants in the real estate investment process has a specific legal relationship with the real estate investment itself. In this section we will look at the linkages between each of them.

The Equity Investor and Mortgage Lender: The Promissory Note

The link between the equity investor and the mortgage lender is the *promissory note* signed by the investor. This specifies that the maker of the note (investor) promises to repay a specific sum of money to the payee (lender). The note can be *negotiable* or *nonnegotiable*. Negotiable notes can be passed to other persons for cash or sold in the market for negotiable notes. Nonnegotiable notes lack this marketability and, for this reason, are used less frequently.

Two common types of promissory notes are used in real estate: *straight notes* and *installment notes*. Straight notes require that only interest be paid during the term of the note and that principal be repaid at the end. Installment notes require periodic interest and principal reduction payments. In the usual case, the note is repaid in the level amortization payment plan, which enables a decreasing portion of a given level periodic payment to be attributed to interest and an increasing portion to principal reduction. It is also possible to only partially amortize the note and make the final payment larger to cover the remaining balance. This final payment is called a *balloon payment* and the mortgage in which it appears is called a *balloon mortgage*.

There are a number of common provisions in promissory notes. Frequently, the same provisions appear in the mortgage (or deed of trust). Together the note and the mortgage make up the agreement between the parties. Some of the provisions typically included are the date and place of the creation of the note, the amount of the note, the names of the payee and the maker, the time in which interest will begin and the effective rate to be charged, the results in the event of a default, and a statement regarding the use of a mortgage as security. Other issues include acceleration provisions, prepayment clauses and penalties, and the use of escrows. In general, for complex transactions, legal counsel is advisable.

The Equity Investor and the Tenant: The Lease

The legal link between the investor and the tenant is the *lease*. This is a type of contract in which one party (lessor) conveys to another (lessee) for consideration the right to use a specified property for a period of time. However, as we have seen, the changing nature of landlord-tenant laws has moved the analysis of leases further away from the law of contracts. Therefore the lease is an instrument that is based on a blend of contract and property law.

To create a valid lease, at least six essential elements must be included:

1. A statement of the correct names and the signatures of the competent parties.
2. An identifiable description of the leased premises, typically including but not limited to the address of the location.
3. A statement of the consideration to be paid.
4. A statement of the purpose(s) for which the premises are expected to be used.
5. A statement of the beginning and ending dates of the leasehold.

6. A statement of the rights and obligations of each party. This may be a simple statement or many pages of clauses and covenants.

Many of the clauses are important for specifying the rights of the lessor and lessee. A well-written lease will help to prevent potential problems. Finally, it is necessary to spend some time carefully examining the clauses in the lease used in the real estate. If real estate is to be viewed as a bundle of rights, then the establishment of leasehold extends certain rights to the lessee. It is of paramount importance to know what right the lessee possesses.

The Equity Investor and Government: Taxation

All levels of government have the authority to impose the burden of taxes. Taxation may consist of taxes on income; taxes on real property, typically used for local purposes; and taxes on the gain from selling assets. In "income tax" systems at the federal and most state levels, the government taxes both income and wealth.

Chapter 7 focuses on the complex and detailed tax system. We will see that not only is tax planning useful, but in many cases it is necessary in order to earn a competitive return. Tax avoidance is expected; tax evasion is illegal and punishable by law.

However, there are other taxes that affect real estate investment. These include personal property taxes, payroll taxes, estate taxes, and others. One of the more controversial issues in recent years has been the extent to which property taxes should be used to finance public expenditures such as schools. The Proposition 13 revolt made the clear point that in the minds of many homeowners and real estate investors, the tax burdens had grown significantly, often to 3 percent or more of market value.

Another way to view taxation is called the *tax capitalization theory*. This notion argues that if, for example, many investors believe that property (or other) taxes will increase in the near future, they will evaluate that expectation in analyzing investments. Thus their investments and the values placed on property will take the tax burden into account.

Whether most or all of the tax burden is "capitalized" into the value of investment property is an empirical question that remains unanswered. Evidence indicates that at least some of the tax burdens on real property are capitalized into selling prices by investors in the real estate market. At the same time, however, the investor is also concerned with the influence of various government programs on the investment's value. For example, the monies collected from the property tax are used to support schools, build roads, support police and fire protection, and so forth. These programs could very well increase the property value. So the investor should be concerned with the net effect: the decrease associated with the property tax and the increase from "quality" neighborhoods.

The Mortgage Lender and the Tenant:
Lender Requirements

The link between the mortgage lender and the tenant is perhaps the weakest of all the legal links between the participants. The lender never encounters the tenant directly. However, if the tenant is not financially secure, this may result in default on the promissory note. Poor tenant selection by the equity investor or management agent may therefore directly affect the mortgage lender.

A major part of the mortgage lender's review of the investor's application for funds is an analysis of the investor's projected income statement. Since the income to be generated from the real estate is directly a function of the tenants' willingness and ability to pay rent, the lender ought to analyze the financial position of major tenants. The lender's willingness to make the loan may be contingent on the type and quality of tenants in the property, particularly in large-scale projects where long-term financing becomes available after the leases are signed.

The lender may require tenants to pass certain income and credit tests. This is especially true in residential income-producing real estate where tenants may not have as easy access to credit markets as large corporations in commercial and industrial property.

The Mortgage Lender and Government:
Restrictions on Lender Behavior

The mortgage lender is linked to the government by a set of legal restrictions placed on the lender. Clearly, the nature of these restrictions depends on the lender involved. Those placed on savings and loan associations, for example, will differ from those placed on commercial banks or life insurance companies. Federally chartered savings and loan associations are largely confined to lending on residential real estate. There are also limits placed on the maximum amount that may be lent on any particular property as well as restrictions on maximum loan-to-value ratios, the length and amount of term loans, and requirements regarding the geographic locations of properties held as loan security.

Commercial banks, however, are permitted to engage in many more financial services. Although banks were not permitted to make real estate loans until after 1913, their interest has since grown to where they represent a major source of real estate loans (Table 5-3). However, there are regulations regarding the use of deposits for real estate loans, including limits on the ratio of mortgages to deposits and loan-to-value restrictions. Banks also do a good deal of short-term (construction) and interim financing which have other requirements.

The Tenant and Government: Evaluating Lessee's Rights

The final link is between the tenant and government. This link involves further restrictions on tenant usage as well as an ongoing interpretation of the lessee's rights. The changing nature of landlord-tenant law has forced many governments to pass new laws to reflect the new legal environment. Laws such as those requiring itemized lists of damages for which charges were deducted when returning security deposits, or those requiring fire alarms and smoke detectors in apartment buildings in some cities and towns, exemplify the changing legal emphasis.

Some observers feel that the government has no business in some of these areas. Builders frequently argue that although the intention may be good, many of the new laws result in higher construction costs and often higher rents charged to tenants. The problem for builders and investors, of course, is that the rents are not always increased in proportion to the increased costs. Sometimes only part of the additional cost is "passed on" to the tenant.

Proponents of government intervention in these areas argue that there is no market mechanism to correct safety, health, or other hazards. Therefore they view the problem as a governmental duty. Whether either side is correct more often than the other is a matter of conjecture. What is clear is that the lessee's rights are continually being refined and reinterpreted with each new governmental action.

OTHER ISSUES IN LEGAL ENVIRONMENT

The legal environment extends far beyond the topics discussed in this chapter so far. During the latter half of the twentieth century, state and local governments took an increasingly active stance in the areas of land-use control under the authority of police power. The real estate investor must take the government's role in this area into account when making investment decisions. The private bundle of rights has become more and more limited by governmental involvement in how real estate may be used.

Land-use control extends beyond resolution of conflicts through zoning and comprehensive planning. Recently, local governments have sought to regulate land on the basis of aesthetic requirements such as sign ordinances, architectural review procedures, and the specification and unique treatment of historically important properties. These areas have traditionally been left to the private market for allocative decisions.

In addition, extensive regulations on the extent, timing, size, and type of urban growth have become a part of the political scene. Courts have consistently sided with local governments who are seeking to plan or limit how their real estate is to be used. These regulations have also included ordinances that put restrictions on types of tenants, unrelated co-inhabitants, and absentee owners. The recent drive to stop condominium conversions is further evidence of the active role government plays in these areas.

Finally, rent control is the ultimate example of governmental limitations on the rights of property owners. Although certain municipalities have had a long history of rent control (most notably New York City), there is a rapidly growing rent control movement spreading throughout the United States. In some states (for example, New Jersey), several cities and towns have implemented rent control ordinances. In others, there is considerable political sentiment for this type of regulation. This development will have a dramatic impact on real estate as an investment if more communities implement such plans. This is an area for real estate investors to keep a careful eye on in the future.

IMPACT OF LEGAL ENVIRONMENT

Because real estate investment analysis is a legal process, a large portion of investing in income-producing real estate in an effective manner involves the use of sound legal advice and planning. Furthermore, since many transactions are or become quite complex, legal problems may easily arise, especially if ownership forms, financing arrangements, tax status, or governmental attitudes change during the life of the investment. Finally, there may be many legal decisions and choices that must be made beyond those briefly discussed in this chapter. This includes various types of transfers of ownership such as wills and inheritance laws, sales contracts, deeds, the use of escrows, gifts, and estate planning, and title assurance and insurance.

It is necessary to have a basic understanding of the legal environment prior to analyzing the financial opportunities associated with the investment. However, merely to possess a descriptive understanding of the various partnership forms or the breakdown of estates is rarely sufficient. *The real estate investor must understand the impact of the legal environment on the decisions he or she faces.* Only then will the legal environment "matter" to the decision maker.

QUESTIONS

5-1. Real estate has long been defined as a "bundle or rights." Why is this useful for analysis purposes?

5-2. What is the difference between *real estate* and *real property*? *Personalty* and *personal property*?

5-3. Various business organizations possess different characteristics according to a number of important variables. Distinguish the major ownership forms according to these variables.

5-4. Name the different types of tenants.

5-5. How do the different levels of government affect real estate investments?

5-6. What are estates? Why are estates valuable?

5-7. What is the difference between *freehold* and *leasehold estates*?

5-8. In recent years, the legal environment has become more important for investors. In what ways can real estate investors benefit from understanding the legal environment before investing?

PROBLEMS

5-1. Suppose two houses of identical size, quality, and condition are for sale in the same neighborhood. One house, however, consists of a fee simple estate as the set of property rights available to a potential buyer. The other is a defeasible fee estate. If the fee simple estate is worth $50,000, how much do you think the defeasible fee estate is worth if there is a 95 percent probability that it *will not* "revert" and become a possessory estate? How much is the defeasible fee worth if there is a 95 percent probability that it *will* "revert" and become a possessory estate?

5-2. "Imagine that you are holding a set of colored pencils bound together with a rubber band. Assume that these pencils represent a bundle of rights. The pencils are of different colors, and if they were of different lengths and thicknesses, made of different materials, and were not all pencils, they would more closely resemble the "bundle or rights" called real property. But even then the simile would be imperfect. Property rights are not sticks, they are more like amoebas, ever-changing in their physical and legal entities."

What is the author's main point? Is this a useful view of real property? How does the "bundle of rights" influence the real estate investment decision?

SELECTED REFERENCES

CORLEY, ROBERT N., PETER J. SHEDD, and CHARLES F. FLOYD, *Real Estate and the Law.* New York: Random House, 1982.

CRIBBET, JOHN E., *Principles of Real Estate Law* (2nd ed). Mineola, N.Y.: Foundation Press, 1975.

FRENCH, WILLIAM B., and HAROLD F. LUSK, *Law of the Real Estate Business* (5th ed.). Homewood, Ill.: Richard D. Irwin, 1984.

HENSZEY, BENJAMIN N., and RONALD M. FRIEDMAN, *Real Estate Law* (2nd ed.). New York: John Wiley, 1984.

KRATOVIL, ROBERT, and RAYMOND J. WERNER, *Real Estate Law* (8th ed.). Englewood Cliffs, N.J.: Prentice-Hall, Inc., 1983.

SIEDEL, GEORGE J., III, *Real Estate Law.* St. Paul, Minn.: West Publishing, 1979.

WRIGHT, ROBERT R., and SUSAN WEBBER, *Land Use in a Nutshell.* St. Paul, Minn.: West Publishing, 1978.

6

THE FINANCING ENVIRONMENT

The environment in which the financing decision occurs is one of the most important for the real estate investor. Financing is frequently a fundamental part of the real estate investment; without financing, many investments would not take place. This chapter begins by analyzing the reasons why real estate investors borrow. It is often said that the typical real estate investor has an advantage over other types of investors in that he or she borrows an amount of funds with only a relatively small amount of cash. In such a case, the investor finances a large portion of the investment by borrowing, pays the cost of obtaining outside debt sources out of the income stream from the investment, and therefore acquires ownership of the property with only a small percentage of equity.

Some investors advocate borrowing as much as possible so that investing in income-producing real estate requires only small amounts of equity and high degrees of "leverage." This school of thought concludes that the use of "other people's money" is the key to making money in real estate.

This chapter deals with the financing environment for real estate investments. The topics include a discussion of why people borrow, why borrowing may and may not be advantageous, and how to evaluate various financing alternatives. Chapter 9 deals with a specific set of financing decisions that face real estate investors.

WHY BORROW?

An individual who wishes to invest in real estate (or other assets) and has enough cash to pay for the investment outright has two choices: pay cash for the entire property or borrow a portion and pay cash for the remaining amount. What should this potential investor do?

Analysis shows that even if individuals have enough cash for this particular investment (but not enough to satisfy all needs), the value of the funds an individual has may be viewed as more valuable than the cost of borrowing. In other words, the investor can acquire more assets by using debt because the same equity can be "stretched" into more investments, more assets, or more consumption. So individuals (and firms) borrow because they believe they will be better off as a result.

In order to consume goods and services now rather than wait, investors must pay a price: the *interest* for the use of the money over the period. It is clear, then, that investors would only borrow if it is perceived to be in their best interests. However, if these situations exist, we would expect to see them borrowing as much as possible all of the time. The problem is that the gains from leverage are associated with increasing amounts of *financial risk*—the probability of defaulting on financial obligations. Obviously, the more debt that is acquired, the higher the required interest payments and the greater the probability of not having enough income to cover obligations. Thus financial leverage is not free or riskless, although no investor borrows without expecting *favorable financial leverage*.

In general, financial leverage is the major reason for borrowing. When the expected rate of return from the investment is greater than the cost of borrowing, favorable financial leverage exists for those who have borrowed to finance the project. If, however, the returns fall short of expectations, and return less than the cost of debt used to finance the investment, *unfavorable financial leverage* exists. Not even the most optimistic real estate investor is happy about unfavorable leverage.

Evaluating Financing Alternatives

If the key financing decision involves the measurement of financial leverage and its impact on the wealth of the investor, it is necessary to compare various financing alternatives in order to decide which would be preferable.

For instance, you could compare the monthly debt services of each loan plan. (This is similar to using the mortgage constant as a cost of borrowing, since the mortgage constant is the proportion of debt service to the original loan.) *The problem with this method is that it is possible to mistakenly choose the more expensive alternative.*

Exhibit 6-1   Should an Investor Borrow as
**   Much as Possible?**

Many real estate investment books tell readers that the biggest advantage to investing in real estate is the use of "OPM" (other people's money). These books provide stories and methods for increasing the return on equity with the use of *financial leverage*. The basic idea is that an investor can "lever" upward the return on the investment by borrowing funds at rates lower than the rate earned on the investment itself. If so, the return on the investor's equity will be higher than if no debt financing were used.

It is quite correct that the use of leverage can increase the rate of return to the equity investor. In fact, if a large percentage of the total financing is debt (as opposed to equity) financing *and* the leverage is *favorable* (i.e., the return on the investment exceeds the cost of debt financing as measured by the effective interest rate on the loans), the return to the equity investor may be astronomical. In this manner, the rate of return from investing in real estate could be as high as 400 or 500 or 700 percent or more!

Does this mean that wise investors should borrow as much as possible when making real estate investment decisions? No, at least not without considering a few additional items. For example, it is important to recognize that the potential gains from financial leverage are not free; the price is additional risk. The risk occurs due to the increased likelihood of default on the debt service payments as a result of unexpected reductions in net operating income. This risk can be expected to result in higher interest costs charged by lenders to investors. If so, there will be a price charged for the ability to lever the investment.

It is also true that the financing choice has an impact on the amount of income taxes the investor will pay. If a large amount of debt is used to finance the investment, the investor will have considerable interest expense. Under the current tax law, interest paid by the investor is a tax-deductible item and may be used to reduce the amount of tax liability owed by the investor. (Note also that homeowners can reduce their taxes in the same manner, so long as the "itemization threshold" is satisfied. This threshold is currently $3,000 for single taxpayers and $5,000 for married taxpayers who file jointly.)

However, simply borrowing money for debt financing (or any other reason) because the interest is tax deductible will not ensure financial success. Like any other market-traded asset, money has its cost. It is likely that the cost of borrowing reflects the deductibility of interest such that the before-tax interest rate would fall substantially if interest deductibility were not allowed by a subsequent change in the tax code. As such, especially for low-income taxpayers, borrowing for tax deductibility reasons is not likely to pay off.

Finally, by the very nature of their existence, owners of corporations (shareholders) receive tax shields from borrowing. First, the interest payments made by the corporation are subtracted from their income when figuring out their taxable income. Second, owners who borrow to finance the purchase of the shares in the corporation receive another round of tax deductions. Dividends that are paid to owners are taxable (after the initial exclusion) and can be reduced through borrowing to finance the purchase of the shares. In this manner, tax shields are valuable to owners, since they will be able to outbid others by borrowing to finance the shares in the firm. Real estate investors can do the same as long as the corporate ownership form is elected.

For example, suppose a loan from Bank A is available for $1,000,000 at a rate of 10.5 percent for twenty years. If the loan is to be repaid in equal monthly payments using a regular amortization schedule, the monthly payment will be $9,980. However, you could borrow the same amount, $1,000,000, from Bank B at a rate of 11.5 percent for thirty years. The monthly payment would be $9,900. By comparing the monthly debt service of the loans, we conclude that the loan from Bank B has a lower debt service. Accordingly, Bank B's loan also has a lower mortgage constant (.00990) compared with Bank A's (.00998). The problem is that despite much widespread use by real estate investors, the loan from Bank B is *not* cheaper than that from Bank A. Simply look at the present value cost of each loan.

Another way to see that the loan with lower debt service is not automatically cheaper is to compare the investor's position at the end of the shorter of the two loans. If the loan from Bank A was accepted, it would be repaid at the end of twenty years. However, if the investor borrowed at Bank B, ten more years of debt service would remain. This situation causes problems for those evaluating alternative financing "packages" by debt service (or mortgage constant).

A better method is one that measures the true cost of the loan or the *effective cost of borrowing*. This net cost distinguishes loans on the basis of the annual interest cost on a time-adjusted basis of borrowing and repaying interest.

A final method evaluates the impact that various loan arrangements can have on the investment value and/or rate of return of the investment. Sometimes this can be done by using the effective cost of borrowing.

THE MECHANICS OF THE MORTGAGE

Once the investor has decided to borrow, he or she must become familiar with the mortgage, since it is the most commonly used financial debt instrument. We might point out that the word *mortgage* can be used as a noun or a verb. The *instrument* of a *mortgage* is the document that provides security to the lender who seeks repayment of a note. In many states, the typical instrument is a trust deed rather than a mortgage, but the results are almost identical. However, an investor may also mortgage a piece of property. In this sense, the investor pledges the property as security in order to receive cash for some purpose. Both uses are permissible and the reader should not be confused.

History of the Mortgage Instrument

The formal use of mortgages began during the fourteenth century in England, although its roots can be traced to the first century B.C. The mortgagee (lender) had most of the property rights. If the mortgagee wished to evict the mortgagor (borrower), he generally could do so. However, the development of common law resulted in more rights for the mortgagor. The mortgage instrument consisted of a description of the property held as security in order to satisfy the note owed. It also specified the one day each year upon which the mortgagor could pay the debt. This was known as *Debt Day*, and the law permitted the satisfaction of the note and the canceling of the mortgage according to the *defeasance clause*.

If the mortgagor failed to pay the debt, he forfeited any interest in the land. This led to the development of the *equitable right of redemption* in the beginning of the seventeenth century. This permitted mortgagors to regain their interests during a grace period after the default. The mortgagors could pay interest and costs to the mortgagee and redeem the property. If the grace period expired, then the mortgagee *foreclosed* and took the property.

This common law led to modern foreclosure practices. Foreclosure today limits the period of redemption of the mortgagor by the mortgagee's action. In modern law, there are two doctrines that may be followed: *strict foreclosure* and *statutory foreclosure*. Strict foreclosure is observed by only a few states and closely resembles common law treatment of mortgagors. Statutory foreclosure permits a taking by the mortgagee only to the extent of the debt, and court proceedings are usually required before an exchange of title can take place.

Analysis of Mortgage Terms

The typical terms of a mortgage loan consist of the interest rate, the amount borrowed relative to the total value (the loan-to-value ratio), the period over which the borrower repays the loan (maturity), and the method and timing of repayment. These interrelationships determine the amount of debt service required each period for repayment of the loan.

Interest rate. The interest rate is the most commonly recognized mortgage lending term. One characteristic of the mortgage market in the past has been the fixed interest rate over the amortization period. This has posed serious problems for mortgage lenders during the high inflation of the last decade. Because the interest rate must include an allowance for inflation risk, the lender must analyze inflation trends over the amortization period. This led to the development of the adjustable rate mortgage, which allows the mortgage interest rate to fluctuate as the market adjusts to supply and demand.

Loan-to-value ratio. The proportion (or percentage) of the total property value represented by the amount borrowed is called the *loan-to-value (L/V) ratio*. For example, an investment with a value of $500,000 against which $400,000 is borrowed has a loan-to-value ratio of .80, or 80 percent. This ratio is partially set by state and federal laws for different types of lenders as well as by lenders' policies. Obviously, the loan-to-value ratio plus the equity-to-value ratio must equal 100 percent. It should also be noted that a higher loan-to-value ratio increases the lender's risk.

A higher loan-to-value ratio means higher leverage and increased risk to the equity investor. If the interest rate and the amortization period are held constant, the loan-to-value ratio, the amount borrowed, and the debt service will be greater. For example, consider 70 and 80 percent loans on a $500,000 property at 10 percent interest. On the 70 percent loan, the interest payment is $35,000 per year. On the 80 percent loan, the interest payment is $5,000 higher.

Amortization term. The amortization term (sometimes called the maturity) is the length of time over which the loan is to be repaid. For example, a twenty-year loan is one that is to be fully repaid at the end of twenty years. As with loan-to-value ratios and interest rates, the amortization term is set partly by state and federal laws and partly by the lenders' policies. If all the other mortgage terms are held constant, a greater amortization term means *lower* debt service.

The Mortgage Constant

The payment on a mortgage is generally referred to as the debt service, which is found by multiplying the mortgage constant by the amount borrowed. The *mortgage constant* relates the interest rate and the amortization term.

Suppose a twenty-five-year loan is made for $500,000 at 11 percent with monthly payments. How much payment is necessary to amortize the loan over the twenty-five years? The mortgage constant is .00980. Multiply this by the amount borrowed to yield a payment of $4,900. The annual payment is twelve times that, or $58,800.

The amortization schedule. One problem that the investor must handle is the allocation of annual debt service between interest and principal repay-

TABLE 6-1 Amortization Schedule for a $100,000 Loan at 10% Interest for 20 Years With Monthly Payments

YEAR	PROPORTION OUTSTANDING	AMOUNT OUTSTANDING	DEBT SERVICE	INTEREST PAYMENT	PRINCIPAL PAYMENT
0	1.00000	$100,000			
1	.98369	98,369	$11,580	$9,949	$ 1,631
2	.96500	96,500	11,580	9,711	1,869
3	.94515	94,515	11,580	9,595	1,985
4	.92256	92,256	11,580	9,321	2,259
5	.89767	89,767	11,580	9,091	2,489
.					
.					
.					
18	.20915	20,915	11,580	2,591	8,989
19	.10976	10,976	11,580	1,641	9,939
20	0.00	0	11,580	604	10,976

ment. Interest is deductible for tax purposes, but principal repayment is not. For instance, a loan for $100,000 at 10 percent interest is made for twenty years with monthly payments. The mortgage constant is .00965, which results in a debt service of $965 per month. Table 6-1 illustrates the distribution of this debt service for the first five years of the mortgage.

The amortization schedule is calculated as follows. First, the proportion outstanding has to be calculated by dividing the mortgage constant for the total term by the mortgage constant for the remaining term. For the first year, we divide .00965 (mortgage constant at 10 percent for twenty years) by .00981 (mortgage constant at 10 percent for nineteen years). Multiplying the proportion outstanding, .98369, by the original loan amount, $100,000, yields the amount outstanding after year 1. The amount outstanding at the end of year 1, $98,369, is subtracted from the original loan amount. This results in $1,631, which is the amount of principal payments made for year 1. In order to find the interest payments made for year 1, subtract the principal payments of $1,631 from the annual debt service of $11,580 ($965 per month times twelve months). The result is interest payments of $9,949 being made for the first year. In year 2, the amount outstanding for the second year would be subtracted from the amount outstanding at the end of the first year to give the principal payments made during year 2. The amortization schedule is also discussed in Chapter 3.

Special Loan Provisions

Modern mortgages include many clauses. Some require that the mortgagor pay additional fees, penalties, or charges. Others require payments at specific times. The investor must be able to evaluate the more common loan provisions.

Early repayment. Although many mortgages extend to twenty or thirty years, few income-producing investments are held that long. In many cases, the property is sold to prepay the loan and satisfy the lien against the property. In other cases, an investor makes payments on the promissory note before they are due. *What effects do these actions have on the rate of return or the value of the investment?*

Assume that the early repayment of a level payment fully amortized loan has no effect on the cost of borrowing, and therefore, on the wealth of the investor. Since the amount to be repaid consists of the present value of the outstanding balance to be paid that year, *the investor bears no additional costs when repaying.* The additional payment is applied directly to the reduction of the principal, which results in lower interest charges in the next period. However, this does not occur if financing costs were paid when the loan was originated.

Financing costs. These are charges assessed by the mortgagee to the mortgagor when making the loan. Typical financing costs include loan origination fees, appraisal fees, recording fees, title insurance, past inspections, and credit reference expenses.

Financing costs (or closing costs as they're more commonly called) are divided into two general categories: costs incurred in placing the mortgage and costs incurred in acquiring the property. The first type is "amortized" on a straight-line basis over the mortgage maturity for tax purposes. The second type can be "capitalized," thereby increasing the property's depreciation. Neither type is tax deductible in the year in which it is paid. The lender usually charges the going rate of interest, then calculates the monthly mortgage payment and the annual percentage rate (APR). The APR reflects the true cost of borrowing.

Prepayment penalties. Some loans also require prepayment penalties to be assessed if the mortgagor chooses to prepay. These penalties are usually a flat 1 to 3 percent of the remaining balance. Another method charges six months' interest at the time of prepayment.

Prepaid interest. In some transactions, the mortgagee seeks prepaid interest when the loan is originated. This buffer is frequently used for short-term loans and construction financing. It is often included as a part of closing costs, although technically it is not a closing cost.

Discount points. This is another charge typically paid by the mortgagor. These points are often added to the loan origination fees but, if treated separately, increase the yield to the lender beyond the rate charged on the loan.

Exhibit 6-2   What Is the APR?

The annual percentage rate, or APR, is the official name for the stated interest rate required by federal law on most financial contracts. It became required on contracts during the 1960s as a result of a series of consumer protection laws aimed at providing a better flow of consumer finance information to borrowers. The idea is that when a borrower sees the APR rate on the contract, he or she will be aware of the "true" cost of borrowing.

The APR has also moved toward standardizing the way in which interest is charged on contracts. While there are still various methods of charging interest, the APR rate must be calculated in a prescribed manner (actually, according to prescribed tables) and requires that such items as payment frequency, compound interest, rate per annum, and certain accompanying charges be evaluated. In this way, the APR seeks to provide a common measure of comparison for consumers who may wish to comparison-shop between more than one financing source.

Note, however, that despite the application and enforcement of the APR legislation, a comparison of APRs on mortgages, for example, will not be sufficient to ensure comparisons of equal costs of borrowing. This is because some items are *not* reflected in the APR rate!

This is due to the fact that in some cases, some charges are not required to be included in the APR calculation, and in other cases, it may not be possible to include them because the amounts are not known when the loan is originated. For example, many of the typical closing costs of a mortgage are required to be included when the lender calculates the APR. However, some are not. These include some expenses associated with credit verification, appraisal fees, and others. In addition, special expenses are rarely included.

Perhaps even more important are the expenses that are expected to occur but are not included in the APR rate because it is difficult or impossible to know their precise amount when the loan is originated. For example, prepayment penalties may be known to exist but are not included because the timing of the charge is unknown. Or, as discussed in the text, the impact of early repayment of the loan with closing costs has an impact on the true cost of borrowing, and yet, since the timing of the early repayment is unknown when the loan is made, there is not any treatment of this issue in the APR. This is because the amount and the timing of the charge have impacts on the borrower's cost of funds.

Mortgage insurance.   Finally, if the loan-to-value ratio of the loan is relatively high, the lender may require private mortgage insurance. This is particularly true of residential single-family loans. Although the mortgage insurance premium is small, typically about one-fourth of one percent of the original loan, it, too, increases the effective cost of borrowing. Typically, a front-end initial premium of about 1 percent is also included.

Other provisions.   These include acceleration clauses, assignments and assumptions, and the use of balloon payments. In addition, there are different tax effects: Certain closing costs are deductible from taxable income. This is particularly important, since these result in tax savings. Prepayment penalties, prepaid interest, and discount points are also tax deductible.

FINANCIAL LEVERAGE

One of the attractions of income-producing real estate is the ability to finance a large portion of the investment with debt. However, the reason why this is so advantageous to the investor is often misunderstood. As we suggested previously, the investor uses debt because he or she believes the rate of return earned by the investment will be greater than the cost of borrowing. This important factor is called *financial leverage.*

Conditions for Favorable Leverage

As discussed earlier in the chapter, if the analysis of financial leverage requires that the investor compare favorable opportunities with the costs of debt financing, it is also necessary to consider the impact of taxes on the financing decision, since income from real estate investments is taxable and the costs of borrowing are tax deductible. Therefore one must decide whether leverage will be favorable or unfavorable.

If an investor anticipates a gain as a result of borrowing, *favorable financial leverage* exists. If the opportunity rate of return from real estate investments is not expected to be greater than the costs of borrowing, favorable financial leverage will not exist. In this case, *unfavorable financial leverage* exists and the investor is better off by minimizing the amount of debt used to finance the investment. Not even the most optimistic real estate investor is happy about negative leverage.

Unfavorable leverage means two things. First, the investor would be better off by not borrowing and by using cash (or perhaps by not investing until later). Unfavorable leverage means that the investor is paying more for the use of funds than the investment is returning. Second, no investor would knowingly undertake unfavorable financial leverage to achieve wealth maximization. In other words, if the cost of borrowing is higher than the expected return, the investor would *lose* by borrowing. To borrow under these circumstances means that the investor is willing to pay more for "other people's money" than for personal funds.

The conditions for favorable leverage can be represented as follows: If

$$r_a \gtreqless k_d (1 - \tau),$$

then

$$r_e \gtreqless r_a. \tag{6-1}$$

where

r_a = expected after-tax return on investment
k_d = expected pretax cost of borrowing
τ = marginal income tax rate
r_e = expected after-tax return on equity

If the after-tax return on the investment is greater than the after-tax cost of borrowing, favorable financial leverage exists because the after-tax return on equity is greater than the return on the overall investment. If the after-tax return on investment is less than the after-tax cost of borrowing, unfavorable financial leverage exists because the after-tax return to the equity holders is less than the after-tax return on the investment. Finally, leverage is "neutral" when the after-tax return on assets is equal to the after-tax cost of borrowing. In this case, the returns on equity and the investment would be identical.

Real estate finance becomes an important part of the analysis because financing decisions play a large part in the investment decision. This determination is made by comparing the impact of the financing option on the rate of return (yield) or investment value of the property.

ALTERNATIVE FINANCING METHODS

Despite the widespread use of conventional fixed-rate, amortized mortgages, modern financing techniques offer several alternatives. Table 6-2 outlines some of the questions which the investor should answer before using any creative financing method. To correctly apply and understand each financing method, the investor should understand the implications for all involved, particularly the lender and the borrower.

The following areas must be carefully analyzed before using any financing method: the mechanics of the technique, the tax implications, the legal aspects of the method, and the decision-making implications.

TABLE 6-2 Analysis of Creative Financing Methods

The following are some basic aspects to consider before using any creative financing method. It is important to analyze both the lender's and the borrower's perspectives.

1. *The mechanics of the technique.* How does it work? What is the expected yield (from the borrower's perspective—the cost of borrowing) both before- and after-tax?
2. *The tax implications.* What are the tax rules related to this financing method? What are the implications for both the lender and the borrower? Are there unique tax implications in the event of default? What unique tax problems does this method create?
3. *The legal aspects of the method.* What legal problems does the method create? How is the legal instrument different from the traditional? What are the typical clauses in such an instrument?
4. *The decision-making implications.* When would such a financing method be used? Under what investment situations would it be more advantageous than other financing methods?

Purchase-Money Mortgage

In a *purchase-money mortgage*, the seller takes back a note from the buyer and retains a lien against the property until the value of the note is satisfied. The major difference between this and a conventional mortgage is that the purchase-money agreement is between the buyer and the seller only. Therefore purchase-money mortgages have very high legal priority in the event of a default. This technique is often used, since financing can affect an offer's attractiveness. Sometimes the investor may lack the necessary equity. However, through negotiation, the seller may accept a purchase-money mortgage with a balloon payment or a second mortgage.

Installment Land Sales Contract

The *installment land sales contract* is used when the buyer can provide only a low down payment. It is similar to the purchase-money mortgage because the financing arrangements are made exclusively between the buyer and the seller. However, the major difference between these two arises in the event of a default. In this method, if the buyer defaults prior to fulfillment of the contract, the seller can recover the full value of the property under contract law. Under a purchase-money mortgage, the defaulting buyer is liable (in most states) for only the balance on the note.

Balloon Payment Mortgages

The balloon payment mortgage is a very general financing technique that requires a large outlay as a final payment (hence the term *balloon payment*). In some forms, the balloon payment amounts to an agreed sales price in a future year, after a period of interest payments. In others, the balloon payment takes place at the end of some period of time over which regular amortized payments were made. This accelerates the repayment of the loan but keeps the level of the repayment of principal plus interest at the original term. This form is sometimes called a *balloon mortgage*.

Junior Liens

Junior liens are claims by creditors against the asset(s) pledged as security for which there exists a senior or prior lien (typically, a first mortgage). These are also called second mortgages and result in a secondary satisfaction in the event of a default and subsequent foreclosure. It should be noted that a purchase-money mortgage may be a junior lien.

Junior liens are inherently more risky from the borrower's point of view due to their secondary priority in claims against the secured assets. To compensate for this risk, lenders often seek higher rates of interest. However, the availability of second mortgages opens up new avenues of finance for the investor. If investment opportunities develop, investors with equity in their property can acquire additional real property interests by using second mortgages and increasing their wealth through favorable financial leverage.

Sale-Leaseback

A *sale-leaseback* is a special financing technique that is used in some markets when more traditional financial arrangements are not acceptable. It is often used between large investors and large manufacturing firms. In sale-leaseback, the investor purchases real estate that is owned and operated by a well-established income-producing firm. At the same time, the investor leases property back to the firm.

In recent years, this form of financing has become quite popular because equity capital is either more expensive or unavailable for commercial real estate investment. In addition, there are advantages to both sides of the transaction. For the leasing firm, this arrangement frees equity for other uses. For the investor, the expected returns from the leaseback are relatively long in term and typically large in size. There are other advantages if the value of the property appreciates at a higher rate than expected. Finally, there are income tax advantages for both sides.

Income and Equity Participations

Income and equity participations allow the institutional lender to acquire an interest in the equity reversion from the property. In these arrangements, the lender participates in future income in addition to receiving the contracted debt service repayment. For this benefit, the lender often accepts a less secure financial position.

The income property mortgage market has developed a wide variety of ways of participating in the income. Examples include taking a percentage of the gross income, net operating income, or the before-tax cash flow and/or a percentage of the income from sale. This participation by the lender increases the yield to the lender on the mortgage loan. Conversely, it increases the cost of borrowing to the investor.

For tax purposes, the payment to the lender under the participation agreement is generally treated as interest paid by the borrower/investor. As such, it is deductible as interest from the investor's taxable income from operations. If the agreement is written as interest payments, the payment due in the year of sale would be deductible like a prepayment penalty.

To illustrate a participation loan, consider the following example. A real estate investor is considering the purchase of a small shopping center. The lender has agreed to make a mortgage for $200,000 at an interest rate of 12.5 percent with monthly payments over twenty years. The mortgage constant is .13632 per year. The annual debt service is $27,264. In addition, the lender requires a participation of 2 percent of the annual effective gross income (EGI). The expected cash flow for years 1 through 5 is shown in Table 6-3.

Table 6-3 also contains the EGI for each year, the operating expenses, and the resulting net operating income. From this the investor subtracts the $27,264 payment on the debt service and the participating interest of 2 percent of EGI each year. The result is the before-tax cash flow.

For tax purposes, the participating amount each year is deductible from the investor's taxable income from operations. While we have constructed this example as participation in the effective gross income, the loans have been written for net operating income or before-tax cash flow participation as well.

Wraparound Mortgage

A wraparound mortgage is a loan which is subordinated to an existing first mortgage and is of a greater amount than the first mortgage. The seller of the real property continues to make payments on the first mortgage using the debt service payments made on the "wrap" by the buyer.

Table 6-3 A Participating Mortgage Example

YEAR	EFFECTIVE GROSS INCOME	OPERATING EXPENSES	NET OPERATING INCOME	DEBT SERVICE	PARTICIPATION INTEREST	BTCF
1	$55,000	$22,000	$33,000	$27,264	$1,100	$4,636
2	57,750	23,100	34,650	27,264	1,155	6,231
3	60,600	26,000	34,600	27,264	1,212	6,124
4	63,600	28,600	34,980	27,264	1,272	6,444
5	66,750	30,000	36,750	27,264	1,335	8,151

A wraparound mortgage usually will be of benefit to both buyer and seller. First, because of the lower interest rate on the first mortgage, it is often in the best interest of both parties to preserve this mortgage, if possible. However, there are situations in which the existing first mortgage should not be kept. If the current loan constant on the first mortgage is higher than tha loan constant available on new loans from conventional sources, the first mortgage should not be retained. Second, since the seller often provides the wrap, more liberal financing terms may be offered than institutions. This should make the property more marketable for the seller since it will be more attractive to potential buyers. Obviously, the holder of the existing low-interest-rate first mortgage is the losing party in the use of the wraparound mortgage.

The following is an example of a situation in which a wrap may be used to the advantage of both buyer and seller. Suppose the owner of a property is interested in selling an investment for $2 million. A buyer is interested in the property but is only willing to make a $400,000 down payment. Suppose more traditional lenders are only willing to lend $1.4 million at a rate of 13 percent. On the basis of this alternative, it does not seem that the deal will go through.

However, the owner has a mortgage on the property which can be "wrapped." The mortgage was originally for $1 million at 8 percent over a twenty-five-year term. Monthly payments on this loan are $7,718. The loan has been in existence for seven years, so the current balance is $882,057.

Because of the existing mortgage, the seller is willing to offer a wrap for $1.6 million at 12 percent with a twenty-five-year amortization schedule with a balloon payment required at the end of five years. Since the wrap is for $1.6 million and the balance on the first mortgage is $882,057, the seller is, in essence, financing $717,943.

The buyer will make monthly payments of $16,851 on the wrap. This is shown in Table 6-4. The total annual payment is $202,212. Table 6-4 also contains the interest-principal split for each payment over the five-year life

TABLE 6-4   A Wraparound Example: Amortization Schedule*

YEAR	ANNUAL PAYMENT	PRINCIPAL PAYMENT	INTEREST PAYMENT	AMOUNT OUTSTANDING
0	—	—	—	$1,600,000
1	$202,212	$10,714	$191,498	1,589,286
2	202,212	12,197	190,015	1,577,089
3	202,212	13,753	188,459	1,563,336
4	202,212	15,366	186,846	1,547,970
5	202,212	17,434	184,778	1,530,536

* See text for assumptions.

TABLE 6-5 Amortization Schedule for the Existing First Mortgage*

YEAR	ANNUAL PAYMENT	PRINCIPAL PAYMENT	INTEREST PAYMENT	AMOUNT OUTSTANDING
0	—	—	—	$882,057
1	$92,616	$22,879	$69,737	859,178
2	92,616	24,800	67,816	834,378
3	92,616	26,803	65,813	807,575
4	92,616	29,081	63,535	778,494
5	92,616	31,423	61,193	747,071

* See text for assumptions.

of the mortgage. From the total payment, the seller must cover the debt service on the existing first loan. The amortization schedule for the existing first loan is shown in Table 6-5.

To calculate the seller's before-tax yield on the wraparound, it is necessary to calculate the before-tax cash flow to the seller. This is shown in Table 6-6. From the total payment of $202,212 on the wraparound, the seller must pay $92,616 on the debt service of the first mortgage. Thus the net to the seller is $109,596. Remember that the seller financed $717,943 for the buyer. The yield on the wrap is approximately 16.6 percent. This is calculated by finding the rate that will equate to expected before-tax cash inflows to the amount financed.

Adjustable Rate Mortgage

Another common alternative financing method is the so-called *adjustable rate loan* (also known as the variable rate loan or the renegotiable rate loan). As

TABLE 6-6 Before-Tax Cash Flows to Seller from the Wraparound Mortgage

YEAR	AMOUNT FINANCED	BEFORE-TAX CASH FLOW
0	$717,943	$109,596
1		109,596
2		109,596
3		109,596
4		109,596
5		893,061*

* This includes the $109,596 from debt service plus the $783,465 net difference between the amount outstanding on the wrap and the first mortgage.

TABLE 6-7 An Adjustable Rate Mortgage Example

A real estate investor is considering the purchase of a duplex for $70,000. The lender has agreed to loan 75 percent of the purchase price with a maturity of twenty-five years with the interest rate adjusted every year. Debt service is payable on a monthly basis. The initial interest rate is 12.5 percent per year for the first year. The investor/borrower expects the interest rate to be as follows for the first five years of the loan:

YEARS	INTEREST RATE PER YEAR
1	12.5%
2	13.5%
3	14.0%
4	12.0%
5	11.0%

the name implies, the interest rate is subject to adjustment, and thus the debt service is subject to the change in some index to which the interest rate is tied.

These types of loans create no unique tax problems for the investor. They do, however, create cash flow forecasting problems, since the investor must forecast the interest rate on the loan for future time periods. In effect, the risk of changes in interest rate is shifted from the lender to the equity investor.

To illustrate the mechanics of such a loan, consider the facts in Table 6-7. The investor is borrowing on an adjustable rate loan of $52,500 (75 percent of $70,000) with the interest rate adjustable every year. The payments on the loan are monthly with a maturity of twenty-five years.

The first year's mortgage constant is .0109. This mortgage constant is then multiplied by the loan amount ($52,500) to result in the monthly payment of $572.44. At the end of year 1, the borrower has an outstanding balance of $52,175.44.

Now we must recalculate the mortgage constant using an annual interest rate of 13.5 percent since this is what the investor expects. What is the maturity of this "new" loan? It is twenty-four years, or 288 six-month periods. The new mortgage constant is .01172. This is multiplied by the amount outstanding

TABLE 6-8   Amortization Schedule for an Adjustable Rate Loan

YEAR	MORTGAGE CONSTANT	AMOUNT OUTSTANDING	ANNUAL DEBT SERVICE	INTEREST	PRINCIPAL
0		$52,500			
1	.010903	52,175.44	$6,869.28	$6,544.72	$324.56
2	.011720	51,863.76	7,336.20	7,024.52	311.68
3	.012162	51,238.25	7,569.20	6,943.69	625.51
4	.010779	50,729.98	6,627.57	6,119.30	508.27
5	.010189	50,076.88	6,202.65	5,549.55	653.10

($52,175.44) to result in the new debt service of $611.35 for each month of the second year. At the end of year 2, the borrower has a balance of $51,863.76.

This process is continued for each year. The final result is shown in Table 6-8. This table shows the amortization schedule for the adjustable rate loan: the debt service for each six-month period at the assumed interest rates, the amount outstanding at the end of each six months, and the allocation between interest and principal for each payment.

As a final note, adjustable rate mortgages may also include points, fees, and prepayment penalties as in a fixed rate mortgage. For tax purposes, the items are treated as in the fixed rate mortgage.

Other Mortgage Instruments

Depending on the plan selected, alternative mortgage instruments allow the investor to acquire a mortgage with a variable interest rate, mortgage term, or debt service repayment schedule. Because these vary with interest rates, the price of the alternative mortgage instrument may be higher or lower than the price of a conventional mortgage.

SUMMARY

The basics of making the real estate financing decision were discussed in this chapter. The costs and benefits of borrowing were analyzed, along with the elements in a mortgage. The concept of financial leverage was presented, and its effects upon a possible investment were analyzed. Some alternative financing methods illustrated the many types of financing packages available to investors. Chapter 7 will turn the focus of discussion towards tax-planning decisions facing a potential or existing investment.

QUESTIONS

6-1. Explain why investors use debt to finance real estate investments.

6-2. What are the principal components of a mortgage?

6-3. Why are loan amortization tables useful to real estate investors?

6-4. What is the effect of early repayment of a mortgage if closing costs are zero? If closing costs are significant?

6-5. What is the necessary condition for leverage to be favorable? Unfavorable?

6-6. What are some of the other methods of financing real estate investments?

PROBLEMS

6-1. A mortgage loan has the following terms:

Amount	$250,000
Interest rate	12%
Maturity	20 years with monthly payments

a. What is the monthly payment?

b. Set up an amortization schedule for years 1 through 5.

c. What is the effective yield if the loan is repaid after five years?

d. How many "points" would the lender charge if the required yield was 12.5 percent?

e. Suppose the lender charged the points calculated in part d and the loan was repaid after five years. What is the effective borrowing cost?

f. Assume that in addition to the points, the lender also charged a prepayment penalty of 6 percent of the outstanding balance. What is the effective borrowing cost?

6-2. "Leverage generally increases both risk and return. So it is neither desirable nor obviously undesirable." Using numerical examples, show how leverage can be favorable, unfavorable, and neutral using the rate of return and wealth-maximizing criteria.

6-3. A lender makes a loan with the same facts as in Problem 6-1 except that the loan has a variable interest rate that adjusts at the end of each year. The interest rates are expected to be as follows:

YEAR	RATE
1	11.5%
2	12.0
3	13.0
4	12.5
5	11.5

a. Calculate the payment for each year.

b. Set up an amortization schedule for years 1 through 5.

SELECTED REFERENCES

BRUEGGEMAN, WILLIAM B., and LEO D. STONE, *Real Estate Finance* (7th ed.). Homewood, Ill.: Richard D. Irwin, 1981.

DASSO, JEROME, and GERALD KUHN, *Real Estate Finance*. Englewood Cliffs, N.J.: Prentice-Hall, Inc., 1983.

EPLEY, DONALD R., and JAMES A. MILLAR, *Basic Real Estate Finance and Investment* (2nd ed.). New York: John Wiley, 1984.

LUSHT, KENNETH M., "A Note on the Favorability of Leverage," *Real Estate Appraiser,* 43 (May-June 1977), 41–44.

MAO, JAMES C. T., "Wealth-Maximizing Criterion for Profitable Leverage in Real Estate Investments," *Real Estate Appraiser and Analyst*, 45 (May-June 1979), 51–54.

MONTGOMERY, J. THOMAS, "Leverage," *Appraisal Journal*, 45 (October 1977), 589–600.

ZERBST, ROBERT H., CHARLES E. EDWARDS, and PHILIP L. COOLEY, "Evaluation of Financial Leverage for Real Estate Investments," *Real Estate Appraiser*, 43 (July-August 1977), 7–11.

7

THE TAX ENVIRONMENT

In the previous chapters we discussed the importance of the market, legal, and financing environments in real estate investment decision making. This chapter analyzes the tax environment for real estate decision making. We concentrate on the impact of the federal income tax laws on investor behavior, cash flows, and valuation.

Recall our discussion of the major participants in the investment decision in Chapter 1. The government, through the tax laws, plays a major role in the overall feasibility of an investment. Real estate has received widespread attention as a "tax shelter." In this chapter we take the government perspective on the tax laws and show how to calculate the government's claim (taxes) on the expected income from operations and sale of real estate investments.

CASH FLOW VERSUS TAXABLE INCOME

It is important to understand the difference between the *cash flow* from a real estate investment and the *taxable income* from the investment. The investor is interested in cash flow—the amount of income after all expenses, including taxes, from the investment. An investment generates two potential sources of cash flow: the after-tax cash flow from operation and the after-tax cash flow from sale, referred to as the after-tax equity reversion. On the other hand, the taxing agency (government) is interested in the taxable income from both operation and reversion (sale or exchange).

**TABLE 7-1   Measurement of Cash Flow
from Operation for Each Year**

	Estimated rent per unit per year
times	Number of units
equals	Potential gross income (PGI)
minus	Vacancy and bad debt allowance
plus	Miscellaneous income
equals	Effective gross income (EGI)
minus	Operating expenses (OE)
equals	Net operating income (NOI)
minus	Debt service (DS)
equals	Before-tax cash flow (BTCF)
minus	Taxes from operation (T)*
equals	After-tax cash flow (ATCF)

* See Table 7-2.

Table 7-1 shows how to measure the expected after-tax cash flows from operation. The investor forecasts these cash flows for each year of operations: the holding period. Table 7-2 measures the expected ordinary income taxes for each year of operations. Table 7-3 measures the after-tax equity reversion from the sale of an investment at the end of the expected holding period. Table 7-4 shows how to calculate taxes due on sale when straight-line depreciation is used.

**TABLE 7-2   Measurement of Taxable Income and Taxes from Operation
for Each Year**

	METHOD 1		METHOD 2
	Effective gross income (EGI)		Effective gross income (EGI)
minus	Operating expenses	minus	Operating expenses
equals	Net operating income (NOI)	equals	Net operating income (NOI)
minus	Interest on debt	minus	Debt service
minus	Depreciation deduction	equals	Before-tax cash flow (BTCF)
minus	Amortized financing costs	plus	Principal
plus	Replacement reserves	minus	Depreciation deduction
equals	Taxable income (TI)	minus	Amortized financing costs
times	Investor's marginal tax rate	plus	Replacement reserves
equals	Taxes from operation (T)	equals	Taxable income (TI)
		times	Investor's marginal tax rate
		equals	Taxes from operation (T)

**TABLE 7-3   Measurement of Expected Cash
Flow from the Sale
of an Investment**

	Estimated selling price (SP)
minus	Selling expenses (SE)
equals	Net sales proceeds (NSP)
minus	Unpaid mortgage balance (UM)
equals	Before-tax equity reversion (BTER)
minus	Taxes due on sale (T')*
equals	After-tax equity reversion (ATER)

* See Table 7-4.

**TABLE 7-4   Taxes Due on Sale
If Straight-Line
Depreciation Method
Is Used**

TAXABLE INCOME	
	Selling price (SP)
minus	Selling expenses (SE)
equals	Amount realized (AR)
minus	Adjusted basis (AB)
equals	Capital gains (CG)

TAXES DUE ON SALE	
	Capital gain
times	Investor's marginal tax rate
equals	Taxes due on sale

Real Estate as a Tax Shelter

As Table 7-2 illustrates, the ordinary taxable income (TI) from operating a real estate investment is

$$TI_t = NOI_t - INT_t - DEP_t + RR_t - AFC_t \qquad (7\text{-}1)$$

where

TI_t = ordinary taxable income from operations in year t
NOI_t = net operating income from the investment in year t
INT_t = interest on debt
DEP_t = depreciation deduction in year t
RR_t = allowance set aside for replacing personal property (replacement reserves) in year t

AFC_t = costs of borrowed funds, such as fees and points, deductible over the life of the mortgage

Taxes from operations are equal to taxable income (TI) multiplied by the marginal tax rate.

It is easy to see how a real estate investment shelters taxes. If the depreciation deduction, interest, and amortized financing costs are equal to the net operating income plus replacement revenues, taxes are equal to zero, since taxable income is zero. Taxes are equal to the taxable income multiplied by the tax rate. If the net operating income and replacement reserves are greater than the depreciation deduction, interest, and amortized financing costs, taxable income is greater than zero. Some of the cash flow is sheltered, but not all of it. If the net operating income and replacement reserves are less than the depreciation deduction and interest costs, the taxable income is negative. This does not mean that cash flow from the investment is negative; instead it means that for *tax purposes*, the investment is generating a loss. Under certain forms of ownership, this loss can be used to offset the investor's other taxable income.

ANALYZING TAX IMPACTS

To analyze the expected taxes from a real estate investment, the investor must do the following:

1. Determine the tax classification of the investment.
2. Determine the status of the investor, that is, corporate or noncorporate.
3. Estimate the investor's marginal rate by examining the investor's taxable income.
4. Estimate the taxable income that arises from both operations and disposition (such as sale, exchange, etc.).
5. Compute the estimated taxes using the expected tax rate and the expected taxable income.

The first step is to determine the tax classification of the investment. For tax purposes, two types of classifications exist. The first classifies real estate into four categories: property held as personal residence, property held for sale to customers, property held for use in a trade or business, and property held for investment. Each of the categories has different tax rules. It should be noted that within the tax code's definition, most real estate investments are classified as trade or business property and *not* investment property.

The second classification comes from the Tax Reform Act of 1986 (TRA 1986). A taxpayer's income has been subdivided into three categories: active, portfolio, and passive income. Table 7-5 depicts the three categories. The basic implication of this categorization is that losses derived from passive activities

TABLE 7-5 Classification of Taxpayer's Income

1. Active Income
   a. Wages
   b. Salaries
2. Portfolio Income
   a. Interest
   b. Dividends
3. Passive Income
   a. Trade or business in which the investor does not materially participate
   b. Rental activities
   c. Limited partnership activities

cannot be used to offset income from either active or portfolio activities. Thus, passive losses may only be used to offset passive income; however, these losses may be carried forward (termed "suspended losses") to offset future passive income. Passive activities are defined as activities in which the investor does not materially participate; specifically included in this are rental and limited partnership activities.

Active participation in real estate rental activities does not change the status to active. However, an exception is granted to individuals who actively participate in a rental real estate activity and who have at least a 10 percent interest. The exception results in a $25,000 loss deduction (total deductions and equivalent credits) against active and portfolio income. A limitation is imposed on this exemption for taxpayers with income greater than $100,000. For every dollar greater than $100,000, the exemption is reduced 50 percent, resulting in a total phase-out for incomes exceeding $150,000. Thus this exception allows taxpayers of medium incomes to offset some of their current rental losses.

The next step is to determine the tax status of the investor. This is important since both tax rates and taxable income are determined differently for the corporate and the noncorporate investor. Certain business organizations, such as partnerships, are not taxed separately. The income from a partnership is taxed on the individual partner's tax return.

Next, estimate the investor's marginal tax rate. Tax rates vary depending on the taxable income of the taxpayer. The crucial one for making investment decisions is the *marginal* rate, which has been reduced from past rates by TRA 1986. Marginal tax rates are as high as 28 percent for the noncorporate investor, while corporate investors face marginal tax rates as high as 34 percent. This means, for example, that the noncorporate taxpayer in a 28 percent bracket would owe twenty-eight cents in taxes out of every one-dollar increase in taxable income. Likewise, a one-dollar decrease in taxable income would save the investor twenty-eight cents in taxes.

The fourth step is to estimate taxable income. The operation and sale

**Exhibit 7-1   Who Benefits from Real
Estate as a Tax Shelter?**

Many people believe that the existence of real estate tax shelter provisions in the federal tax code suggests that real estate as an investment is subsequently enhanced. There are two problems with this approach. First, the tax shelter aspects of the investment are likely to be priced into the asset by the *present* owner such that the *future* investor seeking an investment will be too late. Second, even if the tax shelter benefits are not completely "capitalized" into the market price of the investment before the investment is sold, higher-income investors can place a greater value on the tax shelter than can lower-income investors. This is because of the progressive tax rate schedule that applies to current United States taxpayers.

If the favorable tax provisions of real estate (depreciation write-off, expensing of such items as property taxes and business expenses, etc.) are well known to the clientele of investors interested in certain types of property, it is likely that present prices will reflect the tax shelter provisions. For the future investor, this means that the price will be higher than it would be without the favorable tax law. As such, any advantage to the tax shelter accrues to the "seller" rather than the "buyer," once the law is in place. In fact, if all the tax shelter benefits are capitalized, the only investor who would benefit would be the investor who owned the property prior to the discussion and passage of the new tax law.

Similarly, the fact that a higher tax rate is applied to income for certain individuals suggests that tax savings will also vary according to individuals' income. In some cases, we would expect that low-income investors would not be able to "afford" some investments (such as tax-sheltered limited partnerships), since their prices would be determined by high-income investors. This is because the high-income investors would drive up the price based on the value placed on the tax savings; the higher their tax rates, the greater the tax savings. Thus it is expected that investors in the highest tax brackets would value tax shelter vehicles the most. In the real world, this is frequently the case.

Note that these results occur even though low- as well as high-income investors deduct interest, depreciation, and business expenses when calculating their tax liabilities. The point is not that these deductions are not permitted, but that the investor has already paid for the right to claim the deductions at the time of purchase.

of real estate produces two types of income taxes: tax on ordinary income and capital gains and taxes on preference and adjustment items in the computation of the taxpayer's alternative minimum tax (discussed later). Taxable income is also measured according to the investment's tax classification and the investor's tax status.

The final step is to estimate the taxes using the tax rates and the taxable income. These estimates are then subtracted from the before-tax cash flow (from operation or reversion) to arrive at the estimated after-tax cash flow. We will examine each step in the following sections.

CLASSIFYING REAL ESTATE FOR TAX PURPOSES

The classification of a taxpayer's real property controls the tax influence on the investment. It is extremely important for this reason. The four classifications are property for personal use, property for sale to customers, property for use in a trade or business, and property for investment (for the production of income). Table 7-6 outlines some of the key differences in the tax treatment of each of these.

One distinguishing characteristic of property held for personal use is that all expenses incurred for personal, living, or family purposes as well as expenses for repair or maintenance are nondeductible. Nor is the owner permitted to deduct an allowance for depreciation. In the case of sale, any loss incurred is nondeductible, but a gain is taxed as a short- or long-term capital gain, depending on the holding period. Interest paid on a mortgage loan and real property taxes incurred on a home, however, are deductible if the owner itemizes deductions. The owner of a personal residence is also permitted to defer all or part of the gain realized on a sale if the purchase of another home is made within a specified period of time.

Table 7-6 also shows some important differences between property held for sale to customers and investment property. When the owner of a real estate investment holds it "primarily for sale to customers in the ordinary course of his trade or business," the owner is a *dealer*. On the other hand, if the owner holds property primarily as an investment for the production of income or for use in trade or business, the owner is an *investor*. There are several differences in the treatment of the investor and the dealer in real estate. One key difference is the treatment of income from sales. The dealer's sales are taxed as ordinary income. The investor's sales are classified as capital gains income. In addition, the dealer is not allowed a deduction for depreciation.

One of the major drawbacks on property held for investment purposes is that the interest paid on mortgage indebtedness is subject to limitations for the noncorporate taxpayer. *Investment interest* is defined as interest paid or accrued on indebtedness incurred or continued to purchase or carry property for investment.

TABLE 7-6 Characteristics of Various Classifications of Real Estate for Tax Purposes

TAX CLASSIFI-CATION	DEPRECIA-TION ALLOWANCE	TREATMENT OF GAIN FROM SALE	TREATMENT OF LOSS FROM SALE	TREATMENT OF CHARACTERISTIC FOR TAX PURPOSES				
				OPERATING EXPENSE DEDUCTION	PROPERTY TAX DEDUCTION	INTEREST DEDUCTION	TAX-DEFERRED EXCHANGE	SELLING EXPENSES
1. Personal residence	No	Capital gain (can be deferred)	Loss not deductible	No	Yes	Yes	No	Yes
2. For sale to customers	No	Ordinary income	Ordinary loss	Yes	Yes	Yes (limited)	No	Ordinary business expense
3. Trade or business	Yes	Capital gain (Section 1231)	Fully deductible	Yes	Yes	Yes	Yes	Deductible from sales price
4. Investment	Yes	Capital gain	Deductible (limited)	Yes	Yes	Yes (limited)	Yes	Deductible from sales price

**Exhibit 7-2   Tax Treatment of Owner-
                Occupied Housing**

The tax code differentiates between owner-occupied housing and real estate as an investment asset. This is not surprising, given the importance placed on the single-family home in our society. It is necessary, however, to recognize some of the major differences.

First, expenses associated with ownership of a home are not tax deductible to the homeowner, whereas for the investment, expenses incurred in its renting or maintenance may be used to reduce the tax liability from the investment. Two exceptions to this rule include the deductibility of interest from a homeowner's mortgage and the deductibility of local property taxes on owner-occupied property. As in the case of real estate investment property, homeowners share in this benefit for these two items under the current tax law.

Second, homeowners may not claim depreciation deductions. This is not because owner-occupied housing is physically different from any other type of housing regarding depreciation, but because the law provides depreciation allowances only for real estate investment property.

Third, homeowners may defer capital gains from the sale of their homes indefinitely so long as homes of equivalent value are owned and the new home is purchased within twenty-four months of the sale of the former residence. In addition, there is a special once-in-a-lifetime exclusion of capital gains income for homeowners. At present, if the homeowner is at least fifty-five years old, he or she may claim up to $125,000 of capital gains income as tax-free if the gains accrued from the sales of former residences. Thus, for many owners, this means the elimination of capital gains treatment for owner-occupied homes. While real estate investors may defer capital gains treatment through tax-deferred exchanges, they are not afforded this special rule under the current tax code.

Finally, and perhaps the greatest advantage afforded owner-occupied homes by the tax code, is the omission of the stream of benefits from housing (so-called housing services) from the tax base under the federal tax code. While rent is a taxable item from investment property, the "imputed rent" that accrues to homeowners avoids the tax code. Thus housing services received by owners are untaxed; housing services received by tenants are taxed. This omission emphasizes not only the importance placed on owner-occupied housing in this society but also the special treatment afforded owners of housing compared with renters under the past, current, and, most likely, future tax codes.

Generally, the tax code considers real estate owned and operated for the purpose of deriving rental income to be property used in a trade or business and a passive activity. Transient lodging such as hotels and motels are excluded from this passive activity classification. As previously mentioned, losses derived from passive activities are generally not deductible against active and portfolio income. However, upon the sale of such an activity, any "suspended losses" would be allocated in the following order:

1. Gain from the sale of the passive activity
2. Income from other passive activities
3. Active or portfolio income

Thus, upon the sale of a passive activity, the investor may be able to use some losses against active or portfolio income.

Real estate held for use in a taxpayer's trade or business receives the most favorable treatment. The owner is entitled to deduct all operating expenses related to the investment, as well as an allowance for depreciation.

On the sale of trade or business property held for more than six months, the investor is entitled to treat the gain or loss as a Section 1231 transaction. As we will see, Section 1231 transactions enjoy the greatest tax benefits with respect to capital gains and losses. Also, all interest expenses are deductible, and the investor can take advantage of the tax deferral exchange provisions.

Both the courts and the Commissioner of the Internal Revenue Service agree that any owner who devotes a substantial amount of time to the operation and management of rental units is engaged in a trade or business. Accordingly, a real estate investment will probably be classified as held for use in a trade or business. Most real estate investors, therefore, will enjoy maximum tax benefits.

TAX STATUS AND TAX RATES

Various types of taxes can influence the real estate investment decision. Particularly important are the ordinary income tax, the capital gains tax, and the minimum tax. A real estate investment may generate income that is subject to these taxes. To forecast the expected tax implications of an investment, the investor must know the taxable income and the applicable tax rates. This section discusses the various types of taxes and the tax rates.

Noncorporate Tax Rates

Table 7-7 shows the personal tax rates for 1988 taxable income. Table 7-8 shows the graduated phase-out of the lower 15 percent bracket for incomes above a specified level. Marginal tax rates on personal income are 15 percent

TABLE 7-7 Noncorporate Tax Rates: Taxable Income Year 1988

Single Taxpayers not Qualifying as Heads of Households
$0–$17,850   15%
$17,850 and above   28%
Married Taxpayers Filling Jointly
$0–$29,750   15%
$29,750 and above   28%
Married Taxpayers Filing Separately
$0–$14,875   15%
$14,875 and above   28%
Unmarried Taxpayers Qualifying as Heads of Households
$0–$23,900   15%
$23,900 and above   28%

TABLE 7-8 Graduated Phase-Out Ranges*

Single:
$43,1450–$89,560
Married filing jointly:
$71,900–$149,250
Married filing separately:
$35,960–$113,300
Head of household
$61,650–$123,790

* For incomes falling within this range, an additional 5% tax will be imposed to phase-out the 15% bracket.

and 28 percent, with higher incomes taxed at 28%. All taxpayers are categorized as either unmarried, married filing a joint return (or surviving spouse), head of household, or married filing a separate return.

For example, suppose a taxpayer, married filing a joint return, has a taxable income of $70,000. The taxes due are computed as follows:

Taxes on income up to $29,750 at 15%	$ 4,462
Taxes on income excess at 28%	11,270
Taxes due	$15,732

Suppose the taxpayer makes a real estate investment which generates a taxable income of $10,000. The total taxable income is now $80,000 ($70,000 + $10,000) and taxes due are computed as follows:

Taxes on income up to $29,750 at 15%	$ 4,462
Taxes on income excess @ 28%	14,070
Amount of 15% phase-out [($80,000 − 71,900) × .05]	405
Taxes due	18,937

The taxes increased $3,205 while taxable income increased $10,000. Due to the phase-out of the 15 percent bracket, this investment was subject to a 32.05 percent marginal tax. If the taxpayer's income had already been above the phase-out range, the investment would only have been subject to the 28 percent rate.

Corporate Tax Rates

The investor may also use the corporate form of ownership, which is a separate taxable entity. The income distributed to the investor by the corporation would also be taxed on the investor's individual return. This "double taxation" aspect of the corporation has made it less desirable for investing in real estate. There are, however, other advantages of using the corporate form that may outweigh the double taxation disadvantage. Table 7-9 lists the corporate tax rates beginning July 1, 1987, and after. The 1986 Tax Act reduced the corporate tax rates to relieve some of the double taxation burden but broadened the base to which the rates are applied.

TABLE 7-9   Corporate Tax Rates

$0 to $50,000	15%
$50,001 to $75,000	25%
$75,001 and above	34%

A phase-out rate of 5% is imposed on income between $100,000–$335,000. Thus, corporations with incomes in excess of $335,000 will be subject to a flat rate of 34%.

TAXABLE INCOME FROM OPERATIONS

The taxable income from operations is calculated as shown in Table 7.2. The gross income is adjusted for operating expenses, financing costs, and depreciation deductions. The following sections discuss each of the categories as they relate to the determination of taxable income from operations.

Operating Expenses and Taxes

In general, the expenses of operating, maintaining, and repairing real estate investments are deductible in the year that such expenses are paid or incurred. However, operating expenses are cash outflows, which makes them less valuable to the equity investor compared to the depreciation deduction.

Suppose the investor is in a 28 percent marginal tax bracket. Suppose that the net operating income is $50,000 that year. The investor incurs an unexpected operating expense of $5,000. This reduces the NOI to $45,000. The deductibility of this operating expense reduces the after-tax cost to the investor to $1,400 (28 percent of $5,000). While the expense generated a "tax savings" of $1,400, it cost the investor $3,600.

The test of whether an expenditure is an operating expense or a capital expenditure depends on the nature of the expenditure and its relationship to the operating, care, and maintenance of the property. A repair is deductible, whereas the cost of a capital addition is depreciable over the improvement's useful life. A repair is an expenditure that only maintains the value or useful life of real property. A capital expenditure, on the other hand, increases the useful life or the value of the property, adding to the owner's basis for the property. The costs for capital expenditures can be recovered through a depreciation allowance or upon a taxable disposition of the investment. Since the owner's basis (cost) has increased through the capital expenditure, the tax due on the sale as a result of capital gain would be lowered.

Because repairs and capital improvements are similar, it is often difficult to distinguish between them. The itemization in the table below shows how general types of expenditures are treated for tax purposes.

TYPE OF EXPENDITURE	REPAIR	CAPITAL ADDITION
Roofing	Patching leaks and replacing a limited number of shingles	Installing a new roof or replacing major parts
Wiring	Mending or replacing temporarily	Installing new wiring or replacing most of it
Plumbing	Mending and replacing minor parts	Replacing major units
Fire damage	Cleaning up, removing, and replacing temporarily	Restoring or modernizing damaged facilities

The same problem occurs in the case of an expenditure made in protection of income versus defense of title. Only expenditures to conserve income are deductible. The costs of protecting title must be capitalized as part of the cost of the property and are thus depreciable. The costs of acquiring an investment, such as legal costs and appraisal fees, also are not deductible in the year paid but are added to the depreciable basis and thus are depreciable.

Real estate taxes are deductible by the owner in the year paid or incurred, even on property held for personal use. In the case of a personal residence, however, the taxes are deductible only if the owner forgoes the use of the standard deduction.

Another category that the investor must consider is allowance for replacements. In some instances, the investor should set aside an allowance for the replacement of personal property, such as carpets and appliances. Such reserves, while treated as operating expense for cash flow purposes, are not operating expenses for tax purposes. Therefore replacement reserve allowances must be added to taxable income from operation. Personal property in the investment can be depreciated.

Financing and Taxes

Mortgage financing of real estate investments has four fundamental tax consequences: (1) the mortgage debt is included as part of the depreciable basis; (2) the interest costs are, in general, deductible; (3) borrowed money does not represent taxable income; and (4) the costs associated with placing the mortgage are, in general, not deductible in the year in which they are paid but can be amortized over the life of the loan.

Depreciable basis and the mortgage. First, if an investment is being purchased, the investor can include the amount of any borrowed money used to finance the purchase as part of his or her cost basis when computing the allowance for depreciation. Although only a part of the money is equity, the investor is entitled to take the entire price paid for his or her cost basis. This includes the investor's own money as well as the borrowed money. Thus a substantial portion of the net income from a property may be received as a tax-free allowance for depreciation. The investor is also in a position to increase his or her equity in the investment by paying off the mortgage debt out of the monies contributed by the depreciation allowance.

Suppose an investor is purchasing a property valued at $500,000. Suppose also that the property has a $350,000 mortgage that the investor assumes and in addition invests $150,000 in equity. The total cost of the investment is $500,000 on which the investor would calculate his or her basis for depreciation purposes. The depreciable basis is independent of any mortgage amount. The result is the same regardless of whether an investor buys a property and takes out a new loan, buys a property and assumes an old loan, or buys a property subject to an existing loan.

Interest deductibility. What are the tax effects of various payments and charges made or received by the mortgagor or mortgagee during the life of the mortgage? Repayment of the principal of the mortgage debt is neither income to the mortgagee nor a deductible expense to the mortgagor. However, the payment of interest on a debt is both income to the mortgagee and a deductible item to the mortgagor.

Interest paid by an investor on a mortgage debt is deductible even though the investor might not have assumed personal liability for the debt, as in a purchase subject to an existing loan. The distinction between investment property and property held for trade or business is important because the interest expense paid on a mortgage is subject to limitation if the property is for investment purposes. The limit on the deductibility of investment interest—defined as interest paid or accrued on indebtedness incurred or continued to purchase or carry "property held for investment"—is equal to the sum of net investment income. This applies only to the noncorporate investor.

Real estate investments classified as portfolio activities encompass this deduction, but it does not include interest from passive activities or a personal residence that are basically fully deductible.

Refinancing and tax. The third major advantage of using a mortgage is that borrowed money does not represent taxable income to the borrower. Thus an investor who wishes to liquidate a portion of an investment in real property can do so by borrowing against the property. Unlike personal property, the cash received on borrowing for nonpersonal-use property is not taxable, even though the amount borrowed is in excess of the property's basis. The investor's price for borrowing is the payment of interest, an expense that is normally deductible.

Deductibility of financing costs. The costs of placing a mortgage on nonpersonal-use property are not deductible as expenses in the year in which they are paid. The investor may, however, be entitled to amortize these costs over the life of the mortgage loan. These costs include commissions, brokerage fees, points, and any other expenses of obtaining the loan.

The deduction of the financing cost is taken as an annual amount over the mortgage maturity. For instance, suppose an investor borrows $500,000 against an office building. The investor pays a $1,500 commission for arranging the loan, $1,000 for title insurance in favor of the lender, $750 in legal fees related to the loan, and $10,000 in points to the lender. The loan maturity is twenty years. The total loan costs are $13,250, of which one-twentieth (5 percent) can be deducted each year. Thus the amortized financing costs for annual tax purposes are $662.50.

The unamortized remainder of the costs is deductible in full in the year of sale if the investment is sold prior to the mortgage maturity. Using the same example, suppose the investor sells the property after eight years. The total amount amortized is $5,300 ($662.5 times 8), with a balance of $7,950 ($13,250 minus $5,300) that can be deducted in the year of sale. Any prepayment penalties associated with a mortgage loan are also deductible against operating income in the year paid.

If the loan is taken out against nonbusiness property, such as a personal residence, the financing costs cannot be deducted or amortized. Except for points paid, the costs are not added to the owner's basis. These points are deductible as interest in the year paid.

At-risk limitations.   One additional exception to the deductibility of real estate losses besides passive activities has resulted from the TRA 1986 inclusion of real estate as being subject to at-risk rules. At-risk rules limit the amount of losses an investor may deduct to the amount he or she is actually at-risk or personally liable for. Usually loans in which the investor was not liable (nonrecourse) were excluded; however, with respect to real estate, certain types are included in the amount an investor is at-risk. Loans must be from a qualified lender who may not have an equity interest but may be a related party so long as the terms of the loan are similar to others without these relationships. Loans that are acquired from the seller, which may be the bank itself, cannot qualify as at-risk amounts. Therefore, an investor buying property must be careful when securing a mortgage.

Depreciation Deduction

The third item in the calculation of taxable income from operations is the depreciation deduction. This is the key to the shelter aspect of real estate investing. In order to calculate the depreciation deduction in any year, the taxpayer must determine three factors: the amount being depreciated, the useful life of the asset, and the depreciation method.

What is depreciation?   The depreciation deduction allows the taxpayer to recover the costs of the depreciable property from taxable income. Depreciation produces tax deductions *without* any cash outlay. A maximum depreciation deduction reduces taxable income, which in turn reduces tax liability and increases after-tax cash flow.

Cumulative depreciation deductions usually bear little or no relationship to the *actual* change in the value of the property. Typically, the situation is such that the taxpayer has a deduction for depreciation while the property value is rising. The net result is the creation of a tax-free cash flow.

Two types of property are allowed depreciation deductions:

1. Property used in trade or business
2. Property held for production of income (investment)

Property used by the taxpayer for personal purposes, such as the taxpayer's residence, is not depreciable.

Depreciation is only allowed on property with a limited useful life, such as buildings and machines. Land is not depreciable since it has an infinite useful life. Although certain land improvements such as paving, curbs, and gutters may be depreciable, the depreciation of land improvements in general depends on whether they permanently improve the land or improve it only as long as a particular building remains useful.

The depreciation deduction in any year is the aggregate amount set aside over the useful life of the asset to equal the cost or basis of the property. Therefore, the depreciation deduction depends on

1. Costs or basis (that is, the amount to be depreciated)
2. The period of time over which the asset is to be depreciated
3. The classification of the asset for depreciation purposes

Since much of the investment in a real estate asset is depreciable, the deduction may have three results:

1. All the before-tax cash flow from an investment may be sheltered from taxes.
2. Part of the before-tax flow from an investment may be sheltered.
3. More than the before-tax cash flow from the investment may be sheltered from income taxes. This reduces the taxpayer's other taxable income and other income taxes.

All real estate investments create a tax shelter to some degree. The amount of the tax shelter is determined by the relationship between the depreciation deduction and the net operating income from the investment, the interest payment on mortgage debt, the amortized financing costs, and any adjustment for replacement reserves. The depreciation deduction affects the operating taxable income as well as the taxable income from the sale of the investment.

Determining the depreciable amount.   The first step in estimating the depreciation deduction is to determine the amount to be depreciated. Basis, the term used to describe the value of property for income tax purposes, generally means the cost of the property. The basis is important for determining the amount of annual depreciation deductions and for determining the investor's gain or loss on the property at the time of sale. The total depreciable amount is generally the original cost *plus* the cost of any capital improvements *less* the cost of the land.

Basis includes cash, mortgages, and other real estate given in exchange for the investment. For example, if an investor purchases a property for cash and also assumes a mortgage, the cash and the mortgage amount are combined to form the basis of the investment.

Certain items may affect the cost of an investment and change the depreciable basis. These include expenditures for capital improvements, certain legal fees, and the cost of title insurance. Other items, such as financing costs, do not affect the basis. However, these financing costs are deducted over the life of the mortgage.

To determine the depreciable amount, the investor must allocate the total cost between land and building.

Basis Allocation.   From a tax perspective, a real estate investment consists of a depreciable building and nondepreciable land. The allocation between land and building is based on the market value of each at the time of acquisition. You can determine the allocation by using a professional appraisal or by other methods. For example, suppose you make an investment for a total cost of $100,000. If the building to total value ratio is 75 percent, the depreciable amount is $75,000. On the other hand, if the ratio were to increase to 85 percent, the depreciable amount would increase to $85,000. The increase or decrease in depreciable amount represents a considerable increase or decrease in depreciation deductions, which in turn translates into savings or losses in taxes.

A second means of allocation is to use tax assessor estimates. For instance, suppose the tax assessor has assessed the value of the building at $50,000 and the value of the land at $15,000. This represents a building to total assessed value ratio of $50,000/$65,000, which is equal to 77 percent. Using the ratio, the investor would allocate $77,000 of the $100,000 cost to the building and the remaining $23,000 to land value.

Time depreciated.   Another major factor influencing the depreciation deduction is the length of time over which an investment is to be depreciated. The TRA of 1986 has modified the depreciable lives for real estate. Under the new law, real estate has been divided into two categories: residential real property, which has a life of 27.5 years (including low-income housing), and nonresidential real property, which must be depreciated over 31.5 years. Both types must also be depreciated on a straight-line basis. The effect of this has been to substantially reduce the amount of depreciation deduction the taxpayer is allowed to take.

Depreciation in the year the property is placed in service is based on the mid-month convention. This assumes that an asset is placed in service on the fifteenth of the month regardless of the actual day. Table 7-10 shows

TABLE 7-10   Mid-Month Convention for Residential Real Property Depreciation (27.5 years)

YEAR OF RECOVERY	MONTH PLACED IN SERVICE											
	JAN	FEB	MAR	APR	MAY	JUN	JUL	AUG	SEP	OCT	NOV	DEC
1	.036	.032	.029	.026	.023	.020	.017	.014	.011	.008	.005	.002
2–27	.036	.036	.036	.036	.036	.036	.036	.036	.036	.036	.036	.036
28	.029	.032	.035	.036	.036	.036	.036	.036	.036	.036	.036	.036
29	0	0	0	.002	.005	.008	.011	.014	.017	.020	.023	.026

the percentage deduction for residential property depreciated on a 27.5-year basis for the years in service. To use this table, choose the vertical column which shows the recovery year and move across to the month of depreciation. The percentage will be applied to the total amount to be depreciated. For example, if a real estate investment was placed in service in June, the first year's proportion would be .020 and the second year would be .036. A similar proportion would be used over the balance of the life. If the property is sold before the end of the life, the deduction for the year of disposition is based only on the number of months the property was in service during that year.

Classification of assets.   The final step in determining the depreciation deduction is to select the method. The 1986 tax revision allows real estate investors to use the straight-line method to depreciate residential rental property over 27.5 years and nonresidential real property over 31.5 years.

Certain other types of assets, such as improvements, are subject to accelerated methods of depreciation based upon their ACRS class lives. Table 7-11 depicts the types of real estate assets that would fall into this category. The investor also has the option of depreciating these assets on a straight-line rate. The ACRS methods are applied using a mid-year convention; however, if 40 percent of the assets are acquired in the last quarter of the year, the taxpayer must follow a mid-quarter convention.

Table 7-12 shows the accelerated depreciation percentages for these class lives using the mid-year convention.

The depreciation deduction is computed by multiplying the proportion each year by the depreciable basis. This process is continued for each year.

TABLE 7-11   Class Lives for Certain Real Estate Related Assets

3 year	Property with class lives of 4 or less years (includes such items as carpeting, draperies, furnishings)
5 year	Property with class lives between 4 and 10 years (includes cars, energy-saving devices)
7 year	Property with class lives between 10 and 16 years (includes office equipment, fixtures)
10 year	Property with class lives between 16 and 20 years (includes mobile homes and "prefab" houses)
15 year	Property with class lives between 20 and 25 years (includes landscaping, sidewalks, improvements)
20 year	Property with class lives of 25 years and over (includes sewer pipes and farms)

TABLE 7.12   Depreciation Rates for Certain Asset Class Lives

YEAR OF RECOVERY	CLASS LIFE					
	3	5	7	10	15	20
1	.33	.200	.143	.100	.050	.038
2	.45	.320	.245	.180	.095	.072
3	.15	.192	.175	.144	.086	.067
4	.07	.115	.125	.115	.077	.062
5		.115	.089	.092	.069	.057
6		.058	.089	.074	.062	.053
7			.089	.066	.059	.049
8			.045	.066	.059	.045
9				.065	.059	.045
10				.065	.059	.045
11				.033	.059	.045
12					.059	.045
13					.059	.045
14					.059	.045
15					.059	.045
16					.059	.045
17					.030	.045
18						.045
19						.045
20						.045
21						.017

Component Cost Depreciation

Due to the changes in depreciation from the TRA 1986, the effect of lengthening the recovery periods for depreciation has resulted in lower depreciation deductions and thus less of a tax savings. One solution to this lower deduction is a concept of component cost depreciation.

Real estate is a combination of assets including land, buildings, land improvements, and personal property. If these can be segregated, both land improvements and personal property may be subject to shorter depreciable recovery periods. Land improvements are items such as sidewalks, landscaping, or parking lots. Personal property includes all property contained in or attached to a building but does not include structural components such as heating, wiring, or lighting. Specific recovery periods for these assets can be found in the Internal Revenue Code under the asset depreciation range (ADR) system; however, land improvements generally fall into the fifteen-year, 150 percent declining balance category, and personal property falls into the seven-year, 200 percent declining balance category. The following example demonstrates the benefits of using component cost depreciation.

PROPERTY DESCRIPTION	7-YEAR PROPERTY	15-YEAR PROPERTY	27.5-YEAR PROPERTY
Foundation			$ 60,000
Framing			70,000
Roofing			10,000
Doors			1,000
Windows			2,500
Sidewalks		$ 2,700	
Landscaping		10,000	
Parking lot		5,800	
Fencing		2,500	
Intercom	$ 900		
Security equipment	2,500		
Carpeting	3,000		
Cabinets	5,000		
Shelves	1,200		
Kitchen fixtures	9,600		
Total Capitalized Cost	21,600	21,000	143,500

If component cost depreciation is not used, the entire amount of capitalized costs would be subject to a recovery period of 27.5 years. However, $42,600 is subject to shorter recovery periods if component cost depreciation is used.

Alternative Minimum Tax

In addition to generating ordinary taxable income, a real estate investment also has the potential to generate tax-preference income, which is subject to the minimum tax.

There are two sources of tax preference income from real estate investments: (1) appreciated property given to charities, and (2) accelerated depreciation on property in service prior to 1987. For appreciated property that is donated, the excess appreciation of all donated property is a tax preference item and thus is added back to taxable income. For property in service prior to 1987, an accelerated method of depreciation is available. In the computation of alternative minimum tax, the excess of the accelerated method of depreciation over the straight-line method is a tax preference item. In addition to real estate, there are five other types of tax preferences. As shown in Table 7-13, these are added back to taxable income to arrive at the alternative minimum tax.

Table 7-13 shows how to compute the alternative minimum tax. To calculate this, tax preferences are added to taxable income. Certain adjustments are either added or subtracted to this sum depending on their tax treatment. These adjustments include among others, depreciation of real and personal property in service after 1986, passive activity losses, installment sales of dealer property, alternative net operating loss deduction, and certain itemized deductions.

TABLE 7-13   Calculation of Minimum Taxes on Preference Income (AMT)

	TAXABLE INCOME
plus:	Tax preferences
plus or minus:	Adjustments
equals:	Alternative minimum taxable income
minus:	Exemption

	TAX BASE
times:	21%
equals:	Minimum tax before reduction
minus:	Regular income tax
equals:	Alternative minimum tax

For depreciation of real property in service after 1986, depreciation must be calculated on a forty-year life. When subtracted from the regular depreciation, any excess must be added back; however, following the 27.5-year or 31.5-year life to which the property applies, the amount will result in a reduction of taxable income. Additionally, an exemption is allowed to reduce the minimum tax liability under the TRA of 1986. This amount is $30,000 for single taxpayers and $40,000 for married taxpayers; however, a phase-out of twenty-five percent over certain levels of alternative minimum taxable income is applied. These levels are $112,500 for single and $150,000 for married taxpayers. Thus, when these incomes exceed $232,500 and $310,000, respectively, no exemption will be allowed.

To illustrate, suppose a married real estate investor had taxable income of $150,000. He also had property in service prior to 1986 with an excess of accelerated depreciation over straight-line depreciation of $25,000 and positive adjustments of $40,000. The amount of alternative minimum tax would be as follows:

	Taxable income	$150,000
plus	Tax preferences	25,000
plus/minus	Adjustments	40,000
equals	Alternative minimum taxable income	$215,000
minus	Exemption*	23,750
equals	Tax base	$191,250
times	21%	.21
equals	Minimum tax before reduction	$ 40,163
minus	Regular tax†	35,000
equals	Alternative minimum tax	$ 5,163

* $40,000 − .25 ($215,000 − $150,000).
† Assume the taxpayer's regular tax was $35,000.

Therefore, in addition to the taxpayer's regular tax, he must pay an additional $5,163. This would then reduce the investor's after-tax cash flow.

TAXES ON THE SALE OF AN INVESTMENT

The disposition of a real estate investment is generally referred to as the reversion. The tax impact on the sale of the real estate investment depends on its tax classification and form of ownership. We have already discussed the four tax classifications of property in relation to federal income taxes. This section deals primarily with the tax impact on the individual and the corporate investor from the sale of property held for investment purposes or for use in a trade or business.

For the individual taxpayer, capital gains and losses must be netted together; short-term and long-term gains or losses are computed separately. If a capital gain results, it is subject to tax at the investor's ordinary rate or a maximum of 28 percent. However, if a capital loss is the result, the deduction in the year of sale is limited to $3,000. This must first be used against short-term losses and then long-term losses. Any loss in excess of $3,000 may be carried forward indefinitely, but the distinction between short-term and long-term must remain.

For the corporate taxpayer, capital gains and losses are also netted together and short-term and long-term are kept distinct. However, they are not subject to a minimum tax of 28 percent and losses may only offset gains. Thus, the corporate taxpayer is not allowed to deduct $3,000 of loss against regular income and is further limited in the respect of carrying forward his or her losses. A corporate taxpayer is subject to a three-year carryback and five-year carryforward. Additionally, these corporate carryovers and carrybacks are then classified as short-term. Thus, the taxpayer cannot offset them against future long-term gains.

Table 7.4 illustrates the calculation of taxes due on the sale of the real estate investment. The selling price less selling expenses results in the *amount realized*. Subtract the *adjusted basis* from the amount realized in order to arrive at the *total gain* from the sale. The adjusted basis is the original total cost of the property plus the cost of capital improvements made to the property, less the accumulated depreciation deduction over the holding period. For any nondepreciable investment, such as unimproved land, the adjusted basis equals the original cost.

After arriving at the total gain from the sale, the *capital gain* (loss) on the sale of a real estate investment is multiplied by the investor's marginal tax rate to compute the taxes due on sale.

Capital Gains and Losses

Gains or losses from sale are treated as either short-term or long-term depending on the length of time the investment is owned. If the period of ownership is more than six months, the gain or losses will be long-term. Holding periods of six months or less are short-term and are taxed as ordinary income.

If there are both long-term gains and losses, the investor must compute the net long-term gain. If there are short-term gains and losses, the investor must compute the net short-term gain and loss. A net short-term is treated as ordinary income. A net short-term loss may be used to offset a long-term gain.

All real estate qualifies for capital gains treatment unless it is held primarily for sale to customers in the ordinary course of business. Real estate used in trade or business and held for more than six months qualifies as Section 1231 property. Within the tax guidelines, Section 1231 property receives more favorable tax treatment than other investment real estate, referred to as capital assets. Sale of real estate held as neither a capital asset nor Section 1231 asset results in an ordinary gain or loss, whereas Section 1231 and capital assets receive more favorable tax treatment of gains but have different guidelines for losses.

The disposition of Section 1231 assets can result in more favorable tax treatment than that given to capital assets because (1) a net gain from all sales of Section 1231 assets is taxed as a long-term capital gain, and (2) a net loss from such sales is fully deductible against other income without the limitations imposed on the deductibility of losses of capital assets.

Net long-term losses on capital assets may be deducted from ordinary income. There is a limitation of $3,000 on the deductibility of long-term losses from individuals. Per-year short-term losses for the individual are used dollar for dollar to offset taxable income, subject to the $3,000 limitation. The benefits of the carryforward of a capital loss are available to an individual taxpayer until used up or until his or her death.

For the corporate investor, the full amount of the capital gain is included in a corporation's taxable income before the corporate tax rate is applied. Capital losses can only be deducted against capital gains. A corporation can carry back capital losses for three years to obtain a refund on taxes paid during that period, or it may carry losses forward five years for the same purpose. The benefit of any capital loss must be used in this carryback or carryforward period, or it is lost to the corporate taxpayer.

The disposition of Section 1231 assets can result in more favorable tax treatment than that given to capital assets because (1) a net gain from all sales of Section 1231 assets is taxed as a long-term capital gain, and (2) a net loss from such sales is fully deductible against other income without the limitations imposed on the deductibility of losses of capital assets.

Net long-term losses on capital assets may be deducted from ordinary income. There is a limitation of $3,000 on the deductibility of long-term losses for individuals. Short-term losses for the individual are used dollar for dollar to offset taxable income, subject to the $3,000 limitation. The benefits of the carryforward of a capital loss are available to an individual taxpayer until used up or until his or her death.

For the corporate investor, the full amount of the capital gains is included in a corporation's taxable income before the corporate tax rate is applied. Capital losses can only be deducted against capital gains. A corporation can carry back capital losses for three years to obtain a refund on taxes paid during that period, or it may carry losses forward five years for the same purpose. The benefit of any capital loss must be used in this carryback or carryforward period or it is lost to the corporate taxpayer.

Minimum Taxes on Sale

The second type of taxes to consider on a sale is minimum taxes. The following section discusses minimum taxes for corporate entities.

Minimum taxation of corporations.   The corporate investor calculates the tax preference income by the formula in Table 7-14. Assume the corporation has taxable income of $350,000, including a charitable contribution of appreciated property of $200,000, which had a cost of $50,000. They also have excess depreciation on personal property of $20,000 and a carryforward net operating

TABLE 7-14   Corporate Alternative Minimum Tax

	Taxable income
plus	Tax preferences
plus or	
minus	Adjustments
minus	AMT net operating loss
	Alternative minimum taxable income
minus	Exemption
	Net alternative minimum tax
times	.20
	Alternative minimum tax before credits
minus	Foreign tax credit
	Alternative minimum tax
minus	Regular tax
	Additional tax due (credit carryover)

loss of $70,000. Their regular tax liability for the year amounted to $119,000. The additional taxes due would be computed as follows:

	Taxable income	$350,000
plus	Tax preference	150,000
plus	Adjustments	20,000
minus	Net operating loss	(70,000)
	Alternative minimum taxable income	$450,000
minus	Exemption	0 *
	Net Alternative minimum taxable income	$450,000
		.20
	Alternative minimum tax	$ 90,000
minus	Regular tax	(119,000)
	Additional tax due	0

*Exemption is phased out for incomes over $310,000.

Thus since the alternative minimum tax did not exceed the corporation's regular tax liability, no additional tax is imposed. The purpose for establishing the alternative minimum tax is to ensure that everyone will pay some amount of tax on income generated throughout the year.

Corporate tax preference items must be added back to taxable income. These include, among others, bad-debt reserves, tax-exempt interest, and charitable contributions of appreciated property. These will all increase the base upon which the corporation is taxed. Adjustments may be either added to or subtracted from taxable income. One of the major new items included as a result of TRA 1986 is the depreciation on all of a corporation's personal property. In the computation of AMT, personal property that may have been subject to higher ACRS percentages must be computed using the 150 percent declining-balance method over the asset's class life. The treatment of depreciation of real property acquired after 1986 is handled in the same manner as the noncorporate taxpayer.

In computing alternative minimum taxable income, the new tax law allows a special AMT net operating loss to be deducted from the sum of taxable income and tax preferences. However, it limits the deduction for the AMT net operating loss to 90 percent of that sum. This deduction produces alternative minimum taxable income (AMTI) from which an exemption is subtracted to arrive at net AMTI. The exemption for corporations is $40,000; however, for corporations with net AMTI between $150,000 and $310,000, the exemption is subject to a phase-out of 25 percent, which is calculated similarly to the noncorporate phase-out. From this the allowable foreign tax credit and regular tax are subtracted to arrive at the additional tax the corporation must pay.

However, unlike the noncorporate taxpayer, this amount may be used in future years as a credit to offset future alternative minimum taxes.

To summarize briefly, the sale of a real estate investment creates two potential sources of tax liability: ordinary and capital gains taxes and minimum taxes. The investor must carefully analyze the expected tax consequences *before* undertaking an investment. These taxes are subtracted from the before-tax equity reversion (BTER) to arrive at the after-tax equity reversion (ATER), as shown in Table 7.3. The investor makes the investment decision based on the expected cash flow after taxes for operation and sale.

METHODS OF DEFERRING TAXES ON DISPOSITION

The two most common methods of deferring taxes on the disposition of a real estate investment are *the installment sale* and the *tax-deferred exchange*.

The Installment Sale

When the seller does not receive the entire amount at sale and provides some financing for the buyer, it is possible to defer the tax liability. The installment sale allows the seller to spread the gain from the sale over a period of time instead of reporting it all in the year of the sale. However, tax laws affecting the installment sale have recently been changed. Anyone considering such a sale should seek the most current information.

The installment method of reporting taxable income has advantages over the ordinary method of reporting the entire gain in the year of sale. Some of these considerations follow:

1. Only a pro rata share of the down payment is needed to pay the tax due in the year of sale; if the entire gain were taxable in the year of sale, most of the down payment, or more, might be used in payment in tax on the gain.
2. The seller may postpone the payment of tax on part of the gain until the time in which he or she receives payments that include the proportionate share of the gain.
3. The seller may save some of the total tax if he or she uses the installment method, and if the gain on the sale is taxed as ordinary income. Due to the progressive tax rate structure, the seller's gain will be taxed at lower rates if reported over a period of years than if it is reported all in one year.
4. The seller risks the possibility of changing tax rates. Since taxes are computed according to the tax rates in effect in the year in which the gain is reported, if tax rates decrease in the future, the total tax will be less if the sale is spread out. On the other hand, if the tax rates increase, so will the total tax liability.

Basic requirements.   Basically, in the installment sale method, the buyer pays the seller in a series of payments. The investor is relieved of the obligation to pay tax on income not received and is allowed to include only the "gain" portion of the principal in his or her gross income.

The effect of an installment sale is to spread the gain and tax over the years during which the installment payments are received. This is achieved by applying a gross profit percentage (gain divided by contract price). Losses may not be reported on the installment method. The contract price is the sale price reduced by mortgages or other indebtedness assumed (or taken subject to) by the buyer and payable to a third party. The interest portion of each installment payment is reportable in its entirety as ordinary income, and if no interest is provided for in the agreement, the IRS will impute interest.

Commissions and other selling expenses incurred by the seller are not deducted in determining the sale price, contract price, or payments in the year of sale. the selling expense should be added to the seller's basis. If a minimum amount of interest is not provided for, the IRS will impute interest—each installment payment is divided between interest and principal, and the interest portion will be ordinary income to the seller and deductible interest to the buyer.

With this method of financing, the seller of installment sale property is able to defer tax on the gain received to later years rather than paying the entire amount in the year of sale. In an effort to receive the entire gain from the sale, the seller of installment property could pledge these receivables as collateral on a note, thus receiving the entire gain without immediately paying the taxes on it. To correct this discrepancy the Tax Reform Act of 1986 instituted the proportionate disallowance rule. This measured an investor's total indebtedness against his installment receivables. The result forced the seller to recognize a portion of the gain from installment receivables before they were actually received.

This computation was complex and confusing. Therefore, the Revenue Act of 1987 repealed the proportionate disallowance rule with limitations in three areas. If these receivables are pledged as collateral, then the amount received from the loan is treated as a proceed from the installment receivable. Second, installment sale reporting is generally no longer available to dealers in real property. Lastly, for installment receivables in excess of $5 million, an interest charge is imposed. However, with these limitations in mind, lets take a look at the mechanics of an installment sale.

Installment sale procedure. To illustrate the concepts discussed and the basic mechanics of an installment sale, the following steps are employed:

> Step 1: Compute the after-tax cash flow in year of sale, as illustrated in Table 7-15.
>
> Step 2: Compute the after-tax cash flow each year from installment receipts, as illustrated in Table 7-19.

ATCF in year of installment sale. Table 7-15 shows how to calculate the after-tax cash flow in the year of installment sale. From the cash received (down payment), the investor deducts any selling expenses (such as brokerage

TABLE 7-15 ATCF in Year of Installment Sale

	Down payment
minus	Selling expense
minus	Taxes*
	ATCF in year of sale

* See Table 7-16.

fees) and the taxes due in the year of installment sale. Table 7-16 calculates the tax due in the year of installment sale. The investor's total receipts for tax purposes in the year of sale are the sum of the down payment plus the excess of the mortgage given up over the adjusted basis plus selling expenses. This is then multiplied by the profit percentage, as shown in Table 7-17. This results in the taxable amount in year of installment sale.

TABLE 7-16 Tax in Year of Installment Sale

	Excess of mortgage over adjusted basis and selling expense
plus	Down payment
	Payment in year of sale
times	Profit percentage*
	Taxable portion of principal
	Taxable income
times	Tax rate
	Tax in year of sale

* See Table 7-17.

TABLE 7-17 Profit Percentage on Installment Sale

	Sale price
minus	Selling expenses
minus	Adjusted basis
equals	Total gain
	Sale price
plus	Excess mortgage over basis and selling expenses
minus	Mortgage balance assumed
equals	Contract price
	Total gain
divided by	Contract price
equals	Profit percentage

ATCF from installment receipts.   Table 7-18 shows how to calculate the after-tax cash flow from installment receipts each year. Since the seller is also the lender, the purchaser will make a payment to the seller each year. Some taxes must be paid on the payment received by the seller, that is, ordinary income taxes on the interest portion of the debt service and tax on the gain portion of the principal portion of the debt service. Table 7-19 shows how to calculate the tax on each year's installment payment received by the seller.

Tax-Deferred Exchanges

Section 1031 of the Internal Revenue Code provides an exception to the general rule requiring recognition of gain or loss upon the sale or exchange of property. Under this section, no gain or loss is recognized if the property held for productive use in a trade or business or for an investment is exchanged solely for property of a like kind to be held for productive use in a trade or business or for investment. The application of the section for deferring the taxes due on the disposition of a real estate investment is referred to as the deferred exchange.

Why exchange?   Exchanging real estate rather than selling it and reinvesting the proceeds stems from two basic motivations. The first is that exchanging an investment is an attractive method of marketing real estate when

TABLE 7-18   **After-Tax Cash Flow From Installment Receipts**

	BTCF (debt service)
plus	Balloon payment
minus	Taxes*
equals	ATCF from installment receipts

* See Table 7-19.

TABLE 7-19   **Tax Due on Installment Receipts**

	Principal portion
plus	Balloon payment
	Total principal
times	Profit percentage*
plus	Interest
	Taxable income
times	Tax rate
	Tax on installment receipts

* See Table 7-17.

a sale does not appear possible. The second, and probably the more important motivation, is the availability of income tax deferral. Thus taxes that would be paid on an outright sale may be postponed under the use of the exchange.

To illustrate the importance of the tax deferral concept of the exchange, consider the following simple example. Suppose an investor has a property with a market value of $250,000 and an adjusted basis of $150,000. If the property is sold for an amount realized in cash of $250,000, the taxable income (assuming all capital gains) from the sale is $40,000 (40 percent of the $100,000 total gain). If the investor is in a 40 percent marginal tax bracket, the tax on the taxable capital gain is $16,000. Thus, as a result of the taxes, the investor is left with less capital to reinvest.

The investor, however, must ask the question, Am I better off by selling, paying the tax due on sale, and reinvesting, or by avoiding current taxation by means of the tax-deferred exchange? Since the exchange has other important tax implications (the most important of which is that, in general, the basis of the property given up becomes the basis of the property acquired by the exchange), there is no simple answer to the question.

Basic exchange requirements.   Under Section 1031, no gain or loss is recognized if property held for use in a trade or business or for investment is exchanged solely for property of "like kind" to be held either for productive use in a trade or business or as an investment. The *first requirement* of a tax-deferred exchange is that property must be held for productive use in a trade or business or for an investment.

The exchange qualifies for Section 1031 treatment as long as the properties involved fit into either class. Therefore property held for use in a trade or business may be exchanged for property held for investment, and vice versa. Recall that for tax purposes, real estate is divided into four categories. Property held as a personal residence and property held primarily for sale do not qualify under Section 1031. On the other hand, investment property and property for use in a trade or business may be exchanged and may qualify in any combination: investment for investment, investment for business, or business for business.

The *second requirement* for tax-deferred treatment under Section 1031 is that the properties involved in the exchange must be of "like kind," which refers to the nature or character of the property and not to its grade or quality. Under Section 1031, one kind or class of property may not be tax-deferred exchanged for property of a different kind or class. The fact that any real estate involved is improved or unimproved is immaterial because this relates only to the grade or quality of the property and not to its kind or class.

In general, *like kind* refers to the distinction between real and personal property. Real property may be exchanged for real property as long as the first requirement is met. The exchange of real property for personal property does not qualify under Section 1031 for nontaxable treatment. For example, an exchange of an apartment building will qualify even if it was exchanged for a farm. Also, a commercial building for business use could be exchanged for an apartment building. However, an exchange of an apartment building for government bonds would not qualify under Section 1031 for tax-deferred purposes.

Few real estate exchanges are completely nontaxable for all participants. Property value differences usually require the balancing of the equities with what is known as "boot." Boot can take several forms and, by definition, does not qualify as like-kind property. The *third requirement* of a real estate exchange is the identification of the amount of boot and the amount of taxes due on the exchange.

Boot includes such items as stocks, bonds, cash, notes, or personal property received in a real estate exchange. Boot may also be received in the form of relief from indebtedness, which is treated as a receipt of cash. While boot is generally perceived as value given to entice the other investor to trade, its meaning has greater impact when it is considered in the light of tax consequences to the party who receives it.

How the exchange works. To analyze the real estate exchange, we must do the following:

Step 1: Balance equity positions and identify the value of like-kind and unlike-kind (boot) property.
Step 2: Calculate the realized gain in an exchange.
Step 3: Calculate the recognized gain in an exchange.
Step 4: Identify the taxable gain (the lower of amounts in step 2 or step 3).
Step 5: Calculate the ATCF and equity position after exchange.

Table 7-20 shows how to calculate the value of the equity position for each investor. The investor's equity is the difference between the market value of property given up and the outstanding mortgage debt against the property. In any real estate exchange, the net equity positions must be equal for all parties. There are numerous ways to balance the equity positions. Generally this involves the use of boot, or unlike property, cash, or net loan relief. Table 7-21 calculates the "net equity" position. This is the equity given minus the equity received. If the net equity is negative, it means that the investor must

TABLE 7-20   Calculation of the Equity Position

	Market value of property given
minus	Outstanding mortgage debt
equals	Equity

TABLE 7-21   Calculation of Net Equity Position

	Equity given
minus	Equity received
equals	Net equity*

* If net equity is negative, this indicates the amount of "boot" cash to be paid or of the like-kind property; if positive, it indicates the amount to be received.

give something of equal value, such as cash or other property, like kind or unlike kind.

How to balance equities.   The alternatives for balancing the equities in an exchange include the following:

1. Add cash to investor with lower equity.
2. Add note and mortgage to investor with lower equity.
3. Refinance the property with the higher equity.
4. Add another like-kind investment.
5. Add unlike-kind property (bonds, stocks, etc.)
6. Investor with least equity could pay down the outstanding mortgage, thus increasing equity.
7. Any combination of the above that is acceptable and meets the objectives of each party.

Table 7-22 shows how to calculate what is called the *realized gain*. The realized gain is in essence the gain that the investor would have had if the property had been sold rather than exchanged. The realized gain (Table 7–22) is the market value of the property given, minus the adjusted basis of the property given, minus the transaction costs such as brokerage commission and legal fees.

Next we must calculate the amount of gain that is taxable. Table 7-23

TABLE 7-22   Calculation of the Realized Gain in an Exchange

	Market value of property given
minus	Adjusted basis of property given
minus	Transaction costs
equals	Realized gain on exchange

TABLE 7-23   Calculation of Recognized Gain in an Exchange

	Boot (or cash) received
minus	Boot (or cash) given
plus	Net loan relief*
minus	Transaction costs
equals	Recognized gain†

* Net loan relief is the difference between the mortgage debt on the property given minus the mortgage debt on the property received. It is deemed unlike property (taxable) only to the extent that the debt on the property given up *exceeds* the mortgage on property received.
† The amount of recognized gain subject to taxation cannot exceed the realized gain.

TABLE 7-24   Calculation of the Adjusted Basis of Property Acquired in an Exchange

	Value of property received
minus	Realized gain
plus	Taxable gain*
equals	Adjusted basis of property acquired

* The taxable gain cannot exceed the realized gain.

shows how to calculate the recognized gain in an exchange as follows: the boot received (value of unlike property) or cash, minus the boot (or cash) given, plus the net loan relief, minus transaction costs. The net loan relief in the difference between the two mortgage balances is positive. Thus there is no "negative" net mortgage relief. *The investor pays tax on the lower of the recognized gain or the realized gain.* Thus taxable gain is equal to recognized gain as long as recognized gain does not exceed realized gain.

The final step in analyzing the tax impact of an exchange is to calculate the adjusted basis of the property acquired in the exchange. Table 7-24 shows this calculation. The adjusted basis is the value of the property received minus the realized gain plus the recognized gain.

QUESTIONS

7-1. Distinguish between *cash flow* and *taxable income*. Why should the real estate investor be more concerned with cash flow than with taxable income?

7-2. What are the main elements of a tax shelter?

7-3. Discuss the key differences between the four types of real estate for tax purposes. Which enjoys the most favorable tax rules?

7-4. How are corporations subject to "double taxation"?

7-5. What are the tax consequences of the financing decision?

7-6. How does depreciation affect after-tax cash flow? Illustrate with an example, using the current tax rules.

7-7. What is the alternative minimum tax and how is it calculated?

7-8. What are the two most common methods of deferring taxes on the disposition of real estate investments?

7-9. Should the marginal or the effective tax rate be used in making cash flow projections? Explain.

7-10. How have recent tax law changes limited the attractiveness of real estate as a tax shelter?

PROBLEMS

7-1. Using the example developed in the text on component cost depreciation, compute the tax shield benefit when this method of depreciation is used. Assuming the investor has a marginal tax rate of 28 percent, what is the tax savings?

7-2. Set up the depreciation schedule using the following inputs:

    a. Depreciable basis $5,000,000
        Recovery period   18 years
        Depreciation method   Straight-line
        Marginal tax rate   28 percent
        Placed in service   January

    b. What is the present value of the tax savings discounted at 12 percent?

7-3. Using the facts in Problem 7-2
    a. Calculate the depreciation schedule using component cost depreciation. Assume:
        1. $1 million is seven-year property
        2. $2,750,000 is land improvements
    b. What is the present value of the tax savings discounted at 12 percent?

SELECTED REFERENCES

FISHER, JEFFREY D., and JERROLD J. STERN, "Selecting the Optimal Depreciation Method for Real Estate Investors," *Real Estate Issues*, 7 (Spring-Summer 1982), 21–24.

HENDERSON, GLENN V., and WILLIAM H. WALKER, "Analysis of Installment Sales," *Appraisal Journal*, 47 (October 1979), 485–89.

KAU, JAMES B., and C. F. SIRMANS, *Tax Planning for Real Estate Investors* (3rd ed.). Englewood Cliffs, N.J.: Prentice-Hall, Inc., 1985.

MILBURN, ROBERT D., and STEVEN F. HOLUB, "How the Deficit Reduction Act of 1984 Affects Real Estate," *National Real Estate Investor* (special edition), September 15, 1984.

PRENTICE-HALL, INC., *A Complete Guide to the Tax Reform Act of 1986.* Englewood Cliffs, N.J.: Prentice-Hall, Inc., 1986.

ROBINSON, GERALD J., "Idea for Boosting Depreciation——How to Maximize Deductions with Component Cost Analysis," *Real Estate Tax Ideas,* 16 (November 1987), p. 1–5.

SANDERS, MICHAEL I., and CELIA ROADY, "Tax Legislation: Major Provisions Affecting Real Estate," *Mortgage Banking*, 44 (September 1984), 57–64.

VALACHI, DONALD J., "The Tax-Deferred Exchange: Some Planning Considerations," *Appraisal Journal*, 47 (October 1979), 76–85.

8

OPERATING DECISIONS

One of the major decisions facing investors is the set of operating decisions. These decisions occur throughout the holding period of the investment. As a result, they are often as important as or more important than any of the other decisions the investor is forced to make in real estate investment analysis.

In many real estate investment projects, a careful analysis is frequently overlooked by the investor, the presumption being that the property will manage itself. Although these investors concentrate on the "more glamorous" aspects of real estate investing, such as financing, tax planning, or improvements analysis, few considerations affect the investor's rate of return as much as operating decisions. Since operating decisions are fundamental to successful real estate investing, they affect income and cash flows directly. It is therefore imperative that a careful analysis of operating expenses and the decisions associated with the operation of the project be made. In addition, these decisions must take place periodically throughout the holding period.

Operating decisions affect gross possible income, vacancies, bad debts, and operating expenses. Therefore these items are reflected in net operating income. Determining the rent roll, analysis of vacancies, collection policies, operating expense programs and policies, and some related decisions is the subject of this chapter.

ESTIMATION OF GROSS POSSIBLE INCOME

The rent roll, or the expected rental stream for a specific project, comes from the market analysis discussed earlier in Chapter 4. This "top line" is the beginning of the cash flow statement and is therefore one of the major steps in successful real estate investment analysis.

It is particularly important in real estate to identify the demand forces for the property. The demand will help to determine the economic rent associated with the location of the real estate. Next, the supply must be identified, as the competition will provide valuable information about other projects available for tenants. Together, the market will dictate the price the owner can expect for leaseholds for the subject property.

ESTIMATION OF OPERATING EXPENSES

Another important area in real estate investment analysis is the estimation of the types and amounts of operating expenses associated with the property. Errors in forecasting operating expenses can have a substantial impact on the real estate investment. This is true not only of current owners of property but also of prospective real estate investors.

A Survey of Typical Operating Expenses

Traditionally, for valuation purposes, all the required outlays associated with the regular operation of the property have been called the *operating expenses* of the investment. Expenditures of a more permanent and larger nature that improve, upgrade, or rehabilitate the property are called *capital improvements* and are not regarded as operating expenses.

It is sometimes useful to separate the various operating expenses into categories: variable expenses, fixed expenses, and the reserve for replacement. *Variable expenses* differ from *fixed expenses* in that the former varies with the occupancy and general operation of the property. These items include electricity and water, garbage removal, supplies, repairs, bookkeeping services, management fees, and others. *Fixed expenses* are periodic in nature and in the short run remain constant or level throughout the period, independent of the operation of the property. The best-known fixed expenses are property taxes and property insurance. Recent dramatic changes in property values and thus in property taxes suggest that, in some cases, taxes may not be fixed for the relevant period. In the long run, of course, all expenses tend to vary. However, this categorization is based on the income-reporting period, typically a year. Traditionally, however, since property taxes are based on the tax rate and assessment base, these taxes are treated as fixed each period (year). Other fixed expenses include additional taxes and local fees.

The final expense category is the *reserve for replacement*. This category is frequently misunderstood by beginning investors because it does involve an immediate outflow of cash and is not deductible for tax purposes. It is really a reserve account that is used to set aside funds that will eventually be used to replace worn-out appliances, furniture, or machinery. This reserve adjusts the value of the cash flow to reflect the fact that some of the appliances will need to be replaced in the near future. This is one of the ways that cash flow differs from income for accounting purposes.

Since the funds are not spent each period (monthly, quarterly, semiannually, or annually) like other expenses, the Internal Revenue Service will not permit their deduction from gross income for tax purposes. However, they should be included as an expense item for investment purposes (i.e., when calculating cash flow). By assuming either that the assets to be replaced have economic lives equal to the building (which in most cases is unlikely) or that these assets will not wear out (which is most unlikely if not impossible for most items), failure to include this reserve would result in overstating the value of the property. In any event, inclusion of this expense gives the investor an accurate net operating income figure at each point in time. (This argument can still be made *even* if the investor does not set aside funds for this purpose. The point is that the income and cash flow streams must be evaluated under the realistic assumption that expenditures will be required to replace some of these short-term assets.)

Table 8-1 is a typical operating expense statement for an income-producing real estate project. Note that this statement includes only the expenditures for the past reporting period, in this case one year. In valuing the property, the investor would estimate future expenses and use these to gauge net operat-

TABLE 8-1 Typical Operating Expenses

Variable Expenses
  Utilities
  Repairs and maintenance
  Services
  Administration and payroll
  Supplies
  Decorating
  Management
  Miscellaneous expenses
    Total variable expenses

Fixed Expenses
  Real estate taxes
  Insurance
  Other taxes and fees
    Total fixed expenses

Total Operating Expenses

TABLE 8-2 Replacement Reserve Account

ASSET	NUMBER	COST ($)	EXPECTED ECONOMIC LIFE (YRS)	ANNUAL RESERVE AMOUNT ($)
Refrigerators	24	350	15	560
Stoves	24	300	15	480
Air conditioners	48	150	8	900
Carpeting	24	500	6	2,000
Drapes	24	150	6	600

Total Replacement Reserve = $4,540

ing income. It would be quite reasonable to forecast changes in certain expense items for future periods. It should also be noted that items such as management fees and the reserve for replacement may not be included on past operating expense statements, especially if these were made by the previous owners. This would be true if the previous owner personally managed the property or if he or she failed to establish a reserve for replacement. As already noted, the replacement reserve is not a true expense but rather an account established for valuation purposes. Table 8-2 presents a sample replacement reserve account for an apartment investment.

Data compiled by the Institute of Real Estate Management (IREM) show that the average operating expenses as a percentage of gross possible income per room for residential properties were 13.9 percent for utilities, 5.0 percent for repairs and maintenance, 2 percent for decorating, and about 9 percent for payroll and management. Total variable expenses averaged about 33.2 percent of gross possible income and about 34.5 percent of effective gross income. Total fixed expenses averaged nearly 15 percent. Therefore, for this type of property, total operating expenses averaged about 48 percent of potential gross income and about 50 percent of effective gross income.

Another study by IREM indicated that rent collected for suburban office buildings was typically allocated as follows:

TYPE OF EXPENSE	PERCENT OF PGI
Utilities	15.8%
Janitorial, maintenance, repair	14.6
Real estate taxes	10.2
Insurance and services	3.5
Administration and payroll	5.5
Total expense ratio	49.6%

The study was based on a sample of data from 332 suburban office buildings. The occupancy level for the entire sample was 94 percent. These buildings were within a thirty-mile radius of a metropolitan location, outside the central business district, and had a minimum floor area of 5,000 square feet, at least 80 percent of which was occupied by office space.

Variable Expense Items

Utilities. Utility expenses include most power and water services found in most urban properties, including electricity, gas, heating fuels, telephone charges, sewer or other sanitary system charges, and water. Although many utility expenses are relatively fixed in nature, an investor may be able to restrict unnecessary usage of some of these items by following recommended management prevention techniques. For example, the investor may be able to reduce electricity usage by checking and replacing worn or insufficient insulation in the walls and ceilings and by installing energy-efficient storm windows and thermopane glass. The caulking and weather stripping of windows and doors may further reduce unnecessary electrical usage. Similarly, the investor should regularly check plumbing fixtures for worn rings and seals. As energy becomes more expensive, it will be to the investor's advantage to make the most efficient use of utility services.

Repairs and maintenance. There are two types of repairs and maintenance expenses: those that are minor and are expected to occur at various intervals, and those that are potentially more costly and mostly unexpected. Items typically classified as repairs include breakdowns of elevators, heating and cooling systems, refrigerators and stoves, and other mechanical items. Maintenance items include the general upkeep of the building's common space and the exterior grounds, minor maintenance of appliances on a regular basis (preventive maintenance), and regular maintenance of equipment. When cash flow problems occur in residential income property, some owners tend to postpone certain maintenance and repair items. This deferred maintenance strategy often results in even greater maintenance expenses in the future, falling property values, and very unhappy tenants.

Services. Many items can be better handled by outside professional services. The more obvious ones are garbage removal, regular extermination and pest control, building security, and fire safety control. However, some investors may also be interested in other services such as professional bookkeeping and accounting, maintenance and building cleaning, and window washing. In many ways, the benefits of professional services accrue to both owners and renters. The owners may wish to employ specialists who are more familar with the problems of the job and are trained to handle various situations. Tenants will appreciate the results.

Administration and payroll. Administration and payroll expenses encompass employees who have been hired by the investor (or the management firm) for various tasks. These people include regular maintenance staff, secretarial assistance, groundskeepers, and others. Administrative expenses consist of small operating expenses such as the costs of preparing credit reports on prospective tenants, legal expenses, and petty cash items.

Supplies.   This item refers to materials and small items incidental to the operation of the property. Hardware items and other minor maintenance items purchased by the investor or manager fall into this category. Although supplies constitute a very small percentage of expenses, the owner or manager who neglects this part of the upkeep is inviting trouble in the future.

Decorating.   Sometimes included in services, decorating is listed separately here because it is an important way to ensure an investment's success. The newly redecorated income-producing building allows the investor to attract tenants at the highest rents. It is also regarded as a sign of good management. In many cases, the expenses can easily be justified by the increases in rental receipts.

Management.   This is one of the more controversial expense items. If the owner manages the property himself or herself, then for accounting purposes, there are no management expenses. Since the owner provides the service, the investor would pay a monthly management fee.

Traditionally, management is compensated on a percentage of gross income. Therefore the management firm is useful to reduce vacancies and maximize gross possible income. Management fee percentages vary between 5 and 8 percent for smaller and problem properties. The rate is largely determined by custom and local market conditions.

It is up to the investor to decide whether to hire a management company. Such a company can run the property efficiently and, in the long run, will make more money for the investor.

Fixed Expense Items

Real estate taxes.   Real estate taxes are one of the more permanent expenses that owners of real property must pay. Based on local assessment, these taxes are *ad valorem*, or "according to value." Each state defines the relationship between *assessed value* and *market value* (which requires all property to be assessed at the same percentage). The total amount of tax liability is determined by the tax rate times the assessed value. If the owner feels that the property assessment is too high relative to his or her estimate of market value and the state's assessment-to-market-value ratio, he or she may request a reassessment.

Insurance.   Property insurance is another important area for analysis. Although entire books are available on the subject, the basic purpose for acquiring insurance protection is to reduce or limit unforeseen casualty losses. Insurance firms offer various packages of protection including fire insurance, extended coverage policies (with additional protection against floods, hail, tornadoes, and other disasters), casualty coverage against robbery, theft, and on-the-job accidents, and liability. Property insurance is a fixed expense. In addition, other taxes may be included as fixed expenses. Examples of these are franchise taxes, personal property taxes, or similar levies or fees.

THE ROLE OF PROPERTY MANAGEMENT

Property management is one of the frequently misunderstood areas of analysis. Typically defined as "the branch of real estate composed of renting, supervising, collecting, paying and the overall maintaining and managing of real estate for others,"[1] many investors believe that the expense associated with professional property management is unnecessary. After all, many of the managerial duties and activities may be undertaken by the equity investor. However, since the amount of time required and the types of skills needed may be more than some investors possess, professional property management is a service that warrants consideration. Too, there are other investors for whom the employment of a professional management firm arises out of choice, not necessity.

The decision of whether to employ a management firm is often difficult. The advantages are there, however, for the firm may be more familiar with the market and with the latest construction and maintenance procedures to help increase the efficient use of property. Finally, it may have more resources available for bookkeeping, advertising, and preparing financial reports.

Although these factors and others are helpful, the investor does not acquire them without expense. The decision, then, is whether the services are worth the cost. In many cases, they are.

Evaluating the Impact

One way to determine whether the employment of one or more professional services is "worth it" is to measure its potential impact on the return and value of the investment. For example, if the advice and policies of the property management firm increased the value of the property significantly, it is easy to justify its employment. If, on the other hand, it could not do so and the other services offered were either too expensive or unnecessary, the investor would do better by acquiring the services of others, or of none at all.

Recent studies have shown that property management significantly influ-

---

[1] From the book *Illustrated Encyclopedic Dictionary of Real Estate Terms* by Jerome S. Gross (Englewood Cliffs, N.J.: Prentice-Hall, Inc., 1969).

Exhibit 8-1 What Do Property Managers Do Besides Collect Rent?

Many novice investors regard property managers as rent collectors, and thus the business of property management often suffers from a bad image and reputation. While the collection of rental receipts is one of the functions of the property manager, there are several other tasks with which the manager is also charged.

For example, the leasing, turnover, and inspection programs require extensive planning and coordination between the tenants (both old and new) and the property manager. These activities are frequently fundamental to the smooth operation of the property. In some markets, these activities are vital to the continued success of the property and the goodwill associated with the operation of the investment.

In addition, property managers are usually more familiar with the physical plant than is anyone else, including the owner-investor. If the property manager has detailed knowledge about the property, the manager can provide important inputs into decisions affecting the rehabilitation and/or the long-term maintenance of the property. Also, the property manager may have the valuable technical cost information that can be used to help decide which maintenance programs should be undertaken and which are economically inefficient.

Property managers also represent the owner to the public. As such, there is a public relations aspect to this position. With the rise of consumer protection laws in the area of landlord-tenant relations, the property manager must also be prepared to deal with the media, competition, and others in the community. This is also a valuable service, since the investor does not have to devote time to this aspect of real estate investing.

While there are other tasks property managers may undertake, it should be apparent that these managers can provide a number of services to real estate investors. The "poor relation" image is an unfortunate one; it is often said that effective property management is one of the keys to successful real estate investing.

ences investment values.[2] Since the professionally trained property manager can best deal with factors affecting income and *operating expenses*, he or she is quite valuable to the investor. The following discussion demonstrates some of the other ways in which professional property management may be of considerable help.

[2] See David W. Walters, "Just How Important Is Property Management?" *Journal of Property Management*, 38 (July–August 1973), pp. 164–68; and Austin J. Jaffe, *Property Management in Real Estate Investment Decision-Making* (Lexington, Mass.: Lexington Books, Heath, 1979).

ANALYSIS OF THE IMPORTANCE OF OPERATING EXPENSES

Given that the investor is able to carefully forecast expected operating expenses, there are a number of ways to analyze the relationships between income, expenses, value, return, and risk. These techniques aid in the investment decision-making process and are discussed next.

Operating Expenses and Value

One of the most common ways of valuing property is to estimate an average (or "stabilized") net operating income figure based on market and investment analyses, and capitalize this amount by the appropriate "discount or capitalization rate." If the investor wanted to find out how much value he or she placed on the property, this approach suggests that the investor would make a reliable estimate of net operating income and divide it by the capitalization rate for projects of this risk class and type of investment. The result is an estimate of investment value.

The *operating expense ratio* is defined as follows:

$$OER = \frac{TOE}{EGI} \qquad (8\text{-}1)$$

where

> OER = operating expense ratio
> TOE = total operating expenses
> EGI = effective gross income

Net operating income is determined by multiplying effective gross income by $(1 - OER)$:

$$NOI = EGI \times (1 - OER) \qquad (8\text{-}2)$$

where

> NOI = net operating income

Net operating income is "capitalized" into value by dividing the capitalization rate into the net operating income figure:

$$V = \frac{NOI}{R} \qquad (8\text{-}3)$$

where

> V = investment value
> R = (overall) capitalization rate

For example, using an operating expense estimate of $25,000, if effective gross income is expected to be $50,000, the operating expense ratio would be .50 and net operating income would be $25,000:

$$OER = \frac{\$25,000}{\$50,000}$$

$$= .50$$

and

$$NOI = \$50,000 \, (1 - .50)$$

$$= \$25,000$$

Finally, if the capitalization rate is 10 percent, the investment value is $250,000:

$$V = \frac{\$25,000}{.10}$$

$$= \$250,000$$

Suppose the effective gross income increases by $55,000 due to increased demand for rental space. The analysis shows that the investment value would increase from $250,000 to $300,000, holding everything else constant:

$$OER = \frac{25,000}{55,000}$$

$$= .45$$

and

$$NOI = \$55,000 \, (1 - .45)$$

$$= \$30,000$$

Therefore,

$$V = \frac{\$30,000}{.10}$$

$$= \$300,000$$

The same result would occur, of course, if total operating expenses decreased $5,000 to $20,000, *without an accompanied change in income*. In this case, net operating income would also be $30,000 ($50,000 minus $20,000) and the investment value would also be $300,000.

Finally, the investor could forecast changes in income and expenses and translate those combinations of changes into capitalized value. This is shown in the next section. It is important to emphasize that the calculation of investment value using net operating income as well as other measures of income and an overall capitalization rate is very sensitive to changes in operating expenses.

Although income capitalization is only one method of valuation, operating expenses play a major role in the value of an investment. Since net operating income is the difference between effective gross income and total operating expenses, changes in total operating expenses affect the estimated size of net operating income. Sizable changes in net operating income when divided by the overall capitalization rate result in significant changes in investment value. Therefore a careful analysis of the changes in operating expenses over time is vital to ensure that the investment (and market) values of the property are not seriously damaged.

Similarly, the investor who is able to eliminate unnecessary expenses, or who is able to raise rents by making significant improvements in the physical facilities, can greatly increase the value of the property. One of the benefits of professional property management firms is their ability to eliminate unnecessary expenses and recommend programs for upgrading and rehabilitation that may result in higher rent schedules despite additional outlays. These actions raise net operating income and therefore the value (and return) of the investment.

Operating Expenses, the Operating Expense Ratio, and Value

A question that frequently arises in estimating net operating income is the relationship between changes in operating expenses, changes in the operating expense ratio, and the value of property. This is a very important area, since changes in the operating expense ratio directly result from changes in income as well as expenses.

The operating expense ratio is a key factor in making real estate investment decisions.[3] As a rule of thumb, the investor can predict whether the value of the property will change by comparing the expected changes in rents and expenses with the operating expense ratio. For example, suppose income is only expected to increase at a rate of 5 percent annually but expenses are expected to increase at a rate of 10 percent annually. If the *operating expense ratio* (total operating expenses divided by effective gross income) was less than .50, then investment value would still increase.

---

[3] Austin J. Jaffe and C. F. Sirmans, "The Relationship between Growth Factors, Operating Expense Ratio, and Valuation," *Real Estate Appraiser*, 44 (July–August 1978), pp. 30–34.

The basic relationship is:

If a = expected growth rate in (effective gross) income

b = expected growth rate in (total operating) expenses

Then, OER = operating expense ratio, and

$$\text{value will increase when} \qquad \frac{a}{b} > \text{OER.} \tag{8-4}$$

$$\text{value will remain the same when} \; \frac{a}{b} = \text{OER.} \tag{8-5}$$

$$\text{value will decrease when} \qquad \frac{a}{b} < \text{OER.} \tag{8-6}$$

In this example a/b = .50. If OER < .50, the value will increase. If OER is greater than .50, the value will decline.

This result may seem paradoxical to some readers. In this example, expenses were expected to rise twice as much as income, and yet if the OER was less than .50, the investment value would rise. The explanation is that the investor must pay careful attention to the relationship between operating expenses and the operating expense ratio and determine how these items affect the value of property. The investor simply cannot make a proper decision by only looking at changes in income and expenses.

Gross and Net Income Multipliers

Gross and net income multipliers are reasonably simple investment measures that relate value and effective gross or net operating income. Each has a particular meaning in relation to the analysis of operating expenses. The *gross income multiplier* technique is more commonly used. However, since operating expense levels and, thus, ratios vary among different pieces of property, this technique may be less useful for comparative purposes. However, a well-known article suggests that this technique may be very reliable in making investment decisions.[4]

The gross income multipler (GIM) is defined as follows:

$$\text{GIM} = \frac{\text{MV}}{\text{EGI}} \tag{8-7}$$

where

[4] Richard U. Ratcliff, "Don't Underrate the Gross Income Multiplier," *Appraisal Journal*, 39 (April 1971), pp. 264–71.

MV = market value
EGI = effective gross income
GIM = gross income multiplier

For example, if the effective gross income of an income property is $15,000 per year, and the market value of the property is $100,000, the gross income multiplier would be 6.67:

$$GIM = \frac{\$100,000}{\$15,000}$$

$$= 6.67$$

The investor would then compare this GIM with others for sale in order to evaluate investment alternatives.

The *net income multiplier* (NIM) is defined as value divided by net operating income. It is not used much because the capitalization rate is more commonly used in valuation.

Since $V = NOI/R$, value is also equal to NOI times $1/R$. The net income multiplier (NIM) is defined as $1/R$. For example, if value is equal to $200,000 and net operating income is $20,000, the net income multiplier is 10.0:

$$NIM = \frac{MV}{NOI} \tag{8-8}$$

$$= \frac{\$200,000}{\$20,000}$$

$$= 10.0$$

The net income multiplier is also equal to $1/R$:

$$NIM = \frac{1}{R} \tag{8-9}$$

In addition R, the capitalization rate, may be expressed as the NIM reciprocal:

$$R = \frac{1}{NIM} \tag{8-10}$$

Using the same numbers as in the above example of $V = \$200,000$, NOI = $20,000, and NIM = 10.0, then R is .10, since the capitalization rate is the reciprocal of NIM:

$$R = \frac{1}{10.0}$$

$$= .10$$

In any event, real estate writers and experienced investors urge that a great deal of judgment be used when developing multipliers. Since these measures are relatively simple to compute, the data requirements minimal, and the results easy to interpret, care must be taken to avoid inaccuracies.

To the extent that the gross income multiplier technique is preferred to the net income multiplier, the investor is minimizing the impact that *different sets of operating expenses* can have on various properties. Although comparable properties may vary significantly, comparisons on the basis of gross income multipliers may not pose any significant problems for some income-producing real estate. The problem is when operating expenses vary for other comparable properties. In this event, the net income multiplier (or its reciprocal) is a better measure.

Consider the following alternatives: Projects A and B. Although both have identical expected selling prices and annual effective gross income, the NIM method or direct capitalization using R gives different results. Obviously, an investor would not be indifferent to each project, despite the same GIM. The example shows that Project B requires a greater NIM (or lower R) than Project A. Stated differently, if the capitalization rate, R, was chosen to be 12 percent for both investments, Project B would be valued at \$416,667. Therefore Project A would be preferred if both were viewed as equally risky. Only after the net income multiplier (and the capitalization rate) is considered is the analyst able to choose Project A over Project B. Using the gross income multiplier, the investor does not consider differences in expenses among alternatives.

	A	B
Expected selling price	\$500,000	\$500,000
Effective gross income	\$100,000	\$100,000
Total operating expenses	\$40,000	\$50,000
Net operating income	\$60,000	\$50,000
GIM	5.00	5.00
NIM	8.33	10.00
R	12%	10%

Financial Ratios

Some well-known financial ratios involve operating expenses directly or indirectly. Three of the more common ones are the *operating expense ratio*, the *break-even cash flow ratio*, and the *debt coverage ratio*. Each of these measures is important in the analysis of income, expenses, and productivity of real estate.

A high *operating expenses ratio* may indicate that some expenses currently being charged against the property are unnecessary or that rent levels are too low compared with similar property on the market. The investor should carefully monitor this ratio over time to pick up any danger signals in low or falling net operating incomes.

The *break-even cash flow ratio* is similar to the operating expense ratio except that the debt service is added to expenses as a percentage of gross income. This measure indicates the extent to which the investment is able to provide enough cash flow to pay all the required expenses and financial obligations. If the break-even cash flow ratio approaches 80 to 85 percent, this indicates that the required obligations relative to gross income are reasonably high. Since financial expenses (principal and interest payments) tend to be fixed when a level-payment amortization is used, changes in the break-even cash flow ratio reflect changes in operating expenses, in gross income, or in both of these. In any event, this ratio may help identify periods of tight cash flow and years when the operation of the real estate may require further attention.

The *debt coverage ratio* is net operating income divided by the debt service. A measure of financial risk, it determines the ability of the investment to cover the fixed mortgage payment. Typical ratios for large income-producing properties range from 1.2 to 1.5. The importance of this ratio in terms of operating expenses is that if operating expenses are forecast to increase in the near future, this may result in a lower net operating income (dependent on any expected changes in rental income). If the net operating income falls sharply, the debt coverage ratio may fall dangerously close to 1.00 (or perhaps even less), which would mean serious cash flow problems for the investor. This might occur if operating expenses rose rapidly relative to rental income or if rents fell suddenly due to increasing market risk.

For example, if effective gross income was expected to be $40,000 for the upcoming year, and total operating expenses were estimated to be $20,000, net operating income would be expected to be $20,000. If the debt service for the year is $14,500, the debt coverage ratio is 1.38:

$$\frac{\text{Debt coverage}}{\text{ratio}} = \frac{\text{Net operating income}}{\text{Debt service}} \qquad (8\text{-}11)$$

$$= \frac{\$20,000}{\$14,500}$$

$$= 1.38$$

Suppose operating expenses were expected to increase by 25 percent (to $25,000) for next year without any increase in income. The new debt coverage ratio would be

$$\frac{\$15,000}{\$14,500} = 1.03$$

A debt coverage ratio of 1.03 indicates the lack of safety available to the investor to meet the debt service requirements from net operating income. Therefore analysis of the debt coverage ratio can help identify a changing operating expense position. Table 8-3 summarizes the basic measures and relationships of operating expense analysis.

TABLE 8-3 Summary of Operating Expenses Analysis: Definitions and Ratios

1. Net Operating Income and Value

$$\text{Investment value} = \frac{\text{Net operating income}}{\text{Capitalization rate}}$$

2. Operating Expenses, Operating Expense Ratio, and Value

Increase in investment value   if $\dfrac{\Delta\text{Effective gross income}}{\Delta\text{Operating expenses}} > \text{OER}$

No change in investment value   if $\dfrac{\Delta\text{Effective gross income}}{\Delta\text{Operating expenses}} = \text{OER}$

Decrease in investment value   if $\dfrac{\Delta\text{Effective gross income}}{\Delta\text{Operating expenses}} < \text{OER}$

3. Gross and Net Income Multipliers

Gross income multiplier $= \dfrac{\text{Market value}}{\text{Effective gross income}}$

Net income multiplier $= \dfrac{\text{Market value}}{\text{Net operating income}}$

4. Financial Ratios

Operating expense ratio $= \dfrac{\text{Operating expenses}}{\text{Effective gross income}}$

Break-even cash flow ratio $= \dfrac{\text{Operating expenses} + \text{Debt service}}{\text{Effective gross income}}$

Debt coverage ratio $= \dfrac{\text{Net operating income}}{\text{Debt service}}$

FINANCIAL ANALYSIS OF OPERATING EXPENSES

One of the more vital areas in the analysis of operating expenses is the relationship between fixed expenses, variable expenses, and income. If there are no fixed expenses associated with the property and rents are greater than variable expenses, net operating income will always be positive. However, it is unrealistic to assume that real estate investments will have no fixed expenses. Most have sizable mortgage payments as well. Therefore it is wise to determine how much rental income is needed to "break even" in order to cover variable and fixed expenses. *Break-even analysis* provides this information.

Break-Even Analysis

Since most income-producing properties have fixed expenses, the investor wants to be able to identify the amount of income needed (and, therefore, the number of apartments that must be occupied) in order to break even. The break-even point is the amount of income where revenues would just cover all costs (variable, fixed, and financial expenses). To use this type of analysis, one must make some assumptions about the revenues and expenses of the property.

First, assume that all the rental units are rented at the same rates. Second, estimate the ratio of variable expenses per rental unit and assume that this ratio will be constant for each additional rental unit occupied. Finally, assume that the fixed expenses remain constant throughout the analysis.

Break-even for number of units.   To find the minimum number of rental units that must be occupied in order to break even, we can perform the following analysis.

The following definitions are used:

$$GI = \text{Gross income}$$
$$OE = \text{Operating expenses}$$
$$FE = \text{Fixed expenses}$$
$$ve = \text{Variable expenses per unit}$$
$$gr = \text{Gross rent per unit}$$
$$Q = \text{Number of rental units occupied}$$
$$DS = \text{Debt service}$$
$$TC = \text{Total costs}$$
$$VE = \text{Total variable expenses}$$

Using algebra, we get the following results:

$$TC = OE + DS$$
$$VE = ve \times Q$$
$$GI = gr \times Q$$
$$TC = VE + FE + DS$$

The break-even point for occupied units, BEP(Q), is where gross income equals total costs:

$$\text{Gross income} = \text{Total costs} \qquad (8\text{-}12)$$
$$(gr \times Q) = VE + FE + DS$$

By algebra:

$$gr \times Q - ve \times Q = FE + DS$$

$$Q(gr - ve) = FE + DS$$

$$Q = \frac{FE + DS}{gr - ve} \qquad (8\text{-}13)$$

For example, assume an investor is considering investing in ABC Properties, a fifty-unit, two-bedroom apartment building. Each apartment can be rented at $250 per month. Variable expenses are estimated to be $100 per month per unit, fixed expenses are estimated to be $1,250 per month, and

**Exhibit 8-2   The Value of Break-Even
Analysis**

Break-even analysis is one of the most widely used tools in corporate and real estate financial management. It is a method or analytical technique for studying the relationships between fixed expenses, variable expenses, and income or cash flow. As such, it is helpful in the planning and operations management of real estate investments.

For example, an investor may wish to examine the implications of various policies on the break-even point in number of units of an apartment complex. Alternatively, the analyst may wish to compare several break-even points between different properties when more than one new property is under consideration.

Many property managers and investment analysts regard break-even analysis as one of the basic tools of their trade. In some cases, however, the results of this type of analysis may suggest choices that conflict with the more general investment criteria, such as net present value. For example, the break-even point on a shopping center may occur sooner than on an office building, and yet the financial analysis might suggest that the net present value of the office building exceeds that of the shopping center. In this case, break-even analysis should not result in the choosing of the alternative project, assuming the projects are mutually exclusive. The higher net present value project should be chosen no matter what the break-even analysis suggests.

However, break-even analysis is very useful in showing how sensitive the project is to changes in variable income and expenses in relation to the project's fixed expenses. In this manner, the investor can make use of break-even analysis as a fundamental "nuts and bolts" managerial technique.

the monthly debt service is $4,000. How many apartments must be rented in order to break even?

$$BEP(Q) = (\$100 \times Q) + \$1,250 + \$4,000$$

$$= \frac{\$5,250}{\$150}$$

$$= 35 \text{ units}$$

Therefore the owners of ABC Properties must rent thirty-five of the fifty available units to break even (i.e., achieve a zero cash flow). These results are demonstrated in Table 8-4.

Therefore thirty-five units is the minimum occupancy required to break even, or a 70 percent occupancy rate.

TABLE 8-4   ABC Properties Analysis of Break-Even Cash Flow

Gross income ($250 × 35)		$8,750
Less expenses		
Variable expenses ($100 × 35)	$3,500	
Fixed expenses	1,250	
Operating expenses		$4,750
Net operating income		$4,000
Less debt service		$4,000
If zero, break-even cash flow is correct		$ 0

Break-even for rental income.   It is also possible to calculate break-even points for rental income rather than number of units. This can be useful in cases where there is more than one type of rental unit in a particular investment.

If the break-even point in dollars, BEP($), is consistent with BEP(Q), then gross income must equal total costs:

$$GI = VE + FE + DS \qquad (8\text{-}14)$$

By algebra and substitution:

$$(gr \times Q) - (ve \times Q) = FE + DS$$

$$\frac{GI}{Q}Q - \frac{VE}{Q}Q = FE + DS$$

$$Q\left(\frac{GI - VE}{Q}\right) = FE + DS$$

Since $Q = \dfrac{GI}{gr}$, then

$$\frac{GI}{gr}\left(\frac{GI - VE}{GI/gr}\right) = FE + DS$$

$$GI\left(\frac{GI - VE}{GI}\right) = FE + DS \qquad (8\text{-}15)$$

$$GI\left(1 - \frac{VE}{GI}\right) = FE + DS$$

$$GI = \frac{FE + DS}{1 - \dfrac{VE}{GI}}$$

Using the same numbers from the ABC Properties example, we get results consistent with those in Table 8-4:

$$\text{BEP (\$)} = \frac{\$1,250 + \$4,000}{1 - \dfrac{\$3,500}{\$8,750}}$$

$$= \frac{\$5,250}{.60}$$

$$= \$8,750$$

In other words, $8,750 is needed in rental income per month to break even for this property.

Break-even for rental income per unit. In addition, it may be useful to derive the break-even point in dollars per unit. The algebra is as follows:

$$Q = \frac{FE + DS}{gr - ve}$$

$$Q(gr - ve) = FE + DS$$

$$Qgr - Qve = FE + DS$$

$$Qgr = FE + DS + Qve$$

$$gr = \frac{FE + DS + Qve}{Q} \qquad (8\text{-}16)$$

In this case, the results are consistent because the break-even point in dollars per unit is $250:

$$\text{BEP (\$ per unit)} = \frac{\$1,250 + \$4,000 + 35(\$100)}{35}$$

$$= \frac{\$8,750}{35}$$

$$= \$250$$

Although all the results deal with hypothetical *monthly* income statements, the break-even analysis will work for other periods (i.e., annually) as well. However, the ability to perform useful break-even analyses for annual periods is based on access to annual data. If such data are available and forecasts can be made for the upcoming year, the break-even analysis will work.

Of course, the usefulness of the different break-even methods discussed here vary among analysts, situations, and types of property. The break-even analysis for number of units is best suited for residential income-producing real estate in which all the units are identical in rental price. The methods that measure break-even in dollars and dollars per unit enable the investor to select any gross income and variable expense combination and get a break-even point in dollar terms. Since fixed expenses and debt service are constant, the denominator is always constant for break-even analysis for rental income (in this example, .60) with correct combinations of gross income and variable expenses. Finally, the last method solved for a break-even amount per unit when the number of units was known.

Operating Leverage

Operating leverage[5] is the concept that a relatively small increase in gross income can result in a large increase in net operating income. Using the example of ABC Properties again, we have seen that if thirty-five units are rented at $250 per month, the cash flow will be equal to zero. Similarly, Table 8-5 demonstrates changes in net operating income as a result of changes in occupancy rates.

If, for example, the investor were to increase occupancy from forty to forty-five units (or increase gross income from $10,000 to $11,250), a 12.5 percent increase, the resulting net operating income would increase from $4,750 to $5,500, or 15.79 percent. Therefore a small percentage change in occupancy (or gross income) *levers* net operating income into a larger amount. All of this is due to the manner in which the investor uses fixed expenses. As long as the rent per unit is larger than the variable cost per unit, favorable operating leverage will magnify the changes in occupancy into larger changes in income.

Specification of the percentage change in net operating income resulting from a percentage change in occupancy or gross income is called the *degree of operating leverage* (DOL) and can be calculated at any occupancy level. If the change in net operating income is equal to $\Delta Q(gr - ve)$, since FE is constant, the net operating income at any Q occupancy level is $Q(gr - ve) - FE$, so the percentage change in net operating income is

$$\text{Percentage change in NOI} = \frac{\Delta Q(gr - ve)}{Q(gr - ve) - FE} \tag{8-17}$$

If the percentage change in occupancy is $\Delta Q/Q$, the percentage change in net operating income to occupancy is defined as follows:

$$\text{DOL (at occupancy level, Q)} = \frac{\dfrac{\Delta Q\,(gr - ve)}{Q(gr - ve) - FE}}{\dfrac{\Delta Q}{Q}}$$

$$= \frac{\Delta Q(gr - ve)}{Q(gr - ve) - FE} \times \frac{Q}{\Delta Q}$$

$$= \frac{Q(gr - ve)}{Q(gr - ve) - FE} \tag{8-18}$$

[5] This term, although somewhat related in concept, should not be confused with the term *financial leverage*, which we discussed in an earlier chapter.

TABLE 8-5   ABC Properties Analysis of Operating Leverage

Number of units occupied	30	35	40	45	50
Gross income	$7,500	$8,750	$10,000	$11,250	$12,500
Less expenses:					
Variable expenses	$3,000	$3,500	$4,000	$4,500	$5,000
Fixed expenses	1,250	1,250	1,250	1,250	1,250
Operating expenses	$4,250	$4,750	$5,250	$5,750	$6,250
Net operating income	$3,250	$4,000	$4,750	$5,500	$6,250

Assumptions: Rent per unit = $250
Variable expenses per unit = $100
Fixed expenses = $1,250
Income taxes and bad debts = $0

For example, the degree of operating leverage at forty units is 1.26:

$$\text{DOL at Q} = 40 = \frac{40(250 - 100)}{40(250 - 100) - 1250}$$

$$= 1.26$$

Therefore, for each one percent increase in occupancy after forty units, net operating income will increase by 1.26 percent.

QUESTIONS

8-1. Why should investors analyze gross income and operating expenses?

8-2. "The Internal Revenue Service does not permit investors to subtract the reserve for replacement from effective gross income when calculating taxable income. Therefore a wise investor will omit the reserve from the analysis of cash flow." True or false? Explain.

8-3. What are the typical operating expense items in investment real estate? Over which items do investors usually have control?

8-4. How can property managers be valuable to real estate investors?

8-5. What is the relationship between *operating expenses*, the *operating expense ratio*, and *value*?

8-6. A comparison between gross and net income multipliers reveals potential conflicts in ranking preferences. What implications does this result have for real estate investment analysis?

8-7. What is break-even analysis and how can it be useful for real estate investors?

PROBLEMS

8-1. Using the facts in Table 8-2, set up the replacement reserve account assuming that the investor will invest the annual reserve in an account earning 7 percent interest per year.

8-2. Calculate the operating expense ratio, gross income multiplier, and overall capitalization rate using the following:

Investment value	$1,500,000
Potential gross income	$ 250,000
Vacancy and bad debt losses	5%
Operating expenses	$ 110,000

8-3. Using the facts in Problem 8-2 and the following:

Debt service	$ 105,000

calculate the
a. Break-even cash flow ratio
b. Debt coverage ratio
c. Net income multiplier

8-4. If effective gross income is $10,000 and is expected to increase at the rate of 6 percent per year, and if the operating expense ratio is .60, how high does the expected growth rate in total operating expenses have to be in order for the value of the property to decline? Increase? Stay the same?

8-5. If the rent per unit is $500 per month and variable expenses per unit are $150 per month, what is the break-even number of units if the sum of fixed expenses and debt service is $5,250 per month? What is the break-even point in dollars? Prove your results.

8-6. For the investment in Problem 8-5, what is the degree of operating leverage at ten units? Twenty units? (Note: Assume that $2,000 is the fixed expenses per month.) What does the degree of operating leverage tell the analyst?

SELECTED REFERENCES

Downs, James C., Jr., *Principles of Real Estate Management* (12th ed). Chicago: Institute of Real Estate Management, 1980.

Institute of Real Estate Management, *Income/Expense Analysis: Apartments* (1983 edition). Chicago: Institute of Real Estate Management, 1983.

_____, *Income/Expense Analysis: Office Buildings Downtown and Suburban* (1983 ed.). Chicago: Institute of Real Estate Management, 1983.

Jaffe, Austin J., "The Property Manager: Foremost among the Decision-Makers," *Journal of Property Management,* 42 (November-December 1977), 288–90.

_____ and C. F. Sirmans, "The Relationship between Growth Factors, Operating Expense Ratio, and Valuation," *Real Estate Appraiser,* 44 (July–August 1978), 30–34.

Kelley, Edward N., *Practical Apartment Management*. Chicago: Institute of Real Estate Management, 1976.

Shenkel, William M., *Modern Real Estate Management*. New York: McGraw-Hill, 1980.

Walters, William, Jr., *The Practice of Real Estate Management*. New York: McGraw-Hill, 1980.

9

FINANCING DECISIONS

Real estate financing has become increasingly complex in recent years as the number and types of instruments have proliferated. This chapter deals with several of the financing decisions facing investors. The chapter begins with the simple mechanics of mortgage calculations and then discusses such aspects as the analysis of various mortgage terms and the impact of the financing decision on the net present value of the investment. The financing decision can be evaluated in numerous ways, since a number of financing methods are popular in real estate. Some of the more popular methods are described, along with examples to show how the investor can explicitly evaluate various financing choices.

Chapter 6 analyzed the reasons why an investor would borrow. A major reason is the possibility of financial leverage gains for the investor. Since so much real estate uses financial leverage, it is important to evaluate the principal aspects of a mortgage.

MECHANICS OF THE FINANCING DECISION

The most commonly used financial debt instrument associated with the investment in income-producing real estate is the *mortgage*. Its use has a long tradition in English common law. In addition, the reliance on the level payment, fully amortized loan by many investors, has made this method of amortization standard throughout the industry. However, modern real estate finance has expanded the choices available to real estate investors and, in many ways, the methods of obtaining finance for investing in real estate in the future may be significantly different.

Analysis of Mortgage Terms

The common terms in a mortgage loan are the *interest rate* on the mortgage, the amount borrowed relative to the total value (the *loan-to-value ratio*), the period over which the borrower repays the loan (the *maturity* or *amortization period* of the loan), and the method (*amortization* or the repayment) of the loan. The relationship between these factors determines the amount of *debt service* required each period in order to repay the loan.

Two other concepts are also associated with the mortgage. The *mortgage constant* is a measure of the combined effect of the interest rate and expected maturity of the loan. The *debt coverage ratio* is a measure of the riskiness of the investment from the lender's point of view based on the investment's ability to cover the debt service by its income stream.

Interest rate. The *interest rate* is the most commonly recognized mortgage-lending term. During the past few decades, the use of fixed-rate, level payment mortgages emphasized the extent to which the interest rate was relied on as the important measure and the basis of the cost of borrowing for the mortgagor and as the basic yield for the mortgagee.

However, with unexpected price changes for real property and unexpected inflation throughout the economy during the 1970s, fixed-rate mortgages posed serious problems for mortgage lenders. Since allowances for inflation must be taken into account by lenders prior to lending funds for mortgages, it has become increasingly difficult for lenders to forecast inflation and "price" the standard fixed-rate mortgage.

This, in turn, has led to the growth of many financing alternatives in recent years. For example, the variable-rate mortgage allows the lender to alter the mortgage interest rate as market conditions adjust to changes in supply and demand. The variable-rate mortgage and other new financing options, some of which are discussed later, suggest dramatic changes in the financing of real estate investments in the future.

As a final word on the interest rate, it is clear that a change in the interest rate directly affects debt service. A review of the mathematics of finance in Chapter 3 shows that as interest rates increase, so does debt service, assuming the amortization period and the amount borrowed are held constant. Therefore changes in interest rates translate into changes in the mortgage constant, the debt coverage ratio, and before-tax cash flow.

Loan-to-value ratio. The amount borrowed as a proportion of total property value is called the *loan-to-value ratio*. For example, if a loan of $400,000 is obtained, against which a property valued at $500,000 is held as security, the loan-to-value ratio is .80.

The loan-to-value ratio is subject to state and federal regulations that may vary for different types of lenders and for different types of properties. Frequently, the investor wishes to maximize the loan-to-value ratio because this will maximize the amount of debt used and, therefore, maximize the amount of financial leverage. Although increased financial leverage increases the financial risk of the investment, many investors seek higher amounts of leverage.

The lender, on the other hand, seeks lower loan-to-value ratios because the lower the ratio, the lower the lender's risk. Since the loan-to-value ratio and the *equity-to-value* ratio must equal 100 percent, a lower loan-to-value ratio implies a higher equity-to-value ratio. In other words, the higher the equity-to-value ratio, the greater the equity down payment of the investor. (Another risk measure, the debt coverage ratio, is also used by the lender to assess the risk of various investments. It will be discussed in an upcoming section.)

For a given investment, the higher the loan-to-value ratio, the greater the debt service, assuming a fixed interest rate and amortization period. For instance, consider two loan-to-value ratios of 70 percent and 80 percent on a $500,000 investment. Both loans carry a 12 percent interest rate and both are fully amortized over thirty years. The debt service of the 70 percent loan-to-value ratio loan is $38,795. The debt service of the loan at 80 percent loan-to-value is $44,337, or $5,542 per year higher. The difference is due to the required repayment of $50,000 in additional principal and more interest in the latter case.

Amortization period. Also called the maturity of the loan, the *amortization period* is the length of time over which the loan is to be repaid. For example, a twenty-year loan is one that must be repaid at the end of twenty years. Like loan-to-value ratios and interest rate levels, amortization periods are frequently limited by state and federal regulations. Lender policies also dictate appropriate amortization periods.

Although many traditional investors regard fully amortized loans as the only debt source available, there are three general categories of amortized loans. The first consists of loans for which interest only is paid and no amortization of the principal takes place. The entire principal is due at maturity of the loan. This type of loan is called an *interest-only loan*. In using this loan, the borrower is not required to produce additional amounts of equity capital. Therefore, assuming all else constant, the interest-only debt service is less than the debt service under the amortized loans.

The second category includes loans of various repayment schemes, but all require a larger than typical payment at maturity. A loan of this type is called a *partially amortized loan*, since the final payment includes a large repayment of principal. This final payment is less than the amount borrowed and represents the percentage value of the remaining payments. The final payment is called the *balloon payment*.

The final category is the *fully amortized loan* that is the major repayment plan for much real estate. The most familiar example is the *level payment amortized loan* in which debt service payments are constant throughout the life of the loan, although the breakdown between principal and interest changes each period. For income-producing real estate, the reliance on the level payment, fully amortized loan is lessening. At inflation-adjusted interest rates, the debt service requirements of this loan plan will limit its future use.

With respect to the amortization period, if all the other mortgage terms are held constant, the greater the maturity of the loan, the lower the debt service. Suppose a loan of $100,000 was made at an interest rate of 15 percent, with annual payments for twenty years. The annual debt service is $13,892. If the amortization term is extended to twenty-five years, the debt service would fall to $13,452. So by extending the term of the loan, the debt service declined $440 ($13,892 minus $13,452). The amortization period is measured in years or months, depending on how often payments are made.

Mortgage constant.   The payment on a mortgage is generally referred to as the *debt service*. One way to compute the debt service is to multiply the *mortgage constant* by the amount borrowed. The mortgage constant is the factor that relates the interest rate and the amortization period. Mortgage constants are provided in the tables at the end of the book or can easily be calculated with the following equation:

$$MC = \frac{\dfrac{i}{m}}{1 - \dfrac{1}{\left(1 + \dfrac{i}{m}\right)^{n \times m}}} \tag{9-1}$$

where

      MC = mortgage constant
       i = rate of interest per year
      n = number of years
      m = frequency of compounding per year

Although the mortgage constant is useful in calculating debt service and developing amortization schedules, the reader is cautioned about its application. Use of the mortgage constant as a cost of borrowing and as a measure of financial leverage can lead to serious errors in analysis.

Amortization schedule.   In analyzing real estate, it is necessary to allocate the periodic debt service between interest and principal repayments. The investor can use the mortgage constant to develop the *amortization schedule*. This schedule can be used in the calculation of after-tax cash flow because only the interest portion of the debt service is deductible for tax purposes. Principal repayments offset cash flow but have no effect on taxable income. Thus it is necessary to allocate the debt service between principal and interest.

TABLE 9-1   Amortization Schedule for a $100,000 Loan at 10 Percent Interest for Twenty Years with Annual Payments

YEAR	MORTGAGE BALANCE (BEGINNING OF YEAR)	DEBT SERVICE	INTEREST PAYMENT	PRINCIPAL PAYMENT	MORTGAGE BALANCE (END OF YEAR)
1	$100,000.00	$11,746.00	$10,000.00	$ 1,746.00	$98,254.00
2	98,254.00	11,746.00	9,825.40	1,920.60	96,333.40
3	96,333.40	11,746.00	9,633.34	2,112.66	94,220.74
4	94,220.74	11,746.00	9,422.07	2,323.93	91,896.81
5	91,896.81	11,746.00	9,189.68	2,556.32	89,340.49
.	.	.	.	.	.
.	.	.	.	.	.
.	.	.	.	.	.
16	44,525.22	11,746.00	4,452.52	7,293.48	37,231.74
17	37,231.74	11,746.00	3,723.17	8,022.83	29,208.91
18	29,208.91	11,746.00	2,920.89	8,825.11	20,383.80
19	20,383.80	11,746.00	2,038.38	9,707.62	10,676.18
20	10,676.18	11,743.80	1,067.62	10,676.18	0.00

To develop an amortization schedule, consider the following example. Suppose a loan is made for $100,000 at a 10 percent interest rate, requiring annual payments for a period of twenty years. Using Equation (9-1), the mortgage constant is .11746 and the debt service is $11,746 per year. Table 9-1 illustrates the distribution of debt service between interest and principal.

The amortization schedule is calculated as follows. The beginning outstanding balance of $100,000 is multiplied by the interest rate of 10 percent to get the first year's interest payment, $10,000. Since the total payment is $11,746, the difference of $1,746 represents the repayment of principal. Therefore the outstanding balance at the end of the first year (and the beginning of the second year) is $98,254.00. At the 10 percent interest rate, the second year's interest charge is $9,825.40, leaving a principal reduction of $1,920.60. The mortgage balance at the end of the second year is $96,333.40. This process is repeated until the outstanding balance is zero (that is, at loan maturity).

Debt coverage ratio.   The *debt coverage ratio*, or the ratio of net operating income to debt service, is a measure of the risk of an investment. This ratio is used to evaluate the ability of the income stream to cover the debt service (that is, provide a positive before-tax cash flow to the investor). Traditionally, lenders required debt coverage ratios of 1.15 to 1.50. Now, with debt coverage ratios falling very close to 1.0, current values of this ratio are a lot lower than historical standards and have come under careful scrutiny.[1]

---

[1] For research on the use and importance of debt coverage ratios, see Kenneth M. Lusht and Robert H. Zerbst, "Valuing Income Property in an Inflationary Environment," *Real Estate Appraiser and Analyst*, 46 (July-August 1980), pp. 11–17.

For example, if interest rates rise due to expected inflation, debt service will also rise, assuming everything else is held constant. If net operating income fails to rise or does not rise sufficiently to offset the increased cost of finance, the debt coverage ratio will fall. If this happens, the investor will have difficulty finding financing in periods of tight money.

ANALYSIS OF LOAN PROVISIONS ON COST OF BORROWING

Modern mortgages contain many specific clauses that greatly affect the cost of borrowing. Some clauses require that the mortgagor pay additional fees, penalties, or charges. Others require that payment be made at specific times. The investor must be able to evaluate the effects of special loan provisions on the cost of borrowing. *How do mortgage clauses affect the rate of return or value of the investment?*

Early Repayment

Although many mortgages extend to twenty-five or thirty years, few income-producing investments are held for that long a period. In many instances, the investor would like to prepay the loan and satisfy the lien against the property in order to convey a clear title when selling the property after a shorter period of time. In other instances, an investor may wish to accelerate payments (on a promissory note for example) before the due date. The question is, What effect does early repayment have on the cost of borrowing? Note that we discussed the tax consequences in Chapters 7 and 10.

Let us assume that the decision about whether to borrow has been made and that the investor wishes to repay the loan before it is due for reasons other than altering the financing mix of debt and equity. If the loan is a level payment, fully amortized mortgage, early repayment has no effect on the cost of borrowing and no effect on investor wealth.

This is true because the outstanding balance consists of a set of debt service payments calculated by using the interest rate and amortization period. In accelerating payments, the investor takes the present value of the stream of remaining payments from the "acceleration date" until the end of the amortization period. The present value represents the outstanding balance at the acceleration date. Since the amount to be repaid consists of the present value of the outstanding balance, the investor bears no additional costs.

Therefore, for a mortgage without closing costs, prepayment penalties, or other provisions, the possibility of early repayment does not result in any financial cost to the mortgagor. Since the payment due at the acceleration date is the present value of future debt service payments, discounted by the interest rate that amortized the loan, the proceeds to be paid have been reduced

Exhibit 9-1   Is a Fixed-Rate Mortgage (FRM) Better than a Variable-Rate Mortgage (VRM)?

Many consumer groups have argued that fixed-rate mortgages (FRMs) provide protection against inflation for real estate investors and homeowners and that variable-rate mortgages (VRMs) are devices that enable financial institutions to take advantage of homeowners. Therefore they argue that VRMs should not be permitted in housing markets. While it is true that VRMs differ from FRMs on the basis of inflation protection, it is unlikely that VRMs are intended to take advantage of homeowners any more than any other instrument.

Prior to 1978, FRMs were the only mortgages available on a national basis for homeowners. With the resurgence of inflation and the rapid changes in interest rates that accompany inflation, the reliance on FRMs as the primary instrument used in the financing of real estate led to an unworkable situation. Lenders continued to have difficulty pricing loans when rates were very volatile. Borrowers had considerable difficulty qualifying for loans when interest rates were high due to inflationary expectations. The so-called tilt effect magnified the difficulty as FRM rates reached historic highs of 17 percent.

When the Federal Home Loan Bank Board received permission to grant its version of the VRM in 1979, the adjustable-rate mortgage (ARM) received less than enthusiastic acclaim. It was not unexpected; consumers were used to FRMs and looked with disdain on the new ARMs. However, some consumers welcomed ARMs because the supply of FRMs was at a record low.

Note that variable-rate loans have been in existence in some markets for many years, although this has not been the case in the mortgage market. The issue is frequently viewed as "which type of loan do consumers prefer?" At the same cost, there is no question that consumers will always prefer the FRM over the ARM. However, there is no reason to believe that the ARM will *ever* be available at the same interest rate as the FRM. In fact, theory tells us that the interest rate on an FRM will be higher than the interest rate on an ARM as long as there is interest rate uncertainty in the economy. In the real world, this means always.

The initial experience with ARMs suggests that the premium paid for the right to repay at a fixed rate for a twenty-five- or thirty-year period has varied between 50 and 300 basis points (.5 to 3.00 percentage points) on the mortgage. For some investors, the higher price seems cheap for such protection; for others, the extra interest cost is unnecessary and too expensive. In the future there may be FRMs available, but probably not to the same degree as in the past.

by the savings of future interest charges. However, this does not occur if closing costs were paid when the loan was originated.

Closing Costs

Closing costs are charges assessed by the mortgagee against the mortgagor when the loan is made. Typical closing costs include loan origination fees, appraisal fees, recording fees, title insurance, pest inspections, credit reference expenses, and other similar charges. Other expenses, such as discount points, are sometimes included and we will treat these separately.

Closing costs are divided into two general categories: (1) costs incurred in placing the mortgage and (2) costs incurred in acquiring the property. The first category must be amortized on a straight-line basis over the life of the mortgage for tax purposes. The second type can be capitalized and increases the depreciable basis of the property. Neither type may be deducted for tax purposes in the year paid.

If the costs are incurred and the funds paid, the timing of the payment (that is, at the time of either the creation of the mortgage or the acquisition of the property) is important. The magnitude and timing of the outflows affect the cost of borrowing.

In common arrangements, the lender charges the going rate of interest, depending on the availability of funds and the attractiveness of the client as a mortgagor. The lender then calculates the monthly (or yearly) debt service, assuming a fully amortized loan, the yield-to-maturity of the loan, and as required by the Truth in Lending Act, the annual percentage rate (APR). The APR is said to reflect the true cost of borrowing.

For example, if the mortgagor borrows $50,000 for thirty years and agrees to repay an annual debt service of $5,500 at the end of each of those years, the effective cost of borrowing is 10.44 percent. If closing costs amount to $2,000, paid when the loan is originated, the borrower's cost is viewed differently. The borrower pays $5,500 per year for thirty years as before, but the proceeds borrowed are now reduced to $48,000 ($50,000 minus $2,000). Therefore, since the borrower receives less money but is required to repay according to the schedule *as if* $50,000 were received, the effective cost of borrowing increases.

The effective cost of borrowing $50,000 to be repaid with annual payments of $5,500 for each of thirty years, with $2,000 closing costs paid at the time of loan origination, is 10.95 percent. This rate is more than one-half of a percent higher than the rate without the closing costs. So closing costs make the true cost of borrowing higher than the stated rate.

By law, the APR must include some of the closing costs in order to better represent the cost of borrowing. However, certain fees and expenses are not necessarily included in the APR, so the investor may not really be paying the rate believed. It is important to be able to measure the actual cost of borrowing before any comparisons and decisions can be made.

Finally, some of the closing costs may not result in actual outlays for the mortgage. Loan origination fees, for example, may be charged by the mortgagee's institution to raise the yield of the loan. At this point, it is easy to understand how loan origination fees can dramatically increase the lender's yield. This is further emphasized by the fact that if early repayment occurs and closing costs were assessed to the borrower, the early repayment increases the cost of borrowing. In addition, we must note that *the reported APR does not take into account the likelihood of early repayment.*

Continuing the previous example, suppose the investor wished to repay the loan at the end of year 5. What is the effective cost of borrowing for the loan? The effective cost of borrowing now becomes 11.55 percent, or sixty basis points higher than if the loan were held to maturity. This is because the impact of the closing costs is only spread over five years instead of thirty. Therefore the effective cost of borrowing is directly related to the probability of early repayment, given that closing costs are paid at the beginning of the loan.

The importance of these results should be apparent. Assuming closing costs, it has been shown that not only is the cost of borrowing higher than is stated by the interest rate and possibly the APR but also that if the loan is expected to be repaid earlier than at maturity, the cost rises even more. It can be shown that the earlier the repayment, the greater the rise in effective borrowing cost as a result of the closing costs. It also becomes apparent that the probability of early repayment is a very important estimate, since it can have a dramatic impact on the cost of borrowing. Historical evidence also suggests that only a small portion of the mortgages for income-producing real estate are held to maturity!

Prepayment Penalties

Some loans also require that prepayment penalties be assessed to the mortgagor if the decision is made to prepay. Prepayment penalties are typically included in mortgages on income property investments. These penalties often are measured by a flat percentage (usually 1 to 3 percent) of the remaining loan balance. An alternative method is to charge six or nine months' interest at the time of prepayment.

Prepayment penalties, however charged, increase the cost of the loan to the mortgagor and raise the yield to the mortgagee. In our example, if the prepayment penalties were 3 percent of the outstanding balance, the amount charged would be $1,448. This payment must be made, but unlike closing costs, prepayment penalties are not paid until the prepayment date. However, this also affects the cost of borrowing.

In the example, the fee of \$1,448 paid at the prepayment date increases the effective borrowing rate to 12.02 percent, assuming the same terms, closing costs, and early repayment date. In this case, the prepayment penalty increases the cost of borrowing by forty-seven basis points, so the impact of such penalties may not be as inconsequential as investors presume.

Prepaid Interest

In some transactions, the mortgagee may seek prepaid interest at the time of the origination of the loan. This income to the lender ensures that a buffer is established in the beginning period of the loan. Prepaid interest is frequently used for short-term loans and construction financing. It is often included as part of closing costs, although technically it is not.

The total amount of interest paid to the mortgagee may be the same under a prepaid interest provision, although prepayment of interest clearly affects the cost of borrowing and yield of the loan.

Using the continuing example, if we assume that the lender also required prepaid interest of \$1,000, the outstanding balance to be paid at the early repayment date is \$48,693 (instead of \$48,278). Assuming that the closing costs remained at \$2,000, and the prepayment penalties were now 3 percent of \$48,693, or \$1,461 (instead of \$1,448), the new effective rate of borrowing is 12.05 percent.

Discount Points

Discount points are another typical charge used in the mortgage market. These "points" effectively raise the cost of the loan to the borrower by creating additional finance charges. These charges are often added to the loan origination fees but have a similar effect if treated separately. Of course, points charged to borrowers increase the yield to the lender.

For example, suppose the discount points amount to \$2,000. When this is considered with all the other special provisions, the cost of borrowing increases to 13.26 percent.

Mortgage Insurance

Finally, if the loan-to-value ratio of the loan is relatively high, the lender may require private mortgage insurance. This is particularly true of single-family residential loans. Although the mortgage insurance premium is small, typically about one-quarter of one percent of the original loan, this, too, increases the effective cost of borrowing.

To conclude our example, since the amount borrowed is \$50,000, if the mortgage insurance premium is one-quarter of one percent of the loan per year, this amounts to an additional required premium of \$125 per year. (We assumed only a yearly premium. Usually, a front-end initial premium of about one percent is also included.)

The effect of this provision is clear. Mortgage insurance also results in a higher effective cost for borrowers. If we include the one-quarter of one percent premium charge in the analysis with all the other charges, the effective cost of borrowing becomes 13.56 percent.

Other Provisions

Many other provisions could be analyzed. These include acceleration clauses, assignments and assumptions, and the use of alternative amortization schedules. In addition, there are different tax effects. Certain closing costs and interest are tax deductible. Prepayment penalties reduce taxable income from operation. Discount points may qualify as tax-deductible items.[2] While similar analysis on an after-tax basis would yield different results, the major point is that it is imperative to compare various financing alternatives and to evaluate the impact of the special loan provisions on the cost of borrowing.

Table 9-2 summarizes our cost-of-borrowing example. It is clear that

TABLE 9-2   Summary of Impact on Costs of Borrowing by Various Loan Provisions

DESCRIPTION	EFFECTIVE COST OF BORROWING (%)
1. Basic example:	
$50,000 mortgage, payable in $5,500 annual payments for thirty years	10.44
2. Impact of closing costs:	
$2,000 paid at time of loan origination	10.95
3. Additional impact of early repayment:	
repayment of note at end of five years	11.55
4. Additional impact of prepayment penalty:	
penalty of 3 percent of outstanding balance, paid at time of prepayment	12.02
5. Additional impact of prepaid interest:	
$1,000 paid at time of loan origination (affects outstanding balance and prepayment penalty)	12.05
6. Additional impact of discount points:	
$2,000 paid at time of loan origination	13.26
7. Additional impact of mortgage insurance:	
annual premium of one-quarter of one percent of original mortgage loan	13.56

Each provision assumes that the previous impacts are applicable. Therefore, if some of the provisions do not apply, the effective costs of borrowing are altered. Also, all tax effects are ignored.

[2] Discount points must be amortized if the property is not owner-occupied.

the actual cost of borrowing is directly related to the factors that apply to the investor's mortgage agreement. In this case, assuming that all the factors applied, what appeared to be a relatively low cost of borrowing (10.44 percent) has increased to 13.56 percent. *This represents a 30 percent increase in the actual cost of borrowing to the mortgagor.* This illustrates the importance of mortgage loan provision analysis.

ANALYSIS OF IMPACT OF FINANCIAL LEVERAGE

There are several ways of analyzing financial leverage and its impact on rates of return, risk, and value. We illustrate the most useful methods of analysis in this section.

On Required Rate of Return

One of the ways to demonstrate the effect of financial leverage on the return on equity is to isolate the impact of debt financing and study the potential effects of various financing decisions. The following demonstration illustrates the impact of financial leverage.

We can measure the overall required rate of return from a real estate investment as follows:

$$k_o = k_d(L/V) + k_e(E/V) \qquad (9\text{-}2)$$

where

k_o = overall required rate of return
k_d = cost of debt financing
k_e = required rate of return on equity
L = amount of debt
E = amount of equity
V = value of investment

Using algebra, we get:

$$k_e = \frac{k_o - k_d(L/V)}{E/V} \qquad (9\text{-}3)$$

Since the value of the investments must be the sum of the amounts of debt and equity, it follows that

$$k_e = k_o + (k_o - k_d)L/E \qquad (9\text{-}4)$$

Equation (9-4) demonstrates the impact of different combinations of rates of return and costs of borrowing and their effects on the return on equity. This approach also shows the differing impacts of various combinations of debt and equity sources. Alternative combinations of debt and equity can be measured by L/E, which is frequently called the *debt-to-equity ratio*. It is a well-known measure of the amount of leverage.

For example, assume that $k_o = 15$ percent, $k_d = 12$ percent, and $L/E = 0$. In this case, the rate of return on assets is greater than the cost of borrowing (.15 > .12), but no debt was used (that is, it is totally financed with equity). The rate of return on equity would be

$$k_e = .15 + (.15 - .12).00$$

$$= .15$$

The rate of return on equity is identical to the overall rate of return on investments, which means that there is no leverage effect because no debt is used (that is, $L/E = 0$).

However, consider the case in which $L/E = .25/.75$, or a 25 percent loan-to-value ratio. The rate of return on equity would be 16 percent:

$$k_e = .15 + (.15 - .12)\frac{.25}{.75}$$

$$= .15 + .01$$

$$= .16$$

In this case, because 25 percent of the value of the investment is borrowed, the return on equity increased 6.67 percent as a result of favorable financial leverage.

If the investor were to acquire a relatively large amount of debt, say 80 percent of the total value of the investment, the loan-to-value ratio would be .80 and the debt-to-equity ratio (L/E) would be 4.00. Assuming that k_o and k_d remain the same, k_e would be 27 percent:

$$k_e = .15 + (.15 - .12)\frac{.80}{.20}$$

$$= .15 + .12$$

$$= .27$$

Therefore, by increasing the amount of debt borrowed at a constant rate of k_d, the rate of return on equity increases substantially. This example illustrates the "levering" of return available in real estate investing as a result of the investor's ability to use only small amounts of equity.

However, as the loan-to-value ratio and the debt-to-equity ratio increase, the cost of borrowing also increases. This is because lenders view the investment as more risky, since additional debt must now be satisfied out of the net operating income of the investment. For purposes of illustration, suppose that for loans with loan-to-value ratios of .80, lenders require a 14 percent interest rate. If the expected rate of return on the overall investment remains at 15

**Exhibit 9-2   How Leverage Affects Real
               Estate Investments**

The use of debt financing, or *financial leverage*, affects real estate investments in several ways. The first reason generally given is that the substitution of debt for equity sources (often the investor's own equity) can magnify the rate of return on the investor's equity position. Of course, simply because the investor borrows does not automatically mean that the rate of return will be magnified. The determination that needs to be made so that an investor can decide whether financial leverage will cause a favorable or unfavorable impact is a comparison between the after-tax cost of borrowing and the after-tax rate of return on the project.

If the after-tax cost of borrowing is less than the after-tax rate of return on the project, the investor achieves a favorable result: a financing gain. This is equivalent to saying that the investor's after-tax rate of return on equity exceeds the after-tax rate of return on the investment. In effect, it means the investor is able to "lever upward" the rate of return as a result of borrowing.

Note, however, that if the after-tax cost of borrowing exceeds the after-tax rate of return on the project, an unfavorable result obtains. In this case, the after-tax rate of return on equity will be less than the after-tax return on the investment. The investor would have earned a higher rate of return if more equity instead of debt financing had been used. No borrower is happy about a lower rate of return on equity than that earned on the entire project; no investor will employ debt financing if this condition is expected.

Another impact of leverage is that the greater the amount an investor borrows, the greater the interest that is paid to the lender(s). This is important because, unlike the situation with equity financing, debt financing receives special treatment by the IRS. All interest is tax deductible from ordinary income for both corporations and individuals (assuming the deduction threshold is met by individuals or married taxpayers who file jointly). For corporations, this provides a special feature, since interest expenses reduce taxable income at the company level and owners of the corporation may further reduce their taxable incomes from dividends (or other income) by financing the ownership interest with debt. Once again, the investor may subtract out the interest costs. This type of double counting creates incentives for heavy debt financing in real estate and helps to explain the high loan-to-value ratios of many real estate firms.

For individuals, there is also another reason for the use of debt financing. The ability to diversify an individual's equity into several properties may enhance the investor's portfolio of investments by reducing investment risk and by providing the investor with the opportunity to exert greater control over more real estate than if only equity financing were employed. This reason suggests that investors may borrow funds for real estate acquisitions, especially if they are small, noncorporate investors, in order to spread out their interests into as wide a number of properties as possible.

It is often said that "leverage is the prime mover" of real estate. Few acquisitions are made without it. The cost of mortgage finance is a major concern for builders, large-scale developers, and households. The supply of funds for real estate is generally thought to be an important variable in understanding mortgage and housing markets. Leverage is an important part of modern real estate investment analysis.

percent, the gains from financial leverage would be less than when the cost of borrowing was only 12 percent. The rate of return on equity is now 19 percent instead of 27 percent:

$$k_e = .15 + (.15 - .14)\frac{.80}{.20}$$

$$= .15 + .04$$

$$= .19$$

It is possible to analyze the case in which the cost of borrowing exceeds the overall rate of return on the investment. Next, suppose the cost of borrowing, k_d, is .16, k_o remains at .15, and L/E is 4.00. The return on equity would drop to 11 percent:

$$k_e = .15 + (.15 - .16)\frac{.80}{.20}$$

$$= .15 - .04$$

$$= .11$$

In this case, unfavorable leverage exists. Because the cost of borrowing is greater than the return on assets, unfavorable leverage lowers the rate of return on equity from 15 percent to 11 percent. Furthermore, if the actual return on assets falls short (so that the rate of return is only 10 percent), the impact of borrowing at 16 percent translates into a *negative* rate of return:

$$k_e = .10 + (.10 - .16)\frac{.80}{.20}$$

$$= .10 - .24$$

$$= -.14$$

In this case, the investor loses money because the rate of return is −14 percent. Therefore leverage can increase rates of return and changes in investor wealth very rapidly when it is favorable and can decrease them just as rapidly when it is unfavorable.

On Expected Rate of Return and Risk

The financing of a real estate investment involves the use of two types of funds: debt (mortgage) and equity. The use of debt to finance an investment can have two impacts: the rate of return to the equity position can be increased and so can the expected risk of the equity position. Thus the investor must face this question, Does the increase in the expected return offset the increased risk? If it does, the investor should use the debt. If it does not, the debt should not be used.

To illustrate the impact of borrowing on the expected risk and return, consider the following example.

An investor has the opportunity to invest in an apartment building. The cost of the investment is $500,000. The investment is expected to produce the following net operating incomes:

STATE OF THE WORLD	NOI	PROBABILITY
Pessimistic	$55,000	20%
Most likely	60,000	60
Optimistic	65,000	20

The investor has two financing options:

1. Financing with 100 percent equity and no debt.
2. Financing with 75 percent debt, 25 percent equity. The debt has an interest rate of 10 percent with a maturity of twenty-five years, monthly payments. The debt service is $40,905 per year.

Impact on rate of return.   To illustrate the impact of the two financing options on the rate of return, the following simple rate of return measure is used:

$$EDR = \frac{BTCF}{Equity} \qquad (9\text{-}5)$$

EDR is the equity dividend rate. It is a simple, but widely used, measure of the rate of return from an investment. BTCF is the before-tax cash flow. Equity is the amount of cash required for the investment.

Now look at the example. The *expected* rate of return is the weighted average of the return for each "state of the world" multiplied by the probability for each "state." Thus, in equation form, the expected rate of return is

$$E(EDR) = \sum_{i=1}^{s} p_i(EDR_i) \tag{9-6}$$

where E(EDR) is the expected equity dividend rate, p_i is the probability under each "state of the world," EDR_i is the equity dividend rate under each "state," s is the number of states of the world, and Σ is the summation symbol.

To implement this equation, look at the first financing option. If the investor uses option one, the following would occur:

STATE OF THE WORLD	NOI	DEBT SERVICE	BTCF	EDR	PROBABILITY
Pessimistic	$55,000	$0	$55,000	11%	.2
Most likely	60,000	0	60,000	12	.6
Optimistic	60,000	0	65,000	13	.2

Under the pessimistic state of the world, the investor feels that the NOI would be $55,000. The debt service is zero, since option one involves no debt. The equity investment is thus the total cost of $500,000. The before-tax cash flow (BTCF) is the NOI minus the debt service, or $55,000. The equity dividend rate (EDR) for the pessimistic outcome is

$$EDR = \frac{BTCF}{Equity}$$

$$= \frac{\$55,000}{\$500,000}$$

$$= .11, \text{ or } 11\%$$

The probability of this outcome is 20 percent. Likewise the EDRs for each of the other possible states of the world are calculated as 12 percent for the most likely and 13 percent for the optimistic.

Using Equation (9-5), the expected EDR is

$$E(EDR) = \sum_{i=1}^{s} p_i(EDR_i)$$

$$= .2(.11) + .6(.12) + .2(.13)$$

$$= .12, \text{ or } 12\%$$

So the investor *expects* the investment to generate a 12 percent EDR if financing option one (all equity) is used.

What is the expected EDR (return on equity) if the second financing method is employed? This is illustrated as follows:

STATE OF THE WORLD	NOI	DEBT SERVICE	BTCF	EDR	PROBABILITY
Pessimistic	$55,000	$40,905	$14,095	11.28%	.2
Most likely	60,000	40,905	19,095	15.28	.6
Optimistic	65,000	40,905	24,095	19.28	.2

Under the second financing option, the investor borrows 75 percent, or $375,000, of the total cost. The equity investment is thus $125,000. Under outcome one, the NOI is $55,000. The debt service is $40,905, which leaves $14,095 in BTCF. The equity dividend rate is 11.28 percent ($14,095 divided by $125,000). The probability is 20 percent. The EDR for the most likely outcome is 15.28 percent and 19.28 percent for the optimistic outcome.

The expected equity dividend rate is

$$E(EDR) = \sum_{i=1}^{s} p_i(EDR_i)$$

$$= .2(.1128) + .6(.1528) + .2(.1928)$$

$$= .1528, \text{ or } 15.28\%$$

Now let us compare the rates of return expected for each financing option:

FINANCING OPTION	E(EDR)
Option 1	11.00%
Option 2	15.28

Note that by borrowing money, the expected rate of return on the equity investment increased from 11 to 15.28 percent.

Does this mean that the investor should always use debt? The answer lies in understanding that the risk of the investment has also increased.

Impact on risk.   The risk associated with the use of debt is called *financial risk*. This refers to the probability that the debt obligations will not be met. Note that in the preceding examples, the debt claim has priority over the equity position. Thus the equity position is the "residual" and bears the impact of the risk of investing.

To illustrate the impact of borrowing on the risk, let us define *risk* as the *variation* around the expected rate of return. A measure of variation is the standard deviation, abbreviated by the Greek letter sigma, σ. The equation for calculating the standard deviation, σ, is

$$\sigma = \sqrt{\sum_{i=1}^{s} p_i[\text{EDR}_i - \text{E(EDR)}]^2} \qquad (9\text{-}7)$$

The steps for calculating σ are

1. Calculate the deviation of each possible outcome from the expected EDR [$\text{EDR}_i - \text{E(EDR)}$].
2. Raise this deviation to the second power, [$\text{EDR}_i - \text{E(EDR)}$]^2.
3. Multiply this term by the probability of getting EDR_i (that is, p_i), p_i [$\text{EDR}_i - \text{E(EDR)}$]^2.
4. Sum these products, $\Sigma\, p_i$ [$\text{EDR}_i - \text{E(EDR)}$]^2.
5. Take the square root of this sum.

To illustrate, let us first calculate the standard deviation for financing option one. This is shown as follows:

STATE OF THE WORLD	EDR_i	$\text{EDR}_i - \text{E(EDR)}$	$[\text{EDR}_i - \text{E(EDR)}]^2$	p_i	
Pessimistic	.11	−.01	.0001	.2	.00002
Most likely	.12	0	0	.6	0
Optimistic	.13	.01	.0001	.2	.00002
					$\Sigma = .00004$
	$\sigma = \sqrt{.00004}$				
	$\sigma = \ \ .0063$				

The equity dividend rate under each state of the world (EDR_i) was calculated previously. The expected equity dividend rate, E(EDR), was 12 percent under financing option one. Using the steps outlined, the resulting standard deviation is .0063, or .63 percent.

For financing option two, the same procedure can be followed:

STATE OF THE WORLD	EDR_i	$\text{EDR}_i - \text{E(EDR)}$	$[\text{EDR}_i - \text{E(EDR)}]^2$	p_i	
Pessimistic	.1128	−.04	.0016	.2	.00032
Most likely	.1528	.0	.0	.6	.0
Optimistic	.1928	.04	.0016	.2	.00032
				=	.00064
	$\sigma = \sqrt{.00064}$				
	$\sigma = \ \ .0253$				

Thus for financing option two, the risk is .0253, or 2.53 percent.

What do these numbers mean? Let us summarize as follows:

FINANCING OPTION	EXPECTED RETURN	RISK (σ)
1	11.00%	.63%
2	15.28	2.53

Note that the use of debt increased the expected return on equity from 11 to 15.28 percent. But also note that the risk increased from .63 to 2.53 percent. *Thus expected return and expected risk increased by the use of debt.*

Should the investor use the debt? To answer this question, the investor must ask himself or herself if the increase in return is enough to cover the increased risk. The answer would vary depending on the preference of each investor. For some investors, the answer is yes—meaning that the debt should be used. For others, the answer is no—indicating the debt should not be used.

OTHER FINANCING DECISIONS

There are several other types of financing decisions that have not yet been discussed. These include many types of financing devices used by commercial investors. For example, the use of wraparound mortgage financing is a well-established method of financing in commercial and industrial markets although it has only recently been used in residential markets. In addition, however, the implementation of the due-on-sale clause has removed the possibilities of wraparound financing in many residential markets.

Many seasoned investors frequently note that financing is *the* major part of real estate investing. The basis of their belief lies not in the availability of "cheap" debt financing, but rather in the gains available to creative investors who learn how to structure debt and equity financing packages to solve problems. These problems include cash flow problems, tax motivations, and timing considerations. In this sense, financing methods are always likely to be a major part of real estate investing.

QUESTIONS

9-1. What is the debt coverage ratio and how is it used by lenders and investors?

9-2. What is the mortgage constant? Give an example using the tables in the book.

9-3. What are discount points? What impact do they have on the cost of borrowing? Explain.

9-4. The overall required rate of return can be split into debt and equity components. Illustrate how the required rate of return on equity can be used to show the impact of financial leverage.

9-5. The text also shows how the use of debt financing can increase both the expected return and the expected risk. Therefore, how can the investor determine if debt financing should be used and, if so, how much should be used when making the investment acquisition?

PROBLEMS

9-1. Using Equation (9-1), what happens to the mortgage constant if
   a. The interest rate increases? Decreases?
   b. The mortgage maturity increases? Decreases?
   c. Annual compounding is used instead of monthly compounding?

9-2. Using the following facts, set up the amortization schedule for years 1 through 5:

Mortgage amount	$1,250,000
Interest rate	12.5%
Maturity	20 years/monthly compounding

9-3. Using the facts in Problem 9-2, calculate the effective borrowing cost under the following:
   a. Financing costs of 4 percent of the mortgage amount and the loan is held to maturity
   b. Financing costs of 4 percent of the mortgage amount and the loan is prepaid after five years
   c. Same as part b, but there is also a prepayment penalty of 6 percent of the outstanding mortgage balance

9-4. If the after-tax return on an investment is 8 percent, what is the effect of financial leverage in each of the following conditions?
   a. Pretax cost of borrowing is 10 percent; marginal tax rate is .30.
   b. Pretax cost of borrowing is 10 percent; marginal tax rate is .20.
   c. Pretax cost of borrowing is 12 percent; marginal tax rate is .20.
   d. Pretax cost of borrowing is 12 percent; marginal tax rate is .40.
   e. Pretax cost of borrowing is 15 percent; marginal tax rate is .40.
   f. Pretax cost of borrowing is 16 percent; marginal tax rate is .50.

9-5. Which loan for $30,000 has the lower effective cost of borrowing: a loan at 10.5 percent monthly for twenty years or a loan at 11 percent monthly for thirty years? Which has the lower monthly debt service? Which loan would you prefer as an investor?

9-6. Consider an investment with a market value of $30,000. How does the annual debt service using a 12 percent loan for thirty years fluctuate with a loan-to-value ratio of 50 percent? 75 percent? 90 percent?

9-7. A mortgage loan of $250,000 is made at the rate of 8 percent annually for twenty years.
   a. What is the annual debt service?
   b. What is the breakdown between interest and principal for the first five years?

c. Suppose the lender wants to earn 9 percent. How much must the lender discount the loan?
d. What is the yield assuming no early repayment with the discount in part c?
e. Suppose the loan is repaid after three years with a prepayment penalty of 3.5 percent of the outstanding balance and the discount from part c. What is the yield to the lender?

SELECTED REFERENCES

GAUMNITZ, JACK E., "Leverage and the Rate of Return on Equity in Real Estate Investments: A Note," *Journal of Economics and Business*, 30 (Winter 1978), 155–57.

JAFFE, AUSTIN J., and KENNETH M. LUSHT, "Debt and Value: Issues and Analysis," *Real Estate Appraiser and Analyst*, 49 (Fall 1983), 5–18.

LUSHT, KENNETH M., "Financial Risk, Value, and Capitalization Rates," *Appraisal Journal*, 45 (October 1977), 601–12.

_____ and ROBERT H. ZERBST, "Valuing Income Property in an Inflationary Environment," *Real Estate Appraiser and Analyst*, 46 (July-August 1980), 11–17.

SIRMANS, C. F., *Real Estate Finance*. New York: McGraw-Hill, 1985.

10

REVERSION DECISIONS

In the previous chapters we examined the operating and financing decisions that investors must make in analyzing real estate investments. This chapter discusses the other major area of decisions—those involving the future disposition of an investment. One of the major sources of cash flow is that from future disposition.

To make the investment decision, the investor must make assumptions regarding the expected future value of an investment, how long the investor expects to hold the investment, what method of disposition is to be used, how much the taxes from disposition will be, and others. Thus the expected future disposition influences the decision to invest today.

Reversion decisions must also be made after an investment has been acquired. For example, suppose an investor purchased an apartment building. The investor is constantly reevaluating whether to continue to own or not. The decision is further complicated by the fact that there are various alternative methods of disposition, such as sale, exchange, installment sale, and sale-leaseback. The real estate investor is obviously interested in making the choice that maximizes his or her wealth.

**Exhibit 10-1 Why the Reversion Matters
                        to Investors**

In some simplified analyses of real estate investment projects, investors sometimes examine only the first year's expected net operating income or expected before- or after-tax cash flow. The analysis implies either that the benefit stream is expected to stay constant for the planned holding period or that it will most likely be the same number in perpetuity. To the extent that the reversion represents a sizable portion of the cash flow stream at the end of the holding period, better and more-refined analyses often explicitly treat the reversion when estimating cash flows.

Unless a broad assumption is made about the growth in income or cash flow from the investment, the sale price at the end of the planned holding period must be estimated. This is sometimes a difficult figure to estimate because it is relatively uncertain when the expected holding period is long. Also, if there is a lot of uncertainty associated with the next few years' economic conditions, it becomes difficult to forecast the sale price of the property at some future date.

In addition, the outstanding balance of the mortgage must be calculated if the cash flows are measured to the equity investor. This is because at the time of sale, the mortgage must be satisfied in order to have clear title for conveyance to the purchaser. Furthermore, tax planning is often required so as to ensure that tax liability is legally minimized. This area can become complex if the investor's tax situation is complex.

In general, these factors serve to make the estimate of the equity reversion a major portion of the estimation of cash flows from real estate investments. Studies have shown that the impact of changes in the expected value of the reversion can have a profound impact on the value of the property. Thus the value of the reversion can often be the difference between an acceptable and an unacceptable project.

IMPACT OF REVERSION DECISION
ON INVESTMENT DECISION

Reversion decisions must be considered when making investment decisions. The assumptions made concerning property disposition are an integral part of the investment decision. The investor studies the market and from this analysis assesses the likely return on the investment not only from cash flows during the holding period but from disposition at the end of the holding period as well.

There are various methods of forecasting the probable sale price of the investment at the end of some holding period. One common method is to determine a growth rate and assume the investment will increase by that amount annually throughout the holding period. For example, Mr. X is considering purchasing an apartment building for $100,000. After thorough market analysis, he has determined an expected annual growth rate throughout the period of 1.5 percent. If his expectations are correct, he will be able to sell the property for $100,000 × $(1 + .015)^5$, or $107,728.

Another method of forecasting expected sales price is to derive a market capitalization rate. The property value is determined using the following equation:

$$V = \frac{\text{NOI}}{R}$$

where

V = market value
NOI = expected net operating income
R = capitalization rate

Assume that Mr. X expects net operating income to be $11,000 at the end of the holding period and has derived a market capitalization rate of 10 percent. The property value can be determined as follows:

$$V = \frac{\$11,000}{.10}$$

$$= \$110,000$$

Expected sales price can also be forecast using the market gross income multiplier (GIM). Property value is determined using the following equation:

$$V = \text{EGI} \times \text{GIM} \tag{10-1}$$

where

V = expected value
EGI = expected effective gross income
GIM = expected gross income multiplier

If the expected effective gross income for Mr. X's property is $13,000 and the expected gross income multiplier is 8.5, then Mr. X should expect the value of the apartment building to be $13,000 × 8.5, or $110,500 at the end of the holding period.

Now assuming that Mr. X has forecast the expected sales price for the investment and has a required rate of return of 10 percent, what will happen to the NPV of the investment if the actual sales price varies from the forecast? For illustration purposes, assume that Mr. X has decided to purchase the apartment building for $100,000. Annual after-tax cash flows are expected to be $9,000. After analyzing the market, Mr. X reasonably expects to be

TABLE 10-1   Impact of Sales Price on IRR and NPV

SALES PRICE	IRR	NPV	N
$115,000	10.55%	$2,828.95	7
110,000	10.05	263.16	7
105,000	9.53	−2,302.63	7

TABLE 10-2   Impact of Holding Period on IRR and NPV

SALES PRICE	IRR	NPV	N
$110,000	10.62%	$2,418.43	5
110,000	10.05	263.16	7
110,000	9.74	−1,518.05	9

able to sell the property for $100,000 (net) at the end of the seven-year holding period. Table 10-1 shows the impact of various sales prices on NPV. Note that if Mr. X were overly optimistic in his assumptions and had to sell the investment for only $5,000 less than expected, the NPV would be negative and the return would be less than 10 percent. On the other hand, though, if Mr. X can sell the apartment building for $5,000 more than he expects, the NPV will be $2,829.

In Table 10-1 we assumed that seven years was the optimal holding period for the investment. Could we increase (decrease) our returns by changing the holding period? Holding the sales price ($110,000) constant, what happens to the NPV and IRR if we dispose of the property at the end of five or nine years instead of seven? Table 10-2 illustrates how the return on investment is affected by the holding period. Note that Mr. X can increase his expected returns if he disposes of the property at the end of five years instead of seven.

Thus far we have looked at the impact of reversion decisions on investment decisions assuming *sale* of the property for some amount at the end of some holding period. We have looked at the effects of changes in these assumptions on our rate of return. What if instead of *selling* the property we were to choose some alternative method of disposition? How will this affect the rate of return? Some of the other methods of disposition are discussed in this chapter. Each of these methods involves different investment analysis. We will examine the decision-making implications of these alternatives.

SALE VERSUS CONTINUE TO OPERATE

An important decision facing the real estate investor is that of continuing to operate versus sale. In this section, we illustrate how to make this decision.

Consider a real estate investor (in a 28 percent tax bracket) who owns an apartment investment that was purchased five years ago for $500,000.

The depreciable basis was $400,000. The investor has been using the straight-line method with a 27.5-year life. The investment was financed with a $375,000 fixed-rate mortgage at an interest rate of 10 percent with monthly payments for twenty-five years. The investor estimates that the current selling price is $625,000. Selling expenses would be 7 percent of the selling price.

The investor is trying to decide whether to sell or continue to operate for five more years. The NOI next year is expected to be $68,750 and is expected to increase 2 percent per year. The value of the investment is expected to be $675,000 at the end of this additional five years with selling expenses of 7 percent.

Which option should the investor select (to sell or continue to operate) if the required after-tax rate of return is 15 percent?

ATER from Sale Today

To determine whether to sell or continue to operate, the investor must first compute the after-tax cash flow from sale (or ATER) *now*. This is illustrated in Table 10-3 by subtracting the selling expenses, unpaid mortgage (from Table 10-4), and taxes (from Table 10-5) from the selling price. Table 10-4 is

TABLE 10-3   Expected Cash Flow from Sale Today

	Expected selling price (SP)	$625,000
minus	Selling expenses (SE)	− 43,750
equals	Net sale proceeds (NSP)	581,250
minus	Unpaid mortgage balance (UM)	−353,115
equals	Before-tax equity reversion (BTER)	228,135
minus	Taxes due on sale (TDS)*	− 43,113
equals	After-tax equity reversion (ATER)	$185,022

* See Table 10-5.

TABLE 10-4   Mortgage Amortization Schedule*

YEAR	PROPORTION OUTSTANDING	AMOUNT OUTSTANDING	DEBT SERVICE	INTEREST	PRINCIPAL
0	1.0	$375,000			
1	.99053	371,449	$40,892	$37,341	$3,551
2	.98007	367,526	40,892	36,969	3,923
3	.96851	363,191	40,892	36,557	4,335
4	.95574	358,403	40,892	36,104	4,788
5	.94164	353,115	40,892	35,604	5,288
6	.92606	347,273	40,892	35,050	5,842
7	.90884	340,815	40,892	34,434	6,458
8	.88983	333,686	40,892	33,763	7,129
9	.86882	325,808	40,892	33,014	7,878
10	.84561	317,104	40,892	32,188	8,704

* $375,000 loan at 10% with 25-year maturity, monthly payments.

TABLE 10-5   Expected Taxes Due on Sale Today

	TAXABLE INCOME	
	Expected selling price (SP)	$625,000
minus	Selling expenses (SE)	− 43,750
equals	Amount realized (AR)	581,250
minus	Adjusted basis (AB)	−427,275
equals	Total gain on sale (TG)	$153,975

	TAXES DUE ON SALE	
equals	Total gain on Dale	153,975
times	Investor's marginal tax rate (τ)	× .28
equals	Taxes due on sale (TDS)	$ 43,113

an amortization schedule for the loan that was originated *five years ago*. In other words, the amount outstanding today is the unpaid mortgage in year 5 of the loan ($353,115). Table 10-5 computes the taxes using the standard equations.

Cash Flows from Continuing to Operate

Tables 10-6 and 10-7 compute the after-tax cash flows and taxes from continuing to operate. Table 10-6 computes the after-tax flows (for years 1 through 5) by subtracting debt service and taxes (Table 10-7) from net operating income.

TABLE 10-6   Expected Cash Flow from Operation

		YEAR				
		1	2	3	4	5
	Net operating income (NOI)	$ 68,750	$ 70,125	$ 71,528	$ 72,958	$ 74,417
minus	Debt service (DS)	−40,892	−40,892	−40,892	−40,892	−40,892
equals	Before-tax cash flow (BTCF)	27,858	29,233	30,636	32,066	33,525
minus	Taxes (savings) from operation (TO)*	− 5,083	− 5,921	− 6,502	− 7,112	− 7,752
equals	After-tax cash flow (ATCF)	$ 22,775	$ 23,312	$ 24,134	$ 24,954	$ 25,773

* See Table 10-7.

TABLE 10-7   Expected Taxes from Operation

		YEAR				
		1	2	3	4	5
	Net operating income (NOI)	$ 68,750	$ 70,125	$ 71,528	$ 72,958	$ 74,417
minus	Interest on debt (I)	−35,050	−34,434	−33,763	−33,014	−32,188
minus	Depreciation deduction (D)	−14,545	−14,545	−14,545	−14,545	−14,545
minus	Amortized financing costs (AFC)	− 0	− 0	− 0	− 0	− 0
plus	Replacement reserves (RR)	+ 0	+ 0	+ 0	+ 0	+ 0
equals	Ordinary taxable income (OTI)	19,155	21,146	23,220	25,399	27,684
times	Investor's marginal tax rate (τ)	× .28	× .28	× .28	× .28	× .28
equals	Taxes (savings) from operation (TO)	$ 5,363	$ 5,921	$ 6,502	$ 7,112	$ 7,752

ATER from Continuing to Operate

Table 10-8 computes the after-tax cash flow (ATER) from sale five years from now. The ATER is equal to the selling price, minus the selling expenses, unpaid mortgage ($317,104), and taxes (from Table 10-9).

TABLE 10-8   Expected Cash Flow from Sale

	Expected selling price (SP)	$ 675,000
minus	Selling expenses (SE)	− 47,250
equals	Net sale proceeds (NSP)	627,750
minus	Unpaid mortgage balance (UM)	−317,104
equals	Before-tax equity reversion (BTER)	310,646
minus	Taxes due on sale (TDS)*	− 76,496
equals	After-tax equity reversion (ATER)	$ 234,150

* See Table 10-9.

TABLE 10-9   Expected Taxes Due on Sale

	TAXABLE INCOME	
	Expected selling price (SP)	$ 675,000
minus	Selling expenses (SE)	− 47,250
equals	Amount realized (AR)	627,750
minus	Adjusted basis (AB)	−354,550
equals	Total gain on sale (TG)	$ 273,200

	TAXES DUE ON SALE	
equals	Total gain on sale (TG)	$273,200
times	Investor's marginal tax rate (τ)	× .28
equals	Taxes due on sale (TDS)	$ 76,496

TABLE 10-10 Differential After-Tax Cash Flows of Continuing to Operate Versus Sale

YEAR	ATCF FROM CONTINUE TO OPERATE	ATCF FROM SALE TODAY	DIFFERENTIAL CASH FLOWS
0	$ 0	$185,022	−$185,022
1	22,775	0	22,775
2	23,312	0	23,312
3	24,134	0	24,134
4	24,954	0	24,954
5	259,923	0	259,923

Differential Cash Flows

Table 10-10 illustrates the differential after-tax cash flows of continuing to operate versus selling. The cash flows from selling today are subtracted from the flows of continuing to operate to reach the differential flows. Note that the differential at time point zero is negative, which symbolizes the foregone flow from sale if the investor decides to continue to operate.

NPV and IRR of Continuing to Operate

Table 10-11 illustrates the calculation of the NPV (at 15 percent) and the IRR of continuing to operate. This is done by multiplying the differential after-tax cash flows by present value factors. The NPV is found to be a positive $11,777, which indicates continued operation. The IRR is calculated to be 17.17 percent, and with this information, we can formulate the decision criteria:

1. If the opportunity rate is less than 17.17 percent, then continue to operate.
2. If the opportunity rate is greater than 17.17 percent, then sell (do not continue to operate).

TABLE 10-11 Net Present Value and IRR of Continuing to Operate

YEAR	DIFFERENTIAL AFTER-TAX CASH FLOW	PRESENT VALUE FACTOR AT 15%	PRESENT VALUE
0	$(185,022)	1.0	$(185,022)
1	22,775	.86957	19,804
2	23,312	.75614	17,627
3	24,134	.65752	15,869
4	24,954	.57175	14,267
5	259,923	.49718	129,229
	IRR = 17.17%		Net Present Value = $ 11,777

The opportunity rate referred to here is merely that rate of return an investor can receive on an alternative investment of equal risk. Since the NPV in this case is positive, the investor can conclude that continuing to operate is the best option, since the present value of the inflows from operating exceed the present value of the outflows from not selling.

INSTALLMENT SALE VERSUS OUTRIGHT SALE

An *installment sale* is the sale of property where the buyer agrees to pay the seller in a number of installments rather than a lump sum at the time of purchase.

To understand how an installment sale works, consider the following example: A real estate investor (in the 28 percent marginal tax bracket) is considering the installment sale of a small apartment building. This complex was purchased eight years ago at a total price of $150,000. The investor's depreciable basis was 85 percent of total cost. The straight-line method of depreciation has been used with a recovery life of 27.5 years. The investment was financed with a 12 percent mortgage of $112,500, with monthly payments for twenty-five years.

The installment sale offer that the investor is considering is as follows: a sales price of $250,000 with the buyer assuming a balance of $102,924 of the existing mortgage, making a cash down payment of $37,076, and the seller taking a purchase money mortgage of $110,000 for the remainder at 13 percent interest and annual payments over fifteen years, with a balloon payment for the balance at the end of year 5. The annual payment will be $17,022. Table 10-12 gives the amortization schedule for this purchase money mortgage. The selling expenses are $12,500 (or 5 percent of the selling price).

Alternatively, the investor could sell the investment outright for a price of $250,000 with selling expenses of 5 percent of the selling price. At a required rate of return of 12 percent, which is the better offer: installment or outright sale?

**TABLE 10-12 Mortgage Amortization Schedule
Purchase Money Mortgage**

YEAR	AMOUNT OUTSTANDING	DEBT SERVICE	INTEREST	PRINCIPAL
0	$110,000			
1	107,278	$17,022	$14,300	$2,722
2	104,202	17,022	13,946	3,076
3	100,726	17,022	13,546	3,476
4	96,798	17,022	13,094	3,927
5	92,360	17,022	12,584	4,438

ATCF in Year of Installment Sale

Table 10-13 shows the after-tax cash flow in the year of installment sale. This is computed by subtracting the selling expenses and the taxes (see Table 10-14) from the amount of the down payment. Table 10-14 computes the taxes in the year of installment sale by deriving the taxable gain using the profit percentage (from Table 10-15) and multiplying this gain by the investor's marginal tax rate.

TABLE 10-13 After-Tax Cash Flow in Year of Installment Sale

	Down payment	$ 37,076
minus	Selling expenses	−12,500
minus	Taxes*	−10,174
equals	ATCF	$ 14,402

* See Table 10-14.

TABLE 10-14 Tax in Year of Installment Sale

Taxable income:		
	Excess of mortgage over adjusted basis and selling expenses	$ 0
plus	Down payment	+37,076
equals	Payment in year of sale	37,076
times	Profit percentage*	× .98
equals	Taxable portion of principal	36,334
Tax:		
	Taxable income	36,334
times	Tax rate	× .28
equals	Tax	$ 10,174

* See Table 10-15.

TABLE 10-15 Profit Percentage on Installment Sale

Total gain:		
	Sale price	$ 250,000
minus	Selling expense	− 12,500
minus	Adjusted basis	− 93,336
equals	Total gain	$ 144,164
Contract price:		
	Sale price	$ 250,000
plus	Excess mortgage over basis and selling expenses	+ 0
minus	Mortgage balance assumed	−102,924
equals	Contract price	$ 147,076
Profit percentage:		
	Total gain	$ 144,164
divided by	Contract price	÷147,076
	Profit percentage	98%

Table 10-15 computes the profit percentage by dividing the total gain (selling price minus selling expenses and the adjusted basis) by the contract price (sale price plus the excess mortgage over basis and selling expenses minus the assumed mortgage balance).

ATCF from Installment Receipts

Table 10-16 computes the after-tax cash flow from the installment receipts for years 1 through 5. This after-tax cash flow is simply the before-tax cash flow (or debt service) plus the balloon payment (in year 5), minus the taxes from Table 10-17.

Table 10-17 computes the taxes required to calculate the ATCF from installment receipts. The first step in this computation is to derive the total principal by adding the amount of principal payment (Table 10-12) each year and any balloon payment (Table 10-12). This total is multiplied by the profit percentage (Table 10-15) to derive the taxable income. The tax is the taxable income times the investor's marginal tax rate.

TABLE 10-16   After-Tax Cash Flow from Installment Receipts

		YEAR				
		1	2	3	4	5
	BTCF (debt service)	$17,022	$17,022	$17,022	$17,022	$17,022
plus	Balloon payment	0	0	0	0	92,360
minus	Tax*	4,751	4,748	4,747	4,744	30,085
equals	ATCF	$12,271	$12,274	$12,275	$12,278	$79,297

* See Table 10-17.

TABLE 10-17   Tax Due on Installment Receipts

Taxable income:						
	Principal portion*	$ 2,722	$ 3,076	$ 3,476	$ 3,927	$ 4,438
plus	Balloon payment*	0	0	0	0	92,360
equals	Total principal	2,722	3,076	3,476	3,927	96,798
times	Profit percentage†	× .98	× .98	× .98	× .98	× .98
equals	Profit	2,668	3,014	3,406	3,848	94,862
plus	Interest*	+14,300	+13,946	+13,546	+13,094	+12,584
equals	Taxable income	16,968	16,960	16,952	16,942	107,446
times	Tax rate	× .28	× .28	× .28	× .28	× .28
equals	Tax	$ 4,751	$ 4,748	$ 4,747	$ 4,744	$ 30,085

* See Table 10-12 for the mortgage amortization schedule.
† See Table 10-15 for the profit percentage.

TABLE 10-18   Expected Cash Flow from Sale

	Expected selling price (SP)	$ 250,000
minus	Selling expenses (SE)	− 12,500
equals	Net sale proceeds (NSP)	237,500
minus	Unpaid mortgage balance (UM)	−102,924
equals	Before-tax equity reversion (BTER)	134,576
minus	Taxes due on sale (TDS)*	− 40,366
equals	After-tax equity reversion (ATER)	$ 94,210

* See Table 10-19.

TABLE 10-19   Expected Taxes Due on Sale

	TAXABLE INCOME	
	Expected selling price (SP)	$ 250,000
minus	Selling expenses (SE)	− 12,500
equals	Amount realized (AR)	237,500
minus	Adjusted Basis (AB)	− 93,336
equals	Total income on sale (TG)	144,164
	TAXES DUE ON SALE	
equals	Taxable income from sale (TIS)	144,164
times	Investor's marginal tax rate (τ)	× .28
equals	Taxes due on sale (TDS)	$ 40,366

ATER from Outright Sale

Tables 10-18 and 10-19 are needed to compare an outright sale with the installment sale. This is done by first computing the after-tax equity reversion from the outright sale (selling price, $250,000). The after-tax equity reversion is selling price less selling expenses, unpaid mortgage, and taxes due on sale (Table 10-19).

Differential Cash Flows

Table 10-20 computes the differential after-tax cash flows of installment sale versus outright sale. This differential is simply the installment sale cash flows minus the outright sale cash flow (for each year). Note that at time point zero, the differential is a negative because with the installment sale the investor loses the net of the outright sale proceeds and the installment sale proceeds.

TABLE 10-20 Differential After-Tax Cash Flow of Installment Sale Vesus Outright Sale

YEAR	INSTALLMENT SALE CASH FLOW	OUTRIGHT SALE CASH FLOW	DIFFERENTIAL
0	$14,402	$94,210	$(79,808)
1	12,271	0	12,271
2	12,274	0	12,274
3	12,275	0	12,275
4	12,278	0	12,278
5	79,297	0	79,297

NPV and IRR of Installment Sale

Table 10-21 calculates the NPV and IRR of the installment sale versus the outright sale. The NPV, +$2,467, is calculated by multiplying the differential flows (from Table 10-20) by their respective present value factors at the 12 percent required rate of return. Thus, given the 12 percent required rate, since the NPV is positive, the investor should pursue the installment sale but should not sell outright. The IRR is computed to be 12.90 percent. From this we conclude:

1. If the required rate is less than 12.90 percent, then select the outright sale.
2. If the required rate is greater than or equal to 12.90 percent, then select the installment sale.

TABLE 10-21 Net Present Value and IRR of Installment Sale versus Outright Sale

YEAR	DIFFERENTIAL AFTER-TAX CASH FLOW	PRESENT VALUE FACTOR @ 12%	PRESENT VALUE
0	$(79,808)	1.0	$ (79,808)
1	12,271	.892857	10,956
2	12,274	.797119	9,784
3	12,275	.711780	8,737
4	12,278	.635518	7,803
5	79,297	.567427	44,995
	IRR = 12.90%	Net Present Value = $+2,467	

COMPARING INSTALLMENT SALE OFFERS

In the preceding example, since the required rate of return was 12 percent and the return on the investment was only 12.90 percent (see Table 10-21), the installment was preferable. What happens, though, if the terms of sale are changed? The investor can change the sales price. The down payment can increase, decrease, or remain the same. The purchase money mortgage terms can be altered. As well as changing the amount of the purchase money mortgage, the interest rate and payout period can change. The terms of the loan can be longer or shorter. Payments can be made monthly instead of annually. The balloon payment or mortgage balance can become due after a shorter or longer period of time. The investor's tax rate can change. The required rate of return can increase or decrease. It is necessary to analyze the effect any of these changes would have on the investment decision. For illustration purposes, continuing with the same installment versus outright sale example, let us analyze what would happen, holding all other variables constant, if the installment sale price were changed to $235,000 from $250,000.

ATCF in Year of Installment Sale

Table 10-22 shows the after-tax cash flow in the year of installment sale. Note that this amount ($3,518) differs from the amount in the original example

TABLE 10-22   After-Tax Cash Flow
in Year of Installment
Sale

	Down payment	$ 22,076
minus	Selling expenses	−12,500
minus	Taxes*	− 6,058
equals	ATCF	$ 3,518

* See Table 10-23.

TABLE 10-23   Tax in Year of Installment Sale

Taxable income:		
	Excess of mortgage over adjusted basis and selling expenses	$ 0
plus	Down payment	+22,076
equals	Payment in year of sale	22,076
times	Profit percentage	× .98
equals	Taxable portion of principal	21,634
Tax:		
equals	Taxable income	21,634
times	× Tax rate	× .28
equals	Tax	$ 6,058

($14,402) by $10,884. Table 10-23 computes the taxes in the year of installment sale.

ATCF from Installment Receipts

Since the purchase money mortgage amount remains the same ($110,000), the after-tax cash flow from the installment receipts for years 1 through 5 will not change (see Table 10-16).

ATER from Outright Sale

Tables 10-24 and 10-25 are necessary to compare the outright sale with the installment sale. The after-tax equity reversion is the same as the original example since the terms of the outright sale remain the same.

TABLE 10-24   Expected Cash Flow from Sale

	Expected selling price (SP)	$ 250,000
minus	Selling expenses (SE)	− 12,500
equals	Net sale proceeds (NSP)	237,500
minus	Unpaid mortgage balance (UM)	−102,924
equals	Before-tax equity reversion (BTER)	134,576
minus	Taxes due on sale (TDS)*	− 40,366
equals	After-tax equity reversion (ATER)	$ 94,210

* See Table 10-25.

TABLE 10-25   Expected Taxes Due on Sale

	TAXABLE INCOME	
	Expected selling price (SP)	$ 250,000
minus	Selling expenses (SE)	− 12,500
equals	Amount realized (AR)	237,500
minus	Adjusted basis (AB)	− 93,336
equals	Total income on sale (TG)	144,164
	TAXES DUE ON SALE	
equals	Taxable income from sale (TIS)	144,164
times	Investor's marginal tax rate (τ)	× .28
equals	Taxes due on sale (TDS)	$ 40,366

TABLE 10-26   Differential After-Tax Cash Flow of Installment Sale versus Outright Sale

YEAR	INSTALLMENT SALE CASH FLOW	OUTRIGHT SALE CASH FLOW	DIFFERENTIAL
0	$ 3,518	$94,210	$(90,692)
1	12,271	0	12,271
2	12,274	0	12,274
3	12,275	0	12,275
4	12,278	0	12,278
5	79,297	0	79,297

Differential Cash Flows

The differential after-tax cash flow of installment sale versus outright sale is computed in Table 10-26. Note that the only difference in cash flows in the two examples is in year 1.

NPV and IRR of Installment Sale

Table 10-27 calculates the NPV and IRR of the installment sale versus the outright sale. The NPV is $8,417. Thus, given a 12 percent required rate, since the NPV is negative the investor should pursue the outright sale. The IRR is computed to be 9.19 percent. The investor should change the terms of the agreement such that his or her required rate of return is satisfied.

TABLE 10-27   Net Present Value and IRR of Installment Sale versus Outright Sale

YEAR	DIFFERENTIAL AFTER-TAX CASH FLOW	PRESENT VALUE FACTOR @ 12%	PRESENT VALUE
0	$(90,692)	1.0	$(90,692)
1	12,271	.892857	10,956
2	12,274	.7971194	9,784
3	12,275	.711780	8,737
4	12,278	.635518	7,803
5	79,297	.567427	44,995
	IRR = 9.19%	Net Present Value = $(8,417)	

TAX-DEFERRED EXCHANGE

The tax-deferred exchange is another method of property disposition. The importance of this method is indicated in Section 1031 of the Internal Revenue Code, which provides an exception to the requirement of recognition of gain or loss upon sale or exchange of property. According to this section, no gain or loss is recognized if the property held for productive use in a trade or business or for an investment is *exchanged solely for property of a like kind* to be held for productive use in a trade or business or for investment. The application of the section for deferring the taxes due on the disposition of a real estate investment is referred to as the *deferred exchange*. There are two basic motivations for exchanging real estate rather than selling it and reinvesting the proceeds. One is that the exchange is attractive as a method of marketing real estate when a sale does not appear possible. The other motivation is the availability of income tax deferral.

To illustrate an exchange, the following steps are used:

Step 1: Balance equity positions.
Step 2: Calculate the realized gain in an exchange.
Step 3: Calculate the recognized gain in an exchange.
Step 4: Identify the taxable gain.
Step 5: Calculate the ATCF and equity position after exchange.

To illustrate these concepts, assume that a two-party exchange is being considered by Mr. Dunn and Mr. Roe. Mr. Dunn owns an apartment building with a market value of $660,000 and an outstanding mortgage of $240,000. The adjusted basis of the property is $300,000. Mr. Roe owns an office building with a market value of $750,000 and an outstanding mortgage debt of $450,000. The adjusted basis of the property is $525,000.

Mr. Dunn and Mr. Roe have decided to exchange their investments. Mr. Dunn's transaction costs are $49,500, while Mr. Roe's are $57,000. This includes brokerage fees, legal fees, appraisal fees, and other costs of the exchange. The differences in equities will be balanced by cash.

Balancing Equity Positions

Tables 10-28 and 10-29 explain the method of balancing the equities. The first table lists the pertinent data on each property. The second table computes the equity for both parties by deducting the mortgage debt from the market value. The net equity position is then computed for both parties by subtracting the equity received from the equity given. Note that Mr. Roe owes Mr. Dunn $120,000.

TABLE 10-28 Exchange Property Data

PROPERTY 1	MR. DUNN'S PROPERTY
Market value	$660,000
Mortgage debt	240,000
Adjusted basis	300,000
Transaction costs	49,500

PROPERTY 2	MR. ROE'S PROPERTY
Market value	$750,000
Mortgage debt	450,000
Adjusted basis	525,000
Transaction costs	57,000

TABLE 10-29 Balance Equities on Exchange

A. Mr. Dunn's Equity:

Market value	$ 660,000
minus Mortgage debt	−240,000
equals Equity	$ 420,000

B. Mr. Roe's Equity:

Market value	$ 750,000
minus Mortgage debt	−450,000
equals Equity	$ 300,000

C. Net Equity Position:
Mr. Roe owes Mr. Dunn the difference in equity of $120,000, to be paid in cash:

	MR. DUNN	MR. ROE
Equity given	$ 420,000	$ 300,000
minus Equity received	−300,000	−420,000
equals Net equity	$ 120,000	$(120,000)

Calculation of Realized Gain

Table 10-30 shows how to calculate the realized gain. The realized gain is the gain that the investor would have had if the property had been sold rather than exchanged. It is the market value minus the adjusted basis and the transaction costs. The realized gain is computed in Table 10-30 for both parties.

Calculation of Recognized Gain

The recognized gain and taxable gain are calculated in Table 10-31 by subtracting the boot (or cash) given and the transaction costs, and adding the net loan relief to (or from) the boot (or cash) received. The net mortgage relief is considered unlike property only to the extent that the difference between

TABLE 10-30   Realized Gain on Exchange

	A. Mr. Dunn's Realized Gain:	
	Market value	$ 660,000
minus	Adjusted basis	−300,000
minus	Transaction costs	− 49,500
equals	Realized gain	$ 310,500

	B. Mr. Roe's Realized Gain:	
	Market value	$ 750,000
minus	Adjusted basis	−525,000
minus	Transaction costs	− 57,000
equals	Realized gain	$ 168,000

TABLE 10-31   Recognized Gain on Exchange*

	A. Mr. Dunn's Recognized Gain:	
	Boot (or cash) received	$ 120,000
minus	Boot (or cash) given	− 0
plus	Net loan relief	+ 0
minus	Transaction cost	− 49,500
equals	Recognized gain	$ 70,500

	B. Mr. Roe's Recognized Gain:	
	Boot (or cash) received	$ 0
minus	Boot (or cash) given	−120,000
plus	Net loan relief	+210,000
minus	Transaction costs	− 57,000
equals	Recognized gain	$ 33,000

* The recognized gain is the taxable gain because it is less than the realized gain.

the two mortgage balances is positive. Thus there is no "negative" net mortgage relief. *The investor pays tax on the lower of the recognized gain or the realized gain.*

ATCF and Position After Exchange

The ATCF is computed in Table 10-32. Mr. Dunn receives a positive cash flow of $50,760 while Mr. Roe pays out $186,240. Table 10-33 shows the amount of taxes both investors owe as a result of the exchange.

The equity positions after the exchange are shown in Table 10-34. Mr. Dunn received an office building with a market value of $750,000, with equity of $300,000, and an after-tax cash inflow from the exchange of $50,760. Thus his new equity position is $350,760 after the exchange. Mr. Dunn has deferred taxes on the unrecognized gain (the realized gain minus the recognized gain). Had the investment been sold outright, Mr. Dunn would have had to pay tax on the total realized gain of $310,500.

TABLE 10-32   Cash Flow from Exchange

		INVESTOR	
		MR. DUNN	MR. ROE
	Cash outflow	0	−$120,000
minus	Transaction costs	− 49,500	− 57,000
plus	Cash inflows	+120,000	+ 0
minus	Tax on gain 28% bracket*	−19,740	− 9,240
equals	Net cash flow	$ 50,760	−$186,240

* See Table 10-33.

TABLE 10-33   Taxes Due on Exchange

		MR. DUNN	MR. ROE
	Taxable gain	$70,500	$33,000
times	Marginal income tax rate	× .28	× .28
equals	Tax on gain	$19,740	$ 9,240

TABLE 10-34   Equity Position after Exchange

		INVESTOR	
		MR. DUNN	MR. ROE
	Market value of property given	$ 660,000	$ 750,000
minus	Mortgage debt	−240,000	−450,000
equals	Original equity	$ 420,000	$ 300,000
minus	Transaction: costs	− 49,500	− 57,000
minus	Taxes on recognized gain	− 19,740	− 9,240
plus	Cash given	0	+120,000
equals	New equity position	$ 350,760	$ 353,760

Also after the exchange, Mr. Dunn's adjusted basis has risen from $300,000 to $510,000. This adjusted basis would be allocated to the land and building; since Mr. Dunn's adjusted basis has increased, he will have a larger depreciation deduction after the exchange, thus generating more tax shelter. The new adjusted basis is the value of property received plus taxable gain minus realized gain.

Mr. Roe has acquired an apartment building from the exchange with a market value of $660,000, with equity of $420,000. His original equity position in the office building was $300,000. His new equity position is shown in Table 10-34.

EXCHANGE VERSUS SALE-BUY

As stated earlier, the most important motivation for exchange is the availability of income tax deferral. That is, taxes that would be paid on an outright sale may be postponed under the use of the exchange. However, the avoidance of taxes may not necessarily maximize wealth. The investor must also look at the property's after-tax cash flows over the holding period. Although taxes are deferred in an exchange, the depreciation basis will also be lower in an exchange. Will the benefits of the tax deferral in the exchange outweigh the benefits of increased basis in an outright sale?

To illustrate, assume that Mr. James wishes to buy Mr. Roe's property. Mr. James has $225,000 cash available to acquire the property. Mr. Roe, as before, wants to acquire Mr. Dunn's office building. He plans to hold it for five years, at which time he expects to sell it for $725,000. Selling expenses will be $50,000. Mr. Roe can either sell his apartment complex to Mr. James and with the proceeds buy Mr. Dunn's property, or Mr. Roe can exchange the apartment building for Mr. Dunn's office building and Mr. James can purchase the apartment complex from Mr. Dunn.

Mr. Roe's apartment building is valued at $750,000, with an existing mortgage of $450,000. Net operating income is estimated at $67,500 per year. The adjusted basis of the property is $525,000. Transaction costs from sale or exchange will be $57,000. There is a $525,000 potential mortgage loan available to the buyer. Mr. Roe is in the 28 percent marginal tax bracket.

Mr. Dunn's office building is valued at $660,000 with an existing mortgage of $240,000. The estimated net operating income from the property is $65,000. Transactions costs from sale or exchange will be $49,500. There is a $400,000 potential mortgage available to the buyer. The loan will be amortized over a twenty-five year period at 10 percent with annual payments of $44,067. For depreciation purposes, land/building value will be allocated 25/75 percent. The property will be depreciated over a 31.5-year period using straight-line depreciation.

ATER from Sale Today

Table 10-35 computes the after-tax equity reversion from the sale of Mr. Roe's apartment complex to Mr. James. Net sale proceeds are $693,000. The expected taxes due on the sale are computed in Table 10-36 to be $47,040 or 28 percent of the capital gain of $168,000.

TABLE 10-35   Expected Cash Flow From Apartment Building Sale Today

	Expected selling price (SP)	$ 750,000
minus	Selling expenses (SE)	− 57,000
equals	Net sale proceeds (NSP)	693,000
minus	Unpaid mortgage balance (UM)	−450,000
equals	Before-tax equity reversion (BTER)	243,000
minus	Taxes due on sale (TDS)*	− 47,040
equals	After-tax equity reversion (ATER)	$ 195,960

* See Table 10-36.

TABLE 10-36   Expected Taxes Due on Apartment Building Sale Today

TAXABLE INCOME

	Expected selling price (SP)	$ 750,000
minus	Selling expenses (SE)	− 57,000
equals	Amount realized (AR)	693,000
minus	Adjusted basis (AB)	−525,000
equals	Capital gain on sale (CG)	$ 168,000

TAXES DUE ON SALE

	Taxable income from sale (TIS)	168,000
times	Investor's marginal tax rate (τ)	× .28
equals	Taxes due on sale (TDS)	$ 47,040

Office Building Acquisition

Mr. Roe uses the after-tax equity reversion of $195,960 (Table 10-35) as a down payment to purchase Mr. Dunn's office building for $660,000. In addition to the first mortgage of $400,000, Mr. Roe takes out a second mortgage for $64,040 (8 percent; twenty-five years; $5,999 annually). Therefore the office building can be acquired by Mr. Roe as follows:

Purchase price		$660,000
Down payment	$195,960	
First mortgage	400,000	
Second mortgage	64,040	
	$660,000	

ATCF from Sale-Day

Table 10-37 shows the expected after-tax cash flows from operations for the five-year holding period. The annual debt service is subtracted from the expected NOI each year. Tax savings from operations are subtracted from this figure to find annual after-tax cash flows. Expected tax savings are computed in Table 10-38. Interest and depreciation are deducted from NOI to find ordinary taxable income. This is multiplied by the investor's marginal tax rate (.28) to get tax savings from operation.

TABLE 10-37   Expected Cash Flow from Office Building Operation on Sale-Buy

		YEAR				
		1	2	3	4	5
	Net operating income (NOI)*	$65,000	$66,300	$67,626	$68,979	$70,358
minus	Debt service (DS)	50,066	50,066	50,066	50,066	50,066
equals	Before-tax cash flow (BTCF)	14,934	16,234	17,560	18,913	20,292
minus	Taxes (savings) from operation (TO)*	(1,166)	(1,663)	(2,181)	(2,720)	(3,283)
equals	After-tax cash flow (ATCF)	$13,768	$14,571	$15,379	$16,193	$17,009

* Assume 2% annual increase in NOI.

TABLE 10-38 Expected Taxes from Office Building Operation on Sale-Buy

		YEAR				
		1	2	3	4	5
	Net operating income (NOI)	$ 65,000	$ 66,300	$ 67,626	$ 68,979	$ 70,358
minus	Interest on first mortgage (1)	40,000	39,593	39,146	38,654	38,112
minus	Interest on second mortgage (2)	5,123	5,053	4,977	4,896	4,807
minus	Depreciation deduction (D)	15,714	15,714	15,714	15,714	15,714
plus	Replacement reserves (RR)	0	0	0	0	0
equals	Ordinary taxable income (OTI)	(4,163)	(5,940)	(7,789)	(9,715)	(11,725)
times	Investor's marginal tax rate (τ)	.28	.28	.28	.28	.28
equals	Taxes (savings) from operation	$ (1,166)	$ (1,663)	$ (2,181)	$ (2,720)	$ (3,283)

ATER from Sale in Year 5

Table 10-39 computes Mr. Roe's expected cash flow from sale of the office building in year 5 for $725,000. The after-tax equity reversion is $214,730. The expected taxes from sale (Table 10-40) are computed to be $26,200. The

TABLE 10-39 Expected Cash Flow from Sale in Year 5

		SALE
	Expected selling price (SP)	$ 725,000
minus	Selling expenses (SE)	− 50,000
equals	Net sale proceeds (NSP)	675,000
minus	Unpaid first mortgage balance (UM)	−375,169
minus	Unpaid second mortgage balance (UM)	− 58,901
equals	Before-tax equity reversion (BTER)	240,930
minus	Taxes due on sale (TDS)*	− 26,200
equals	After-tax equity reversion (ATER)	$ 214,730

* See Table 10-40.

TABLE 10-40 Expected Taxes Due on Sale in Year 5

	TAXABLE INCOME	
	Expected selling price (SP)	$ 725,000
minus	Selling expenses (SE)	− 50,000
equals	Amount realized (AR)	675,000
minus	Adjusted basis (AB)	−581,430
equals	Total gain on sale (TG)	$ 93,570

	TAXES DUE ON SALE	
	Total gain on sale (TG)	93,570
times	Investor's marginal tax rate (τ)	× .28
equals	Taxes due on sale (TDS)	$25,200

adjusted basis ($581,430) is the original basis ($495,000) less accumulated depreciation ($78,570) plus the land value ($165,000).

Exchange Alternative

Table 10-41 shows the results of Mr. Roe exchanging his apartment building for Mr. Dunn's office building and Mr. Dunn selling the newly acquired apartment building to Mr. James. Mr. Roe exchanges the apartment building for the office building for his net equity ($243,000) and owes a first mortgage of $400,000 and a second mortgage of $17,000. The second mortgage is amortized over twenty-five years at 11 percent with annual payments of $2,019.

Mr. Dunn receives his net equity ($370,500), of which $353,000 is in cash and $17,000 is the second mortgage. Mr. James buys the apartment building for $750,000 with $225,000 down and a $525,000 first mortgage.

By exchanging with Mr. Dunn, Mr. Roe owes a total of $417,000 ($400,000 + $17,000) in loans. If Mr. Roe sells instead of exchanging, his debt is $464,040. The difference ($47,040) is capital gains taxes paid on the sale.

ATCF from Exchange

Table 10-42 computes the expected after-tax cash flow from operations for the five-year holding period. The annual debt service is subtracted from the expected NOI each year. Taxes (savings) from operations are subtracted from this figure to find annual after-tax cash flows. Expected taxes (savings) are computed in Table 10-43. Interest and depreciation are deducted from NOI to find ordinary taxable income. This is multiplied by the investor's marginal tax rate (.28) to find taxes (savings) from operation. Note that the differences between the cash flows from sale-buy and exchange are due to mortgage and depreciation differences.

ATER from Sale in Year 5

Table 10-44 computes Mr. Roe's expected cash flow from sale of the office building in year 5. The after-tax equity reversion is 216,116. The expected taxes from sale (Table 10-45) are computed to be $67,640. The adjusted basis ($433,430) is the original basis ($369,000) less accumulated depreciation ($58,570) plus the land value ($123,000).

IRR of Sale/Buy versus Exchange

Table 10-46 calculates the IRR of sale-purchase versus the IRR of exchange. Note that the IRR of the sale-purchase (9.366 percent) is lower than the IRR of the exchange (10.359 percent).

TABLE 10-41 Results of Exchanges

PROPERTY	MKT VALUE	EXISTING LOAN	EQUITY	CASH GIVES	CASH RECEIVES	PAPER GIVES	PAPER RECEIVES	TRANS. COSTS	NET EQUITY	NEW LOAN	OLD LOAN	NET LOAN PROCEEDS
Roe has	750,000	450,000	300,000					57,000	243,000			
Roe gets	660,000	400,000	260,000			17,000			243,000			
Dunn has	660,000	240,000	420,000					49,500	370,500	400,000	240,000	160,000
Dunn gets	750,000	450,000	300,000		70,500				370,500			
Dunn has	750,000	450,000	300,000						300,000	525,000	450,000	75,000
Dunn gets					283,000		17,000		300,000			
James has				225,000					225,000			
James gets	750,000	525,000	225,000						225,000			
				225,000	353,500	17,000	17,000	106,500				235,000
				235,000	106,500							
				460,000	460,000							

TABLE 10-42 Expected Cash Flow from Operation on Exchange

			YEAR			
		1	2	3	4	5
	Net operating income (NOI)	$65,000	$66,300	$67,626	$68,979	$70,358
minus	Debt service (DS)	46,286	46,286	46,286	46,286	46,286
equals	Before-tax cash flow (BTCF)	18,714	20,014	21,340	22,693	24,072
minus	Taxes (savings) from operation (TO)*	3,121	3,679	4,180	4,703	5,247
equals	After-tax cash flow (ATCF)	$15,593	$16,335	$17,160	$17,990	$18,825

* See Table 10-43.

234

TABLE 10-43 Expected Taxes from Operation on Exchange

| | | YEAR | | | | |
		1	2	3	4	5
	Net operating income (NOI)	$65,000	$66,300	$67,626	$68,979	$70,358
minus	Interest on first mortgage (I)	40,000	39,593	39,146	38,654	38,112
minus	Interest on second mortgage (I)	1,870	1,854	1,836	1,815	1,793
minus	Depreciation deduction (D)	11,714	11,714	11,714	11,714	11,714
plus	Replacement reserves (RR)	–0–	–0–	–0–	–0–	–0–
equals	Ordinary taxable income (OTI)	11,416	13,139	14,930	16,796	18,739
times	Investor's marginal tax rate (τ)	.28	.28	.28	.28	.28
equals	Taxes (savings) from operation (TO)	$3,196	$3,679	$4,180	$4,703	$5,247

Depreciation basis = [(Sales price − Unrecognized gain)] .75 ÷ 31.5, or $\dfrac{(660,000 - 168,000).75}{31.5}$

TABLE 10-44 Expected Cash Flow from Sale (Exchange)

	Expected selling price (SP)	$ 725,000
minus	Selling expenses (SE)	− 50,000
equals	Net sale proceeds (NSP)	675,000
minus	Unpaid mortgage balance (UM) (1)	−375,169
	(2)	− 16,075
equals	Before-tax equity reversion (BTER)	283,756
minus	Taxes due on sale (TDS)*	− 67,640
equals	After-tax equity reversion (ATER)	$ 216,116

* See Table 10-45.

TABLE 10-45 Expected Taxes Due on Sale in Year 5 (Exchange)

TAXABLE INCOME		
	Expected selling price (SP)	$ 725,000
minus	Selling expenses (SE)	− 50,000
equals	Amount realized (AR)	675,000
minus	Adjusted basis (AB)	−433,430
equals	Total gain on sale (TG)	$ 241,570

TAXES DUE ON SALE		
	Total gain on sale (TG)	241,570
times	Investor's marginal tax rate (τ)	× .28
equals	Taxes due on sale (TDS)	$ 67,640

TABLE 10-46   IRR of Sale-Buy versus Exchange

YEAR	SALE/PURCHASE	YEAR	EXCHANGE
0	$ (195,960)	0	$ (195,960)
1	13,768	1	15,593
2	14,571	2	16,335
3	15,379	3	17,160
4	16,193	4	17,990
5	17,009	5	18,825
	$+214,730		$+216,116
	IRR = 9.366%		IRR = 10.359%

SALE-LEASEBACK

Another method of property disposition is the *sale-leaseback*. This is an arrangement under which a property owner sells the property and simultaneously takes back a lease. The terms of such a lease are generally written to the requirements of the parties involved. The lease is typically for a number of years, with renewal options. The rental payments are typically sufficient to amortize the price of the property over the term of the lease and yield a desired rate of return to the investor.

To illustrate, assume that as a real estate developer, you have just been approached by a representative of Dixieland Incorporated (DI), a national convenience store chain, about constructing a Dixieland convenience store. DI has purchased a site for $30,000, will construct the store at a cost of $60,000, and desires to sell the land and its improvements to you for $100,000. So, under the terms set forth in fifteen-year lease, you will lease the property to DI for $17,000 per annum. DI will pay all costs related to maintaining the store, but you must pay the $2,000 per annum property taxes and you retain ownership of the land and building at the end of the fifteen years. You estimate that at the end of year 15, the building and the land will be worth $105,000. Selling expenses at that time will be $7,000. You have decided to use the straight-line depreciation method with a zero salvage value, and the useful life is 31.5 years. The current value (for depreciation purposes) of the building is $60,000. Your tax rate is currently 28 percent and you plan to finance with your own equity (100 percent) and desire a 10 percent after-tax rate of return. Should you accept DI's offer?

ATCF from Lease

The first step in solving this problem is to determine the annual cash flows to the lessor (buyer). These cash flows are computed in Table 10-47 by subtracting the debt service (0) and operating expenses ($2,000) from the lease revenues

TABLE 10-47   Expected Cash Flow from Operation

	Effective gross income (EGI)	$17,000
minus	Operating expenses (OE)	− 2,000
equals	Net operating income (NOI)	15,000
minus	Debt service (DS)	− 0
equals	Before-tax cash flow (BTCF)	15,000
minus	Taxes (savings) from operation (TO)*	− 3,666
equals	After-tax cash flow (ATCF)	$11,334

* See Table 10-48.

TABLE 10-48   Expected Taxes from Operation

	Effective gross income (EGI)	$17,000
minus	Operating expenses (OE)	− 2,000
equals	Net operating income (NOI)	15,000
minus	Interest on debt (I)	− 0
minus	Depreciation deduction (D)	− 1,905
minus	Amortized financing costs (AFC)	− 0
plus	Replacement reserves (RR)	+ 0
equals	Ordinary taxable income (OTI)	13,095
times	Investor's marginal tax rate (τ)	× .28
equals	Taxes (savings) from operation (TO)	$ 3,666

($17,000) to obtain the before-tax cash flows ($15,000). The after-tax cash flows ($11,334) are found by subtracting the taxes (Table 10-48) from the before-tax cash flows. The taxes are computed by deducting depreciation and interest expenses from the NOI and then multiplying this figure (taxable income of $13,095) by the investor's tax rate (28 percent). The annual cash flows are $11,334 for fifteen years.

ATER from Sale

The second step (Table 10-49) is to compute the after-tax equity reversion from the sale in year 15. This figure is found to be $90,559 by deducting selling expenses, the unpaid mortgage, and taxes of $7,441 (from Table

TABLE 10-49   Expected Cash Flow from Sale

	Expected selling price (SP)	$105,000
minus	Selling expenses (SE)	− 7,000
equals	Net sale proceeds (NSP)	98,000
minus	Unpaid mortgage balance (UM)	− 0
equals	Before-tax equity reversion (BTER)	98,000
minus	Taxes due on sale (TDS)*	− 7,441
equals	After-tax equity reversion (ATER)	$ 90,559

* See Table 10-50.

TABLE 10-50   Expected Taxes Due on Sale

	TAXABLE INCOME	
	Expected selling price (SP)	$105,000
minus	Selling expenses (SE)	− 7,000
equals	Amount realized (AR)	98,000
minus	Adjusted basis (AB)	− 71,425
equals	Total gain on sale (TG)	$ 26,575

	TAXES DUE ON SALE	
	Total gain on sale (TG)	26,575
times	Investor's marginal tax rate (τ)	× .28
equals	Taxes due on sale (TDS)	$ 7,441

10-50) from the selling price of $105,000. Table 10-50 computes the taxes due on sale by deducting the selling expenses and adjusted basis from the selling price to calculate the total gain. The total gain ($26,575) is then taxed at the investor's marginal tax rate (28 percent) to yield the taxes ($7,441).

NPV and IRR of Sale and Leaseback

In the third step (Table 10-51), the net present value is computed by subtracting the present value of the investment from the sum of the present value of

TABLE 10-51   NPV and IRR of Buy and Leaseback

YEAR	EQUITY (E)	AFTER-TAX CASH FLOW (ATCF)	AFTER-TAX EQUITY REVERSION (ATER)	PRESENT VALUE FACTOR @ 10% (PVF)	PRESENT VALUE
0	−$100,000			1.0	−$100,000
1		$11,334		.90909	10,304
2		11,334		.82645	9,367
3		11,334		.75132	8,515
4		11,334		.68301	7,741
5		11,334		.62092	7,038
6		11,334		.56447	6,340
7		11,334		.51316	5,816
8		11,334		.46651	5,287
9		11,334		.42410	4,807
10		11,334		.38554	4,370
11		11,334		.35049	3,972
12		11,334		.31863	3,611
13		11,334		.28966	3,783
14		11,334		.26333	2,985
15		11,334	$90,559	.23939	$ 24,392
				IRR = 11.06%	NPV = +$7,828

the cash flows and reversion. If this figure is negative, then a reject decision is made, and the reverse is true if it is positive. In this project, the NPV was positive, so the developer accepted the project. If the annual lease revenue had been negotiated at a lower amount, one might have rejected the project (since this may have made the NPV zero). The IRR turned out to be 11.06 percent, which is above the required 10 percent, and further substantiates that the decision to buy and lease back is worthwhile.

SALE-LEASEBACK VERSUS CONTINUE AS IS

Continuing with the previous sale-leaseback example, assume that Dixieland Incorporated *also* has the option to build the convenience store, occupy it for fifteen years, and then sell it. Construction costs will not change. DI will use straight-line depreciation with a zero salvage value, and the useful life is 31.5 years. The basis is $60,000. DI's tax rate is 28 percent. DI plans to finance with its own equity (100 percent) and requires a 10 percent after-tax rate of return. Should DI sell and lease back the property or retain ownership for fifteen years?

ATER from Sale Today

The first step in solving this problem is to determine the cash flow that DI receives for disposition of the property in year zero. DI sells the property at a $10,000 pretax gain ($100,000 − $90,000). The gain is taxed as ordinary income at the investor's 28 percent rate. The after-tax proceeds from sale are, therefore, $10,000 × .72, or $7,200.

ATCF from Lease

The second step is to compute the annual cash flows to DI from the lease. DI leases the property for $17,000 per annum. The annual ATCF from the lease is calculated by multiplying the lease expense ($17,000) by one minus the tax rate (1 − .28), which amounts to $12,240 per year.

ATCF from Continuing to Operate

The third step (see Table 10-52) is to compute the ATCF from retaining ownership and continuing to operate for fifteen years. The cash flow in year zero for the construction of the building is −$90,000. The cash flows in years 1 through 15 (Table 10-54) are computed by adding the property tax expense

TABLE 10-52   Expected Cash Flow from Operation

	Effective gross income (EGI)	$ 0
minus	Operating expenses (OE)	− 2,000
equals	Net operating income (NOI)	− 2,000
minus	Debt service (DS)	− 0
equals	Before-tax cash flow (BTCF)	− 2,000
minus	Taxes (savings) from operation (TO)*	− (1,093)
equals	After-tax cash flow (ATCF)	$ 907

* See Table 10-53

TABLE 10-53   Expected Taxes from Operation

	Effective gross income (EGI)	$ 0
minus	Operating expenses (OE)	− 2,000
equals	Net operating income (NOI)	− 2,000
minus	Interest on debt (I)	− 0
minus	Depreciation deduction (D)	− 1,905
minus	Amortized financing costs	− 0
plus	Replacement reserves (RR)	+ 0
equals	Ordinary taxable income (OTI)	− 3,905
times	Investor's marginal tax rate (τ)	× .28
equals	Taxes (savings) from operation (TO)	$(1,093)

(−$2,000) to the depreciation deduction (−$1,905) and multiplying by the investor's marginal tax rate (.28) (see Table 10-53).

ATER from Disposition in Year 15

The fourth step is to compute the after-tax equity reversion from the sale in year 15. This figure is found to be $90,559.

NPV and IRR of Sale-Leaseback versus Continue to Operate Differential

The final step (Table 10-54) is to compute the net present value (at 10 percent) of the differential cash flows. The cash flows from continuing to operate are subtracted from the flows from the sale-leaseback to reach the differential after-tax cash flows, which are multiplied by present value factors to compute NPV. The NPV is found to be −$10,896. Thus, given the 10 percent required rate, since the NPV is negative, the investor should not continue to operate but should sell and lease back.

TABLE 10-54 NPV and IRR of Sale-Leaseback versus Continue to Operate

YEAR	SALE-LEASE	OCCUPY-SALE	DIFFERENTIAL	PRESENT VALUE FACTOR @ 10% (PVF)	PRESENT VALUE
0	$ 7,200	−$90,000	$ 97,200	1.0	$97,200
1	(12,240)	907	(11,333)	.90909	(10,303)
2	(12,240)	907	(11,333)	.82645	(9,366)
3	(12,240)	907	(11,333)	.75132	(8,515)
4	(12,240)	907	(11,333)	.68301	7,741)
5	(12,240)	907	(11,333)	.62092	(7,037)
6	(12,240)	907	(11,333)	.56447	(6,397)
7	(12,240)	907	(11,333)	.51316	(5,816)
8	(12,240)	907	(11,333)	.46651	(5,287)
9	(12,240)	907	(11,333)	.42410	4,806)
10	(12,240)	907	(11,333)	.38554	(4,369)
11	(12,240)	907	(11,333)	.35049	(3,972)
12	(12,240)	907	(11,333)	.31863	3,611)
13	(12,240)	907	(11,333)	.28966	(3,283)
14	(12,240)	907	(11,333)	.26333	(2,984)
15	(12,240)	90,559	102,799)	.23939	24,609)

IRR = 11.49%   NPV = − $10,869

SUMMARY

This chapter examined the reversion decisions that the real estate investor must make. Reversion decisions deal with future expectations of an investment's value, such as when to dispose of an investment, how much the property is expected to increase or decrease in value over the holding period, and which method of disposition to choose. All of these decisions are made by calculating the net present value (or internal rate of return).

In the next part we explore in more detail the various investment criteria for investment decisions and the risk associated with real estate investments.

QUESTIONS

10.1. How does the reversion affect the investment decision?

10-2. The discussion in the book demonstrates that investment analysis continues after the property has been purchased, since the investor must constantly decide whether to sell the property or continue to hold it. How does the after-tax equity reversion affect the investor's decision?

10-3. What is an installment sale? Under what conditions would an installment sale be a possibility?

10-4. Tax-deferred exchanges are another method of property disposition. What are the basic steps in exchanging real property?

10-5. What is the most important consideration for a tax-deferred exchange?

10-6. What is a sale-and-leaseback arrangement?

10-7. In several examples in this chapter, the analysis concentrated on the difference in cash flows between the options under study. Why is this approach often useful in real estate decision making?

PROBLEMS

10-1. Using the sale versus continue-to-operate example developed in the chapter, what would happen to the decision if
   a. The estimated current selling price is higher than $625,000? Lower?
   b. The expected NOI grows at a lower rate than 2 percent? Higher?
   c. The expected value at the end of the holding period is lower than $675,000? Higher?
   d. The required after-tax rate of return is 12 percent? 20 percent?

10-2. Using the installment-versus-outright-sale example developed in the chapter, what would happen to the decision with the following changes?
   a. The installment sale has a price greater than $250,000.
   b. The interest rate on the purchase money mortgage was greater than 13 percent.
   c. The outright selling price was less than $250,000.

SELECTED REFERENCES

HENDERSON, GLENN V., and WILLIAM H. WALKER, "Analysis of Installment Sales," *Appraisal Journal*, 47 (October 1979), 485–89.

JAFFE, AUSTIN J., and C. F. SIRMANS, *Real Estate Investment Decision Making*. Englewood Cliffs, N.J.: Prentice-Hall, Inc., 1982.

SIRMANS, C. F., *Real Estate Finance*. New York: McGraw-Hill, 1985.

VALACHI, DONALD J., "The Tax-Deferred Exchange: Some Planning Considerations," *Appraisal Journal*, 47 (October 1979), 76–85.

11

TRADITIONAL INVESTMENT CRITERIA

In this chapter we begin our analysis of the various criteria used in making investment decisions. The previous chapters discussed how to forecast the expected outflows and inflows, measured in terms of cash flows. Our task now is to apply some criteria so that we can compare these cash flows. We analyze the various traditional measures—rules of thumb and appraisal techniques. The next chapter discusses the more sophisticated discounted cash flow models.

To make the investment decision we have two methods: compare what the investment is worth with what it cost or compare the expected rate of return with that required. All the criteria are simply techniques for obtaining measures of worth or rates of return. We now consider the various rules of thumb used to measure value and rate of return.

RULES-OF-THUMB CRITERIA

The rules-of-thumb criteria fall into two classes: the payback methods (or their reciprocal, rates of return) and the average rate-of-return methods (see Table 11-1). Note that the overall capitalization rate is simply the reciprocal of the net income multiplier. Likewise, the equity dividend rate and the after-tax rate are reciprocals of the before-tax and after-tax cash flow multipliers.

TABLE 11-1   Rules of Thumb: A Summary

I. Payback methods
   A. Multipliers

      1. Gross income multiplier (GIM) $= \dfrac{\text{Total investment}}{\text{Gross income (potential or effective)}}$

      2. Net income multiplier (NIM) $= \dfrac{\text{Total investment}}{\text{Net operating income}}$

      3. Before-tax cash flow multiplier $= \dfrac{\text{Equity investment}}{\text{BTCF}}$

      4. After-tax cash flow multiplier $= \dfrac{\text{Equity investment}}{\text{ATCF}}$

   B. Rates of return

      1. Overall capitalization rate (R) $= \dfrac{\text{Net operating income}}{\text{Total investment}}$

      2. Equity divided rate (EDR) $= \dfrac{\text{BTCF}}{\text{Equity investment}}$

      3. After-tax return (ATR) $= \dfrac{\text{ATCF}}{\text{Equity investment}}$

II. Average rates of return

      1. Average rate on net operating income $= \dfrac{\text{Average net operating income}}{\text{Total investment}}$

      2. Average rate on before-tax cash flow $= \dfrac{\text{Average before-tax cash flow}}{\text{Equity investment}}$

      3. Average rate on after-tax cash flow $= \dfrac{\text{Average after-tax cash flow}}{\text{Equity investment}}$

General Characteristics

These rules of thumb have a number of general characteristics in common. First, all these measures can be derived from data available from the forecast cash flow for the investment. The necessary cash flow items include gross income, net operating income, and before-tax and after-tax cash flow. Other items required are total investment costs and total (or initial) equity. All of these measures are easily found by calculating the ratios of costs to cash flow (or income) or the ratios of cash flow (or income) to costs.

    Second, many of these rules attempt to measure the same conceptual item: either as a multiplier or as a rate of return. The difference is that each measure relates different levels of expected cash flow to equity or to total investment. For example, the equity divided rate (EDR) is similar to the after-tax rate (ATR) except that the cash flow of the former is before-tax while the latter is after-tax. With the same denominator (equity), the after-

**Exhibit 11-1   How Can Rules of Thumb
                            Be Used?**

In several instances, the real estate investment rules of thumb can be used by investors. For example, some investors may wish to compare the results of the analysis using the rules of thumb with the results using discounted cash flow models. The rules of thumb provide "quick and dirty" approximations of more rigorous analysis.

The rules of thumb can also be used as guidelines before the more-detailed analysis is performed. In this way, the analyst begins to get the feel for the property and can see how well the various numbers stack up against each other. Also, the rules of thumb may be adequate for some investment decisions. The issue about the usefulness of the rules of thumb is not how robust and complex other methods are in comparison, but how predictive are the simple measures. In some cases, the single-period ratios, multiples, and rates of return will provide a sufficient amount of information about the property's investment characteristics.

It has become quite common to downplay the use of the rules of thumb as investment criteria. The growth of the use of discounted cash flow models in many markets has led to their demise. For several decades, however, these methods were the standard measures used in real estate markets, including large-scale developments. In modern investments, they continue to have a following and are regarded as helpful, if not quite as important as they once were. These measures have their purpose, and it seems unlikely that multi-period models will ever completely replace them.

tax rate will obviously be different from the before-tax equity dividend rate as long as there are tax consequences. The point is that these measures produce different results that may precipitate different investment decisions.

Third, these techniques are unadjusted for the time value of money. Typically, these are "single-period measures." This means that the multipliers and rates of return are calculated using only a single-period measure of income or cash flow, which severely constrains the usefulness because income (or cash flow) typically changes over time.

In the case of the average rate of return, the average income and cash flow (see Table 11-1) are (1) only averages and thereby prone to significant undervaluing in some periods and overvaluing in others, (2) unadjusted for the timing of the cash flows and, therefore, less useful from an investment standpoint, and (3) inconsistent with investment criteria using the time value of money concept. Finally, since none of these criteria measures change in the expected future income of cash flow streams, they are generally imprecise and subject to error.

Payback Period Methods

The *payback period* is simply the number of years necessary to recover the initial investment from an investment's future cash flow. It is often expressed in reciprocal form, that is, as a rate of return.

In equation form, the payback method is expressed as

$$\text{Payback period} = \frac{\text{Investment cost}}{\text{Income}} \qquad (11\text{-}1)$$

Alternatively, in the rate form:

$$\text{Rate of return} = \frac{1}{\text{Payback period}}$$

$$= \frac{\text{Income}}{\text{Investment cost}} \qquad (11\text{-}2)$$

As we noted earlier, there are five measures (or levels) of income from the operation of a real estate investment:

1. Potential gross income
2. Effective gross income
3. Net operating income
4. Before-tax cash flow
5. After-tax cash flow

Payback periods (or rates of return) for these five types of inflow can be calculated by using Equations (11-1) and (11-2).

Gross income multiplier.   One of the most widely used payback methods for estimating both market and investment value is the *gross income multiplier* (GIM). The GIM can be expressed as

$$\text{GIM} = \frac{\text{Total investment}}{\text{EGI}} \qquad (11\text{-}3)$$

The GIM simply tells the analyst how many years it would take to recover the total investment cost (purchase price) if all the gross income were allocated to recovery. To illustrate, the investor is considering purchasing a quadraplex with an asking price of $165,000. The estimated effective gross income in the first year is $18,240 (see Table 11-4). So the GIM is

$$\text{GIM} = \frac{\$165,000}{\$18,240}$$

$$= 9.05$$

An Example: A Small Rental Property

To illustrate the various traditional investment criteria, consider an investor interested in buying a quadraplex (four-unit) rental housing property. The asking price is $165,000. The investor is in a 28 percent marginal tax bracket and anticipates owning the property for five years, at which time the property is expected to be sold for $200,000.

The present rent per unit is $400 per month. The potential annual gross income, therefore, is $19,200 and is expected to increase 5 percent per year throughout the holding period. Vacancy and bad debt allowance are estimated at 5 percent of potential gross income. Annual operating expenses, assumed to increase proportionately each year, are estimated as follows:

Management fees (5% of EGI)	$ 912
Property taxes	1,000
Utilities (water and sewer)	450
Maintenance	450
Replacement reserves (constant)	1,125
Insurance	500
	$4,437

The depreciation schedule is shown in Table 11-2 using the following:

Total basis	$168,000*
Depreciable basis	$143,250†
Nondepreciable basis	$ 24,750
Method	straight-line
Recovery period	27.5 years

* This is the cost of $165,000 plus the acquisition costs of $3,000.
† This is the building value of $140,250 plus the acquisition costs of $3,000.

TABLE 11-2 Depreciation Schedule

YEAR	BASIS	STRAIGHT-LINE DEPRECIATION
0	$143,250	
1	138,041	$ 5,209
2	132,832	5,209
3	127,623	5,209
4	122,414	5,209
5	117,205	5,209
		$26,045

TABLE 11-3   Amortization Schedule

YEAR	PROPORTION OUTSTANDING	AMOUNT OUTSTANDING	DEBT SERVICE	INTEREST	PRINCIPAL
0	1.0	$123,750			
1	.99325	122,915	$15,640	$14,805	$ 835
2	.98564	121,973	15,640	14,698	942
3	.97707	120,912	15,640	14,579	1,061
4	.96741	119,717	15,640	14,445	1,195
5	.95653	118,371	15,640	14,294	1,346

The amortization schedule is as shown in Table 11-3 using the following:

Mortgage amount $123,750
Interest rate   12%
Maturity   25 years (monthly)
Financing costs $ 6,200*
* Estimated at approximately 5% of the
mortgage amount.

Hence, if all the gross income were used and the gross income were constant each year, it would take approximately 9.05 years to recover the total cost of the investment.

Net income multiplier (overall rate).   A second type of payback criteria is calculated by using net operating income (NOI) instead of gross income. The method is typically called the *overall capitalization rate*. Thus, using Equation (11-2), the overall rate is

$$\text{Overall capitalization rate } (R) = \frac{\text{NOI}}{\text{Investment cost}} \qquad (11\text{-}4)$$

This overall capitalization rate is sometimes called the "free and clear" rate of return.

Again referring to our example, the investment considered has a purchase price of $165,000 and a net operating income (see Table 11-4) in the first year of $13,803. The overall rate is

$$R = \frac{\$13,803}{\$165,000}$$

$$= 8.4\%$$

Note that the NOI varies every year in our example, so the overall rate will change as well.

In payback form, the net income multiplier (NIM) is the reciprocal of the overall rate, using Equation (11-1):

$$\text{NIM} = \frac{\$165,000}{\$13,803}$$

$$= 11.95$$

TABLE 11-4 Expected Cash Flow From Operation

		YEAR			
	1	2	3	4	5
Potential gross income (PGI)	$19,200	$20,160	$21,168	$22,226	$23,338
minus Vacancy and bad debt allowance (VBD)	(960)	(1,008)	(1,058)	(1,111)	(1,167)
plus Miscellaneous income (MI)	0	0	0	0	0
equals Effective gross income (EGI)	18,240	19,152	20,110	21,115	22,171
minus Operating expenses (OE)	(4,437)	(4,659)	(4,892)	(5,136)	(5,393)
equals Net operating income (NOI)	13,803	14,493	15,218	15,979	16,778
minus Debt service (DS)	(15,640)	(15,640)	(15,640)	(15,640)	(22,742)†
equals Before-tax cash flow (BTCF)	(1,837)	(1,147)	(422)	339	(5,964)
minus Taxes (savings) from operation (TO)*	(1,494)	(1,270)	(1,034)	(783)	(3,895)
equals After-tax cash flow (ATCF)	$(343)	$ 123	$ 612	$ 1,122	$ (2,069)

* See Table 11-5.
† $15,640 + $7,102 = $22,742
(Debt service + prepayment penalty)

249

So it would take almost twelve years to recover the total investment cost if all the net operating income were allocated to recovery.

Before-tax cash flow multiplier (equity dividend rate). The third pay-back period method is the *equity dividend rate* (EDR), or the *cash-on-cash return*. The before-tax cash flow (BTCF) is used to calculate the rate. In equation form, the equity dividend rate is

$$EDR = \frac{\text{Before-tax cash flow}}{\text{Equity investment}} \qquad (11\text{-}5)$$

Note that with this method, the cost of the investment is measured by the amount of equity rather than by the total investment costs.

In our example, the investment has a total cost of $165,000, of which $123,750, or 75 percent, is financed with a mortgage and $41,250 with equity. The BTCF is −$1,837 in the first year. The equity dividend rate is

$$EDR = \frac{-\$1,837}{\$41,250}$$

$$= -4.5\%$$

In multiplier form, the reciprocal of the EDR is

$$\text{Before-tax cash flow multiplier} = \frac{\$41,250}{-\$1,837}$$

$$= -22.46$$

Note that since the BTCF in the first and most subsequent years is negative, the equity dividend rate and its reciprocal are useless in our example. It is necessary under this circumstance to use one of the other payback period methods for analysis.

After-tax cash flow multiplier (after-tax rate). The final payback rate of return is calculated by using the after-tax cash flows rather than before-tax cash flows. In equation form, the *after-tax rate* (ATR) is

$$ATR = \frac{\text{After-tax cash flow}}{\text{Equity investment}} \qquad (11\text{-}6)$$

Since the ATCF is −$343 (Table 11-4) in the first year, the ATR is

$$ATR = \frac{-\$343}{\$41,250}$$

$$= -0.83\%$$

Average Rate of Return Methods

The second major category of rules-of-thumb techniques—the *average* (or accounting) *rates of return*—is not as popular. An average rate of return is calculated by dividing an investment's average annual income (or average before- or after-tax cash flow) by the total investment or equity costs. In equation form, the average rate of return is expressed as

$$\text{Average rate of return on total investment} = \frac{\text{Average cash flow}}{\text{Investment cost}} \quad (11\text{-}7)$$

The three common forms of the average rate of return method are described next.

Average rate on net operating income. This is very similar to the over-all capitalization rate. For example, if the net operating income of the investment is constant each period, the average rate on net operating income and the overall capitalization rate are identical. The average rate on net operating income is expressed as

$$\text{Average rate on net operating income} = \frac{\text{Average NOI}}{\text{Total investment}} \quad (11\text{-}8)$$

This measure gives the average rate of return on net operating income to investment cost over an expected number of years.

In our example, the average rate on net operating income is

$$\text{Average rate on net operating income} = \frac{\$15,254}{\$165,000}$$

$$= 9.24\%$$

Using the figures from Table 11-4, the average NOI was computed as follows:

YEAR	NOI
1	$13,803
2	14,493
3	15,218
4	15,979
5	16,778

$$\text{Average NOI} = \frac{\$76,271}{5}$$

$$= \$15,254$$

Note that this differs from the overall capitalization rate of 8.4 percent calculated earlier in the chapter. This method averages yearly NOI, whereas the previous example was calculated using NOI from the first year's operations.

Average rate on before-tax cash flow. This calculates the average before-tax cash flow as a percentage of equity investment. Therefore the average rate on before-tax cash flow is defined as

$$\text{Average rate on before-tax cash flow} = \frac{\text{Average BTCF}}{\text{Equity investment}} \quad (11\text{-}9)$$

From our example, we can get the following results:

$$\text{Average rate on before-tax cash flow} = \frac{-\$1{,}764}{\$41{,}250}$$

$$= -4.28\%$$

Using the figures from Table 11-4, the average BTCF numerator was computed as follows:

YEAR	NOI
1	−$1,837
2	− 937
3	− 422
4	+ 339
5	− 5,964
	−$8,821

$$\text{Average BTCF} = \frac{-\$8{,}821}{5}$$

$$= -\$1{,}764$$

Since the average before-tax cash flow is negative, the average rate on before-tax cash flow will not be useful to the investor in this instance.

Average rate on after-tax cash flow. This average rate of return is calculated in the same way as the before-tax cash flow but on an after-tax basis. This measure is defined as

$$\text{Average rate on after-tax cash flow} = \frac{\text{Average ATCF}}{\text{Equity investment}} \quad (11\text{-}10)$$

Continuing with the quadraplex example, we can get the following results:

$$\text{Average rate on after-tax cash flow} = \frac{-\$111}{\$41{,}250}$$

$$= -0.27\%$$

Using the figures from Table 11-4, the average ATCF was computed as follows:

YEAR	ATCF
1	$ (343)
2	123
3	612
4	1,122
5	(2,069)
	($555)

$$\text{Average ATCF} = \frac{(\$555)}{5}$$
$$= (\$111)$$

This rate will not be useful either due to the negative average cash flow.

Note that it requires more calculations to determine the average rate on after-tax cash flow, as Table 11-5 shows. Interest payments on the loan decrease as the loan is being amortized. Since the interest portion is deductible, taxable income varies each period. Depreciation is also deducted, assuming that $143,250 is depreciable over 27.5 years. The straight-line method is used, so the amount deductible from taxable income is constant each year. Taxable income or loss multiplied by the tax rate (28 percent) is equal to the tax liability or savings. The tax savings is added to the BTCF to yield annual ATCF.

Adjusting for reversion. The average rate of return methods can be modified to adjust the average income and cash flow figures to reflect the fact that the selling price is expected at the end of some holding period. Although this adjustment is an improvement, the adjusted average rates of return still contain several problems.

Using the preceding example, we see that the property sale has the following effect on the average rate on net operating income:

Total net operating income (over 5 years)	$ 76,271
Net sales proceeds (after 5 years)	190,000
Total cash return	266,271
Cost of total investment	(165,000)
Income	$101,271

Average income: ($101,271 ÷ 5 = $20,254)

$$\text{Adjusted average rate on net income} = \frac{\$\ 20,254}{\$165,000}$$
$$= 12.28\%$$

TABLE 11-5 Expected Taxes from Operation

		YEAR				
		1	2	3	4	5
	Effective gross income (EGI)	$18,240	$19,152	$20,110	$21,115	$22,171
minus	Operating expenses (OE)	(4,437)	(4,659)	(4,892)	(5,136)	(5,393)
equals	Net operating income (NOI)	13,803	14,493	15,218	15,979	16,778
minus	Interest on debt (I)*	(14,805)	(14,698)	(14,579)	(14,445)	(21,396)‡
minus	Depreciation deduction (D)†	(5,209)	(5,209)	(5,209)	(5,209)	(5,209)
minus	Amortized financing costs (AFC)	(248)	(248)	(248)	(248)	(5,208)§
plus	Replacement reserves (RR)	1,125	1,125	1,125	1,125	1,125
equals	Ordinary taxable income (OTI)	(5,334)	(4,537)	(3,693)	(2,798)	(13,910)
times	Investor's marginal tax rate (τ)	.28	.28	.28	.28	.28
equals	Taxes (savings) from operation (TO)	$ (1,494)	$ (1,270)	$ (1,034)	$ (783)	$ (3,895)

* See Table 11-3.
† See Table 11-2.
‡ This is the sum of the interest deduction in year 5 ($14,294) plus the prepayment penalty (6% of the mortgage amount outstanding, or $118,371 × .06 = $7,102).
§ This is the unamortized balance.

If we include the impact of the before-tax equity reversion on the average rate on before-tax cash flow, we get:

Total before-tax cash flow	$ (8,821)
Before-tax equity reversion	71,629
Total cash return	62,808
Cost of equity investment	(41,250)
Average cash flow: ($21,558 ÷ 5 = $4,312)	$21,558

$$\text{Adjusted average rate on before-tax cash flow} = \frac{\$\ 4,312}{\$41,250}$$
$$= 10.46\%$$

Finally, if we include the impact of the after-tax equity reversion on the average rate on after-tax cash flow, we calculate the after-tax equity reversion as follows:

Taxes due on sale:	$190,000
Net sales proceeds	
Less adjusted basis (168,000 − 26,045)	141,955
Equals total gain	48,045
After-tax equity reversion:	
Net sales proceeds	$190,000
Less unpaid mortgage	(118,371)
Less taxes on capital gain and recapture	(13,453)
Equals after-tax equity reversion	$ 58,176

Therefore the adjusted average rate on after-tax cash flow is:

Total after-tax cash flow (over 5 years)	($555)
Plus after-tax equity reversion (after 5 years)	58,176
Total cash return	57,621
Cost of equity investment	41,250
Cash flow	$16,371
Average cash flow: ($16,371 ÷ 5 = $3,274)	

$$\text{Adjusted average return on after-tax cash flow} = \frac{\$\ 3,274}{\$41,250}$$
$$= 7.94\%$$

TABLE 11-6   Expected Cash Flow from Sale

	Expected selling price (SP)	$200,000
minus	Selling expenses (SE)	−10,000
equals	Net sale proceeds (NSP)	190,000
minus	Unpaid mortgage balance (UM)	−118,371
equals	Before-tax equity reversion (BTER)	71,629
minus	Taxes due on sale (TDS)*	−13,453
equals	After-tax equity reversion (ATER)	$ 58,176

* See Table 11-7.

TABLE 11-7   Expected Taxes Due on Sale

TAXABLE INCOME

	Expected selling price (SP	$200,000
minus	Selling expenses (SE)	−10,000
equals	Amount realized (AR)	190,000
minus	Adjusted basis (AB)	−141,955
equals	Total gain on sale (TG)	$ 48,045

TAXES DUE ON SALE

	Total gain on sale (TG)	48,045
times	Investor's marginal tax rate (τ)	×.28
equals	Taxes due on sale (TDS)	$ 13,453

TABLE 11-8   Summary of Average Rates of Return for Quadraplex Investment

	WITHOUT REVERSION	WITH REVERSION
Average rate on net operating income	9.24%	12.28%
Average rate on before-tax cash flow	(4.28)	10.46
Average rate on after-tax cash flow	(0.27)	7.94

Table 11-8 summarizes the results of this example. Note that in all cases, the rates of return increase with inclusion of the expected sales proceeds and decrease if taxes are considered.

Decision Rules

How does the investor use the rules-of-thumb criteria to make an investment decision? For example, an investment with a gross income multiplier of 5 for an investment means nothing by itself. The investor must compare this with something in order to make the decision.

In using the payback methods, the investor wants to minimize the payback period. If expressed as a rate, the investor wants to maximize this rate of return. In our example, the investment has a calculated net income multiplier of 11.95, so the investor compares this with multipliers of rates on similar investments. If similar properties have multipliers of 14, the investor may conclude that the first project is preferable because it has the shorter payback period. However, whether the investment is "acceptable" or not is a more difficult question.

In using the average rate of return measures, the investor prefers investments with the highest expected rates of return. A rate of return of 9 percent for the quadraplex investment is preferred to another with a return of 8 percent, using the same measure.

Perhaps a more important consideration is the fact that there are no standards against which the analyst may gauge the acceptability of a particular investment. In the case of payback methods, what is the maximum acceptable payback period? How is it determined? In the case of rates of return, what is an acceptable rate of return? How is this determined? Also, how can an investor account for differences in risk?

Limitations of Rules of Thumb

One of the most serious problems with these measures is that the rate of return varies according to the measure used. Furthermore, we could compare these rates of return with better measures, such as the internal rate of return, and get totally different results.

The most serious defect in both the payback methods and the average rates of return measures is that no provision is made for the discounting of the future cash flow. Consider the hypothetical investments in Table 11-9. The investor can only acquire one project and each costs $100,000.

Each investment expects to return the effective gross income during the years indicated. If the investor were to use the gross income multiplier to decide which investment is preferable, investments A, B, and C would all be equally attractive, since each has a GIM of 4.

However, a more careful look indicates that as long as there is a time value of money, investment B would be preferable to C, and both would be preferable to A, if acceptable at all. The time value of money consideration implies that for the same amount, the investor prefers income (or cash flow) in the present rather than the future. In this example, investments A, B, and C are expected to return $25,000 at the end of year 1. However, investments B and C promise $125,000 in returns over four years while investment A promises only $100,000. Even if a "zero capitalization rate" is used, investment A is unacceptable for a four-year holding period, since it only promises to return $100,000 over four years for a $100,000 outlay. However, the GIM method fails to distinguish investment A from investment B or investment C.

TABLE 11-9 Expected Before-Tax Cash Flows for Investments A, B, C, and D

	ALTERNATIVE INVESTMENTS			
YEAR	*A*	*B*	*C*	*D*
0	($100,000)	($100,000)	($100,000)	($100,000)
1	25,000	25,000	25,000	—
2	25,000	50,000	—	—
3	25,000	—	—	—
4	25,000	50,000	100,000	—
5	—	—	—	150,000

TABLE 11-10   Expected Before-Tax Cash Flows for Investments R, S, and T

| | ALTERNATIVE INVESTMENTS | | |
YEAR	R	S	T
0	($150,000)	($150,000)	($150,000)
1	25,000	50,000	75,000
2	50,000	50,000	50,000
3	75,000	50,000	25,000

The GIM approach also views investments B and C as identically attractive. A closer look indicates that investment B is preferable to investment C for any positive time value of money. This is because, for identical amounts of income, we prefer to have the cash now rather than later. Therefore the GIM approach fails to select investment B over C, even though the former is clearly preferable. Finally, if we use the GIM, investment D is never really considered, since it "pays back" after the other three. Therefore there are serious doubts about the use of payback methods as investment criteria.

Moreover, the rules of thumb are inappropriate when cash flows change over the investment holding period. To illustrate this point, consider the investments in Table 11-10.

The positive numbers represent the before-tax cash flows for each investment. Each investment requires $150,000 equity, and only one can be selected. The cash flows from investment R are expected to increase as shown. The before-tax cash flows are constant for investment S and are decreasing for investment T.

The average rate on before-tax cash flow is clearly identical for all the investments: $50,000 ÷ $150,000 = 33.33 percent. Using this measure, the investor may conclude that all are equally attractive. A more careful examination suggests that if money has a time value, investment T is the most attractive because it returns more cash flow more quickly, and investment R is the least attractive for the same reason.

RATIO ANALYSIS

The financial feasibility of a real estate investment can also be measured, to a limited extent, by several ratios. These ratios show relationships between the various parts of the cash flow statement. From the investor's standpoint, analyzing the cash flow statement is useful both as a way to anticipate future conditions and as a starting point for planning action that will influence the future cash flow.

Ratios in real estate investment analysis fall into two groups: leverage and operating activity ratios and profitability ratios. Table 11-11 lists the

TABLE 11-11 Ratio Analysis

RATIO		EQUATION	QUADRAPLEX EXAMPLE†
A. Leverage and operating ratios			
1. Mortgage debt to property value ratio (loan-to-value ratio)	=	$\dfrac{\text{Mortgage outstanding}}{\text{Property value}}$	$\dfrac{123{,}750}{165{,}000} = .75$
2. Debt coverage ratio	=	$\dfrac{\text{NOI}}{\text{Debt service}}$	$\dfrac{13{,}803}{15{,}640} = .88254$
3. Default ratio	=	$\dfrac{\text{Operating expenses plus debt service}}{\text{Effective gross income}}$	$\dfrac{4{,}437 + 15{,}640}{18{,}240} = 1.10071$
4. Total asset turnover ratio	=	$\dfrac{\text{Effective gross income}}{\text{Property value}}$	$\dfrac{18{,}240}{165{,}000} = .11055$
5. Operating expense ratio	=	$\dfrac{\text{Operating expenses}}{\text{Effective gross income}}$	$\dfrac{4{,}437}{18{,}240} = .24326$
B. Profitability ratios*			
1. Profit margin	=	$\dfrac{\text{ATCF}}{\text{EGI}}$	$\dfrac{5{,}089}{18{,}240} = .27900$
2. Return to equity on total investment	=	$\dfrac{\text{ATCF}}{\text{Total investment}}$	$\dfrac{5{,}089}{165{,}000} = .03084$
3. Return on equity	=	$\dfrac{\text{ATCF}}{\text{Equity}}$	$\dfrac{5{,}089}{41{,}250} = .12337$
4. "System of financial analysis"	=	$\dfrac{\text{EGI}}{\text{Property value}} \times \dfrac{\text{ATCF}}{\text{EGI}}$	$\dfrac{18{,}240}{165{,}000} \times \dfrac{5{,}089}{18{,}240} = .03084$

* Also see the ratios in Table 11-1.
† These are calculated using the first year's estimated cash flows.

various ratios that we will now discuss. For the sake of analysis, we will assume a positive cash flow of $5,089.

Leverage and Operating Ratios

One of the investor's major concerns is the liquidity of the investment. Will the investment be able to meet the financial obligations related to operating and debt costs? There are five useful ratios for this type of analysis.

Mortgage debt to property value ratio (L/V).   One of the most commonly used financial leverage measures is the mortgage debt to property value ratio (also known as the loan-to-value ratio). This measures the relationship between the mortgage debt outstanding and the property value. In equation form:

$$L/V = \frac{\text{Mortgage debt outstanding}}{\text{Property value}} \qquad (11\text{-}11)$$

Debt coverage ratio (DCR).   The debt coverage ratio (DCR) measures the extent to which net operating income can decline and still cover the financial obligations (debt service). In equation form, the debt coverage ratio is

$$DCR = \frac{\text{Net operating income}}{\text{Annual debt service}} \qquad (11\text{-}12)$$

This ratio is widely used by lenders to measure the financial feasibility of an investment. If the debt coverage ratio falls below 1, the investment is unable to meet the obligation from operating income. The investor must take remedial action by investing more equity or borrowing to meet the financial obligation.

Default ratio (DR).   This also measures the financial feasibility of an investment from the lender's perspective. In equation form:

$$DR = \frac{\text{Operating expenses plus debt service}}{\text{Effective gross income}} \qquad (11\text{-}13)$$

The default ratio (also called the break-even ratio) measures an investment's ability to cover all the expenses of operations and the debt service.

Total asset turnover ratio (TAT).   This measures the ratio of effective gross income (EGI) to the total value of the investment. In equation form:

$$TAT = \frac{\text{EGI}}{\text{Property value}} \qquad (11\text{-}14)$$

The TAT is also the reciprocal of the gross income multiplier that we discussed in the previous section.

Operating expense ratio (OER). The operating expense ratio (OER) measures the relationship between total operating expenses and effective gross income (EGI). In equation form:

$$OER = \frac{\text{Operating expenses}}{\text{Effective gross income}} \qquad (11\text{-}15)$$

The greater the OER, the greater the proportion of effective gross income used to cover operating expenses.

Profitability Ratios

A number of profitability ratios were discussed earlier in the chapter. Profitability is the net result of a number of policies and decisions. Profitability ratios show the combined effects of liquidity, management, and debt on operating results. In addition to the ratios discussed previously (see Table 11-1), there are ratios for profit margin and the return to equity on total investment.

Profit margin ratio. Computed by dividing after-tax cash flow by effective gross income, this ratio gives the profit per dollar of gross income:

$$\text{Profit margin} = \frac{\text{ATCF}}{\text{EGI}} \qquad (11\text{-}16)$$

A low profit margin relative to other properties could indicate that an investment's rents are relatively low or that its operating costs are relatively high, or both.

Return to equity on total investment. The ratio of after-tax cash flow to total investment measures the return on the total investment:

$$\text{Return on total investment} = \frac{\text{ATCF}}{\text{Total investment}} \qquad (11\text{-}17)$$

However, this ratio is not as appropriate for the investor as the return on equity.

Return on equity. The ratio of after-tax cash flow to equity also provides a rate of return measure:

$$\text{Return on equity} = \frac{\text{ATCF}}{\text{Equity}} \qquad (11\text{-}18)$$

This is precisely the same measure as the after-tax rate discussed as one of the payback period methods.

"System of financial analysis."   It is possible to break down the return to equity on total investment into the product of two ratios: the total asset turnover ratio and the profit margin ratio:

"System of financial analysis" = Total asset turnover × Profit margin   (11-19)

$$= \frac{EGI}{\text{Property value}} \times \frac{ATCF}{EGI}$$

$$= \frac{ATCF}{\text{Property value}}$$

Therefore the product of the total asset turnover and the profit margin is another way of calculating the return to equity on total investment.

Limitations of Ratio Analysis

Although the ratios discussed are widely used in investment decision making, they are subject to the following limitations:

1. The ratios can be distorted by many factors. For example, understating operating costs (such as excluding management fees) can deflate the operating expense ratio.
2. It is difficult to generalize about whether a particular ratio is "good" or "bad." For example, a high debt coverage ratio may look good to the lender but may indicate that the investor is underleveraged.
3. Most investments have some "good" and some "bad" ratios. Consequently, it is often difficult to tell whether the investment is financially feasible.

Ratio analysis is useful despite these problems, but investors should make adjustments where necessary. Conducted with good judgment, this type of analysis can provide useful insights into an investment's operations. A number of published sources provide data on ratios for numerous types of investments, including shopping centers, apartments, and office buildings.

TRADITIONAL APPRAISAL METHODS

The three traditional appraisal methods are the market comparison, income, and cost approaches. These methods can also be used, and should be used, as investment criteria by the real estate investor, since he or she is particularly interested in the market value of the property. Real estate appraisal advocates the use of the comparison approach as the best method for value estimation. Obviously the investor does not want to pay more than the market value for the investment, even if it is worth more to him or her.

Exhibit 11-2 Appraisal Methods for Investors

One of the tools available to real estate investors is the set of appraisal methods. These techniques have a long tradition that dates back to the early part of this century. Commonly known as "the three approaches to value," the appraisal methods may be useful because investors may be familiar with the techniques from appraisal work, the methods may be applicable for investment purposes, or the methods may be familiar to others associated with the project and may therefore be helpful in communicating ideas about the potential investment.

For example, the *cost approach to value* estimates the value of the site and the improvements based on the concept of replacement cost. Investors who have expertise in development may wish to consider the option of reconstructing the property under consideration if the cost of doing so is less than the market price they will have to pay in order to acquire the property. In this situation, the cost approach provides helpful information to investors about an important option available to them.

The *income approach to value* is often used by investors for income-producing property. In recent years, more and more investors are employing relatively sophisticated income approaches, often using computers and spreadsheet software.

The *sales comparison approach* may provide information to the investor about the relative values of attributes (number of bedrooms, bathrooms, fireplaces, etc.), as well as entire properties in the market in which the investment property under consideration is located. This approach is useful in determining whether the assumptions and estimates made in the financial analysis are consistent with the workings of others in the same market. If market values of similar types of property are vastly different from the results obtained in the financial analysis, this is a danger signal and suggests that the investor needs to reexamine the premises and estimates of the investment analysis.

In many ways, the traditional appraisal methods can be used by investors. These methods can be used to estimate market values for comparison purposes, can demonstrate the market values of attributes in similar properties, or can serve as alternative investment techniques to help the investor do a better job in performing the financial analysis.

The Market Comparison Approach

Using the market comparison (or direct sales comparison) approach, the investor estimates value by comparing the subject property with similar properties in the market. Recently sold comparables are selected, and the appraiser identifies and adjusts for the factors that affect the value. In essence, the skilled interpretation of recent sales in the marketplace of similar property leads to the value estimate.

The comparison approach removes the bias a particular investor might have regarding future income appreciation or depreciation and internal rate of return. The comparison approach gives an indication of the expectations of and the return sought by the "typical" investor. This decision-making process is reflected in the market price of recent sales.

The most serious limitation of the comparison approach is the lack of sales data. The appraiser (investor) must have an adequate number of truly comparable sales in order to estimate the value. Since no two properties are exactly alike, the appraiser (investor) must adjust for differences to arrive at a final value estimate. In general, there are five major categories of adjustments:

1. *Time.* Since sales are historical, the comparables should be adjusted for time. For example, suppose the investor observed a comparable that sold six months ago. How have things changed over this period? Has there been new construction of this type of property? Have factors influencing demand for the property changed? What has the inflation rate been over the period? All of these considerations will influence value, either positively or negatively. Taking these factors into consideration, how much would the property sell for today?

2. *Location.* The location of a property can have a significant impact on the value. Obviously, if the comparable is in the same neighborhood, no adjustment will be necessary. If the comparable is in a different neighborhood, the investor must compare the relative advantages and disadvantages of each neighborhood. An adjustment must be made to reflect these differences.

3. *Financing.* Different methods of financing can have a significant impact on the behavior of investors and on the selling prices in the market. It is important to know what type of financing is available at the present time and the terms of financing on the comparable property as well.

4. *Conditions of sale.* The appraiser (investor) must be certain that the buyers and sellers are motivated by ordinary market motives. Factors such as the inclusion of a significant amount of personal property in the sale, inordinate bargaining strength, unusual pressure, and a poorly informed buyer or seller can render a sale useless as a comparable.

5. *Physical characteristics.* This category of adjustments involves many factors, such as size of building, number of rooms, age of the comparable, and lot size.

The appraiser (investor) should select a set of comparables and adjust these to the five key categories. The investor is asking the question, What would the comparable have sold for if it were like the subject property?

Uses of the market comparison approach.   The appraiser-investor typically places heavy reliance on the market comparison approach for value estimation. The market comparison approach may be used for investment properties if an adequate number of sales have occurred. It is generally possible to find data on the sale of apartments, office buildings, shopping centers, and other types of income properties.

Market comparison approach procedure. There are five steps involved in the market comparison approach:

1. Research the market to identify similar properties for which pertinent data are available.
2. Qualify the comparables according to terms, motivating forces, and authenticity.
3. Compare the attributes of each of the comparable properties in relation to time, location, physical characteristics, conditions of sale, and financing.
4. Consider the disparities between the comparable and the subject. The probable effect on the selling price of each comparable must be determined to derive individual market value indications for the property being appraised.
5. Formulate an opinion of the market value of the property being appraised from this analysis.

Because the sales chosen as comparables have a definite bearing on the value estimate, research of the market should be thorough. As far as the nature of the sale is concerned, the financing, bargaining strength, knowledge of buyer and seller, and other significant details of the transaction should be considered. These factors are as important in establishing comparability as are the physical characteristics of the property. In essence, the appraiser is looking for any market "imperfections" that cause the observed selling price of a comparable to be different from the market value.

In making the comparison between the selected comparables and the subject property, the appraiser must note all significant differences among properties. This provides a basis for adjusting the comparables to give an indication of value of the property being appraised. After considering all the data, the appraiser formulates an opinion of value for the subject property.

Market comparison approach example. Consider the situation in our earlier example. The investor is interested in buying a quadraplex. There are three comparable properties shown with the price per unit and per room. Note that the sales price ranges from $44,250 to $45,000 per unit. The sales price per room ranges from $9,000 to $11,063. Also given is the gross income multiplier, which ranges from 111 to 117.

If necessary, adjustments are made for comparables. In this example, we did not adjust for time, location, or condition of the building. Note that all the comparables are very similar to the subject property.

The subject property contains sixteen rooms. Multiplying the number of rooms by the estimated value per room results in a total value ranging from $144,000 to $177,008. The final value estimate depends on the reliability of each comparable. Comparable number 1 was considered most similar to the subject property, so most attention was given to its value indications.

To use this value estimate to make the investment decision, the investor compares this estimated market value with the asking price for the property. The asking price for the subject property is $10,313 per room. The investor would probably conclude that the property is reasonably priced, since the value indicated from the market comparison approach is $10,500 per room. The investor uses this estimate as the standard for making the investment decision.

Limitations of the market comparison approach.   The major limitation of the direct sales comparison approach is that an adequate number of comparable sales may not be available. Even if such sales can be found, changes that have occurred over time may diminish the comparability of each sale. Market conditions may have changed due to increases or decreases in supply or demand for a particular type of property.

For example, is it prudent to use an apartment complex sold one year ago as a comparable when operating expenses have increased substantially over the period? In this event, it is difficult to determine what type of adjustment should be made for these differences. Since the direct sales comparison approach may be of little use during times of rapidly changing market conditions, the income approach to value may be better suited to derive the necessary adjustment.

Another problem with the market approach is that it is based on past prices and trends. Adjusting these to reflect current market conditions is difficult. To the extent that sales are lacking or the data used by the appraiser are adequate, the estimate of the value of the subject property under current market conditions is limited.

The Cost Approach

The basic concept on which the cost approach relies is the principle of substitution. According to this argument, no investor would be willing to pay more for a property than the cost of building a property of equal utility. The cost approach may be particularly relevant to the investor who is considering a new project. Suppose the value estimate of the cost approach is lower than the value estimate of the market and both estimates of value are well supported. Such a situation may indicate that a shortage of the particular type of property exists, since demand has pushed the price to a level above the cost of construction. In this situation, the prudent action is to build a new structure, so the cost approach is used to make the investment decision.

Uses of the cost approach.   The cost approach is probably the most difficult of the three approaches to apply accurately. Thus the situations in which it is most applicable are those in which data are lacking for the market comparison and income approaches. Churches, public buildings, and special-use properties are often appraised in this manner because the other approaches are somewhat inapplicable. The application of the cost approach to investment property helps to make the "build versus buy" decision or helps to determine the feasibility of a renovation or conversion.

Cost approach procedure.   Estimate value using the cost approach by following these steps:

1. Estimate the land (site) value as if vacant.
2. Estimate the reproduction cost new or replacement cost new of the basic improvements and other structures (excluding any that were included as part of the land value).
3. Estimate in dollar amounts the loss in value (depreciation) caused by (a) physical deterioration, (b) functional deficiencies, and (c) adverse economic influences.
4. Deduct accrued depreciation from the improvements' reproduction cost new to arrive at a depreciated cost estimate.
5. Add the land value (from step 1) to the depreciated cost estimate (from step 4) to arrive at a value estimate.

The first step in the cost approach is to estimate the land value. This is typically done using the comparison approach discussed earlier.

The second step is to estimate the cost of the improvements. This is accomplished by using reproduction cost or replacement cost. *Reproduction cost* is the cost of producing an exact replica of the subject property. *Replacement cost* is the cost of producing a building with utility equal to that of the subject property. If reproduction cost is used, problems in cost estimation arise if the building is old and functionally obsolete. Such a building would not be built today, and therefore cost data on such construction are lacking. If replacement value is used, there may be a problem in determining the type of building with the same utility as the subject. Since replacement cost eliminates the functional obsolescence in a structure, a depreciation deduction for this item is inappropriate.

Typically, reproduction cost is estimated by the appraiser according to three major techniques: the *quantity survey method*, the *unit-in-place method*, and the *comparative unit method*.

The quantity survey method involves determining the quantity and costs of materials, supplies, equipment, and labor necessary for construction. This is the most costly and time-consuming method.

The unit-in-place method separates the structure into its major components and estimates what it costs for each of these major components to be "put in place." These components include foundation, floor, plumbing, wiring, heating, cooling, exterior walls, partitions, roof decks, and roof cover.

The unit comparison method of cost estimation is based on square-foot or cubic-foot units. Reproduction cost is derived in terms of dollars per unit based on known costs of similar structures, adjusted for time, location, and physical differences. These unit cost figures can be obtained from local contractors or cost services such as Boeckh's *Building Valuation Manual* or Marshall's *Valuation Service*. To the extent that the subject varies from the benchmark structure, adjustments are necessary to the cost figure.

Once the cost is estimated, allowances for accrued depreciation must be figured. Depreciation—the loss in value—is commonly measured by the *straight-line method* and the *breakdown method.*

The straight-line method depreciates property based on its age and expected life. There are various ways in which to apply this method. Physical life or economic life may be used as the basis for measurement. Physical age is an easily quantifiable measure, but it may not accurately reflect the condition of the property if maintenance and repairs are either better or worse than average. If effective age is used, the appraiser must make a subjective decision regarding the appropriate age of the property.

Because of its simple concept, the straight-line method usually does not reflect the actual market situation. Too many factors affecting accrued depreciation cannot be accounted for by this method. Therefore the breakdown method of depreciation estimation is generally used.

In the breakdown method of depreciation, there are three types of depreciation: (a) physical deterioration, (b) functional obsolescence, and (c) economic obsolescence. *Physical depreciation* is the adverse effect on value caused by deterioration of condition as a result of wear and tear. *Functional obsolescence* is the adverse affect on value resulting from problems in design, structure, or material that causes a loss of utility. *Economic obsolescence* is due to adverse influences outside the property itself.

Both physical deterioration and functional obsolescence may be curable or incurable. *Curable* items are those that can be economically corrected, such as painting and outdated plumbing fixtures. *Incurable* items are those that cannot be corrected physically or are not economically feasible to correct at present.

The depreciated value of the improvements is calculated by deducting the depreciation estimate from the estimated cost. If there are any site improvements on smaller structures, the depreciated cost of these should be estimated using the same procedures. Items such as parking lots, fences, landscaping, and swimming pools should be considered in this step.

Cost approach example. To illustrate value estimation using the cost approach, continue with the quadraplex example. The investor has an apartment building that comprises 3,750 square feet. The estimated reproduction cost from comparable properties recently constructed is $34 per square foot. The building is almost new, so it is estimated that the loss in value from physical depreciation is zero. There is no economic or functional loss in value. The land value is estimated at $28,000.

Using these assumptions, the value under the cost approach would be:

1. Reproduction cost:

3,750 sq. ft. times cost of $34 per sq. ft.	$127,500
Fireplace	6,000
Drives, walks, landscaping, parking	8,000

2. Loss in value:

Physical depreciation—none	0
Economic depreciation—none	0
Functional depreciation—none	0

3. Depreciated value of building and other improvements is

$127,500 + $6,000 + $8,000 − 0	141,500
4. Estimated land value	28,000
5. Total value = land value + depreciated building value	169,500

Limitations of the cost approach. There are certain limitations of the cost approach to value with which the investor should be familiar.

Cost Equals Value. One limitation is that the cost approach assumes that cost minus depreciation is equal to value. Even with newly constructed improvements, this may not be true. In some instances, the market value may be greater or less than the cost. This is possible if the improvements do not make the best use of the site or if market demand is in equilibrium and additional properties of a particular type are not required at that time. Because it costs $169,500 to build the quadraplex does not necessarily mean that this is its total value.

Another problem with the cost-equals-value assumption is that the cost is difficult to measure accurately. If several contractors are asked to bid on the same job, variations in these estimates may be as high. So which is the best cost estimate? Obviously, this is not easily resolved. Additional problems regarding the cost estimate may arise depending on the method the appraiser uses.

Depreciation Estimates. Another problem in the application of the cost approach concerns the estimate of depreciation. Depreciation in the cost approach is the loss in value between a new and a used structure, and because the estimation of depreciation is highly subjective, it is open to substantial error.

Identification of the various forms of depreciation is one problem, but proper measurement is an even greater shortcoming of the cost approach. Reliance on the cost approach should be limited to cases in which the property is relatively new and does not suffer from significant functional or economic obsolescence. In the final analysis, we simply do not know very much about estimating depreciation in appraising theory or practice.

The Income Approach

The major objective of real estate investors is to maximize their wealth from investments. *Value* is defined as the present worth of the expected future stream of income received from ownership of the property. The amount an investor is willing to pay to acquire a property takes into account the expected annual cash flow as well as the reversion at the end of the holding period.

Operationally, the definition of value is expressed in the following equation:

$$V = \frac{I}{R}$$ (11-20)

where

V = value
I = expected income stream
R = rate of capitalization

Uses of the income approach. The income approach can be applied to all properties that generate an income stream. Information regarding the type of return investors are seeking can usually be obtained through market research or various methods of rate synthesis. Traditionally, appraisers develop an estimate of the net operating income and the appropriate rate of capitalization from which an estimate of value is made from market analysis.

The income approach also is able to adjust for changes in market factors more rapidly than the cost or direct sales comparison approaches. Since these latter approaches depend on historical data, they may not reflect changes in financing, income, expenses, or appreciation. With the income approach, it is possible to make appropriate changes to income and expenses as soon as they are known. If market comparison methods are used to develop a capitalization rate, they will also reflect any changes in market expectations.

Income approach procedure. The steps outlining the traditional income approach to value estimation are as follows:

1. Estimate potential gross income.
2. Estimate and deduct a vacancy and bad debt loss allowance to derive effective gross income.
3. Estimate and deduct expenses of operation to derive net operating income.
4. Estimate remaining economic life (or the duration) and pattern of the projected income stream.
5. Select an applicable capitalization method and technique.
6. Develop the appropriate rate or rates.
7. Select the method to derive a value estimate using the income approach.

The basic premise of the income approach is expressed as shown in Equation (11-20). Because the income referred to in this relationship is net operating income (NOI), the first three steps in the procedure are designed to estimate it.

Once NOI is determined, the appropriate rate must be derived. Step 4 indicates that economic life and pattern of the income stream should be considered before selecting a capitalization method.

There are three traditional methods used to derive capitalization rates. The first method extracts the rate from sales in the market. Table 11-12 illustrates three recently sold properties that are similar to the quadraplex investment being valued. The rate is derived from the market (as shown in Table 11-12) using Equation (11-20).

When deriving a rate from the market, it is important that the properties be highly similar in terms of age, location, quality, condition, and other significant factors, as are these properties. Since these sales occurred at the same point in time, market and financing conditions should be very similar.

The second method of rate derivation is called the *band of investment*, or mortgage-equity analysis. This method considers the return required by the mortgage, as indicated by the annual mortgage constant (MC), and the return required by equity, as indicated by the equity dividend rate (EDR). Mortgage and equity returns are weighted by the proportion they contribute to total value. The rate (R) is derived using the following:

$$R = L/V \text{ (MC)} + E/V \text{ (EDR)} \tag{11-21}$$

Since the equity dividend rate is negative in our quadraplex example, the band of investment method will not be useful in this instance. Let us assume a 5 percent equity dividend rate. Let us also assume that the investor expects to obtain a 75 percent loan at 12 percent, with a twenty-five-year term. The overall capitalization rate is calculated as follows:

$$.75 \times .12637 = .09478$$
$$.25 \times .05 = \underline{.01250}$$
$$R = .10728 \text{ or } 10.73 \text{ percent}$$

TABLE 11-12   Quadraplex Example: A Capitalization Rate Range

	SALE 1	SALE 2	SALE 3
PGI	$ 18,480	$ 19,200	$ 19,200
− VB *	924	960	960
= EGI	17,556	18,240	18,240
− OE †	4,213	4,378	4,378
= NOI	$ 13,343	$ 13,862	$ 13,862
SP	$180,000	$177,000	$180,000
Indicated $R =$	$ 13,343	$ 13,862	$ 13,862
	$180,000	$177,000	$180,000
=	7.41%	7.83%	7.70%

* Estimated at 5% of PGI.
† Estimated at 24% of EGI.

To satisfy the requirements of the mortgage and equity, the investor would pay the price indicated by capitalizing the NOI of the property at a rate of .1073 percent. Since the information used in the band of investment is taken from the market, the rate derived by this method should be an indication of the overall capitalization rate in the market.

A third method of deriving the capitalization rate is called the *Ellwood technique*. In addition to cash flow, this method takes equity buildup into account through mortgage amortization and increases (or decreases) in value as sources of holding period for the investment.

While the mathematical derivation of the Ellwood method for the overall rate is beyond our present discussion, the Ellwood equation for determining the overall rate is

$$R = y - mc \, {}^{+\text{dep}}_{-\text{app}} \, (1/S_{\overline{n}|y}) \tag{11-22}$$

where

R = overall rate

y = equity yield rate, the required before-tax rate of return to equity

m = ratio of mortgage to value (loan-to-value ratio)

c = mortgage coefficient $(c = y + p \, (1/S_{\overline{n}|y}) - f)$

dep = proportion depreciation in the property value for the holding period

app = proportion appreciation in the property value for the holding period

$1/S_{\overline{n}|y}$ = sinking fund factor at a rate y for the holding period

p = proportion of loan paid off over the holding period

n = length of holding period

f = annual mortgage constant

Income approach example. The quadraplex example illustrates application of the income approach to value, using the Ellwood method to develop a capitalization rate.

The investor is considering an investment with an approximate NOI of $14,000 in the first year. As stated earlier, the loan is obtained for 75 percent of the property value at an interest rate of 12 percent for twenty-five years with monthly payments. The property is expected to appreciate in value by 15 percent over the five-year holding period, and the investor requires an equity yield rate of 10 percent.

The overall capitalization rate is calculated as follows, using Equation (11-22):

$$R = y - mc \, {}^{+\text{dep}}_{-\text{app}} \, (1/S_{\overline{n}|y})$$

$$R = .10 - .75 \, (-.0192642) - .15 \, (.163797)$$

$$R = .10 - (-.0144482) - .0245696$$

$$R = .0898786$$

Using the NOI of $14,000, the value of the quadraplex is

$$V = I/R$$

$$V = \frac{\$14,000}{.09}$$

$$V = \$155,555.56, \text{ or } \$155,600 \text{ (rounded)}$$

According to the Ellwood method, the estimated value is $155,600. The investor could pay $155,600 for the property, given the assumptions, and earn a before-tax rate of return of 10 percent on the equity investment.

Limitations of the income approach.   The main limitation of the income approach is that its application is precluded if a property does not produce income, as in the appraisal of single-family residential housing. However, most properties purchased by investors have some expected cash flow, so the use of the income approach is possible in these cases.

Another limitation of the income approach is the development of appropriate "cap" rates. Any of the methods for developing rates are subject to question. In many instances, the appraiser is forced to use rates that are not taken directly from the market, so it is important that the method the appraiser uses to derive the rate parallel the method used by the investor.

Another problem in the development of rates is the projection of future change in the property value. Perhaps the appraiser can gain some insight regarding expectations through a market study. On many smaller investments, appreciation may be expected to provide a significant portion of the overall return. Since an investor is not sure if properties will appreciate in the future, there is likely to be a divergence of opinion among appraisers, investors, brokers, and developers about the proper rate of appreciation or depreciation. Therefore the selection of a rate deemed to be appropriate will often spark controversy, since a subjective element is introduced into the capitalization process.

QUESTIONS

11-1. What are the general characteristics of the rules-of-thumb criteria?

11-2. What is the relationship between the overall capitalization rate and the net income multiplier?

11-3. What are average rate of return measures?

11-4. How can the reversion be included in the average rate of return calculations?

11-5. "A major problem using the rules-of-thumb criteria is that they lack sound decision rules." True or false? Explain.

11-6. What are the typical ratios used in analyzing real estate investments?

11-7. What is another name for the "return on equity" ratio?

11-8. What are the limitations of ratio analysis?

11-9. Traditional appraisal approaches can also be used in real estate investment analysis. Illustrate how the three appraisal approaches can be used by investors.

11-10. What is the "income approach to value"?

PROBLEMS

11-1. "Market value is an interesting and useful input to the investment decision process, but more importantly, the investor is concerned with the present worth of the partial interest that represents the investor's planned investment interest." Demonstrate why market value estimation is a useful input to the investment decision.

11-2. Demonstrate how appraisal techniques can be used by investors.

11-3. You have been given the assignment to appraise a single-family house. The house has 1,500 square feet of living area. Analysis of construction costs indicates a per-square-foot cost of $30. The house has an effective age of ten years and an estimated economic life of fifty years. Changing neighborhood characteristics have had a negative influence of $1,000 on the value. An examination of similar lots indicates a value of $10,000 for the land value. What is the market value estimate of the property?

11-4. For the appraisal assignment in Problem 11-3, you also observe the following: An analysis of the market indicates the following:

CHARACTERISTIC	SUBJECT PROPERTY	COMPARABLE 1	COMPARABLE 2
Sale price	—	$50,000	$48,000
Time	11/85	9/85	7/85
Location	—	Same	Same
Financing	Conventional	Same	Same
Size	1,500 sq. ft.	1,650 sq. ft.	1,400 sq. ft.
Age	10 yrs.	12 yrs.	8 yrs.
Garage	2-car	Same	None

a. Housing prices have been increasing at the rate of 0.8 percent per month.
b. Each additional square foot is valued at $25.
c. Each additional year of age reduces value by $250.
d. A two-car garage is valued at $5,000.
What is the estimate of value of the subject property?

11-5. Using the following information, estimate the value using the Ellwood valuation model:

NOI	$100,000
L/V	75%
Interest rate	9%
Maturity	20 years/annual payments
Holding period	8 years
Change in value	20% appreciation
Before-tax equity yield	16%

SELECTED REFERENCES

American Institute of Real Estate Appraisers, *The Appraisal of Real Estate* (8th ed.). Chicago: American Institute of Real Estate Appraisers, 1983.

ELLWOOD, L. W., *Ellwood Tables for Real Estate Appraising and Financing* (3rd ed.). Chicago: American Institute of Real Estate Appraisers, 1970.

GETTEL, RONALD E., *Real Estate Guidelines and Rules of Thumb.* New York: McGraw-Hill, 1976.

LUSHT, KENNETH M., "Measuring Rate of Return: Two Rules of Thumb versus the Internal Rate," *Appraisal Journal,* 46 (April 1978), 245–56.

PAGE, DANIEL E., "Criteria for Investment Decision Making: An Empirical Study," *Appraisal Journal,* 60 (October 1983), 498–508.

PYHRR, STEPHEN A., "Mathematics of Real Estate Finance," in *Financing Income-Producing Real Estate,* ed. James A. Britton, Jr., and Lewis O. Kerwood, pp. 310–55. New York: McGraw-Hill, 1977.

SIRMANS, C. F., and JAMES R. WEBB, "Mortgage Equity Analysis, Again?!" *Appraisal Journal,* 47 (January 1979), 44–52.

Society of Real Estate Appraisers, *An Introduction to Appraising Real Property.* Chicago: Society of Real Estate Appraisers, 1978.

WENDT, PAUL F., *Real Estate Appraisal—Review and Outlook.* Athens, Ga: University of Georgia Press, 1974.

12

DISCOUNTED CASH FLOW MODELS

In the preceding chapter we summarized many of the traditional methods that investors use to make investment decisions. We also explained why these methods are often faulty and prone to inconsistent investment choices. A more rigorous method is described in this chapter. This method, called *discounted cash flow models*, has been used for some time by financial analysts but has only recently been applied to real estate investment analysis.

After the analyst forecasts cash flows, these measures are used to choose projects that are consistent with the investor's personal objectives. However, the possibility of changing cash flow streams, growth or decline in the expected future selling price, and various other concerns regarding financing policy and tax planning may dramatically affect the investment choice. Therefore any acceptable approach must address these issues.

This chapter examines the two discounted cash flow models typically used in practice: the *net present value* approach and the *internal rate of return* method. Both of these capital-budgeting techniques have been designed for the real estate equity investor. In addition, we compare the two techniques, and we show that if the investor's objective is to maximize investment wealth, the use of net present value as an investment criterion will ensure that the best projects will be selected. This implies that at least in some cases, the use of the internal rate of return as an investment criterion will lead to suboptimal choices.

Finally, some alternative discounted cash flow models are presented. These represent modifications of the basic models. Many investors seem to prefer some of the modified models based on recent survey results. The chapter concludes with a brief discussion of the importance of discounted cash flow models.

THE DISCOUNTED CASH FLOW APPROACH

Modern real estate investment analysis has generally adopted the discounted cash flow approach to valuation. There are many reasons why this approach is favored. First, it can measure cash flows throughout the life of the investment, as well as the impact of the reversion at the time of sale. Second, the measure of benefits used, after-tax cash flows, is selected because this measure takes into account factors such as operating expenses, financial expenses, depreciation and interest, tax shelter, and taxation. Third, the after-tax equity reversion takes into account the selling expenses, if any, and the repayment of outstanding principal. Fourth, this approach permits any or all of these variables to change over time, at individual rates of change, if the analyst believes such changes are necessary. Fifth, since expected cash flows in the future and the expected equity reversion at a future selling date are not received by the investor *today*, this technique incorporates a consideration of the time value of money to permit the adjustment of actual dollars into present value, time-adjusted dollars. Finally, the various types of risk may be incorporated into the discounted cash flow approach. In addition, changing risk levels may also be treated, although this may become a difficult task. Therefore, for these and other reasons, the discounted cash flow approach enjoys a prominent place among investment criteria for real estate investment analysis.

The use of discounted cash flow models requires the understanding of more technical methods of analysis, additional data requirements and estimates, and additional time and effort on the part of the analyst. We believe that familiarity with the basic approach and an understanding of the concept of discounted models can help investors improve their analysis of potential real estate investment, and in many cases, eliminate reliance on the traditional rules of thumb.

The Models

The real estate investment process provides a framework for systematically analyzing information to use when choosing among alternative investment opportunities.

Recall from Chapter 2 that the equity valuation model measures the investment value of equity, the net present value of equity, and/or the internal rate of return on equity. The investment value of equity (E) is defined as

$$E = \sum_{t=1}^{n} \frac{\text{ATCF}_t}{(1 + k_e)^t} + \frac{\text{ATER}_n}{(1 + k_e)^n} \tag{12-1}$$

**Exhibit 12-1 The Benefits of Discounted
Cash Flow Models**

There are several reasons why discounted cash flow models have become the standard tool in many modern real estate investment studies. They are more explicit in their ability to evaluate factors, they are less restrictive in their measurement, and they are general enough to be adapted to a wide variety of real estate projects. For these and other reasons, discounted cash flow models have enjoyed enormous popularity in schools as well as in the field.

For example, most real estate investments promise changing cash flow levels each year. Discounted cash flow models can easily accommodate this feature; simpler methods use averages. Also, the specific timing of each cash flow can be treated as it is expected to occur. Since the existence of the time value of money is an important aspect of investing, discounted cash flow models permit the investor to analyze not only the magnitude of the cash flows but also the timing of the flows. Finally, discounted cash flow models permit the investor to separate the cash flow into different components for special analysis. For example, if some portions of the cash flow are regarded as being riskier than others, this can easily be evaluated using these models.

Discounted cash flow models have been computerized, and several commercial programs are currently available. With the development of spreadsheets such as *VisiCalc* and *Lotus 1-2-3*, these models are likely to become even more popular. In the past, some investors avoided these models because they were operationally complex—a relatively large number of calculations were required. With the new computerized technology, this issue has disappeared.

It should also be noted that discounted cash flow models will not ensure that the investor will not make mistakes. What these models do is to take into account a large number of parameters affecting real estate and to explicitly account for each parameter in a carefully controlled and logical way. The investor is often able to test the "sensitivity" from changes in one or more of these parameters and observe the likely impact on the results. Many real-world investors and financial managers believe this is the real advantage of the discounted cash flow models.

The net present value of equity (NPV_e) is defined as

$$NPV_e = \sum_{t=1}^{n} \frac{ATCF}{(1 + k_e)^t} + \frac{ATER_n}{(1 + k_e)^n} - (MV - MD) \qquad (12-2)$$

The internal rate of return on equity (IRR_e) is the value that satisfies the following equation:

$$0 = \sum_{t=1}^{n} \frac{\text{ATCF}_t}{(1 + \text{IRR}_e)^t} + \frac{\text{ATER}_n}{(1 + \text{IRR}_e)^n} - (\text{MV} - \text{MD}) \qquad (12\text{-}3)$$

These models constitute basic discounted cash flow analysis.

The calculation of the investment value of equity (E) is equal to the discounted value of after-tax cash flows from operations over the expected holding period and the discounted value of the after-tax equity reversion at the time of sale, discounted by the required rate of return on equity. The result represents the greatest amount that the specific investor is justified in paying to acquire the property rights of the investment. This amount must be compared with the amount of equity required of the investor, which when added to the presumed amount of mortgage debt, equals the acquisition price.

The net present value of equity (NPV_e) is equal to the difference between the investment value of equity and the down payment required of the equity investor. In effect, the investment value of equity represents the benefits from the investment, and the down payment represents the costs. Thus the net present value is the difference between costs and benefits.

The internal rate of return on equity (IRR_e) is the rate of return such that the discounted value of after-tax cash flows and the discounted value of the after-tax equity reversion are equal to the required equity investment. This expected rate of return is compared with the required rate of return on equity to evaluate the investment's attractiveness.

Some Issues in Discounted Cash Flow Analysis

Real estate investment is basically a capitalization process: investors give up a known, certain amount in exchange for an expected, but uncertain, stream of future cash flows. Capitalization is the conversion of an expected future stream of benefits into a present value sum. Therefore capitalization of income or cash flow is an integral part of investment analysis.

There are four major reasons why discounted cash flow models are superior to the traditional methods discussed in Chapter 11: (1) changing income (and cash flow) streams, (2) changing levels of risk, (3) differing size and types of expected future benefits, and (4) the time value of money concept.

Changing benefit streams. Unlike other investments such as corporate bonds and some common stocks, the financial benefits of real estate investments vary each period. In the case of apartment houses, for example, despite the fixing of contract rent and the predominance of level-payment amortized mortgages, operating expenses may vary significantly throughout the leasing period. This causes net operating income to vary. As net operating income varies, so does before-tax cash flow with the fixed debt service payment.

Furthermore, discounted cash flow techniques rely on after-tax cash flow payments in calculating value and return. Chapters 1 and 11 showed that after-tax cash flow differs from before-tax cash flow by the amount of income tax to be paid each period. Since income taxes are calculated by the investor's tax rate times the amount of taxable income, changes in taxable income (or the tax rate) will result in changes in after-tax cash flow. The cash flow statement in Chapter 1 also showed that taxable income varies according to changes in interest payments and depreciation allowances (if an accelerated depreciation method is used). Therefore since the equity valuation model uses after-tax cash flow as a measure of benefits, changes in net operating income, interest payments, depreciation allowances, or tax rates expected in the future will result in the changing benefit stream from the investment.

Finally, if rental and income payments vary due to monthly lease agreements, or if vacancies vary, or if bad debt problems are particularly relevant, effective gross income and potential gross income will vary. If multiple financing options are used, causing financial expenses to vary from period to period, measures relating to the equity position also may be altered. These possibilities suggest that changing benefit streams are more likely to occur than not, and as a result, discounted cash flow models are much more suited to handling these problems.

Changing levels of risk.   Since financial and economic markets are dynamic in nature, events frequently occur that affect the risk/return opportunities of investments. For example, at the time the investment is being evaluated, there is a certain amount of market risk associated with the investment, as discussed in Chapter 4. If the amount of risk is expected to vary over the expected holding period of the investment, the analyst is concerned with the fact that as the riskiness of the investment increased (decreased), the investment value would fall (rise) in response to the change in risk. Similarly, changes in the required rate of return on equity would occur in proportion to changes in the riskiness of the investment.

Discounted cash flow models are better suited to handle this measurement problem than direct capitalization or other single-period rules of thumb. In some cases, the necessary adjustment can be made to income estimates when risk is expected to increase. Other models show that expected increasing risk levels result in falling values of income or cash flows. Finally, complex models may be used to account for expected changes in future risk levels in a discounted cash flow approach. Although this development is beyond the scope of this book, it demonstrates the fact that discounted cash flow models can be extremely flexible and therefore are valuable for real estate analysts.

Some investors suggest that increasing the capitalization rate by using traditional rules of thumb has the same effect as raising the risk-adjusted discount rate used in discounted cash flow models. In some cases, it may be possible to get consistent or identical results. However, in view of other limitations and problems with the earlier techniques, the measurement of expected changes in risk is best handled in the discounted cash flow approach.

Differing sizes and types of benefits.   Another advantage is the ability to accurately account for income or cash flow figures that are expected to vary significantly from year to year. Traditional techniques have either disregarded future benefit streams that were expected to be significantly different from the current one, averaged the expected income or cash flow for the next few years, or stabilized the benefits in some fashion. The ability of discounted cash flow models to reflect the expected size of the income or cash flow in the year in which it is expected to occur is a major improvement over other techniques.

Real estate investment analysis often involves property where an income is earned over the holding period and appreciation in value is expected to be realized at the time of sale. Thus the investor actually expects to receive two types of benefits: periodic cash flow receipts and a lump-sum cash flow at the end of the holding period. These benefits cause significant problems for investors using rules of thumb.

Discounted cash flow models can adequately account for both types of benefits. Furthermore, estimates of benefit sizes can be made without specifying the capitalization rate or investment value. Discounted cash flow procedures also help the investor to account for rising property values, equity buildup, or rising income levels due to changes in demand. The investor who uses rules of thumb either takes rough averages of the changing variables, assumes the changes have no effect on the investment and does nothing about them, or is unable to evaluate the effects of these changes on income-producing real estate.

Time value of money.   Finally, discounted cash flow techniques are important due to the existence of the time value of money in productive market economies. The concept of the time value of money is critical to investment decisions because returns from the investment often occur at various intervals throughout the holding period. The present value of all the expected income or cash flow payments is less than the sum of the payments, even without inflation or risk, and the analyst must evaluate investments on a time-adjusted basis. Discounted cash flow models help the investor to take into account the *timing* and the amount of payments and receipts. Then this factor is incorporated into the decision criteria.

The traditional single period measures either ignore the time value of money or assume these are consistent with discounted cash flow models. However, the former action leads to inferior investment choices while the latter is more general and flexible and therefore preferable.

Discounted cash flow models were developed due to the effect of declining values of future benefits. As we will see, comparisons based on total dollar receipts (income, cash flows, etc.) disregard the measurement of the time value of money and therefore result in a wrong choice. This point is demonstrated in the following example. An investor wishes to decide between investments G and H. Each costs the same amount. Investment G is expected to yield $100 per year for ten years. Investment H is expected to yield $1,000 at the end of the tenth year. Each investment is believed to be in the same risk class. Should the investor assume that these two are similar? Obviously, the answer is no. Although both yield the same "total dollars" of benefits, $1,000, investment G will yield some return each year. Since investment H is not expected to return any dollars until the end of ten years, the time value of money theory says that investment G is preferred to investment H at any positive discount rate.

Therefore discounted cash flow analysis can be a powerful and useful tool for analysts. It forms the framework for most modern real estate investment analysis and is flexible enough to permit adjustments according to market changes. Finally, it permits a treatment of the time value of money considerations which are so crucial in making financial decisions.

Uncertainty, Future Cash Flows, and Market Efficiency

If we lived in a world where we knew with certainty *what* and *when* future cash flows would occur, making investment decisions would be much easier. In such a world, however, there would not be any investment problems. The investor would simply calculate rates of return and values of various choices and *know* what each alternative was truly worth. But, in such a world, *everyone* would know what each asset would be worth. Although investment analysis might still exist, investment values would always equal market values.

In the real world, future cash flows from real estate investments and changes in those cash flows are *not* known with certainty. Therefore investment analysis is risk analysis. But it is possible to view it as the analysis of the quality of data as well as the acquisition of technical skill to identify, measure, and evaluate the uncertainty. As we will see in Chapter 13, there are various ways to incorporate risk into the discounted cash flow framework.

If we believe that the analysis of data will yield valuable information about prospective investments, this implies that other analysts might also learn about the risk and possible returns from the investment by analyzing the same data. If so, there may be little reason to believe that one side of the market has more information than the other. Therefore the determination of market values may reflect the information available to the market. If this is the case, it may be impossible for investors using market information to outperform others in the market unless the investor has (1) particular or unusual skills, (2) unusual investment requirements, (3) an exceptionally quick response time, or (4) a short-run string of luck.

Of course, the availability of information depends on *market efficiency*, or the rate and extent to which information is incorporated into market prices. If the market is very efficient, the available information is quickly reflected in selling prices of assets in that market. If inefficient, the acquisition of

**Exhibit 12-2   DCF Models Do Not Predict
the Future**

Some investors, upon their first exposure to discounted cash flow models, believe that the intent of the models is to predict the future. Since the method requires that the investor make estimates about future items such as rents, expenses, sales prices, tax liability, and future income levels and thus future income tax rates and other variables, some novices believe that the analyst is predicting the future. To them, if the estimates prove to be in error, the analysis has no meaning.

This is incorrect and indicates a misunderstanding of the intention and application of discounted cash flow models. These models do not predict the future; they merely use the available information at the time the analysis is being done and attempt to use the information to make an intelligent and analytical decision.

When an investor makes an investment decision, the best he or she can hope to do is to properly evaluate all the available information about the property and the market at the current time. Thus real estate investment analysis is often called *ex ante* valuation, or analysis based on expected, but uncertain, events. When viewed in this manner, the use of discounted cash flow models seeks to provide as much information as possible in an organized manner to enable the investor to compare one project with others. There is no prediction in the sense that the quality of the analysis is based on the predictive power of the estimates.

If one were to use actual, past data, this would be a different type of study. It is called *ex post* valuation and serves as empirical verification of past experience. Real estate investors use this procedure to help form expectations about the future. As such, ex post analysis can provide valuable inputs for ex ante real estate investment analysis.

The best test of the use of discounted cash flow models is not whether the results predict the future, but how many hidden or misunderstood factors the analysis has revealed for the real estate investor. If few or none, simpler methods such as the rules of thumb are likely to work just as well. If several factors are illuminated and, for the first time, subject to closer examination, discounted cash flow models are likely to be indispensable. In no case should the investor measure the success of the discounted cash flow analysis based on the prediction of the future.

superior information about market activity suggests opportunities for *arbitrage returns*, or the identification of undervalued assets available for sale.

Discounted cash flow analysis is often deemed useful whether markets are efficient or not. In inefficient markets, this technique can be used to identify projects that are undervalued. In efficient markets, discounted cash flow analysis can be one of the techniques that assists investors in maintaining market efficiency.

CALCULATING THE INVESTMENT VALUE OF EQUITY (*E*)

We can now develop the *investment value of equity* (*E*) model. This model provides the investor with an approach that can then be compared with the market (or asking) price to see if it is an acceptable investment. This measure emphasizes the equity position of the investor and values two major components: *after-tax cash flow* and *after-tax equity reversion*. Of course, emphasis is also placed on the decision rules for making the analysis.

Present Value of After-tax Cash Flow

The preceding example calculated investment values using cash flows as measures of benefits. In valuing the portion attributable to the equity holder, the analyst can choose which type of cash flow measure to use. However, there are many reasons why an investor would prefer to use an after-tax cash flow figure.

Chapter 1 defined *after-tax cash flow* as net operating income less debt service less tax payments. This can be represented as

$$\text{ATCF}_t = \text{NOI}_t - \text{DS}_t - \text{T}_t \tag{12-4}$$

where

ATCF_t = after-tax cash flow in the *t*th period
NOI_t = net operating income in the *t*th period
DS_t = debt service in the *t*th period
T_t = income tax liability in the *t*th period

Furthermore, we can split debt service into two components: interest expense and principal amortization:

$$\text{DS}_t = \text{I}_t + \text{A}_t \tag{12-5}$$

where

I_t = interest expense in the *t*th period
A_t = principal amortization in the *t*th period

Recall that income taxes are calculated by multiplying the investor's marginal tax rate times net operating income plus the replacement reserve less interest expense less depreciation, or

$$\text{T}_t = \tau(\text{NOI}_t + \text{RR}_t - \text{I}_t - \text{D}_t) \tag{12-6}$$

where

$$\tau = \text{investor's marginal tax rate}$$
$$\text{RR}_t = \text{reserve for replacement in the } t\text{th period}$$
$$\text{D}_t = \text{depreciation allowance in the } t\text{th period}$$

By substituting Equations (12-5) and (12-6) into Equation (12-4) we get:

$$\text{ATCF}_t = \text{NOI}_t - (\text{I}_t + \text{A}_t) - \tau(\text{NOI}_t + \text{RR}_t - \text{I}_t - \text{D}_t) \qquad (12\text{-}7)$$

Note that the depreciation allowance affects the after-tax cash flow only in the last term of Equation (12-7). The benefits of depreciation result from a reduction in income tax liability and, in this way, depreciation allowances increase the after-tax cash flow to the investor.

Therefore we can calculate the discounted value of the after-tax cash flows with this basic model:

$$\text{PV of ATCF} = \frac{\text{ATCF}_1}{(1 + k_e)^1} + \frac{\text{ATCF}_2}{(1 + k_e)^2} + \frac{\text{ATCF}_3}{(1 + k_e)^3} + \cdots + \frac{\text{ATCF}_n}{(1 + k_e)^n}$$

$$= \sum_{t=1}^{n} \frac{\text{ATCF}_t}{(1 + k_e)^t} \qquad (12\text{-}8)$$

where

$$\text{PV of ATCF} = \text{present value of after-tax cash flow stream}$$
$$k_e = \text{required rate of return on equity}$$

This formula represents the discounted value of after-tax cash flows for the expected holding period. It permits after-tax cash flow estimates to be constant each period as in an annuity, or permits the cash flows to vary from year to year as in the typical investment.

Present Value of After-tax Equity Reversion

However, Equation (12-8) fails to take into account *the expected selling price at the end of the nth year, the satisfaction of the unpaid mortgage note, or taxes due at the time of sale* (capital gains, recapture, or minimum taxes). A better valuation model would take account of these factors, since these affect the cash flow to the investor at the time of sale. Therefore the analyst needs to incorporate these considerations into one model. Equation (12-9) provides the necessary measure: *the after-tax equity reversion*:

$$\text{ATER}_n = \text{SP}_n - \text{SE}_n - \text{UM}_n - \text{GT}_n \qquad (12\text{-}9)$$

where

ATER_n = after-tax equity reversion at the end of the nth period
SP_n = estimated net selling price at the end of the nth period
UM_n = unpaid mortgage balance at the end of the nth period
GT_n = taxes on total gain at the end of the nth period
SE_n = selling expenses

Since ATER does not result in a positive cash flow for the investor until the nth period (year), the value of this component can be found as follows:

$$\text{PV of ATER} = \frac{\text{ATER}_n}{(1 + k_e)^n} \qquad (12\text{-}10)$$

where

PV of ATER = present value of after-tax equity reversion

Therefore, by combining Equations (12-8) and (12-10), we get the complete equity valuation model:

$$E = (\text{PV of ATCF}) + (\text{PV of ATER})$$

$$= \frac{\text{ATCF}_1}{(1 + k_e)^1} + \frac{\text{ATCF}_2}{(1 + k_e)^2} + \frac{\text{ATCF}_3}{(1 + k_e)^3} + \cdots + \frac{\text{ATCF}_n}{(1 + k_e)^n} + \frac{\text{ATER}_n}{(1 + k_e)^n} \qquad (12\text{-}11)$$

$$= \sum_{t=1}^{n} \frac{\text{ATCF}_t}{(1 + k_e)^t} + \frac{\text{ATER}_n}{(1 + k_e)^n}$$

Whenever ATER_n is positive, analysts who neglect the impact of the after-tax equity reversion and rely solely on the after-tax cash flow benefits will calculate a lower value than desirable. Therefore the inclusion of the reversion is important to valuing income-producing real estate, and Equation (12-10), which measures the investment value of equity (E), is a more realistic model.

As an example, suppose we wish to value an investment with the following five-year net operating income stream and expected selling price at the end of the fifth year:

YEAR	NOI	SP
1	$10,000	
2	12,000	
3	15,000	
4	15,000	
5	20,000	$150,000

Assume that the reserve for replacements is $2,000 per year, interest payments vary according to a level-payment amortization schedule of $50,000 borrowed at 9 percent annually for twenty-five years, and depreciation is deducted on the basis of $75,000 over a depreciable life of 27.5 years using the straight-line method. The investor's marginal tax rate is .28.

Using these data, we can calculate the annual tax liability, using Equation (12-6):

YEAR	NOI ($)	+	RR ($)	−	I ($)	−	D ($)	=	T* ($)
1	10,000		2,000		4,500.00		2,727		1,366.44
2	12,000		2,000		4,484.70		2,727		1,900.72
3	15,000		2,000		4,468.02		2,727		2,745.39
4	15,000		2,000		4,449.85		2,727		2,750.48
5	20,000		2,000		4,430.09		2,727		4,156.01

*See the following table.

A table can now be developed to calculate the annual after-tax cash flow, using Equation (12-7):

YEAR	NOI ($)	−	I ($)	−	A ($)	−	T ($)	=	ATCF ($)
1	10,000		4,500.00		170.00		1,336.44		3,993.56
2	12,000		4,484.70		185.30		1,900.72		5,429.28
3	15,000		4,468.02		201.98		2,745.39		7,584.61
4	15,000		4,449.85		220.15		2,750.48		7,579.52
5	20,000		4,430.09		239.97		4,156.01		11,173.99

Finally, the after-tax equity reversion can be calculated, using Equation (12-9):

YEAR	SP ($)	−	UM ($)	−	GT ($)	=	ATER ($)
1							
2							
3							
4							
5	150,000		48,982.60		24,817.80		76,199.60

If we assume k_e equal to 12 percent, we can get the two components of E:

$$\text{PV of ATCF} = \frac{\$3,993.56}{(1.12)^1} + \frac{\$5,429.28}{(1.12)^2} + \frac{\$7,584.61}{(1.12)^3} + \frac{\$7,579.52}{(1.12)^4} + \frac{\$11,173.99}{(1.12)^5}$$

$$= \$24,449.79$$

$$\text{PV of ATER} = \frac{\$76,199.60}{(1.12)^5}$$

$$= \$43,237.70$$

Therefore the investment value of equity (E) is \$65,896.84, using Equation (12-11).

$$E = \$24,449.79 + \$43,237.70$$
$$= \$67,687.49$$

The analyst would be willing to pay up to \$67,687.49 in equity for the property. The following discussion examines the decision rules in more detail.

THE NET PRESENT VALUE DECISION RULES

When using investment models, it is important to decide whether an investment is acceptable or not and, if so, how attractive it is relative to other alternatives, especially if some of these are mutually exclusive. In fact, one of the major criticisms of the rules of thumb has been the lack of consistent decision rules. For example, how short a payback period should the minimally acceptable project have if payback methods are used? How high can the gross income multiplier become before the investment ceases to be attractive? Clearly, there are no objective answers to these questions. The traditional answers often result in more rules of thumb.

Using the investment value of equity model developed in this section, we can define an acceptable investment project as one that minimally earns the required rate of return. Using Equation (12-11), we get a value for E. Since the initial amount of mortgage debt, MD, must be known in order to calculate the debt service, we next develop an investment value for the *total investment* by adding E and MD. Then this sum is compared with the market value. If this value (E + MD) is greater than market's sales price (or market value), the investor should invest in the project because it would earn more than the required rate of return and increase the investor's wealth. If the market value is greater than the sum of E and MD, the investor would not be able to achieve the required rate of return and should reject it.

Therefore, if the investment value for the total capital is greater than the market value, this excess value is the *net present value* of the investment. As long as the net present value is greater than zero, investment in the project will increase the investor's wealth and the investor should accept all projects with positive net present values.

Decision Rule 1: Using investment value of equity and mortgage debt, if

$$(E + \text{MD}) \geq \text{MV, then NPV} \geq 0, \text{ and if}$$
$$(E + \text{MD}) < \text{MV, then NPV} < 0.$$

Following the example, E is calculated to be \$67,687.49 and MD is \$50,000. Since \$117,687.49 is greater than \$75,000, the decision rule tells the investor to accept the investment (NPV is equal to \$42,687.49).

An alternative approach is to develop a decision rule using E directly. Since Equation (12-11) calculates E, some analysts might prefer a decision rule using E, which indicates whether or not to accept the investment. This can be accomplished by modifying Decision Rule 1 as follows:

Decision Rule 2: Using investment value of equity, if

$$E \geq (MV - MD), \text{ then NPV} \geq 0, \text{ and if}$$

$$E < (MV - MD), \text{ then NPV} < 0.$$

Using the numbers from the example, \$67,687.49 is greater than \$25,000, so this decision rule also tells the investor to accept the investment.

Obviously, Decision Rules 1 and 2 are consistent. Both provide identical measures of net present value. Both indicate whether or not the wealth of the investor will increase if the investment is acquired.

CALCULATING THE INTERNAL RATE OF RETURN ON EQUITY (IRR$_e$)

An alternative framework for making real estate investment decisions uses a measure called the *internal rate of return*. It is similar to net present value but potentially inconsistent with the foregoing techniques. The *internal rate of return* is defined as the annual rate that equates the present value of the cash inflows with the present value of the cash outflows. In real estate investment analysis, the *internal rate of return on equity* (IRR$_e$) is the measure preferred by most investors.

The Internal Rate of Return Calculation

The internal rate of return on equity, IRR$_e$, in equation form is represented as follows:

$$0 = \frac{ATCF_1}{(1 + IRR_e)^1} + \frac{ATCF_2}{(1 + IRR_e)^2} + \frac{ATCF_3}{(1 + IRR_e)^3}$$

$$+ \cdots + \frac{ATCF_n}{(1 + IRR_e)^n} + \frac{ATER_n}{(1 + IRR_e)^n} - (MV - MD) \qquad (12\text{-}12)$$

$$= \sum_{t=1}^{n} \frac{ATCF_t}{(1 + IRR_e)^t} + \frac{ATER_n}{(1 + IRR_e)^n} - (MV - MD)$$

Using the numbers from the example discussed earlier, we get the following internal rate of return on equity:

$$0 = \frac{\$3,993.56}{(1 + IRR_e)^1} + \frac{\$5,429.28}{(1 + IRR_e)^2} + \frac{\$7,584.61}{(1 + IRR_e)^3} + \frac{\$7,579.52}{(1 + IRR_e)^4}$$

$$+ \frac{\$11,173.99}{(1 + IRR_e)^5} + \frac{\$76,199.60}{(1 + IRR_e)^5} - (\$75,000 - \$50,000)$$

$$IRR_e = 42.22\%$$

In this case, 42.22 percent represents the yield or time-adjusted rate of return to the equity investor.

Technically, however, a multiperiod internal rate of return cannot be calculated directly. The analyst must (a) approximate the internal rate of return by trial-and-error and center in on the value, (b) use a calculator or computer to approximate the answer using one of several mathematical techniques, or (c) find the rate of return, IRR_e, that makes E equal to $(MV - MD)$ (i.e., where NPV = 0). This last suggestion is actually the condition under which the internal rate of return on equity is derived.

THE INTERNAL RATE OF RETURN DECISION RULE

After a value for IRR_e is derived, the analyst must evaluate the attractiveness of the investment. The following decision rule can be quite helpful.

Decision Rule 3: Using internal rate of return on equity, if

$$IRR_e \geq k_e, \text{ then } NPV \geq 0, \text{ and if}$$

$$IRR_e < k_e, \text{ then } NPV < 0.$$

In this example, 42.22 percent is greater than 12.00 percent, so the investor should invest in the project.

A few words of clarification are in order. First, although the use of the investment value of equity model and the internal rate of return on equity are closely related, there are some important differences. A comparison of Decision Rules 1 and 2 with Decision Rule 3 reveals that in all the rules, a favorable project is indicated by a positive net present value. Whenever one of the rules indicates an "accept" signal, the other two will indicate it as well. Therefore it is impossible to get conflicting "accept-reject" signals between the net present value (investment value of equity) and internal rate of return (on equity) techniques. Second, although the decision rules are consistent about final outcomes, they do not rank projects identically. Finally, despite the close relationship between these two approaches, there is much to lose if the analyst chooses the internal rate of return as a "matter of preference."

WHICH DCF TECHNIQUE SHOULD BE USED?

One of the most frequently discussed issues in the capital budgeting literature is the comparison between net present value and internal rate of return. A summary of the important issues is presented here.

Either Technique Chooses an Identical Set of Investments

It is possible to decide whether an investment is acceptable by using either the internal rate of return method or the net present value method. Consider an investment that has a net present value greater than zero. This means that the discounted value of the benefits, *at some discount rate*, is greater than the investment outlay. At a higher discount rate, the net present value will be lower.[1] Suppose further that the net present value is still positive at the higher discount rate. At some discount rate, the net present value is equal to zero. This rate is also equivalent to the internal rate of return.

Therefore, whenever the net present value is greater than zero, the internal rate of return will be greater than the discount rate used to calculate the NPV. In these cases, both criteria indicate "accept." For conventional cash flow streams, this result will always hold. A similar demonstration can be made when net present values are negative. If the internal rate of return is less than the discount rate, both criteria indicate "reject."

The conclusion is important: Since both criteria provide the same results with respect to choosing attractive investment opportunities, either may be used to make the accept-reject decision. Either technique will choose the identical set of investments because the criteria provide identical decisions. However, *both techniques will not rank projects identically*. When considering mutually exclusive projects, this observation is essential to avoid selecting investments that conflict with the goal of wealth maximization.

Ranking Problems Between the Techniques

If two (or more) alternative investments are mutually exclusive or if capital is limited, ranking problems may occur when comparing the results under the net present value and internal rate of return criteria. These problems can occur when the projects are of different sizes or when the timing of the cash flows is substantially different. However, these conditions are insufficient to obtain ranking differences between the investments.

For example, suppose we are considering two mutually exclusive alternatives: investments A and B.[2] Each requires outlays of $25,000 in equity. (Table 12-1 compares their expected after-tax cash flows and estimated after-tax

---

[1] An exception is if the cash flow stream is nonconventional (i.e., if negative cash flows are expected to occur during the life of the investment after one or more positive cash flows). Therefore, throughout our discussion, a conventional cash flow stream is assumed and defined as a cash outflow followed by a series of cash inflows.

[2] As an example of two investments being mutually exclusive, consider the case in which both investments are considered for the same site.

TABLE 12-1   Example of Two Mutually Exclusive Investments

| | INVESTMENTS | | | |
| | A | | B | |
YEAR	ATCF ($)	ATER ($)	ATCF ($)	ATER ($)
0	(25,000)		(25,000)	
1	15,000		1,000	
2	5,000		2,000	
3	2,000	20,000	4,000	40,000

equity reversions.) Each has an expected holding period of three years. Upon examination of each project's cash flows, we see that investment A's are higher in the beginning of the holding period and the equity reversion is relatively small. Investment B has minimal cash flows but a large equity reversion.

Using the discounted cash flow model, we can calculate the net present value at various discount rates. It is also possible to calculate the internal rate of return for each investment (shown in Table 12-2). These results indicate that the net present value of each investment declines as the required rate of return on equity increases. However, due to the difference in timing of the cash flows, the net present value of investment B falls more quickly.

Figure 12-1 presents different net present values as a function of the discount rate. Both investments A and B are plotted on the graph. Note that when k_e is relatively low, the net present value of B is greater than the net present value of A. If the discount rate is greater than about 15 percent, the

TABLE 12-2   Results of Net Present Value and Internal Rate of Return Analyses

| | INVESTMENTS | |
k_e (%)	A ($)	B ($)
0	17,000	22,000
5	12,825	15,775
10	9,298	10,620
15	6,290	6,313
20	3,704	2,685
25	1,464	(392)
30	(489)	(3,020)
35	(2,204)	(5,278)
40	(3,717)	(7,230)
IRR$_e$	28.68%	24.32%

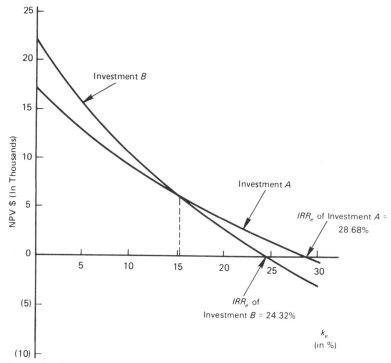

Source: Austin J. Jaffe and C. F. Sirmans, *Real Estate Investment Decision Making*, 1982,
p. 418. Reprinted by permission of Prentice-Hall, Englewood Cliffs, NJ.

Figure 12-1   NPV as a Function of k_e for Investments A and B.

net present value of A is greater than that of B.[3] Since the internal rate of
return is equal to the rate of discount when the net present value is equal
to zero, the IRR_e for investment A is 28.68 percent and the IRR_e for investment
B is 24.32 percent. Therefore the IRR_e for A is greater than for B, independent
of the value of the required rate of return on equity.[4]

But suppose the required rate of return for investments of this type is
12 percent. Using the net present value criterion, the investor finds the net
present value is higher for investment B than for investment A. At the same
time, the internal rate of return is higher for investment A. This is the ranking
problem that can develop when using net present value and the internal
rate of return to compare alternatives.

Table 12-3 summarizes the problem. The net present value method favors

[3] Actually, the specific value for the "crossover point" is 15.10 percent in this example.

[4] Recall that if $k_e > IRR_e$, then NPV < 0 and the investment would be rejected. This is
shown at rates higher than 28.68 percent and 24.32 percent for investments A and B, respectively.

TABLE 12-3   Possible Ranking Problems Using Net Present Value and Internal Rate of Return

	INVESTMENTS	
	A	B
Net Present Value*		∨
Internal Rate of Return	∨	

* At certain required rates of return on equity.

investment B over A, if $k_e < 15.10$ percent. The internal rate of return method favors investment A over B in all cases. Given that these investments are mutually exclusive, the investor is forced to choose either A or B even though there is a conflict between the criteria. So which investment should be acquired and why?

Thus the investor would choose one investment if the net present value method is used and the other if the internal rate of return is used. What can the investor do?

One way to solve this problem is to evaluate the investor's wealth position under each alternative. In choosing B, the investor is better off because the net present value is greater. By choosing A, the internal rate of return is higher, but the net present value is lower. Therefore, following the internal rate of return rule results in the selection of a project that is less valuable for the investor *despite its higher rate of return*. This result may shock those who prefer the internal rate of return approach. Nonetheless, the investor would not benefit by choosing the investment with the lower net present value, even if it has a higher internal rate of return.

The Reinvestment Rate Issue

Another basis for comparison is what happens to the cash flows earned by an investor during the investment period. Is there any difference in the *presumption* about the reinvestment of cash flows using the net present value method or the internal rate of return method?

Some may argue that there is no reinvestment presumption at all, since E and IRR_e do not imply that anything must be done with the cash flows. In other words, the investor may be just as well off by spending the cash flows as by reinvesting them. However, to the extent that the analyst must value the opportunity cost of the reinvested proceeds by spending the cash flows, it seems much more appropriate to use the discount rate, k_e, rather than IRR_e as the rate. Following this line of reasoning, the internal rate of return method poses a problem regarding the choice of a reinvestment rate.

Nonexistent or Multiple Rates of Return

It is possible to have two or more internal rates of return that are *each mathematically correct*. These occur when negative cash flows are expected to appear in a future period with positive cash flows expected the period(s) before and after the negative one(s). This condition renders the calculation of internal rate of return useless.

In the event that more than one value for IRR_e solves the formula, the investor would have a difficult time deciding the investment's rate of return. Is it the higher one (30 percent) or the lower one (10 percent) or both? Let us assume that the required rate of return is in between (20 percent). If the "right" rate of return is 30 percent, the investor rejects the investment. However, it could be either. The analyst cannot determine what to do if a multiple solution is found.

Some analysts suggest solving for E, using the required rate of return on equity of 20 percent in this case. If the net present value is greater than zero, accept the investment and the problem is solved. What this means is that one must use the net present value approach to make the decision because the internal rate of return method will not result in a solution in this case.

ADVANCED TECHNIQUES AND MEASURES OF PERFORMANCE

Additional methods have been developed to improve previous measures or to evaluate different problems. This brief section introduces some of the concepts and techniques typically found in more advanced books.

Profitability Index (PI)

One of the criticisms of the internal rate of return techniques is that comparisons on the basis of values of IRR_e failed to consider the size of the investments. To deal with this problem, analysts relied on the *benefit-cost ratio* (sometimes called the profitability index). This provided a measure of "benefits per dollar of cost" and corrected a shortcoming of the internal rate of return.

For real estate investments, *the profitability index* (PI) is defined as

$$PI = \frac{E}{MV - MD}$$

$$= \frac{\sum_{t=1}^{n} \frac{ATCF_t}{(1 + k_e)^t} + \frac{ATER_n}{(1 + k_e)^n}}{MV - MD} \tag{12-13}$$

The profitability index, therefore, is the ratio of the investment value of equity, E, to the required equity outlay ($MV - MD$) for investment alternatives.

When the investment value of equity is greater than or equal to the equity outlay, the investor should accept the investment. When the investment value of equity is less than the equity outlay, the investment should be rejected.

Another way of specifying the decision rule follows.

PI Decision Rule: Using the profitability index, if

$$PI \geq 1.00, \text{ then NPV} \geq 0, \text{ and if}$$
$$PI < 1.00, \text{ then NPV} < 0.$$

Since the profitability index is a ratio of the present value of the equity benefits to initial equity cost, if this ratio is greater than 1.00, the benefits will exceed the costs, the net present value of the investment is positive and the investment should be accepted. If the ratio is less than 1.00, the present value of the benefits is less than the costs, and the net present value of the project is negative. In this case, the investment should be rejected.

Adjusted Internal Rate of Return (AIRR)

The *adjusted internal rate of return* (AIRR) category contains a number of techniques that were motivated by dissatisfaction with the original internal rate of return. The typical adjustments deal with either the reinvestment rate problem or the possibilities of the multiple rate of return problems. Some models deal with both.

The results vary, although some of the advanced models avoid some of the internal rate of return problems. Much of this work was done by analysts such as Strung,[5] who sought to get a rate of return method free of the problems outlined in the previous section.

The major difficulty with these models is that for the most part, no new information is derived by a "perfected internal rate of return." After all, if there are ranking problems compared to net present value, differences will remain between the investment value of equity approach and the adjusted internal rate of return approach. If a particular model solves all the inconsistencies with wealth-maximization criteria (i.e., maximizing net present value), then nothing new is gained because the net present value result is already available. The point is that this argument raises some serious questions about the benefits to be gained by investors using these measures.

Financial Management Rate of Return (FMRR)

One of the more highly regarded measures is the *financial management rate of return* (FMRR). Developed in 1975, it has attracted a wide following

---

[5] Joseph Strung, "The Internal Rate of Return and the Reinvestment Presumptions," *Appraisal Journal*, 44 (January 1976), pp. 23–33.

**Exhibit 12-3   Which DCF Model Should
Investors Use?**

For several years, a raging controversy has developed over which of the two major discounted cash flow models investors should use in financial decision making, including real estate investment analysis. Many investors and several textbook writers prefer the internal rate of return. Many authors and fewer real-world investors prefer the net present value model. Some authors and investors advocate their own models, either as modifications or extensions of the basic model or as different formulations. Some advocate the use of both the internal rate of return and the net present value models under the idea that "more techniques are better than fewer techniques."

The question often raised is, Which model should investors use? Theory suggests that if the goal of the investor is to maximize his or her wealth through investing, the net present value model (or one of several variations) will rank and select projects in a manner that is consistent with this goal. Therefore it is well suited to many investment problems.

On the other hand, practitioners have always been uncomfortable with the idea of basing decisions on net present value numbers and have traditionally preferred rates of return. The most popular calculation in modern real estate investment analysis is the internal rate of return. Although this model is subject to criticism about some of its assumptions (as is the net present value model), this rate of return measure is superior to several others in that it provides a "rate of return per annum" and properly evaluates the return over the entire period under analysis.

In many ways, the choice between using the net present value and the internal rate of return can be reduced to identifying investor objectives and personal tastes. There is little question that the latter has been the favorite in many real estate and other financial markets. On the other hand, the theoretical superiority of the former suggests that it should prevail if effective decision making is sought.

If the goal of the investor is to add as much wealth to his or her portfolio as possible from the real estate market, the use of net present value to select and, more importantly, to rank investment alternatives *cannot* be duplicated by the internal rate of return method. If a client or a superior requests an internal rate of return calculation, the analyst would be wise to provide it—in addition to performing the net present value analysis!

in a very short time.[6] It is basically a rate of return model that purports to solve the reinvestment presumption problem and the possibility of multiple rates of return. It uses a holding period rate of return measure that may result in differences from an internal rate of return calculation.

There are many attractive elements about the FMRR model. However, much of the conceptual basis and the reinvestment presumptions have been questioned in recent years. Still, it is too early to judge the degree of acceptance and the amount of reliance placed on this technique.

THE IMPORTANCE OF DISCOUNTED
CASH FLOW MODELS

Discounted cash flow models are fundamental to modern real estate investment analysis. Since they are more flexible and robust than traditional appraisal techniques and investment rules of thumb, they are likely to provide more and, in some cases, better information. However, the use of these techniques does not imply that the analyst can foretell the future. Although the analyst is required to estimate what cash flows will be in the future, this is done with available information at the time he or she is making the investment decision. It is presumed that there is uncertainty associated with the valuation estimate. It is for this reason that risk analysis is required in order to better decide whether or not the investment should be purchased.

Thus the investor does not predict the future using discounted cash flow models; no one can do that except perhaps fortune tellers. Discounted cash flow models permit the analyst to systematically evaluate several economic effects on the investment choice in a world of uncertainty. Since the basic discounted cash flow models imply that risk analysis can be captured through the use of the appropriate discount rate or the required rate of return on equity, net present value and internal rate of return models can be used as shown. However, on the issue of risk analysis, the analyst begs the question if the measurement of risk is presumed at the start of the analysis. Therefore it is necessary to explicitly incorporate risk analysis into discounted cash flow models. This is done in the next chapter.

QUESTIONS

12-1. What are the basic discounted cash flow models?

12-2. "Discounted cash flow models are useful whether real estate markets are efficient or inefficient." True or false? Explain.

12-3. The text lists four reasons why discounted cash flow models are better tools for real estate investors than traditional methods. What are these reasons?

---

[6] Stephen D. Messner and M. Chapman Findlay III, "Real Estate Investment Analysis: IRR versus FMRR," *Real Estate Appraiser*, 41 (July–August 1975), pp. 5–20.

12-4. What is the investment value of equity? Why is the figure useful?

12-5. What is the internal rate of return on equity? How is this rate of return used?

12-6. What is the relationship between Decision Rules 1 and 2 using the investment value of equity? Between Decision Rules 1, 2, and 3?

12-7. There are several issues involved in comparing the internal rate of return and the net present value methods. What are the issues?

12-8. What is the profitability index? How does it compare with the other discounted cash flow models and criteria?

12-9. What is the FMRR? Describe how it is calculated and compare it with the other models, especially the internal rate of return.

12-10. Do investors who use discounted cash flow models need to predict the future? Why or why not?

PROBLEMS

12-1. Consider the following set of cash flows and reversion:

	INVESTMENT	
YEAR	ATCF ($)	ATER ($)
0	(10,000)	
1	10,000	
2	20,000	
3	20,000	
4	25,000	50,000

a. What is the net present value of equity if k_e equals 10 percent?
b. What is the net present value of equity if k_e equals 15 percent?
c. What is the present value of equity if k_e equals 25 percent?
d. What is the internal rate of return on equity?
e. Should the investment be accepted under all cases?

12-2. A real estate investor is considering an investment with the following expected cash flows and reversion:

	INVESTMENT	
YEAR	ATCF ($)	ATER ($)
1	10,000	
2	10,500	
3	12,000	
4	11,000	
5	13,000	
6	10,000	140,000

What is the maximum that the investor can pay and earn a 15 percent rate of return?

12-3. Another investor is considering an investment that has a total cost of $500,000. The following information is obtained from analyzing the market:
   a. Rent = $200 per unit per month
   b. Number of units = 50
   c. Vacancies = 7 percent
   d. Operating expenses = $48,000
   e. Loan-to-value ratio = .80
   f. Interest rate on mortgage = 10 percent
   g. Maturity of mortgage = 25 years (with annual payments)
   h. Depreciable basis = 85 percent of total cost
   i. Depreciation method = straight-line
   j. Useful life = 27.5 years
   k. Expected reversion growth = 10 percent over holding period
   l. Holding period = 5 years
   m. Tax rate = .28
   n. Required rate of return on equity = .16
   o. Rental growth rate = 5 percent per year
   p. Operating expense growth rate = 5 percent per year
   q. Financing costs = $16,000 amortized over life of mortgage
   r. Prepayment penalty = .06 of outstanding balance
   Should the investor buy the project? Why or why not?

12-4. Consider the following set of cash flows and reversion:

	INVESTMENT	
	ATCF	ATER
YEAR	($)	($)
0	(100,000)	
1	10,000	
2	8,000	
3	19,000	
4	20,000	
5	15,000	
6	−10,000	
7	30,000	
8	15,000	140,000

   a. What is the net present value, using k_e = 15 percent?
   b. What is the profitability index?
   c. What is the adjusted internal rate of return, using r = 8 percent?
   d. What is the adjusted internal rate of return, using r = 12 percent?
   e. What is the FMRR, using r = 10 percent?
   f. What is the net terminal value, using r = 15 percent?
   g. What is the net present value of the net terminal value of equity, using r = 14 percent?

12-5. There is an office building for sale at a price of $3 million. The building is 60,000 square feet of which one-sixth is common area. The building leases space at $12 per square foot, per year, and is operating at a 90 percent occupancy rate. Rents are expected to grow at a rate of 5 percent per year and the occupancy rate should remain constant over the next ten years. The building is currently divided into fifty units with each renting five parking spaces per month at $5 per month, per space. In addition, each of the tenants at the end of the year must contribute equally to the $15,000 of common area maintenance costs. The building currently has operating expenses of 40 percent of effective gross income, and these are expected to increase by 5 percent each year. Financing available to the investing company consists of two mortgages. The first mortgage is $2 million at a 12 percent interest rate of twenty-five years. Financing costs will be 5 percent with an additional 5 percent prepayment penalty on the outstanding balance. In addition, the seller will offer the buyer a second mortgage of $500,000 of the purchase price at a rate of 15 percent over the investor's seven-year expected holding period. Should the investing company purchase the building if it has a 34 percent marginal rate and requires a 15 percent return?

12-6. An apartment building is available for purchase for a price of $3,500,000. The complex contains a total of 225 units in which 100 are one-bedroom units and 125 are two-bedroom units. The following additional information is available.

One bedroom:
  Rent = $350/month
  Vacancy rate = 6%

Two bedroom:
  Rent = $400/month
  Vacancy rate = 8%

Rental growth rate = 5%

Operating expenses in the first year =
  $426,060
  Operating expense growth rate = 7%
Land to value = 20%
Depreciable life = 27.5 years
Financing:
  1st mortgage = $2,000,000
    Interest rate = 13%
    Term = 25 yrs. (monthly payments)
    Points = 4
    Prepayment penalty = 6% of
      outstanding balance

Replacement Reserve Account
  # of refrigerators = 10
    Cost per unit = $350
    Expected economic life = 15 yrs.
  # of stoves = 10
    Cost of unit = $300
    Expected economic life = 15 yrs.
  # of carpets = 25
    Cost per unit = $500
    Expected economic life = 6 yrs.
  # of drapes = 25
    Cost per unit = $150
    Expected economic life = 6 yrs.

2nd mortgage = $800,000
  Interest rate = 16%
  Term = 15 yrs. (monthly payments)

The investor believes that in 6 years the building will increase in value approximately 14% to an expected selling price of $4,000,000. Selling expenses are expected to be 8%. The investor is currently subject to a 28% marginal tax rate which is expected to remain constant throughout the holding period. If the investor requires a 14% rate of return, should the projected project be accepted?

SELECTED REFERENCES

COOPER, JAMES R., and STEPHEN A. PYHRR, "Forecasting the Rates of Return on an Apartment Investment: A Case Study," *Appraisal Journal*, 41 (July 1973), 312–37.

HANFORD, LLOYD D., JR., "The Use of Discount Cash Flow Analysis," *Real Estate Appraiser*, 39 (November–December 1973), 31–34.

HETTENHOUSE, GEORGE W., and JOHN J. DEE, "A Component Analysis of Rates of Return in Real Estate Investment," *American Real Estate and Urban Economics Association Journal*, 4 (Spring 1976), 7–22.

HIGGINS, ROBERT C., and R. HUGH CUNNINGHAM, "Computerized Calculations—Rate of Return and Risks in Commercial Property," *Appraisal Journal*, 38 (January 1970), 37–49.

JAFFE, AUSTIN J., "Is There a 'New' Internal Rate of Return Literature?" *American Real Estate and Urban Economics Association Journal*, 5 (Winter 1977), 482–502.

————, and C. F. SIRMANS, *Real Estate Investment Decision Making*. Englewood Cliffs, N.J.: Prentice-Hall, Inc., 1982.

MESSNER, STEPHEN D., and M. CHAPMAN FINDLAY III, "Real Estate Investment Analysis: IRR versus FMRR," *Real Estate Appraiser*, 41 (July–August 1975), 5–20.

ZERBST, ROBERT H., "Evaluating Risks by Partitioning the IRR," *Real Estate Review*, 9 (Winter 1980), 80–84.

13

RISK ANALYSIS

The preceding chapter developed and illustrated the two basic discounted cash flow models. This chapter explicitly introduces risk into the analysis. The importance of the analysis of risk cannot be overemphasized. Discounted cash flow analysis in a world of certainty is relatively straightforward and simple once the mechanics have been learned. After the costs and benefits have been estimated, the outcome of the investment becomes a function of the likelihood of success or failure. It is not surprising that the analysis of risk has occupied the minds of numerous financial writers for the past thirty years as they have attempted to identify, measure, and analyze the effects of risk on rates of return and values.

This chapter begins with a brief discussion of the importance of risk analysis in real estate discounted cash flow models. It then reviews the various generations of risk analysis beginning with the early methods of analysis, the traditional and standard techniques, and the modern risk measures. All of these techniques can be viewed as extensions of the basic discounted cash flow models.

INTRODUCING RISK INTO DISCOUNTED CASH FLOW MODELS

Because we live in an uncertain world, investors cannot forecast future cash flows with complete accuracy. However, the development of better information, techniques of analysis, and an understanding of the conceptual relationships between parameters in the world can reduce the risk the investor faces when making investment decisions. This is one of the primary motivations for analyzing real estate investment projects.

Given that all investment decisions are made with an element of risk, risk analysis is very relevant. Without it, the decision might easily be less favorable. Also, since all decisions involve risk, it is impossible to avoid it. Therefore these next two chapters provide various measures, decision rules, and analyses for decision makers who want to choose between alternatives in an uncertain world.

Why Risk Analysis is Essential

In a world without risk, all outcomes would be known with certainty. Therefore the probability of receiving an amount of cash flow in a future year would be 100 percent certain. Real estate investment analysis in such a world would be a relatively easy pursuit: select those projects with the highest discounted after-tax cash flows and after-tax equity reversions over the required investment costs.[1] This is the precise method of investment analysis suggested by Chapter 12. However, once we allow for the fact that few cash flows or reversions *are* known with certainty, the problem of risk is introduced. The following demonstrates why risk analysis is so important.

Imagine an investor who is faced with deciding which, if any, of three mutually exclusive investments to acquire. Suppose the investor estimates the after-tax cash flows for each alternative as shown in Table 13-1.[2]

Assuming that the acquisition cost of each of these investments is identical, the investor might initially decide on investment X, which promises to yield $1,000 per year *regardless of the state of the world*. On the other hand, the investment promises to return $500 per year if the factory does not locate in the city, *but* $1,500 per year if it does. (The presumption, of course, is that the location decision of the factory owners will increase the demand for investment Y, which may be an apartment building to house workers.) Investment Y may be preferable to investment X, since a positive decision by the factory owners would increase the after-tax cash flow by $500 per year under this alternative. Finally, the investor may be interested in investment Z *despite* the low estimates of after-tax cash flow under two outcomes, since the third has such a favorable impact. (The presumption is that without rent control and with a restrictive growth policy, the investor would receive higher cash flow payments than if rent control or urban growth were permitted.)

---

[1] Note that in a world of certainty, the future benefits (or costs) would be discounted by the risk-free rate. This is the rate at which consumers and producers have to be compensated annually in order for them to give up their respective consumption and investment plans.

[2] For illustrative purposes, Table 13-1 ignores the after-tax equity reversion and assumes that each after-tax cash flow for each "state of the world" is constant for each year of the expected holding period.

TABLE 13-1   After-Tax Cash Flow Estimates for Investments X, Y, and Z for Different States of the World*

		$
Investment X		
ATCF$_x$		1,000
Investment Y		
ATCF$_{y1}$	(if factory does not locate in city)	500
ATCF$_{y2}$	(if factory locates in city)	1,500
Investment Z		
ATCF$_{z1}$	(if city passes rent control ordinance)	−250
ATCF$_{z2}$	(if city defeats rent control ordinance)	0
ATCF$_{z3}$	(if city defeats rent control ordinance *and* adopts a "no-growth" policy)	4,500

* Assume that the after-tax cash flow for each state of the world of each investment is constant each year.

However, the investor would be unable to make a very effective decision without considering whether these different states were likely to occur. The following cases demonstrate why.

In scenario I, suppose the investor is suspicious of the announcement that the factory will locate in the city. Also, suppose rent control is likely, although adoption of a no-growth policy is remote. Given these beliefs, the investor can make *probability estimates* about the likelihood of the occurrence of the events. Alternatively, suppose the investor has more faith in the announcement. The investor could assign a higher probability to the estimate of after-tax cash flows if the factory is expected to locate in the city, and assuming everything else is the same, the investor would view alternatives differently. We can call this situation scenario II.

Finally, imagine scenario III, where the factory owners convince the investor that there is a strong possibility of locating in the investor's city, the possibility of rent control legislation in the city is reduced, and the prospects for restrictive land-use controls through a no-growth policy are greater than before. The investor could analyze these effects as well.

Table 13-2 shows that investment X might be favored in scenario I, investment Y might be preferred in scenario II, and investment Z might be selected in scenario III. The word "might" is important, as we will see.

To understand the results in Table 13-2, a few terms must be defined. *Probability* is defined as the chance or likelihood that an event will occur. Thus, if there is no chance of this happening, the probability is zero. If the likelihood of an event occurring is certain, the probability is 100 percent. Therefore any probability of occurrence must be between zero and 100 percent.

Mathematically, we can represent probabilities as p_i, so that $0 \leq p_i \leq 1$ for all values of i (that is, the states of the world). In addition, the sum of all probabilities must equal one:

$$\sum_{i=1}^{m} p_i = 1.00 \tag{13-1}$$

TABLE 13-2   Expected After-Tax Cash Flows for Investments X, Y, and Z Under Three Scenarios

Scenario I: Factory Favors Alternative City; No-Growth Policy Is Unlikely

INVESTMENTS

X		Y		Z	
ATCF ($)	p(ATCF)	ATCF ($)	p(ATCF)	ATCF ($)	p(ATCF)
1,000	1.00	500	.75	−250	.40
		1,500	.25	0	.50
				4,500	.10

$\overline{\text{ATCF}} = \$1,000$	$\overline{\text{ATCF}} = \$750$	$\overline{\text{ATCF}} = \$350$

Scenario II: Factory Favors Investor's City: No-Growth Policy Is Unlikely

INVESTMENTS

X		Y		Z	
ATCF ($)	p(ATCF)	ATCF ($)	p(ATCF)	ATCF ($)	p(ATCF)
1,000	1.00	500	.40	−250	.40
		1,500	.60	0	.50
				4,500	.10

$\overline{\text{ATCF}} = \$1,000$	$\overline{\text{ATCF}} = \$1,100$	$\overline{\text{ATCF}} = \$350$

Scenario III: Factory Favors Investor's City; Rent Control Is Unlikely; No-Growth Policy Is More Likely

INVESTMENTS

X		Y		Z	
ATCF ($)	p(ATCF)	ATCF ($)	p(ATCF)	ATCF ($)	p(ATCF)
1,000	1.00	500	.40	−250	.20
		1,500	.60	0	.50
				4,500	.30

$\overline{\text{ATCF}} = \$1,000$	$\overline{\text{ATCF}} = \$1,100$	$\overline{\text{ATCF}} = \$1,300$

where

m = number of occurrences or states of the world

To account for the various probabilities and their effects on the outcome, we must compute *expected values*. An expected value is the sum of each possible outcome multiplied by their probability of occurrence. Mathematically, the *expected after-tax cash flow* for each year is

$$\overline{\text{ATCF}}_t, = \text{ATCF}_{1t} \times p_t + \ldots + \text{ATCF}_{mt} \times p_{mt}$$

$$= \sum_{i=1}^{m} \text{ATCF}_{it} \times p_{it} \tag{13-2}$$

where

$\overline{\text{ATCF}}_t$ = expected after-tax cash flow for the tth year

ATCF_{it} = after-tax cash flow if the ith state of the world occurs in the tth year

p_{it} = probability of the ith state of the world in the tth year

Table 13-2 demonstrates how expected after-tax cash flow estimates change as a result of shifts in probabilities. This, of course, affects the attractiveness of investment opportunities. In scenario I, the uncertainty about the location decision results in investment X having the highest after-tax cash flow estimate. In scenario II, investment Y has the highest estimate of after-tax cash flow. With scenario III, the highest estimate of after-tax cash flow is found in investment Z.

At this point, the problem is to decide which of these investments, if any, should be chosen. Given the goal of wealth maximization, it seems logical that decision rules similar to the NPV decision rules in Chapter 12 could be developed to account for expected values. However, will this modification be sufficient to enable the investor to select the one consistent with personal goals?

The answer is no. However, the use of expected after-tax cash flows is a step in the right direction. The next logical step is to develop a method for estimating the *expected net present value of equity*, using expected after-tax cash flows and the expected after-tax equity reversion as calculation inputs. As we will see, the expected net present value and its subsequent decision rules will not solve the problem of risk because there is no reason to believe that all projects are equally risky.

To develop a measure of expected net present value of equity, we must define the *expected after-tax equity reversion*. When the discounted value of the expected after-tax equity reversion is added to the expected after-tax cash flow stream, discounted for the time value of money, the result is the expected net present value of equity. The expected after-tax equity reversion is equal to the possible after-tax equity reversion values for each state of the world times the probability of occurrence:

$$\overline{\text{ATER}}_n = \text{ATER}_{1n} \times p_{1n} + \text{ATER}_{2n} \times p_{2n}$$
$$+ \ldots + \text{ATER}_{mn} \times p_{mn}$$
$$= \sum_{t=1}^{m} \text{ATER}_{in} \times p_{in} \qquad (13\text{-}3)$$

where

$\overline{\text{ATER}}_n$ = expected after-tax equity reversion in the nth year

ATER_{in} = after-tax equity reversion if the ith state of the world occurs in the nth year

p_{in} = probability of the ith state of the world in the nth year

Therefore the discounted value of each expected after-tax cash flow and the discounted value of the expected after-tax equity reversion are equal to the expected net present value of equity when the required equity outlay is subtracted.[3]

$$\overline{\text{NPV}} = \frac{\text{ATCF}_1}{(1 + k_f)^1} + \frac{\text{ATCF}_2}{(1 + k_f)^2}$$

$$+ \ldots + \frac{\text{ATCF}_n}{(1 + k_f)^n} + \frac{\overline{\text{ATER}_n}}{(1 + k_f)^n} - (\text{MV} - \text{MD}) \qquad (13\text{-}4)$$

$$= \sum_{t=1}^{n} \frac{\overline{\text{ATCF}_t}}{(1 + k_f)^t} + \frac{\overline{\text{ATER}_n}}{(1 + k_f)^n} - (\text{MV} - \text{MD})$$

where

$\overline{\text{NPV}}$ = expected net present value of equity
k_f = risk-free rate

Returning to the example involving investments X, Y, and Z, if each expected after-tax cash flow is anticipated for a period of ten years, if each has a $5,000 required equity outlay, and if the risk-free rate is assumed to be 4 percent, we get the results reported in Table 13-3.

As we observed before, the expected cash flow outcomes vary as a result of the changes in probabilities and, now, as a result of the discounting process. It should be pointed out that the risk-free rate is chosen in the calculation of expected net present value of equity because risk is now accounted for by the probability distributions that affect the expected after-tax cash flows. As a result, the risk-free rate is the appropriate discount rate.

The results of expected net present values of equity in Table 13-3 for each investment under each scenario indicate preferences identical with the earlier analysis (Table 13-2). However, this is due to the assumption that each expected cash flow stream is an annuity, each requires the same amount of equity outlay, and each has an identical expected holding period. The fact that investment X under scenario I, investment Y under scenario II, or investment Z under scenario III might not be preferred for non-annuity expected cash flow streams or for investments with differing holding periods is not germane to this discussion. Instead we are primarily concerned with whether the development of expected net present values of equity will permit us to choose one alternative over another.

Unfortunately, it will not. We cannot be sure, for example, that investment Y is preferable to investments X and Z in scenario II because we do not

---

[3] This equation assumes that the after-tax cash flows in each year are statistically independent of each other and of the after-tax equity reversion.

TABLE 13-3 Expected Net Present Values for Equity for Investments X, Y, and Z Under Three Scenarios

---

SCENARIO I

$$\overline{NPV_X} = \sum_{t=1}^{10} \frac{\$1,000_t}{(1+.04)^t} - \$5,000 = \$3,110.90^*$$

$$\overline{NPV_Y} = \sum_{t=1}^{10} \frac{\$750_t}{(1+.04)^t} - \$5,000 = \$1,083.17$$

$$\overline{NPV_Z} = \sum_{t=1}^{10} \frac{\$350_t}{(1+.04)^t} - \$5,000 = -\$2,161.19$$

SCENARIO II

$$\overline{NPV_X} = \sum_{t=1}^{10} \frac{\$1,000_t}{(1+.04)^t} - \$5,000 = \$3,110.90$$

$$\overline{NPV_Y} = \sum_{t=1}^{10} \frac{\$1,100_t}{(1+.04)^t} - \$5,000 = \$3,921.99^*$$

$$\overline{NPV_Z} = \sum_{t=1}^{10} \frac{\$350_t}{(1+.04)^t} - \$5,000 = -2,161.19$$

SCENARIO III

$$\overline{NPV_X} = \sum_{t=1}^{10} \frac{\$1,000_t}{(1+.04)^t} - \$5,000 = \$3,110.90$$

$$\overline{NPV_Y} = \sum_{t=1}^{10} \frac{\$1,100}{(1+.04)^t} - \$5,000 = \$3,921.99$$

$$\overline{NPV_Z} = \sum_{t=1}^{10} \frac{\$1,300}{(1+.04)^t} - \$5,000 = \$5,544.16^*$$

---

* Designates the preferred investment.

know whether or not investment Y is a more risky investment. *As a result, adopting the goal of maximization of expected net present value of equity may be an improvement over the goal of maximization of net present value of equity independent of the likelihood of various states of the world occurring, but only if we are confident that risk is consistent for all projects under consideration.*

What we need is a method of analyzing risk in relation to expected net present value in order to compare projects on a sound basis. This requires the use of measures of risk based on the variability or dispersion of values. Two well-known measures of this type are the *variance* and *standard deviation*. These techniques were introduced in Chapter 4 and are discussed later in the chapter when they are used to measure risk. At this point, it is sufficient to understand the problem of risk and why it is essential that investors explicitly take it into account when making investment choices.

**Exhibit 13-1 Risk Analysis Is What
Investment Analysis Is All
About**

Real estate students and novice investors often seem to have peculiar preconceptions about the main objective of real estate investment analysis. Many believe that tax planning is the major part of the analysis. Others treat the financing decision as the primary focus. Still others regard the forecasting of income, cash flows, and property value growth rates as the chief elements in the process. While all of these activities have major roles, none gets at the actual crux of the real estate investment process. The real basis of investment analysis is the identification, measurement, and assessment of risk and the ways the investor can deal with risk. This activity is called *risk analysis*.

Risk analysis is fundamental because the calculation of cash flows (including income, expenses, financing costs, depreciation, future selling prices, and other items) would be a more mechanical exercise if risk did not exist. In such a world, all properties would easily and precisely be priced, and owners would know exactly what their rates of return would be for each investment. Competition would force prices of properties to their correct levels and the net present values of all investments would be zero; investors would purchase properties and would earn the market rate of return on each property. In this case, the rate of return would equal the risk-free rate.

In the real world, risk is an element in everyday life. The explicit specification of cash flow items attempts to provide the analyst with as much fundamental information as possible so that he or she can identify differences in properties and differences in their expected levels of risk. If the investor is successful, only "superior" projects will be purchased and less attractive ones will be rejected. Risk analysis may help investors sort out the array of available investment vehicles based on their expected returns and levels of risk.

This does not suggest that if an investor purchases a property, he or she is guaranteed to obtain an increase in investor wealth. Since all investment analysis is based on expectations, investors do the best they can with the information, skills, and judgment they possess *before* the project is selected. In a world with risk, the best analysis will not always ensure a successful venture; sometimes things go wrong, economic conditions change, or new information that is detrimental to the investment becomes available subsequent to the purchase. Note that this does not mean that the investor made any mistakes in performing the risk analysis prior to the acquisition of the investment. It merely means that, in retrospect, the analyst's best efforts did not result in a successful investment.

Risk analysis is what the investor needs to concentrate on once the mechanical aspects of investment analysis are understood. Computers are for calculating; investors are for thinking and analyzing. Real estate investment analysis is actually risk analysis.

ACCOUNTING FOR RISK IN DISCOUNTED CASH FLOW MODELS

There are many ways of accounting for risk and uncertainty using discounted cash flow models. Although others could be added, we include some of the well-known techniques: (a) conservatism, (b) risk-adjusted discount rates, (c) certainty-equivalent approach, (d) measures of variability, (e) decision trees and sensitivity analysis, (f) probabilistic modeling and simulation, and (g) modern capital market measures.

Conservatism

A rudimentary method of assessing risk is to choose low estimates of cash benefits, choose high estimates of cash outflows (costs), and evaluate the net benefits using a relatively high discount rate. These actions result in a low value estimate or a high required rate of return estimate. If the analyst accepts the project as a good investment, he or she feels even more anxious to make the purchase because this analysis assumed bad outcomes in every case. So a conservative outlook regarding benefits and costs limits potential projects to the best alternative.

The problem with this method is that if the estimates used are more conservative than what the analyst believes will occur, and if the analyst seeks to maximize his or her wealth, conservative action results in the exclusion of some projects that would be acceptable under "normal conditions."

Risk-Adjusted Discount Rates

We noted in an earlier chapter that as the risk associated with an investment rises, the nominal (or market) interest rate (or required rate of return) on that investment increases as the risk is incorporated into the discount rate. The analyst accomplishes the same thing by applying higher risk-adjusted discount rates in order to lower the investment value of the project.

Conceptually, this approach is not difficult. However, some analysts find it hard to assess discount rate levels for each type of risky investment as well as the relevant increase in rates due to the perceived increase in risk levels.

The Certainty-Equivalent Approach

The certainty-equivalent approach offers an alternative to the risk-adjusted discount approach. This approach argues that it is conceptually equivalent and operationally easier to account for the risk associated with the likelihood of the cash flows than it is to account for the time value of money using the risk-free discount rate.

Here the analyst applies a *certainty-equivalent coefficient* to each income or cash flow payment. This coefficient may vary from 0.00 to 1.00 depending on the degree of certainty associated with the receipt of the payment. Typically, one expects cash flows in the immediate future to be more easily estimated than those in the distant future. In the instance of one year, a certainty-equivalent coefficient of almost 1.00 would be multiplied by the expected cash flow. Those expected five years hence may warrant a coefficient of .50. The final year's cash flow is far less certain, so .20 may be used. Obviously, the analyst must decide on the relative sizes of the certainty equivalents based on when the cash flow will occur. In this sense, the risk of the cash flow not occurring is accounted for independently of the consideration of the time value of money.

The certainty-equivalent approach is attractive for a number of reasons. First, it provides a conceptual basis for accounting for risk which is consistent with more traditional methods. Second, it may be easier to use because risk and the time value of money are treated separately. This may be important depending on the risk characteristics of the project in question. Third, the certainty-equivalent approach requires no new information over the risk-adjusted discount rate approach. Finally, it is easier to derive investment results when risk is not constant over time. Since risk tends to be resolved over time, this last condition offers a strong argument for its adoption.

Measures of Variability

Traditionally, measures of risk and uncertainty in finance measure the expected variability of cash flows from the expected value. The most common of these measures are the *variance* and the *standard deviation.*

There are many reasons why these measures are useful. First, both are operationally consistent with each other because, by definition, the standard deviation is the square root of the variance. Second, both use deviations of outcomes from expected values to measure the degree of variability around the mean. If the expected values are identical, we use variability in the distribution of outcomes to measure risk.

Finally, modern statistical analysis demonstrates that *confidence intervals* and *hypothesis testing* are possible using these measures of variability. Confidence intervals permit analysts to develop a range of possible outcomes based on the expected value and the variance (or standard deviations) of outcomes. Hypothesis testing permits the analyst to statistically investigate the likelihood of achieving certain goals or objectives. Although these techniques are complex, they are very useful in providing information about risk. However, they are also beyond the introductory nature of this book (see the "Selected References" at the end of this chapter).

Decision Trees and Sensitivity Analysis

Two additional well-known techniques for measuring risk are *decision trees* and *sensitivity analysis*. Decision trees require the analyst to estimate the likelihood of each outcome at every expected decision point in the future. In this manner, the analyst will grasp an understanding of the relationships between each decision and the probabilities of occurrence. Sensitivity analysis is the estimation of investment values by systematic alteration of the inputs. This technique is characterized by the question "What if . . . ?" In other words, the analyst might ask, "What if effective gross income fell by ten percent?"

These techniques are helpful in judging the linkages and inputs of various investment decisions (decision trees) and the sensitivity of value of return to changes in certain input values (sensitivity analysis). Furthermore, this type of analysis is available to most analysts in real estate investment.

Probabilistic Modeling and Simulation

A logical extension of decision trees and sensitivity analysis is the incorporation of random elements directly into the decision-making process. *Probabilistic modeling* involves the use of subjective probability distributions around various input variables. For example, the analyst estimates the distribution of outcomes around effective gross income, operating expenses, debt service, growth rates in income and expenses, growth rate in property values, and others. The probabilistic model then uses this information to make a valuation estimate. *Simulation* is an integral part of this process, since the distributions of inputs for a large set of observations are typically generated by a computer program. Many computer services now offer these types of programs to investors.

Modern Capital Market Measures

The final method measures risk by integrating risk and return into a modern capital market approach. This involves measuring the risk of an asset as a function of variability with other investments ("covariability"), or with the real estate market in general rather than variability of its own possible outcomes. This *covariance* is essential to modern portfolio theory.

To the extent that the risk of real estate investments is viewed as a function of the relationship between the expected returns of one investment and the expected returns of other investments in the market, the development of market measures of risk incorporating principles of diversification, portfolio theory, and capital market theory may be useful. Recent attempts to modify financial models for real estate investments have made some gains in this direction, although more development is expected.

EXAMPLES OF RISK ANALYSIS

The Certainty-Equivalent Approach

The certainty-equivalent approach incorporates risk separately from the consideration of the time value of money by accounting for it in the *numerator* (the cash flows) rather than the denominator of the discounted cash flow model. This factor is the *certainty equivalent of the expected cash flow*.

   Following traditional analysis, the certainty-equivalent factor is derived by answering the question, *What is the smallest certain after-tax cash flow (ATCF*) for which the investor would be willing to give up the expected, risky, after-tax cash flow (ATCF) and still be indifferent?* Mathematically, we can represent this factor by the symbol α:

$$\alpha = \frac{\text{ATCF}^*}{\text{ATCF}} \text{ (so that } 0 < \alpha \le 1) \tag{13-5}$$

where

$$\alpha = \text{certainty-equivalent factor}$$
$$\text{ATCF}^* = \text{certain after-tax cash flow}$$
$$\text{ATCF} = \text{expected (but risky) after-tax cash flow}$$

If we allow values of α to vary over all t periods, the investment value of equity can be written as follows:

$$E = \sum_{t=1}^{n} \frac{\alpha_t \text{ATCF}_t}{(1 + k_f)^t} + \frac{\alpha_n \text{ATER}_n}{(1 + k_f)^n} \tag{13-6}$$

where

$$\alpha_t = \text{certainty-equivalent factor in the } i\text{th year}$$
$$k_f = \text{risk-free rate}$$

   If the use of the certainty-equivalent approach also provides an estimate of the investment value of equity, then for some values of α_t and $(k_e - k_f)$:

$$E = \sum_{t=1}^{n} \frac{\alpha_t \text{ATCF}_t}{(1 + k_f)^t} + \frac{\alpha_n \text{ATER}_n}{(1 + k_f)^n} = \sum_{t=1}^{n} \frac{\text{ATCF}_t}{(1 + k_e)^t} + \frac{\text{ATER}_n}{(1 + k_e)^n} \tag{13-7}$$

It also follows that for some values of α_t and $(k_e - k_f)$, the net present values are equivalent in these models:

$$\begin{aligned}
\text{NPV}_e &= \sum_{t=1}^{n} \frac{\alpha_t \text{ATCF}_t}{(1 + k_f)^t} + \frac{\alpha_n \text{ATER}_n}{(1 + k_f)^n} - (\text{MV} - \text{MD}) \\
&= \sum_{t=1}^{n} \frac{\text{ATCF}_t}{(1 + k_e)^t} + \frac{\text{ATER}_n}{(1 + k_e)^n} - (\text{MV} - \text{MD})
\end{aligned} \tag{13-8}$$

TABLE 13-4 Example for Certainty-
Equivalent and Risk-
Adjusted Discount Rate
Comparisons

	INVESTMENT Q	
YEAR	ATCF ($)	ATER ($)
0	(17,000)	
1	2,000	
2	4,000	
3	6,000	12,000

As an example, suppose an investor wishes to compare the risk-adjusted discount rate technique with the certainty-equivalent approach for the following expected after-tax cash flow and after-tax equity reversion stream (investment Q in Table 13-4).

If cash flows in the near future are believed to be less risky than cash flows in the distant future, the investor would be more willing to accept lower, certain, after-tax cash flows (ATCFs*) in the distant future than in the near future. This is identical to saying the investor believes that $\alpha_1 > \alpha_2 > \alpha_3$.

Suppose that by the method presented earlier, the investor determines the following values for $\alpha_t: \alpha_1 = 0.95$, $\alpha_2 = 0.90$, and $\alpha_3 = 0.85$. The net present value, using the certainty-equivalent approach, would be $1,756.97, assuming a risk-free rate of 4 percent:

$$NPV_e = \frac{0.95(\$2,000)}{(1.04)^1} + \frac{0.90(\$4,000)}{(1.04)^2} + \frac{0.85(\$6,000)}{(1.04)^3} + \frac{0.85(\$12,000)}{(1.04)^3}$$
$$- \$17,000$$
$$= \$1,756.97$$

According to the NPV decision rules, any positive value indicates that the investment should be accepted.

Suppose the risk premium $(k_e - k_f)$ is equal to 11 percent. The appropriate discount rate to be used is the sum of the risk-free (k_f) and the risk premium $(k_e - k_f)$ or the required rate of return on equity (k_e). To calculate the net present value using the risk-adjusted discount rate approach, k_e is equal to 15 percent:

$$NPV_e = \frac{\$2,000}{(1.15)^1} + \frac{\$4,000}{(1.15)^2} + \frac{\$6,000}{(1.15)^3} + \frac{\$12,000}{(1.15)^3} - \$17,000$$
$$= -\$401.00$$

However, using the risk-adjusted discount rate approach, the investor would reject the investment. In this case, a comparison between the risk-adjusted discount rate approach and the certainty-equivalent approach results in a conflict about whether to accept the investment.

Proponents of the certainty-equivalent approach argue that acceptance of the investment makes sense, since the net present value is positive. However, users of risk-adjusted discount rates argue that at a 15 percent discount rate, the investment should be rejected because the net present value is negative. The resolution of this matter depends on the investor's ability to estimate certainty-equivalent factors.

The Variance as a Risk Measure

In the example of investments X, Y, and Z developed earlier in this chapter, the analysis of alternative investments using expected after-tax cash flows presumed all of the projects were equally risky. Because all sets of cash flows were of the same risk class, any differences in the expected after-tax cash flow were a function of the probabilities of occurrence of different states of the world. The *variance* is a measure of dispersion, or deviation away from the expected value.

As an example, suppose the investor must choose between three mutually exclusive projects: investments E, F, and G, as shown in Table 13-5. The investor estimates various after-tax cash flows for each state of the world and assigns subjective probability estimates to the likelihood of occurrence.

A review of the table indicates that the expected after-tax cash flow of each investment is identical. Therefore a measure must be developed to determine the relative riskiness of each investment. The variance of the expected after-tax cash flow is one such measure.

The variance is defined as σ_t^2, so that

$$\sigma_t^2 = \sum_{i=1}^{m} (\text{ATCF}_{it} - \overline{\text{ATCF}_t})^2 p_{it} \tag{13-9}$$

TABLE 13-5   Expected After-Tax Cash Flows for Investments E, F, and G with Various States of the Economy*

STATE OF THE ECONOMY	PROBABILITY OF STATE OCCURRING	INVESTMENTS E	F	G
		($)	($)	($)
Recession	.20	500	750	900
Normal	.60	1,000	1,000	1,000
Boom	.20	1,500	1,250	1,100

$\overline{\text{ATCF}_t}$ of investment E = \$500(.20) + \$1,000(.60) + \$1,500(.20) = \$1,000

$\overline{\text{ATCF}_t}$ of investment F = \$750(.20) + \$1,000(.60) + \$1,250(.20) = \$1,000

$\overline{\text{ATCF}_t}$ of investment G = \$900(.20) + \$1,000(.60) + \$1,100(.20) = \$1,000

* Note that these after-tax cash flows are for the tth year.

where

σ_t^2 = variance of expected after-tax cash flows for the tth year
$ATCF_{it}$ = after-tax cash flow if the ith state of the world occurs in the
            tth year
$\overline{ATCF_t}$ = expected after-tax cash flow for the tth year
p_{it} = probability of the ith state of the world in the tth year

The variances for investments E, F, and G can be calculated by using this equation (Table 13-6). It is not surprising that the tighter the probability distribution around the expected after-tax cash flow, the smaller the variance. As a measure of risk, the lower the variance, the lower the risk.

Graphically, we can see the probability distributions of investments E, F, and G in Figure 13-1. Here the distribution is "widest" for investment E

TABLE 13-6   Variances of Expected After-Tax Cash Flow for Investments E, F, and G*

σ_t^2 of investment E = ($500 − $1,000)^2.20 + ($1,000 − $1,000)^2.60 + ($1,500 − $1,000)^2.20
            = $100,000
σ_t^2 of investment F = ($750 − $1,000)^2.20 + ($1,000 − $1,000)^2.60 + ($1,250 − $1,000)^2.20
            = $25,000
σ_t^2 of investment G = ($900 − $1,000)^2.20 + ($1,000 − $1,000)^2.60 + ($1,100 − $1,000)^2.20
            = $4,000

* Note that these variances are for the tth year and that the dimension of the variance is in "dollars squared."

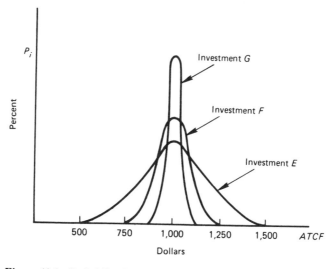

Figure 13-1   Probability Distributions for Investments E, F, and G.

Source: Austin J. Jaffe and C. F. Sirmans, *Real Estate Investment Decision Making*, 1982, p. 448. Reprinted by permission of Prentice-Hall, Englewood Cliffs, NJ.

and "tightest" for investment G, which corresponds to the magnitudes of our risk measure.

Recall that earlier in the chapter, we showed that projects could be ranked on the basis of expected after-tax cash flow if risk was presumed constant for all projects. However, if the expected after-tax cash flows for projects under consideration are equivalent, as in the cases of investments E, F, and G (see Table 13-5), the investor will be neutral about these investments only if the risk is the same for all. In this example, the risk varies with the project (see Figure 13-1) and a new measure is needed. The variance of the after-tax cash flow shows that investment G would be preferred over investment F, and investment F over investment E (see Table 13-6).

These results indicate that the investor can now analyze expected values and risk together when making investment choices. This ability, as we will subsequently show, is useful in forming a very robust criterion.

The Standard Deviation as a Risk Measure

A popular measure of risk, the *standard deviation*, is the square root of the variance:

$$\sigma_t = \sqrt{s_t^2} \tag{13-10}$$

where

σ_t = standard deviation of expected after-tax cash flows for the tth year

The standard deviations of investments E, F, and G are shown in Table 13-7. Note that the greater the variance, the greater the standard deviation. So it does not matter whether the investor calculates variances or standard deviations in order to identify the investment with the lowest risk; either will provide the same information.

TABLE 13-7   Standard Deviations of Expected After-Tax Cash Flows for Investments E, F, and G*

σ_t of investment E $= \sqrt{100,000}$
$= \$316.23$
σ_t of investment F $= \sqrt{25,000}$
$= \$158.11$
σ_t of investment G $= \sqrt{4,000}$
$= \$63.25$

* Note that these standard deviations are for the tth year and note that the dimension of the standard deviation is in "dollars."

Some simple examples. As a review of the use of the expected value, variance, and standard deviation criteria for choosing investments, it may be useful to consider a few simple examples. In each case, the investor's task is to choose the investment that is consistent with the goal of expected wealth maximization, taking risk into account.

Example 1: An investor is confronted with a choice between investments A and B, with the expected values, variances, and standard deviations shown in Table 13-8. Since the expected after-tax cash flow in year t of investment A is greater than that of investment B and the risk, as measured by the variance (and the standard deviation) of the cash flows in year t, is the same for each investment, it is safe to conclude that the investor would prefer investment A over B. Since the risk is identical, the investor would choose the investment with the higher expected after-tax cash flow.

Example 2: Imagine an investor who is confronted with a choice between two other investments, C and D, with the expected values, variances, and standard deviations shown in Table 13-9.

In this case, since the expected after-tax cash flows are the same, the investor must consider possible differences in risk. It is clear that since the variance (and the standard deviation) are greater for investment D than for investment C, the investor would prefer investment C. In cases where the

TABLE 13-8 Expected Values, Variances, and Standard Deviations for Investments A and B

	INVESTMENT	
	A	*B*
$\overline{ATCF_t}$	$200	$100
$\sigma_t{}^2$	25	25
σ_t	$ 5	$ 5

TABLE 13-9 Expected Values, Variances, and Standard Deviations for Investments C and D

	INVESTMENT	
	C	*D*
$\overline{ATCF_t}$	$200	$200
$\sigma_t{}^2$	25	36
σ_t	$ 5	$ 6

expected values are the same, the investor would always prefer less risk, and therefore the investment with the lower variance (and standard deviation) is chosen.

Example 3: Imagine that the investor is given yet another choice between investments E and F, with the expected values, variances, and standard deviations shown in Table 13-10. In this case, the expected after-tax cash flow in year t is greater for investment F than for investment E. However, the risk is also greater. Although investment F expects to return a higher after-tax cash flow than does investment E, the cash flow stream is more risky. So which investment should be selected?

Although the analysis was quite straightforward in Examples 1 and 2, it is more difficult in Example 3. Specifically, we need the theory of utility to decide the issue and it will be shown in the next chapter. However, some authors have advocated the use of the coefficient of variation to choose between investments E and F.

TABLE 13-10 Expected Values, Variances, and Standard Deviations for Investments E and F

	INVESTMENT	
	E	F
$\overline{\text{ATCF}}_t$	$100	$200
$\sigma_t{}^2$	25	36
σ_t	$ 5	$ 6

The Coefficient of Variation as Risk Measure

The *coefficient of variation* is defined as the standard deviation divided by the expected value:

$$v_t = \frac{\sigma_t}{\overline{\text{ATCF}}_t} \qquad (13\text{-}11)$$

where

v_t = coefficient of variation of expected after-tax cash flows for the tth year

The coefficient of variation can be used to evaluate choices when the expected value *and* risk of one alternative are greater than those of another. In the case of investments E and F, the coefficients of variation are equal to .05 and .03, respectively (as shown in Table 13-11).

TABLE 13-11   Coefficients of Variation for Investments E and F

	INVESTMENT	
	E	F
v_t	$\$5 \div \$100 = .05$	$\$6 \div \$200 = .03$

Using the coefficient of variation, the investor concludes that the "risk per dollar of expected value" is greater for investment E than for investment F, and therefore investment F is preferred over investment E. The coefficient of variation may be viewed as an attempt to standardize the amount of risk per unit of value.

The trouble with the coefficient of variation as an investment decision rule for risky investments is that *it may not always work*. So it must be discarded, as the next example will show.

Example 4:   An investor is given a choice between two final investments, G and H, with the probability distributions shown in Table 13-12.

TABLE 13-12   Expected Probability Distributions for Investments G and H

INVESTMENT			
G		H	
ATCF$_i$ ($\$$)	p_i	ATCF$_i$ ($\$$)	p_i
100	1.00	200	.50
		400	.50

Given the probability distributions for each after-tax cash flow, variances, standard deviations, and coefficients of variation can be calculated for year t. These are shown in Table 13-13.

TABLE 13-13   Expected Values, Variances, Standard Deviations, and Coefficients of Variation for Investments G and H

	INVESTMENT	
	G	H
ATCF$_t$	$\$100$	$\$\ 300$
σ_t^2	0	10,000
σ_t	$\$\ 0$	$\$\ 100$
v_t	.00	.33

It is clear that the expected after-tax cash flow and the variance (and standard deviation) of one alternative (investment H) are greater than those of the other (investment G). Therefore this example is a possible candidate for using the coefficient of variation.

However, a review of the probability distribution of investment H indicates that something is wrong with the measure if investment G is preferable to investment H. The proof is, of course, that no matter which outcome occurs (that is, whether it is $200 or $400), either would be preferable to the outcome under investment G ($100). Therefore, despite the fact that the coefficient of variation criterion indicates otherwise, investment H will always be preferred.

Therefore the coefficient of variation fails as a useful criterion for choosing among risky alternatives. However, it *is* possible to develop useful decision rules for making these choices, as we will see.

The Mean-Variance Decision Criterion

Since an investor must be able to evaluate risky investment opportunities in a manner consistent with his or her goals and risk preferences, a decision rule would be useful for this purpose. The rule developed here is commonly called the *mean-variance decision criterion*. It says that investment 1 is preferable to investment 2 if

   a. The expected after-tax cash flow of investment 1 is greater than or equal to the expected after-tax cash flow of investment 2, and the variance of the expected after-tax cash flow of investment 1 is less than the variance of the expected after-tax cash flow of investment 2

                                                        or
   b. The expected after-tax cash flow of investment 2 and the variance of the expected after-tax cash flow of investment 1 are less than or equal to the variance of the expected after-tax cash flow of investment 2[4]

To demonstrate the applicability of the rule, refer to Examples 1 through 4. In Example 1, investment A is preferable to investment B because A's expected cash flows are greater than B's and the variances are equal. Investment C is preferable to investment D in Example 2 because C's variances are less than D's and their expected cash flows are equal. However, for Examples 3 and 4, the decision rule cannot indicate which is preferred. In both investment

----

[4] The validity of this rule here depends on (a) investments 1 and 2 having annuity after-tax cash flow streams, (b) after-tax equity reversion values being equal to zero or an annuity payment, and (c) each investment being of equal length. If these conditions are not satisfied, the investor must modify the parameters used to account for the differences between the investments. This is done by using expected net present value instead of expected after-tax cash flows and expected variance of the net present value of after-tax cash flows instead of the expected variance of the after-tax cash flows.

F and investment H, the expected cash flows *and* variances are greater than for investment E and investment G, respectively. As a result, this decision rule cannot decide the outcomes based on the criterion established.

MODERN RISK ANALYSIS

Sensitivity Analysis

Sensitivity analysis is defined as the repetition of multiple estimations of calculations using a known model, by systematically varying the inputs to the model to evaluate the impact of changes on the expected results. This technique can be viewed as a set of questions in the following form:

If_____ is changed from_____ to _____ , what impact does this change have on the net present value of equity?

As an example, suppose we consider investment S with the expected cash flows and reversion given in Table 13-14. The net present value of equity, ΔE, for investment S is $4,730.60, using a required rate of return on equity, k_e, of 15 percent.

To see what impact a change in after-tax cash flow has on net present value, study the results in Table 13-15. These show various estimates of after-tax cash flow each period (t) when the net present value of equity is equal to 15 percent. Note that a small increase in the estimated after-tax cash flow stream substantially increases the net present value of equity. Thus, for investment S, the investor is "sensitive" to changes in the level of after-tax cash flows.

TABLE 13-14 Expected Cash Flows for Investment $

YEAR	ATCF ($)	ATER ($)
0	($25,000)	
1	5,000	
2	5,000	
3	5,000	
4	5,000	
5	5,000	
6	5,000	25,000

**Exhibit 13-2   Other Methods of Risk
                 Analysis**

In addition to the traditional methods of risk analysis discussed in the text, several others have been developed. Each of the other methods has its own advantages and disadvantages for real estate investors. Some are likely to become increasingly popular in the future as computers become more widely available.

One method of risk analysis is called *statistical inference*. This approach employs classical statistics to assess the likelihood of success or failure in meeting a certain investment objective. For example, this type of analysis provides information on the prospects for achieving a positive net present value, given the current estimates of cash flows and the variance of the flows. If the probability is high, the investor is likely to regard the investment as an attractive one.

Another method of risk analysis is called *simulation*. This approach introduces probability distributions around inputs in order to capture various outcomes of several parameters. For example, the rent level is an estimate in traditional analysis. In simulation, a distribution of rent levels is used to indicate that in the real world, rents are not known with certainty. The amount of uncertainty can be captured by the likely outcomes (i.e., the probability distributions). In the end, the results using this type of approach provide a great deal more information than do simple, best-guess estimates.

The final new method of risk analysis is based on the *portfolio theory* and selection revolution that has occurred in security markets during the past twenty years. The development of portfolios of investments based on the benefits associated with diversification has changed much thinking in the financial community. In the case of real estate, this area is just beginning with the development of real estate investment vehicles such as mortgage-backed securities, REITs, and other financial instruments secured or otherwise related to real estate. In the future, it is likely that real estate investors will also concern themselves with the gains associated with diversification and the reduction of risk through the adoption of portfolio selection procedures.

The analyst might also want to test various growth rates for the after-tax cash flow stream. Since investment S is estimated to return $5,000 in after-tax cash flow per year, it has a zero percent annual growth rate in after-tax cash flows (Table 13-16).

In this case, as the expected growth rate increases, the net present value of equity climbs at a decreasing rate. Therefore the analyst is less concerned about estimating the correct growth rate in after-tax cash flow than about

TABLE 13-15   Results of Sensitivity Analysis: ATCF$_t$

ESTIMATED ATCF$_t$ ($)	NET PRESENT VALUE OF EQUITY* ($)
1,500	(8,515.09)
4,000	838.14
5,000	4,730.60
6,000	8,515.09
8,000	16,084.05

* Assuming ATER$_n$ = $25,000 for n = 6.

TABLE 13-16   Results of Sensitivity Analysis: Growth Rate in ATCF$_t$

ESTIMATED GROWTH RATE IN ATCF$_t$ (%)	NET PRESENT VALUE OF EQUITY* ($)
0	4,730.60
1	5,133.83
3	5,966.65
5	6,841.49
10	9,219.16
20	14,900.69

* Assuming ATCF$_t$ = $5,000 for t = 1 and ATER$_n$ = $25,000 for n = 6.

the magnitude of the cash flow each period (ATCF$_t$), since the impact on net present value is lessened in this case.

Also, the analyst could examine the sensitivity of net present value to different annual growth rates in property values to see how these affect the values of the after-tax equity reversion. Obviously, changes in the after-tax equity reversion will affect the net present value of equity. Table 13-17 gives the results of this sensitivity analysis for investment S. It is easy to see that changes in the expected growth rate in after-tax equity reversion exert a sizable impact on the net present value of equity for investment S given an expected holding period of six years in this case. Note, however, that the slope of this sensitivity function is less steep than that for estimated after-tax cash flow each period, but greater than for the growth rate in after-tax cash flow.

Finally, an analyst may want to examine these changes in combination with each other. For example, taking an initial cash flow of $1,500 with a 1 percent growth in cash flows and no growth in the reversion, the estimated net present value of equity would be −$8,395.60, using 15 percent as the required rate of return on equity. On the other hand, if the analyst wanted to calculate the net present value of equity with an initial cash flow of $8,000 and an expected growth rate of 20 percent in the after-tax cash flow and after-tax equity reversion, this can be done as well. In this case, the net present value of equity is $53,821.27, using k_e, equal to 15 percent.

TABLE 13-17 Results of Sensitivity Analysis: Growth Rate in ATER$_n$

ESTIMATED GROWTH RATE IN ATER$_n$ (%)	NET PRESENT VALUE OF EQUITY* ($)
0	4,730.60
3	6,827.96
6	9,254.04
12	15,255.87
15	18,922.41
20	26,195.50

* Assuming ATCF$_t$ = \$5,000 for $t = 1, 2, \ldots, 6$.

Sensitivity analysis, therefore, demonstrates the impact of misestimating cash flows, equity reversions, the required rate of return on equity, or any combination of parameters.[5] It is quite valuable to investors and analysts for this reason.

Whether sensitivity analysis is valuable as a method for analyzing risk is another matter. Its advocates generally feel that, as a risk measure, this technique minimizes the risk of low rates of return (and low net present values) by examining a number of outcomes with various types of inputs.

QUESTIONS

13-1. Why is risk analysis essential to real estate decision making?

13-2. What is the expected net present value of equity? Why is it more useful than the net present value of equity, assuming certainty?

13-3. There are several traditional methods of accounting for risk. What are these methods and what are their shortcomings?

13-4. This book illustrates the certainty-equivalent approach. How does this method compare with the more traditional risk-adjusted discount rate method?

13-5. What are the variance and standard deviation measures of risk?

13-6. "The tighter the distribution around the expected value, the lower the risk." True or false? Explain.

13-7. Show that if two investment opportunities have the same expected values, the investment with the lower variance and lower standard deviation will be preferred.

13-8. What is the coefficient of variation? Why does it fail as a risk measure?

13-9. What is sensitivity analysis and how is it used in real estate investing?

13-10. Do you think risk analysis is useful in actual real estate investing? Why or why not?

[5] The reader should keep in mind the types of inputs that would cause ATCF and ATER to vary. These include rents, vacancies, operating expenses, financing terms, tax rates, depreciation rules, and others.

PROBLEMS

13-1. An investor is offered the following three investments:

	INVESTMENT		
	S	T	U
p	ATCF ($)	ATCF ($)	ATCF ($)
.25	1,000	2,000	2,500
.50	3,000	3,000	3,000
.25	5,000	4,000	3,500

    a. What are the expected after-tax cash flows for each investment in each tth year?

    b. Which investment would an investor prefer?

    c. Prove why certain investments are preferable to others.

13-2. Using a numerical example, demonstrate how the certainty-equivalent approach can be inconsistent with the risk-adjusted discount rate model.

13-3. Calculate the coefficient of variation for the investment chosen in Problem 13-1. Is this a useful measure? Explain.

13-4. An investor is considering the purchase of a parcel of land.

    a. If the investor pays $45,000 for the land, what will be the rate of return if the land sells for $50,000 one year from purchase?

    b. Suppose the investor formulates the following expectations:

STATE OF THE WORLD	PROBABILITY	EXPECTED SELLING PRICE
1	.05	$48,500
2	.80	80,000
3	.15	55,000

What is the expected rate or return? What is the standard deviation of the expected rate of return?

SELECTED REFERENCES

COOPER, JAMES A., and CATHY A. MORRISON, "Using Computer Simulation to Minimize Risk in Urban Housing Development," *Real Estate Appraiser*, 39 (March–April 1973), 15–26.

FINDLAY, M. C., S. D. MESSNER, and R. A. TARANTELLO, "Risk Analysis in Real Estate," *Real Estate Appraiser and Analyst*, 45 (July–August 1979), 27–38.

KAPPLIN, STEVEN D., "Financial Theory and the Valuation of Real Estate under Conditions of Risk," *Real Estate Appraiser*, 42 (September–October 1976), 28–37.

MARTIN, WILLIAM B., JR., "A Risk Analysis Rate-of-Return Model for Evaluating Income-Producing Real Estate Investments," *Appraisal Journal*, 46 (July 1978), 424–42.

Miles, Mike, and Michael Rice, "Toward a More Complete Investigation of the Correlation of Real Estate Investment Yield to the Rate Evidenced in the Money and Capital Markets: The Individual Investor's Perspective," *Real Estate Appraiser and Analyst*, 44 (November–December 1978), 8–19.

Wofford, Larry E., "A Simulation Approach to the Appraisal of Income Producing Real Estate," *American Real Estate and Urban Economics Association Journal*, 6 (Winter 1978), 370–94.

14

APPLYING THE
INVESTMENT PROCESS:
A CASE STUDY

In the previous chapters we outlined and discussed the real estate investment process. In this chapter we apply this decision-making process in a detailed case format. The investment situation involves a real estate investor considering the purchase of a small apartment building.

We first review some of the basic elements of a real estate investment strategy. Then we "walk" the investor step by step through the decision-making process. The reader is encouraged to work all the numerical calculations and use the text as an answer key. Only by such a detailed analysis will the mechanics of real estate investment decision making be understood.

Obviously, a case study cannot examine in detail all the relevant elements. Any decision-making situation contains judgmental aspects. Thus our interpretation and judgment (decisions) may be different from yours. Indeed, this is a key concept in investment decision making. Decisions are based on expectations. How to formulate the expectations and "judge" our expectations is the important learning element in any case study.

ELEMENTS OF AN INVESTMENT STRATEGY

Investment analysis involves identifying the factors that influence risk and return of alternative investments. There are several key elements in the development of an investment strategy. These include diversification, legal environment, choices of ownership entity, choices of management strategy, choices of financing options, tax planning, choices of decision criteria, and inflation expectations. Let us discuss each of these elements.

Exhibit 14-1   The Importance of Strategy

In the end, successful real estate investment analysis requires the adoption of an investment strategy. Without a well-defined and well-developed strategy, the investor may find that he or she seems lost and bewildered. It is imperative that the investor begin to formulate both short-term and long-term strategic plans prior to acquiring any interests in property.

For example, some investors may seek real estate investments for cash flow; some may be interested in speculative land that is likely to appreciate; others may have alternative objectives.

The development of a general investment strategy forces the analyst to formulate specific goals for the investment portfolio. These goals will help determine the types of real estate investments that should be considered and those that should be avoided. There are far more investment choices available than some investors realize. As a result, care must be taken to concentrate investment efforts only in markets where projects that meet the investor's objectives can be acquired and where the investor has some skill or expertise.

In addition, long-term strategic planning is essential in developing lifelong goals and objectives for estate building. Real estate can be a fundamental cornerstone in creating personal wealth; real estate investment analysis can be used to build net worth. One of the principal components of long-term planning is the fact that the power of compound interest becomes a major factor if harnessed over a long period of time. Although it is difficult to "save and invest for the future," especially during the earlier years of a professional adult's life, the rewards can be astronomical in the later years.

Finally, investors who adopt strategic plans can take advantage of investment opportunities as they occur, since these investors position themselves so as to have an equity base for investment purposes and are likely to have a strong credit relationship with local bankers and business leaders. This should not be taken lightly. Just as expectations about the future affect the current prices of real estate, expectations about your future are likely to affect your ability to obtain financing, assistance in specialized ventures, and an inside track on potential joint ventures in the local economy. Strategy is an important component of a long-term successful real estate investor.

Diversification

To make optimal decisions, resources must be allocated to real estate in consideration with other types of investments, such as stocks and bonds. This area of investment analysis is referred to as *portfolio analysis*. A portfolio is a combination of different types of investments or investments with different characteristics. Through diversification, investors can lower the overall risk to which they are exposed.

Diversification involves investing equity into a number of different investments. An ideal portfolio of investments is one in which the returns for each investment are inversely related to each other.

One method of diversification would be to choose the same type of real estate investment but in a spatially varied fashion. A particular investor, for example, may prefer residential investments. He or she could diversify the real estate portfolio by spreading investments across different housing markets.

An investor could also diversify equity capital into different types of real estate investments (residential and commercial) *and* different locations for the various investments (i.e., different neighborhoods, cities, or even states). In this case, the investor may be able to improve the investment portfolio by carefully analyzing different expectations regarding the type and location of property.

Legal Environment

The development of a real estate investment strategy must include an understanding of the legal environment. The legal environment affects the investment decision in a number of ways. For example, the type of legal estate involved in the transaction can dramatically affect the value of the investment. The value of real property can significantly differ depending on the estate's limitations, duration, and conception. Therefore the investor must understand the legal implications involving investing and making a real estate investment strategy.

To analyze an investment strategy, the investor has two choices: accept the legal environment as a constraint and work within it to achieve his or her financial outcome or adopt a more active stance regarding the legal environment and use the law to his or her best interests.

While the first is a more passive approach, it should not be viewed as less aggressive or less ambitious. It seeks to achieve financial results, given a set of expectations and legal outcomes that legal counsel will support.

The second approach views the legal environment as a changing area which can be molded to fit the particular situation and requirements. In this case, the analyst seeks legal counsel as an active participant in the decision-making process.

Ownership Entity

Another important issue is the choice of business entity for ownership. Since this choice can mean the difference between the achievement of financial objectives or bankruptcy, or between fixed (or limited) liability and complete (or unlimited) liability in the event of suit against the owner, the choice of ownership entity is not to be overlooked. Furthermore, the choice of ownership varies according to the rights of control and operation which may lead to problems concerning the ownership of property.

Management Strategy

Another important consideration is an analysis of the managerial decisions during the period of ownership. Many things occur during this time that affect the value of the property.

Because many operating decisions are delegated to the property manager when one is employed, the property manager may be one of the most important participants in the real estate investment process. Many of the production, operations, and financial decisions made by this person (or firm) may determine an investment strategy for the owner.

Financing Options

Financing is another major area. The investor must answer some important questions such as, What is the appropriate level of debt? Is there an appropriate time to refinance in the case of a level-payment amortized loan? Should second-mortgage sources be sought in order to expand the holdings of real estate investments when an attractive property becomes available? The answers to these and other questions involve dealing with financing policy, and the solutions are not easily derived.

Tax Planning

Income taxation has a great impact on real estate investment decisions. The cash flow on which to make investment decisions is the amount after taxes. The amount of taxes depends on the taxable income and the investor's tax rate. A real estate investment strategy for income-producing property must involve considerable tax planning. The tax implications at the time of sale are also important.

In general, since income taxation remains one of the basic ways in which federal and state governments collect money, tax planning is a necessary prerequisite for maximizing the equity investor's wealth. Those who choose to analyze projects on a before-tax basis can select inferior projects over better ones or in many cases overstate values or expected returns.

Decision Criteria

There are various methods of measuring expected returns and investment values. The more traditional criteria are called rules of thumb because they are more easily used and require fewer data for analysis. The more sophisticated criteria require more data and more complex estimation procedures, and they employ a stronger conceptual basis. The investor interested in developing a real estate investment strategy must decide on which criterion (or criteria) the decision will be made. For some investors, many measures and criteria will be used to provide as much relevant information as possible. For others, experience may show that only a select few are needed. Finally, a few investors may rely only on one or two approaches to make the investment decision.

Effective real estate investment decision making requires that the investor make the best choice, given his or her objectives and a set of alternatives. Implicit in this statement is the presumption that a wrong choice is costly in terms of giving up expected income, cash flow, or wealth.

Inflationary Environment

In the past few years, inflation has soared to double digits in the United States. Many observers believe inflation will probably continue for many years to come. Real estate is traditionally regarded as an inflation hedge because some empirical evidence shows that the nominal value of property has increased at a faster rate than other goods. Although this really represents a change in relative prices due to changing demand, it nonetheless supports the notion that real estate investments provide real rates of return to investors.

THE INVESTMENT STRATEGY: A CASE STUDY

To illustrate the development of the real estate investment strategy, we will use a detailed case study of an apartment building investment. While it is impossible to illustrate all the problems faced by an investor, this example is a step-by-step discussion of an investment strategy based on the investment process discussed in the preceding chapters.

Step 1: Identifying Investor Objectives

The initial step is to identify the objectives of the investor. There are several different reasons for investing, such as inflation hedge and cash flow.

The investor in this project decides that he wants to earn a 13 percent rate of return per year on his equity investment on an after-tax basis over the anticipated holding period of eight years. The investor anticipates selling the property at the end of year 8. This desired rate of return is determined after considering the other investment opportunities and the relative risk of the project. The investor's major objective is to decide whether the project is expected to generate the required return of 13 percent.

Step 2: Analysis of the Investment Environment

The second step is to analyze the environment in which the investment decision is made. This consists of three categories: market, legal, and sociopolitical.

Market analysis. Two major categories of risk include the possibility that an investment will not generate the expected level of net income (business risk) and the possibility that income increases will not keep pace with inflation (purchasing power risk). Market analysis is designed to aid the investor in identifying the factors that influence these categories of risk.

The basic components of a market study include

1. Definition and delineation of the market area for an investment.
2. Analysis of the demand factors. Demand for housing is dependent on the number of households, income levels, and other demographic aspects, such as sex, age, and education.
3. Analysis of supply factors. This includes the existing competition in the market area, a survey of projects currently under construction, and an understanding of projects under consideration. It is most difficult to obtain information about this latter category. However, real estate lenders, appraisers, brokers, developers, and other real estate professionals can provide this type of information. Vacancy rates for existing competition should be carefully considered along with rent levels and operating expenses.
4. The physical aspects of any proposed or existing project must be reviewed. Such factors as the compatibility with existing uses, size, shape, topography, zoning regulations, density requirements, and deed restrictions must be analyzed.

The market study must also provide information about such items as anticipated rent levels, vacancy rates, and forecasts of future property values.

To analyze the market for the investment, the investor collects data for a sample of comparable properties. Table 14-1 summarizes some of this information. The investor has information on the comparable properties in the price range similar to the subject property. Information on the date of sale, sale price, number of apartments, number of vacant apartments, average square footage per apartment, number of rooms, effective gross income, operating expenses, and net operating income can be found in Table 14-1.

Table 14-2 summarizes various units of comparison for each of the comparable properties. We have calculated the price per apartment, price per room, price per square foot, gross income multiplier, average rent per unit per month, average rent per room per month, average rent per square foot per month, operating expense ratio, overall rate, and vacancy rate for each comparable sale. From this information, the investor formulates expectations about the marketplace. Note that rent for the comparables ranges from $285 to $325 per month per unit. Note also that the vacancy rate is between zero and

TABLE 14-1 Comparable Apartment Sales

COMPA-RABLE	DATE OF SALE (MONTHS AGO)	SALE PRICE	NUMBER OF APARTMENTS	NUMBER OF VACANT APARTMENTS	NUMBER OF ROOMS	AVERAGE SQUARE FEET PER APARTMENT	EFFECTIVE GROSS INCOME	OPERATING EXPENSES	NET OPERATING INCOME
1	2	$300,000	16	1	64	1,000	$ 54,000	$24,000	$30,000
2	6	330,000	18	2	67	950	62,400	29,900	32,500
3	8	475,000	24	1	100	925	86,900	39,000	47,900
4	1	545,000	28	0	110	1,100	92,400	38,900	53,500
5	5	525,000	30	2	120	1,050	105,800	52,000	53,800
6	6	510,000	25	1	105	1,125	86,400	38,000	48,400
7	3	500,000	26	0	105	1,100	93,600	42,100	51,500
8	10	410,000	22	2	96	1,000	69,600	29,000	40,600
9	5	590,000	36	3	140	1,025	120,500	59,500	61,000
10	1	800,000	40	3	170	1,100	142,000	60,500	81,500

TABLE 14-2 Units of Comparison for Apartments*

COMPA-RABLE	PRICE PER APART-MENT	PRICE PER ROOM	PRICE PER SQUARE FOOT	GROSS INCOME MULTI-PLIER	AVERAGE RENT PER UNIT/MONTH	AVERAGE RENT PER ROOM/ MONTH	AVERAGE RENT PER SQ. FT./ MONTH	OPERATING EXPENSE RATIO	OVERALL RATE	VACANCY RATE
1	$18,750	$4,688	$18.75	5.56	$300	$70.31	$0.3000	.4444	.1000	6.25%
2	18,333	4,925	19.30	5.29	325	77.61	.3421	.4792	.0985	11.11
3	19,792	4,750	21.40	5.47	315	72.42	.3405	.4488	.1008	4.17
4	19,464	4,955	17.69	5.90	275	70.00	.2500	.4210	.0982	0
5	17,500	4,375	16.67	4.96	315	73.47	.3000	.4915	.1025	6.67
6	20,400	4,857	18.13	5.90	300	68.57	.2667	.4398	.0949	4.00
7	19,231	4,762	17.48	5.34	300	74.29	.2727	.4498	.1030	0
8	18,636	4,271	18.64	5.89	290	60.42	.2900	.4167	.0990	9.1
9	16,389	4,214	15.99	4.90	304	71.73	.2966	.4938	.1034	8.33
10	20,000	4,706	18.18	5.63	320	69.61	.2909	.4261	.1019	7.5

* Calculated from data in Table 14-1.

TABLE 14-3   Assumptions from Market Analysis

1. Investment type: Apartments
2. The asking price is $475,000.
3. The total number of rentable units is twenty-five. The average number of square feet per unit is 1,125. The total number of rooms is 110.
4. The age of the investment is ten years.
5. Rents are expected to range from $285 to $325 per unit per month.
6. Vacancy and bad debt losses are expected to be between 3 and 7 percent per year.
7. Rents are expected to increase at an annual rate between 3 and 7 percent.
8. Demand is expected to be strong. Evidently there is a growing demand.
9. The location is excellent relative to shopping and employment centers.
10. The building is in good condition with little deferred maintenance. This should help keep demand strong.

11.11 percent. Table 14-3 summarizes the assumptions based on this comparison.

Legal analysis. A second major category of risk is legislative (legal) risk. This is the possibility that the government will change the laws and introduce restrictions and regulations that cause incomes and/or property values to decline. Examples of this type of change would be increased taxation, change in zoning ordinances, and the exercising of the right of eminent domain.

Legal risk can also arise from the relationships between the other participants in the investment process (see Figure 1-2 in Chapter 1). For example, there may be deed restrictions that limit the use of the property or outstanding mortgage liens against the property that create a "cloud" in the title.

The investor must realize that *property rights* are bought and sold in the real estate market. The investor must be certain that the seller possesses the property rights. The buyer (investor) cannot acquire more rights than the seller has to sell. Table 14-4 illustrates the assumptions from the legal analysis.

Sociopolitical analysis.   Another area to be analyzed involves potential social constraints related to an investment. While a project may be legally permissible, it may not be feasible from society's point of view. Social controls in real estate investment analysis have received increased attention in recent years.

TABLE 14-4   Assumptions from Legal Analysis

1. The property conforms to current building code and zoning restrictions.
2. There is no threat of rent control in the community.
3. Property rights to be acquired are fee simple, subject to existing easements and government restrictions.
4. Current easements do not appear to have a significant impact on the value.
5. The current liens are property taxes (not in arrears) and an existing mortgage (nonassumable) that will be paid off on sale.

TABLE 14-5   Assumptions from Sociopolitical Analysis

1. There appear to be no sociopolitical problems associated with this investment.
2. The comprehensive zoning ordinance has been in effect and there do not appear to be any major developments in this area.
3. Local citizen groups are supportive of this type of investment.
4. Landlord-tenant law should not impose any problems on this investment.

A real estate investment creates *external* effects on the neighborhood and society in general. Some of these external effects are *positive* while others are *negative*. Potential external effects and their possible benefits and costs affect the risk and return expected from an investment. Examples of these effects include increased traffic and lowered (or increased) property values.

In this case, the apartment building's value should reflect these external effects. If it were a proposed project, the investor would be more concerned with the sociopolitical constraints. Is there any adverse neighborhood reaction to the investment? Table 14-5 indicates no expected sociopolitical problems with the investment.

Step 3: Forecast of Cash Flows

The third step in the development of the investment strategy is to forecast the expected cash flows (both in and out) for the expected holding period (length of ownership). The cash inflows are derived from two sources: the annual cash flows from rental collections and the cash flow from the disposition (typically sale) of the investment. The investor is interested in the expected after-tax cash flow from these two sources. This represents the amount of cash that the investment is expected to generate after all obligations, including income taxes, have been met.

Cash flows are those that the project is *expected* to generate. The investor will not know the *actual* cash flows until the investment has been acquired, operated, and sold. This is what investing is all about—sacrificing outflows for expected inflows. There is always the possibility that an investment will not produce the investor's expected level of cash flow. To formulate the expected cash flows, the investor must make decisions and assumptions regarding operations, financing, reversion, and tax planning.

Operating decisions.   To formulate the expected cash inflow, the investor must make assumptions regarding the operation of the investment. This operating plan should include expenses such as maintenance, repairs, utilities, property taxes, and insurance.

Table 14-6 shows the projected level of operating expenses in the first year. Total operating expenses are forecast to be $37,665 in the first year.

TABLE 14-6 Forecast First-Year Operating Expenses

EXPENSE CATEGORY	AMOUNT	% OF MOST LIKELY EGI (ROUNDED)
Real estate taxes	$10,044	12%
Insurance	2,511	3
Utilities	10,044	12
Administrative (management)	6,696	8
Maintenance and operation	8,370	10
Total operating expenses	$37,665	45

These expenses are expected to increase at a rate between 3 and 7 percent each year.

In the first year, the expected operating expenses require approximately 45 percent of the effective gross income (EGI). The investor must compare this expected level of expenses with that of the competition. After doing so, the investor decides that the operating expense ratio (OER) will probably vary between 42 and 50 percent (see Table 14-2).

Financing decisions. The next area of analysis of formulating the expected cash flows is the financing decisions. Financing involves two sources: debt and equity.

Table 14-7 summarizes the financing decision assumptions. Total mortgaged debt is $375,000 and the equity required is $115,000. Note that the equity is the sum of the down payment ($475,000 − $375,000) plus the cost of replacing the mortgage (15,000).

TABLE 14-7 Financing Decision Assumptions

DEBT FINANCING

1. The investor can borrow $375,000 from a local lender. This results in a loan-to-value ratio of about 80 percent.
2. The mortgage interest rate is 11 percent.
3. The mortgage maturity is twenty-five years with monthly payments.
4. Financing costs, including points and fees, are 4 percent of the amount borrowed, or $15,000 ($375,000 times .04).
5. Prepayment penalties are 3 percent of the outstanding balance.

EQUITY FINANCING

1. The equity investment is $100,000 plus the $15,000 financing costs. Total equity is thus $115,000.
2. The desired rate of return on the equity position is 13 percent after tax.

TABLE 14-8 Mortgage Amortization Schedule

Total cost: $475,000
Amount borrowed: $375,000
Interest rate: 11%
Maturity term: 25 years
Payments: Monthly
Annual mortgage constant: .1176
Debt service: $44,105

YEAR	PROPORTION OUTSTANDING	AMOUNT OUTSTANDING	DEBT SERVICE	INTEREST PAYMENT	PRINCIPAL PAYMENT
0	1.0	$375,000			
1	.99199	371,996	$44,105	$41,101	$3,004
2	.98305	368,644	44,105	40,754	3,352
3	.97308	364,905	44,105	40,366	3,739
4	.96196	360,735	44,105	39,934	4,170
5	.94955	356,081	44,105	39,451	4,654
6	.93570	350,888	44,105	38,912	5,193
7	.92025	345,094	44,105	38,311	5,794
8	.90301	338,629	44,105	37,640	6,465

The required rate of return on the equity is 13 percent. This rate reflects the risks to which the equity position is exposed (business risk, inflation risk, legal risk, and financial risk).

Table 14-8 gives the mortgage amortization schedule. This shows the distribution between interest and principal for each year of the holding period. The debt service is expected to be $44,105 per year.

Reversion decisions.   The second category of cash flow is that from the expected sale of the investment. The investor must forecast the expected changes in the property value over the expected holding period. The investment horizon is eight years. Table 14-9 summarizes the reversion decision assumptions.

Tax-planning decisions.   The last major area of analysis in forecasting the expected cash flows is tax planning. Table 14-10 lists the assumptions for tax planning. The important elements are the tax rate and the depreciation deduction. The amount of the depreciation deduction depends on the deprecia-

TABLE 14-9 Reversion Decision Assumptions

1. Property values are expected to increase between 3 and 5 percent per year.
2. Selling expenses (brokerage fees, legal fees, etc.) are estimated to be 10 percent of the selling price.

TABLE 14-10 Tax-Planning Assumptions

1. The investor is in a 28 percent marginal tax bracket that is not expected to change over the holding period.
2. The building has a value of $403,750 (or about 85 percent of the total cost). The depreciable basis is thus $403,750.
3. The useful life of the building for tax purposes is 27.5 years with a zero salvage value.
4. The investor will use the straight-line depreciation method.
5. The alternative minimum tax is not applicable.

TABLE 14-11 Depreciation Schedule

Total cost:	$475,000
Depreciable amount:	$403,750
Nondepreciable amount:	$71,250
Useful life:	27.5 years
Depreciation method:	straight-line

YEAR	BOOK VALUE	AMOUNT	CUMULATIVE
0	$403,750		
1	389,068	$14,682	$ 14,682
2	374,386	14,682	29,364
3	359,704	14,682	44,046
4	345,022	14,682	58,728
5	330,340	14,682	73,410
6	315,658	14,682	88,092
7	300,976	14,682	102,774
8	286,294	14,682	117,456

ble basis, useful life, and depreciation method. Table 14-11 gives the depreciation schedule based on the assumptions in Table 14-10.

Table 14-12 summarizes the assumptions necessary to forecast the expected cash flows. These assumptions are based on the market, financing, operations, reversions, and tax-planning analyses. The investor has formulated expectations on three possible "states of the world": most likely, optimistic, and pessimistic. These three possible outcomes provide information regarding the "sensitivity" of the investment decision based on the assumptions. It is obvious that the investor will not know the actual state of the world until he or she buys, operates, and sells the property. The investor must, however, make a decision today based on the expectations. The next section develops the expected after-tax cash flows from operations and sale under these three possible outcomes.

The expected cash flow from operations. Using the assumptions from the preceding analysis, the expected after-tax cash flows from operations,

TABLE 14-12   Summary of Assumptions for Investment Inputs

INPUT		ASSUMPTIONS
Purchase price		$475,000
Number of units		25
Rents	Optimistic	$325 per month expected to increase 7% per year
	Most likely	$300 per month expected to increase 5% per year
	Pessimistic	$285 per month expected to increase 3% per year
Vacancies	Optimistic	3% per year
	Most likely	5% per year
	Pessimistic	7% per year
Operating expenses	Optimistic	$37,665 in the first year expected to increase 3% per year
	Most likely	Expected to increase 5% per year
	Pessimistic	Expected to increase 7% per year
Financing		$375,000 mortgage; 11% interest rate; monthly payments for 25 years; prepayment penalties of 3% of outstanding balance; 4% financing costs
Depreciation		Straight-line: useful life of 27.5 years Depreciable basis of $403,750
Holding period		8 years
Reversion price	Optimistic	Value is expected to be $725,000
	Most likely	Value is expected to be $675,000
	Pessimistic	Value is expected to be $575,000
Selling expenses		10% of value
Tax rate		28% marginal tax rate; the alternative minimum tax is not applicable
Equity		Total equity investment of $115,000; desired after-tax rate of return on equity is 13%

under the most likely, optimistic, and pessimistic outcomes, are given in Tables 14-13 through 14-18.

Tables 14-13 and 14-14 show that for the most likely outcome, the investment generates a negative taxable income each year. Note that using these most likely assumptions, rents are estimated to be approximately $425 per unit per month at the end of eight years, up from the initial $300.

Table 14-15 gives the ATCF for the optimistic assumptions. Under these assumptions, rents after eight years are estimated to be approximately $520 per month per unit. Since rents are rising much faster than operating expenses, NOI, and thus ATCF, almost double over the eight-year projected holding period.

Table 14-17 gives the expected ATCF from operations under the pessimistic assumptions. Here, rents are forecast to be approximately $350 per unit per month at the end of the holding period. Also, note that the investment generates a tax shelter for each year of the holding period and that in every year BTCF is negative. The ATCF is positive due to the tax shelter benefits. The investment does, however, have a declining expected ATCF for each year.

TABLE 14-13 Expected Cash Flow from Operations: Most Likely Assumptions

					YEAR			
	1	*2*	*3*	*4*	*5*	*6*	*7*	*8*
	Potential gross income (PGI)	$ 90,000	94,500	99,225	104,186	109,396	114,865	120,609	126,639
minus	Vacancy and bad debt allowance (VBD)	$ 4,500	4,725	4,961	5,209	5,470	5,743	6,030	6,332
plus	Miscellaneous income (MI)	$ 0	0	0	0	0	0	0	0
equals	Effective gross income (EGI)	$ 85,500	89,775	94,264	98,977	103,926	109,122	114,578	120,307
minus	Operating expenses (OE)	$ 37,665	39,548	41,526	43,602	45,782	48,071	50,475	52,998
equals	Net operating income (NOI)	$ 47,835	50,227	52,738	55,375	58,144	61,051	64,103	67,309
minus	Debt service (DS)	$ 44,105	44,105	44,105	44,105	44,105	44,105	44,105	54,264†
equals	Before-tax cash flow (BTCF)	$ 3,730	6,122	8,633	11,270	14,039	16,946	19,998	13,045
minus	Taxes (savings) from operation (TO)*	$ (2,394)	(1,627)	(815)	45	955	1,920	2,943	(1,672)
equals	After-tax cash flow (ATCF)	$ 6,123	7,748	9,448	11,225	13,084	15,026	17,055	14,717

* See Table 14-14 for tax computation.
† This includes a prepayment penalty of $10,159 on the mortgage.

TABLE 14-14 Taxes from Operations: Most Likely Assumptions

		YEAR							
		1	2	3	4	5	6	7	8
	Effective gross income (EGI)	$ 85,500	89,775	94,264	98,977	103,926	109,122	114,578	120,307
minus	Operating expenses (OE)	$ 37,665	39,548	41,526	43,602	45,782	48,071	50,475	52,998
equals	Net operating income (NOI)	$ 47,835	50,227	52,738	55,375	58,144	61,051	64,103	67,309
minus	Interest on debt (I)	$ 41,102	40,754	40,366	39,934	39,451	38,912	38,311	47,800*
minus	Depreciation deduction (D)	$ 14,682	14,682	14,682	14,682	14,682	14,682	14,682	14,682
minus	Amortized financing costs (AFC)	$ 600	600	600	600	600	600	600	10,800
plus	Replacement reserves (RR)	$ 0	0	0	0	0	0	0	0
equals	Ordinary taxable income (OTI)	$ (8,548)	(5,809)	(2,910)	160	3,411	6,857	10,510	(5,973)
times	Investor's marginal tax rate (τ)	0.28	0.28	0.28	0.28	0.28	0.28	0.28	0.28
equals	Taxes (savings) from operation (TO)	$ (2,394)	(1,627)	(815)	45	955	1,978	2,943	(1,672)

* This includes a prepayment penalty of $10,159, deductible as interest for tax purposes.

TABLE 14-15 Expected Cash Flow from Operations: Optimistic Assumption

		YEAR							
		1	2	3	4	5	6	7	8
	Potential gross income (PGI)	$ 97,500	104,325	111,628	119,442	127,803	136,749	146,321	156,564
minus	Vacancy and bad debt allowance (VBD)	$ 2,925	3,130	3,349	3,583	3,834	4,102	4,390	4,697
plus	Miscellaneous income (MI)	$ 0	0	0	0	0	0	0	0
equals	Effective gross income (EGI)	$ 94,575	101,195	108,279	115,858	123,969	132,646	141,932	151,867
minus	Operating expenses (OE)	$ 37,665	38,795	39,959	41,158	42,392	43,664	44,974	46,323
equals	Net operating income (NOI)	$ 56,910	62,400	68,320	74,701	81,576	88,982	96,958	105,544
minus	Debt service (DS)	$ 44,105	44,105	44,105	44,105	44,105	44,105	44,105	54,264†
equals	Before-tax cash flow (BTCF)	$ 12,805	18,295	24,215	30,596	37,471	44,877	52,853	51,280
minus	Taxes (savings) from operation (TO)*	$ 147	1,782	3,548	5,456	7,516	9,741	12,142	9,033
equals	After-tax cash flow (ATCF)	$ 12,657	16,513	20,667	25,140	29,955	35,136	40,710	42,246

* See Table 14-16 for tax computation.
† This includes a prepayment penalty of $10,159 on mortgage.

TABLE 14-16 Taxes from Operations: Optimistic Assumptions

		1	2	3	4	YEAR 5	6	7	8
	Effective gross income (EGI)	$ 94,575	101,195	108,279	115,858	123,969	132,646	141,932	151,867
minus	Operating expenses (OE)	$ 37,665	38,795	39,959	41,158	42,392	43,664	44,974	46,323
equals	Net operating income (NOI)	$ 56,910	62,400	68,320	74,701	81,576	88,982	96,958	105,544
minus	Interest on debt (I)	$ 41,102	40,754	40,366	39,934	39,451	38,912	38,311	47,800*
minus	Depreciation deduction (D)	$ 14,682	14,682	14,682	14,682	14,682	14,682	14,682	14,682
minus	Amortized financing costs (AFC)	$ 600	600	600	600	600	600	600	10,800
plus	Replacement reserves (RR)	$ 0	0	0	0	0	0	0	0
equals	Ordinary taxable income (OTI)	$ 527	6,364	12,672	19,486	26,844	34,788	43,364	32,262
times	Investor's marginal tax rate (τ)	0.28	0.28	0.28	0.28	0.28	0.28	0.28	0.28
equals	Taxes (savings) from operation (TO)	$ 147	1,782	3,548	5,456	7,516	9,741	12,142	9,033

*This includes a prepayment penalty of $10,159, deductible as interest for tax purposes.

TABLE 14-17 Expected Cash Flow from Operations: Pessimistic Assumptions

		YEAR							
		1	2	3	4	5	6	7	8
	Potential gross income (PGI)	$ 85,500	88,065	90,707	93,428	96,231	99,118	102,091	105,154
minus	Vacancy and bad debt allowance (VBD)	$ 5,985	6,165	6,349	6,540	6,736	6,938	7,146	7,361
plus	Miscellaneous income (MI)	$ 0	0	0	0	0	0	0	0
equals	Effective gross income (EGI)	$ 79,515	81,900	84,357	86,888	89,495	92,180	94,945	97,793
minus	Operating expenses (OE)	$ 37,665	40,302	43,123	46,141	49,371	52,827	56,525	60,482
equals	Net operating income (NOI)	$ 41,850	41,599	41,235	40,747	40,124	39,353	38,420	37,312
minus	Debt service (DS)	$ 44,105	44,105	44,105	44,105	44,105	44,105	44,105	54,264†
equals	Before-tax cash flow (BTCF)	$ (2,255)	(2,506)	(2,870)	(3,358)	(3,981)	(4,753)	(5,685)	(16,952)
minus	Taxes (savings) from operation (TO)*	$ (4,069)	(4,042)	(4,036)	(4,051)	(4,091)	(4,156)	(4,248)	(10,072)
equals	After-tax cash flow (ATCF)	$ 1,814	1,536	1,165	693	109	(597)	(1,437)	(6,881)

* See Table 14-18 for tax computation.
† This includes a prepayment penalty of $10,159 on the mortgage.

TABLE 14-18 Taxes from Operations: Pessimistic Assumptions

		YEAR							
		1	2	3	4	5	6	7	8
	Effective gross income (EGI)	$ 79,515	81,900	84,357	86,888	89,495	92,180	94,945	97,793
minus	Operating expenses (OE)	$ 37,665	40,302	43,123	46,141	49,371	52,827	56,525	60,482
equals	Net operating income (NOI)	$ 41,850	41,599	41,235	40,747	40,124	39,353	38,420	37,312
minus	Interest on debt (I)	$ 41,102	40,754	40,366	39,934	39,451	38,912	38,311	47,800*
minus	Depreciation reduction (D)	$ 14,682	14,682	14,682	14,682	14,682	14,682	14,682	14,682
minus	Amortized financing costs (AFC)	$ 600	600	600	600	600	600	600	10,800
plus	Replacement reserves (RR)	$ 0	0	0	0	0	0	0	0
equals	Ordinary taxable income (OTI)	$ (14,533)	(14,437)	(14,413)	(14,468)	(14,609)	(14,842)	(15,173)	(35,970)
times	Investor's marginal tax rate (τ)	0.28	0.28	0.28	0.28	0.28	0.28	0.28	0.28
equals	Taxes (savings) from operation (TO)	$ (4,069)	(4,042)	(4,036)	(4,051)	(4,091)	(4,156)	(4,248)	(10,072)

* This includes a prepayment penalty of $10,159, deductible as interest for tax purposes.

The declining ATCF results from the fact that rents are not rising as fast as operating expenses, which causes NOI to decline.

The expected after-tax cash flow from sale. The expected after-tax cash flow from sale (ATER) is given in Tables 14-19, 14-21, and 14-23 for the most likely, optimistic, and pessimistic assumptions regarding future values of the property. Tables 14-20, 14-22, and 14-24 give the taxable income and the taxes due on sale for these three possible outcomes.

Step 4: Applying the Decision-Making Criteria

The preceding section developed the expected cash flow from operations and sale. We now turn to the decision-making criteria: rules of thumb, appraisal methods, and discounted cash flow models.

TABLE 14-19   Expected Cash Flow from Sale in Year 8: Most Likely Assumptions

	Expected selling price (SP)	$ 675,000
minus	Selling expenses (SE)	$ 67,500
equals	Net sales proceeds (NSP)	$ 607,500
minus	Unpaid mortgage balance (UM)	$ 338,630
equals	Before-tax equity reversion (BTER)	$ 268,870
minus	Taxes due on sale (TDS)*	$ 69,987
equals	After-tax equity reversion (ATER)	$ 198,883

* See Table 14-20 for calculation of taxes due on sale.

TABLE 14-20   Taxes Due on Sale in Year 8: Most Likely Assumptions

	Expected selling price (SP)	$ 675,000
minus	Selling expenses (SE)	$ 67,500
equals	Amount realized (AR)	$ 607,500
minus	Adjusted basis (AB)	$ 357,545
	Total gain on sale	$ 249,955
minus	Investor's marginal tax rate (τ)	0.28
equals	Taxes due on sale (TDS)	$ 69,987

TABLE 14-21   Expected Cash Flow from Sale in Year 8: Optimistic Assumptions

	Expected selling price (SP)	$ 725,000
minus	Selling expenses (SE)	$ 72,500
equals	Net sales proceeds (NSP)	$ 652,500
minus	Unpaid mortgage balance (UM)	$ 338,630
equals	Before-tax equity reversion (BTER)	$ 313,870
minus	Taxes due on sale (TDS)*	$ 82,587
equals	After-tax equity reversion (ATER)	$ 231,283

* See Table 14-22 for calculation of taxes due on sale.

TABLE 14-22   Taxes Due on Sale in Year 8: Optimistic Assumptions

	Expected selling price (SP)	$ 725,000
minus	Selling expenses (SE)	$ 72,500
equals	Amount realized (AR)	$ 652,500
minus	Adjusted basis (AB)	$ 357,545
equals	Total gain on sale	$ 294,955
times	Investor's marginal tax rate (τ)	0.28
equals	Taxes due on sale (TDS)	$ 82,587

TABLE 14-23   Expected Cash Flow from Sale in Year 8: Pessimistic Assumptions

	Expected selling price (SP)	$ 575,000
minus	Selling expenses (SE)	$ 57,500
equals	Net sales proceeds (NSP)	$ 517,500
minus	Unpaid mortgage balance (UM)	$ 338,630
equals	Before-tax equity reversion (BTER)	$ 178,870
minus	Taxes due on sale (TDS)*	$ 44,787
equals	After-tax equity reversion (ATER)	$ $134,083

* See Table 14-24 for calculation of taxes due on sale.

Rules of thumb.   Some alternative rules of thumb are shown in Table 14-25. These include the gross income multiplier (GIM), overall rate, equity dividend rate (EDR), after-tax rate (ATR), debt-coverage ratio (DCR), and operating-expense ratio (OER). Each is calculated using the most likely, optimistic, and pessimistic assumptions.

**TABLE 14-24   Taxes Due on Sale in Year 8:
Pessimistic Assumptions**

	Expected selling price (SP)	$ 575,000
minus	Selling expenses (SE)	$ 57,500
equals	Amount realized (AR)	$ 517,500
minus	Adjusted basis (AB)	$ 357,545
equals	Total gain on sale	$ 159,955
times	Investor's marginal tax rate (τ)	0.28
equals	Taxes due on sale (TDS)	$ 44,787

How does the investor decide whether or not to invest, using these rules of thumb? Obviously, the investor needs a standard of comparison.

To illustrate, the GIM for each of the comparable properties is shown in Table 14-26. These can be used as the standard by which to make the decision. By comparing the gross income multiplier of the subject property (5.56) with those of the comparables, we see that the subject property appears to be at the upper end of the range. This indicates that the property may be somewhat overpriced relative to the market. For example, the market GIM appears to be around 5.75. Using this and the subject property EGI of $85,500, we get a value estimate of

$$\text{Value} = 5.75 \ (\$85,500) = \$491,625$$

The debt-coverage ratio (DCR) is widely used by mortgage lenders. It is the ratio of the NOI to the debt service. In this case, the DCR in the first year is 1.08 in the most likely outcome. This would probably fall at the lower end of the acceptable range for most mortgage lenders.

The various other rules of thumb shown in the table are used in the same manner as the GIM or the DCR. The investor compares these with a standard and accepts or rejects the investment. Note that the rules of thumb

TABLE 14-25   Rules of Thumb Using First-Year Cash Flow from Operation*

	STATE OF THE WORLD		
RULE OF THUMB	MOST LIKELY	OPTIMISTIC	PESSIMISTIC
1. Gross income multiplier (GIM)	5.56	5.02	5.97
2. Overall rate	10.07%	11.98%	8.81%
3. Equity dividend rate (EDR)	3.24%	11.13%	−1.96%
4. After-tax rate (ATR)	5.32%	11.01%	1.58%
5. Debt-coverage ratio (DCR)	1.08	1.29	.95
6. Operating expense ratio (OER)	.44	.40	.47

* Calculated using cash flows in Tables 14-13, 14-15, and 14-17.

TABLE 14-26   Rules of Thumb for Comparable Sales*

COMPA-RABLE	GROSS INCOME MULTIPLIER	OVERALL RATE	EQUITY DIVIDEND RATE†	DEBT-COVERAGE RATIO†	OPERATING EXPENSE RATIO
1	5.56	.1000	4.72%	1.13	44.44%
2	5.29	.0985	4.11	1.12	47.92
3	5.47	.1008	5.06	1.14	44.88
4	5.90	.0982	3.99	1.11	42.10
5	4.96	.1025	5.71	1.16	49.15
6	5.90	.0949	2.68	1.08	43.98
7	5.34	.1030	5.92	1.17	44.98
8	5.89	.0990	4.33	1.12	41.67
9	4.90	.1033	6.07	1.17	49.38
10	5.63	.1019	5.47	1.15	42.61

* Calculated using data in Table 14-2.
† This was calculated assuming that the comparables were financed with a 75% mortgage at an interest rate of 11% with monthly payments over 25 years.

do not always lead to the same accept/reject decision. An investment that may be acceptable using the GIM may be unacceptable using the EDR method. The investor should compute all the various rules of thumb and arrive at the investment decision after analyzing each one.

Appraisal methods. A second set of decision-making criteria consists of the traditional appraisal methods discussed in Chapter 11. These methods of valuation are the direct sales comparison approach, the cost approach, and the income approach. Each of these methods provides the investor with an estimate of value for the subject property. These estimates can be used in making the investment decision.

Table 14-27 gives the estimated value of the property using the *cost approach*. The investor estimates the land market value at $71,250. Site improvements, such as paving and landscaping, have an estimated reproduction cost (new) of $24,500. The depreciated value is estimated at $21,325. The apartment buildings have a reproduction cost (new) of $25 per square foot for a total of $703,125. However, given the physical condition, the depreciated value is estimated at $421,875. The total indicated value of the property using the cost approach is $514,000.

Under the *direct sales comparison* approach, the value of the property is estimated using the comparable sales obtained in the market. As we noted in Chapter 11, there are various units of comparison. Table 14-28 gives the unadjusted prices per room, unit, and square foot for each comparable and the unadjusted indication of the value for the subject property. These unadjusted estimates provide a fairly wide range in the value of the subject property.

Table 14-29 gives the adjustment grid for selected comparable sales. Given the data in Table 14-1, the investor decided that comparable numbers

TABLE 14-27 Cost Approach Summary: 25-Unit Apartment

PROPERTY COMPONENT	REPRO-DUCTION COST	PERCENT DEPRE-CIATION	DEPRE-CIATED VALUE	MARKET VALUE
Land:				
3 acres @ $23,750 per acre, or 25 apartment units @ $2,850 per unit				$ 71,250
Site improvements:				
Utilities	$ 6,500	5%	$ 6,175	
Paving	12,000	20	9,600	
Walkways	2,000	15	1,700	
Landscaping	3,000	0	3,000	
Outside lighting	1,000	15	850	
Total	$ 24,500			$ 21,325
Buildings:				
Apartments (28,125 sq. ft. @ $25)	$703,125	40	$421,875	$421,875
				$514,450
Indicated value from cost approach			(rounded)	$514,000

3, 4, 6, and 7 were the most similar to the subject property. In addition, analysis of the various units of comparison (price per unit, price per room, price per square foot) indicates that price per room is probably the best unit of comparison.

The adjustment grid (Table 14-29) indicates an adjusted price per room of about $4,600. This results in an estimated value of about $506,000 ($4,600 times 110 rooms). Note that the comparables have been adjusted for time, location, and building condition. Using the direct sales comparison approach, it appears that the property's market value is within the $500,000 to $510,000 range.

The third appraisal method is the *income approach*. Under this approach, the value is estimated by capitalizing the property's income stream. As we noted in Chapter 11, there are three major income methods: direct capitalization of NOI using a market-extracted overall rate, direct capitalization using a weighted-average capitalization rate, and the mortgage-equity method.

Table 14-30 gives the *market-extracted overall rate* for each comparable and the indicated value for the subject property. The overall rate was calculated for each comparable by dividing the NOI by the sale price. For example, comparable number 1 had an NOI of $30,000 and a sale price of $300,000.

TABLE 14-28 Unadjusted Market Comparison Approach Estimates

COMPA-RABLE	UNADJUSTED PRICE PER ROOM*	INDICATED VALUE—SUBJECT PROPERTY	UNADJUSTED PRICE PER UNIT*	INDICATED VALUE—SUBJECT PROPERTY	UNADJUSTED PRICE PER SQ. FT.*	INDICATED VALUE—SUBJECT PROPERTY
1	$4,688	$515,680	$18,750	$468,750	$18.75	$527,344
2	4,925	541,750	18,333	458,325	19.30	542,813
3	4,750	522,500	19,792	494,800	21.40	601,875
4	4,955	545,050	19,464	486,600	17.69	497,531
5	4,375	481,250	17,500	437,500	16.67	468,844
6	4,857	534,270	20,400	510,000	18.13	509,906
7	4,762	523,820	19,231	480,775	17.48	491,625
8	4,271	469,810	18,636	465,900	18.64	524,250
9	4,214	463,540	16,390	409,750	15.99	449,719
10	4,706	517,660	20,000	500,000	18.18	511,313

* Calculated from sales data.

TABLE 14-29   Adjustment Grid for Comparable Sales

| FACTOR | COMPARABLE SALE* | | | |
	3	4	6	7
Sale price	$475,000	$545,000	$510,000	$500,000
Number of rooms	100	110	105	105
Price per room	4,750	4,955	4,857	4,762
Time adjustment	+ 5%	0	+ 4%	+ 2%
	(+238)		(+194)	(+ 95)
Condition of building	0	− 15%	− 10%	0
		(−743)	(−486)	
Location	− 10%	+ 10%	0	− 5%
	(−475)	(+496)	0	(−238)
Net adjustment	−237	−247	−292	−143
Value per room	$ 4,513	$ 4,708	$ 4,565	$ 4,619
Indicated value of subject property (110 rooms)	$496,430	$517,880	$502,150	$508,090

* See Table 14-1.

TABLE 14-30   Value Using Market-Extracted Overall Rate

COMPARABLE*	OVERALL RATE†	INDICATED VALUE— SUBJECT PROPERTY‡
1	.1000	$478,000
2	.0985	485,300
3	.1008	474,200
4	.0982	486,800
5	.1025	466,300
6	.0949	503,700
7	.1030	464,100
8	.0990	482,800
9	.1033	462,700
10	.1019	469,100

* See Table 14-1.
† This is the NOI of each comparable divided by its sale price, as reported in Table 14-2.
‡ This is the subject property's estimated NOI ($47,800) divided by the rate from each comparable.

This results in an overall rate of 10 percent ($30,000/$300,000). Using this rate and the subject property's estimated NOI of $47,800 in year 1, the indicated value is $478,000. This process was repeated for each comparable. Using this approach, it appears that a value estimate of $490,000 to $500,000 would be reasonable.

Another income approach method is to capitalize the NOI using a *weighted-average overall rate*, defined as

$$R = L/V\,(MC) + E/V\,(EDR) \tag{14-1}$$

where

R = overall rate
L/V = loan-to-value ratio
MC = annual mortgage constant
E/V = equity-to-value ratio
EDR = equity dividend rate

Using the loan-to-value ratio of 75 percent, an interest rate of 11 percent with a maturity of twenty-five years (monthly), and an equity dividend rate of 5 percent (see Table 14-26):

$$R = .75(.1176) + .25(.05)$$
$$R = .0882 + .0125$$
$$R = .1007$$

The indicated value would be

$$V = \$47,800/.1007$$
$$V = \$475,000 \text{ (rounded)}$$

Thus the asking price of $475,000 appears to be the same using these appraisal methods.

Recall from our discussion of the appraisal model in Chapter 11 that the total value of an investment can be defined as the value of the mortgage plus the present value of the cash flows to the equity. This is called the *mortgage-equity method*. In equation form:

$$V = V_M + V_E \tag{14-2}$$

where

V = total value
V_M = value of the mortgage
V_E = value of the equity

Using the before-tax cash flows, the value of the equity position (V_E) can be written as

$$V_E = \sum_{t=1}^{n} \frac{BTCF_t}{(1+y)^t} + \frac{BTER_n}{(1+y)^n} \tag{14-3}$$

where

$BTCF_t$ = expected before-tax cash flows in year t
$BTER_n$ = expected before-tax equity reversion in the year of sale
y = required rate of return on equity (before tax)

Returning to our example, suppose the investor's required (before-tax) return is 13 percent. Using the "most likely" forecasts of the BTCF and BTER

TABLE 14-31   Present Value of Equity Using Before-Tax Cash Flows

YEAR	BTCF	BTER	PVF @ 13%	PV
1	$ 3,730		.88496	$ 3,301
2	6,122		.78315	4,794
3	8,633		.69305	5,983
4	11,270		.61332	6,912
5	14,039		.54276	7,620
6	16,946		.48032	8,140
7	19,998		.42506	8,500
8	13,045	$268,870	.37616	106,045
			Total Equity Value =	$151,295

shown in Table 14-31, the present value of these cash flows is approximately $151,000. Since the mortgage value (amount) is $375,000, the total value of the investment would be

$$V = \$375,000 + \$151,000$$
$$V = \$526,000$$

This means that the investor could pay up to $526,000 for the investment and earn an expected yield of 13 percent. A price more than this would mean that the expected yield would be less than 13 percent, and vice versa. Using this mortgage-equity valuation approach, the investment seems to be acceptable to the investor. Note that if the investor-required before-tax yield on equity was increased (decreased), the value of the investment would decrease (increase).

Discounted cash flow models.   The third major set of investment criteria consists of the discounted cash flow (DCF) models. As the name implies, the DCR models take the forecast cash flows and discount them back to the present. Thus the investor has the present worth of the expected cash flows.

The best DCF model is called the *net present value* (NPV) technique in which the investor calculates the total present value of the cash flows and compares this with the cost of investing. Under the NPV criterion, the investor invests if the NPV is positive. The investor does not invest if the NPV is negative. These decision rules make sense intuitively. They say: Compute the present worth of the expected cash flows at the desired rate of return; compare this present worth with how much it costs to invest; if the costs exceed the present worth of the cash flow, do not invest; if the present worth of the cash flows exceeds the costs, do invest.

Tables 14-32, 14-33, and 14-34 give the net present value of the ATCF from operation and the ATER from the sale at the end of eight years. Recall that the equity investment was $115,000. These present values were calculated using a 13 percent rate of return. These cash flows are taken from the most likely, optimistic, and pessimistic outcomes. The after-tax cash flows represent

TABLE 14-32   Present Value of After-Tax Flows at 13% Rate: Most Likely Assumptions

YEAR	EQUITY*	ATCF†	ATER‡	PRESENT VALUE FACTOR AT 13%	PRESENT VALUE
0	$(115,000)			1.00000	$(115,000)
1		$ 6,123		.88496	5,419
2		7,748		.78315	6,068
3		9,448		.69305	6,548
4		11,225		.61332	6,885
5		13,084		.54276	7,101
6		15,026		.48032	7,217
7		17,055		.42506	7,249
8		14,717	$198,883	.37616	80,348
				Net Present Value = $	11,835

* This is the asking price ($475,000) minus the mortgage ($375,000) plus the financing costs ($15,000).
† See Table 14-13.
‡ See Table 14-19.

the amount going to the equity position after all expenses, debt service, and taxes have been paid.

Column 5 of Tables 14-32, 14-33, and 14-34 contains the present value factor at the desired 13 percent rate of return on equity. Recall that the investor's objective is to decide whether or not the investment would yield a 13 percent rate of return on the equity investment of $115,000. The present value factors were taken from the present value tables in the Appendix. These factors, when multiplied by the expected cash flows in the respective years, give the present value of these cash flows, as shown in column 6.

TABLE 14-33   Present Value of After-Tax Flows at 13% Rate: Optimistic Assumptions

YEAR	EQUITY	ATCF*	ATER†	PRESENT VALUE FACTOR AT 13%	PRESENT VALUE
0	$(115,000)			1.0000	$(115,000)
1		$12,657		.88496	11,201
2		16,513		.78315	12,932
3		20,667		.69305	14,323
4		25,140		.61332	15,419
5		29,955		.54276	16,258
6		35,136		.48032	16,877
7		40,710		.42506	17,304
8		42,246	$231,283	.37616	102,891
				Net Present Value = $	92,206

* See Table 14-15.
† See Table 14-21.

**TABLE 14-34 Present Value of After-Tax Cash Flows at 13% Rate:
Pessimistic Assumptions**

YEAR	EQUITY	ATCF*	ATER†	PRESENT VALUE FACTOR AT 13%	PRESENT VALUE
0	$(115,000)			1.0000	$(115,000)
1		$1,814		.88496	1,605
2		1,536		.78315	1,203
3		1,165		.69305	807
4		693		.61332	425
5		109		.54276	59
6		(597)		.48032	(287)
7		(1,437)		.42506	(611)
8		(6,881)	$134,083	.37616	47,848
				Net Present Value = $(63,951)	

* See Table 14-17.
† See Table 14-23.

To interpret the present value numbers in column 6, look at Table 14-32. This table gives the ATCF for the most likely assumptions. In year 5, the investment is expected to generate $13,084 in ATCF. However, the present value of this $13,084 is $7,101. This means that at the desired rate of return of 13 percent, the investor is willing to pay $7,101 for the right to receive $13,084 five years later.

The net present value of the cash flow is found by adding the numbers in column 6. Note that the net present value for the most likely assumptions is $11,835. The net present value of the cash flows under the optimistic assumptions is $92,206. Likewise, the net present value is ($63,951) for the pessimistic assumptions. Under the most likely assumptions the investment is acceptable, since the NPV is positive. This means that the present value of the cash inflows at a rate of 13 percent is greater than the equity outflow. Thus the investment is "worth" $11,835 more than it "costs."

A second discounted cash flow method is the internal rate of return (IRR). Recall from Chapter 12 that the IRR is the rate that will make the present value of the cash inflows equal to the present value of the cash outflows. Using the most likely estimates of the cash flows (see Table 14-32), the IRR is 14.70 percent. Under the optimistic forecasts, the IRR is 25.01 percent. With the pessimistic forecasts, the IRR falls to 1.64 percent.

To make the investment decision using the IRR method, compare the calculated IRR using the expected cash flows with the required rate. If the expected rate of return exceeds the required rate, then the investment is acceptable. In the case for the most likely forecasts, the calculated (expected) IRR is 14.70 percent. The required rate is 13 percent. Thus the project appears acceptable.

Step 5: The Investment Decision

Now that the investor has established the objective and the investment environment, forecasted the cash flows, and applied the investment criteria, should he pay $475,000 for the investment?

Table 14-35 summarizes the results of the various investment criteria. Note that some of these indicate an accept decision, whereas others indicate a reject decision. The rules of thumb recommend rejection. However, the results for the proposed investment are very close to the market standard. The appraisal methods result in an acceptance. Generally, the direct sales comparison approach is the most widely advocated. The more sophisticated discounted cash flow models, using the most likely forecasts of cash flow, recommend acceptance.

For the most likely outcome, the NPV of the investment is $11,835. Using the NPV decision rules, the investor should make the investment.

The investment would be made under the optimistic outcome. The investment should not be undertaken under the pessimistic assumption.

Suppose the investor assigned the probabilities in Table 14-36 to the three possible "states of the world." The investor believes that there is an 80 percent chance of the most likely assumption occurring. There is a 10 percent probability of the optimistic or pessimistic outcomes. Multiply these probabilities times the net present value of each state in order to find the expected net present value. Thus it would appear that the project is one worth considering

TABLE 14-35   Summary of Investment Criteria

CRITERION	PROPOSED INVESTMENT	STANDARD	ACCEPT-ABLE
Rule of thumb			
GIM	5.56*	5.75	Yes
DCR	1.08*	1.15	No
EDR	3.24%*	5%	No
Appraisal methods			
Cost approach	$475,000	$514,000	Yes
Direct sales comparison	$475,000	$505,000	Yes
Income approach			
Direct capitalization	$475,000	$500,000	Yes
Weighted-average capitalization	$475,000	$475,000	Yes
Mortgage equity	$475,000	$526,000	Yes
Discounted cash flow models			
Net present value	$11,835*	$ 0	Yes
IRR	14.7%*	13%	Yes

* Using the most likely estimates of the expected cash flows.

TABLE 14-36   Expected Net Present Value

STATE OF THE WORLD	PROBABILITY	NET PRESENT VALUE	EXPECTED NPV
Optimistic outcome	.10	$92,206	$ 9,221
Most likely outcome	.80	11,835	9,468
Pessimistic outcome	.10	(63,951)	$(6,395)
		Expected NPV =	$12,294

as an investment. The investor could obviously reassess the likelihood of the various states of the world and recalculate the expected NPV.

What should the investor do? Obviously, many assumptions have been made. This, however, is what investing is all about. Investment is giving up cash today (equity) in return for expected, but risky, cash inflow in the future. The investor must formulate the expectations explicitly. While no investor knows the actual outcome, this does not mean that he cannot form expectations about the future. The critical question is, How certain is the investor that his expectations are correct? Obviously, under some possible outcomes the investor should invest, whereas under others he should not. The important lesson for the investor is to examine each assumption and expectation carefully, thus reducing the risk as much as possible. The investment decision is only as good as the expectations on which it is based.

The Offer

Using the analysis, the investor decides to make an offer on the property of $465,000. Other factors in the offer are as follows:

1. The offer is contingent on the investor being able to obtain a $375,000 mortgage at an 11 percent rate with monthly payments over twenty-five years.
2. Property taxes, of $10,044 for the current year, are to be prorated between the seller and the buyer at closing.
3. The seller is to provide the buyer with a termite inspection at a cost of $250.
4. The buyer is to obtain a title insurance policy at a cost of $1,000 (to be paid by the buyer).
5. Transfer tax, estimated at $6,000, is to be split 50/50 between the seller and the buyer.
6. Hazard insurance policy at a cost of $2,000 paid in advance for the current year is to be prorated at closing.
7. Loan origination fees of $15,000 are to be paid by the buyer.
8. The seller has seventy-two hours to accept the offer.
9. Closing is set for January 1, 19XX.
10. The seller is to deliver a general warranty deed.
11. The seller is to provide evidence of marketable title.

12. The buyer is to make an earnest money deposit of $5,000. This will become part of the buyer's equity if the offer is accepted.

13. Other costs of the transaction will be as follows:

Buyer:	
Document preparation	$ 500
Appraisal fees	1,000
Survey	500
Recording fees	100
Legal fees	2,000
Seller:	
Legal fees	$ 750
Broker's commission	25,000
Termite inspection	250
Mortgage balance	275,500

The Counteroffer and Acceptance

The seller reviews the offer and decides to accept all items except the price. The seller counteroffers at a price of $475,000.

This appears acceptable to the buyer, who accepts the counteroffer. Now the buyer and the seller have a binding sales contract.

Closing the Transaction

Table 14-37 contains the closing statement for this transaction. Note that the purchase price is $500,000. The buyer has deposited $5,000 and will borrow $375,000 on the first mortgage. The real property taxes have been paid by the seller, but since the closing is taking place at the beginning of the year, the buyer essentially reimburses the seller. The buyer is incurring a total cost of the transaction of $35,144. However, $10,044 of this is for the property taxes, an operating expense item. Basically the buyer is incurring acquisition

TABLE 14-37 The Closing Statement

Seller	Sam Jones		Buyer	John Smith
Spouse	Mary		Spouse	Judy
Address	3928 Gourrier		Address	405 Ave. F
	Baton Rouge, LA			Bogalusa, LA Phone (504) 927-2345
Phone (504) 769-8575 Mortgagee American Bank			Lender Union Federal Phone (504) 732-2798	
Attorney Walt Smith Phone (504) 346-6442			Attorney Neal Vincent Phone (504) 387-9417	

	Buyer		Seller	
	Debit	Credit	Debit	Credit
1. Consideration	$475,000			$475,000
2. Earnest Money Deposit		$ 5,000		

	Buyer		Seller	
	Debit	Credit	Debit	Credit
3. Real Property Taxes	10,044			10,044
4. Mortgage Payment				
5. Mortgage Interest Adjustment				
6. Mortgage Assumption				
7. Buyer's Mortgage		375,000		
8. Preparation of Loan Documents	500			
9. Loan (origination) Fee	15,000			
10. Mortgage Discount				
11. Real Estate Transfer Tax	3,000		$ 3,000	
12. Deed Preparation				
13. Lien				
14. Appraisal Fee	1,000			
15. Termite Certificate			250	
16. Agent's Commission			25,000	
17. Survey	500			
18. Fire Insurance	2,000			2,000
19. Legal Fees	2,000		750	
20. Title Insurance	1,000			
21. Recording	100			
22. Credit Report				
23. Fuel Oil				
24. Seller's Mortgage			275,500	
Debit/Credit Totals	$510,144	380,000	304,500	$487,044
Balance Needed to Close		130,144		
Balance Due to Seller			182,544	
Totals	510,144	510,144	487,044	$487,044

costs of about $10,000 and financing costs (see item 9) of $15,000 for a total of about $25,000, as was expected. This represents about 5 percent ($25,000/ $475,000) of the purchase price. The buyer needs about $130,144 to close the transaction. The resulting equity investment (excluding the property taxes) is approximately $125,000, or $10,000 more than expected because the purchase price increased due to the resulting costs of acquiring the property.

Since the acquisition costs increased the cost of the investment, the criteria analyzed in the previous section are not precise. However, viewing the previous analyses we know that the investment would still be attractive.

DEVELOPMENT EXAMPLE*

This example shows some of the additional analysis needed to make an investment decision when the investor will both develop and operate an income-producing property.

1. The development phase will start in January with the acquisition of a building site. The costs of site acquisition, preparation, and building construction are presented in Table 14-38.

TABLE 14-38 Acquisition and Development Cost Schedule

	JAN.	FEB.	MAR.	APR.	MAY	JUN.	JUL.
DISBURSEMENTS							
HARD COSTS							
Land	450000						
Site Improvements		50000	100000	85000			
Building Shell				30000	150000	87000	210000
Garage							30000
Tenant Improvements							
Furniture, Fixtures, Equipment							
TOTAL HARD COSTS	450000	50000	100000	115000	150000	87000	240000
SOFT COSTS					5000		10000
Marketing							
Architect & Engineer	20000		20000		20000		
Cons. Loan Fee							
Cons. Loan Interest		2070	2641	3816	5027	6752	7651
Permanent Loan Fee	0						
Start-Up	8500						
Miscellaneous							7500
Property Taxes		7500		7500			
TOTAL SOFT COSTS	28500	9570	22641	11316	30027	6752	25151
TOTAL COSTS	478500	59570	122641	126316	180027	93752	265151
Period surplus/-deficit	−478500	−59570	−122641	−126316	−180027	−93752	−265151
Cumulative surplus/-deficit	−478500	−538070	−660711	−787028	−967055	−1060807	−1325957
TOTAL FINANCING NEEDED	478500	59570	122641	126316	180027	93752	265151
Financing Sources							
Construction Loan Draw	216022	59570	122641	126316	180027	93752	265151
Equity Contributions	262478						
Construction Loan Payment							
TOTAL FINANCING OBTAINED	478500	59570	122641	126316	180027	93752	265151
Construction Loan Balance	216022	275592	398233	524550	704577	798329	1063479
Construction Loan Rate	NA	11.500%	11.500%	11.500%	11.500%	11.500%	11.500%

* This example was provided by Michael Giliberto of Southern Methodist University.

2. Upon completion the property will be placed in service. The following assumptions are used to develop the operating pro forma:

Purchase price	$3,204,697* (includes land cost of $450,000)
Selling Costs	4%
PGI (year 1)	$500,000
Income Growth Rate	5%
Vacancy/Collection Loss	5%
Operating Expenses	35% of EGI
Value Growth Rate	3%
Permanent Loan Amount	$2,560,000
Annual Interest Rate	9%
Loan Term	25 years (monthly payments)
Loan Fee	2%
Prepayment Penalty	1%
Marginal Tax Rate	28%
Straight-line depreciation	over 31.5 years
Holding Period	5 years
Required After-Tax Yield	13%

* Based on acquisition and development cost (see below).

The investor is subject to the passive activity loss limitation.

						QUARTERLY SUMMARY			
AUG.	SEP.	OCT.	NOV.	DEC.	TOTAL	1	2	3	4
					450000	450000	0	0	0
300000	105000	80000			235000	150000	85000	0	0
30000	75000	15000			1657000	0	267000	615000	775000
	45000	120000	120000	90000	150000	0	0	135000	15000
15000	15000	23000	24000	35000	375000	0	0	45000	330000
330000	240000	238000	839000	125000	97000	0	0	15000	82000
					2964000	600000	352000	810000	1202000
10000	10000	10000			45000	0	5000	30000	10000
					60000	40000	20000	0	0
					0	0			
10192	13548	16073	18604	26823	113197	4711	15596	31390	61500
					0	0	0	0	0
					8500	9500	0	0	0
					0	0	0	0	0
					22500	7500	7500	7500	0
20192	23548	26073	18604	26823	249197	60711	48096	68890	71500
350192	263548	264073	857604	151823	3213197	660711	400096	878890	1273500
−350192	−263548	−264073	−857604	−151823					
−1676149	−1939697	−2203770	−3061374	−3213197					
350192	263548	264073	857604	151823		660711	400096	878890	1273500
350192	263548	264073	857604	151823	2950719	398233	400096	878890	1273500
					262478	262478	0	0	0
					0	0	0	0	0
350192	263548	264073	857604	151823	3213197	660711	400096	878890	1273500
1413671	1677219	1941292	2798896	2950719					
11.500%	11.500%	11.500%	11.500%	11.500%					

3. The developer provided $262,478 of equity at the start of the project. All additional costs were funded with an open-ended construction loan. This loan carries an interest rate of 11.5%.

4. During the development phase there is essentially no taxable income or expense. Instead, most of the costs form the basis of the property, i.e., they are capitalized. These costs will be recovered through depreciation, starting at the time the building is placed in service. The exception is the start-up cost totaling $8,500. It is amortized over 5 years.

5. When the building is completed the investor/developer will use the proceeds of the permanent loan to repay the construction loan. Note that the construction loan balance at that time will be $2,950,719. The permanent loan of $2,560,000 does not provide enough to pay off the construction loan. Therefore, the investor will have to put an additional $390,719 into the project.

Investment Analysis

The operating pro forma for this property is presented in Table 14-39. To complete the investor's analysis, it is necessary to identify the after-tax equity

TABLE 14-39 Pro-Forma Operating Statements and Reversion Estimates

YEAR:	1	2	3	4	5
Potential Gross Income	500000	525000	551250	578813	607753
less Vacancy/Collection	−25000	−26250	−27563	−28941	−30388
Effective Gross Income	475000	498750	523688	549872	577365
less Operating Expenses	−166250	−174563	−183291	−192455	−202078
Net Operating Income	308750	324188	340397	357417	375288
less Debt Service	−257801	−257801	−257801	−257801	−257801
Before Tax Cash Flow	50949	66386	82596	99616	117486
Net Operating Income	308750	324188	340397	357417	375288
less Interest	−229241	−226562	−223631	−220426	−216920
Depreciation	−87493	−87493	−87493	−87493	−87493
Amort. of Start-Up	−1700	−1700	−1700	−1700	−1700
Amort. of Loan Fee	−2048	−2048	−2048	−2048	−2048
Taxable Earnings pre PALL	−11732	6384	25524	45749	67126
% PAL Disallowed	100%	100%	100%	100%	100%
PAL Allowed This Year	0	0	0	0	0
PAL Added to Carryforward	−11732	0	0	0	0
PAL Offset by Carryforward	0	6384	5348	0	0
Cum. PAL Carryforward	−11732	−5348	0	0	0
Taxable Earnings post PALL	0	0	20176	45749	67126
Federal Income Tax	0	0	−5649	−12810	−18795
Before Tax Cash Flow	50949	66386	82596	99616	117486
less Federal Income Tax	0	0	−5649	−12810	−18795
After Tax Cash Flow	50949	66386	76946	86806	98691

TABLE 14-39 (Cont.)   Pro-Forma Operating Statements and Reversion Estimates

YEAR:	1	2	3	4	5
Estimated Selling Price					3715122
less Selling Costs					−148605
Net Sales Proceeds					3566517
less Mortgage Balance					−2387774
Prepayment Penalty					−23878
BTCF from Reversion					1154865
Net Sales Proceeds					3566517
less Original Cost					−3204697
plus Accum. Depreciation					437467
Total Gain					799287
less Accum. PAL					0
Capital Gain					799287
Capital Gain Tax Liability					−223800
Ordinary Income Tax Items					
from Sale					
Unamortized Fee					−40960
Prepayment Penalty					−23878
Excess Accum. PAL					0
Ordinary Income Tax					18155
BTCF from Reversion					1154865
less Ordinary Income Tax					18155
Capital Gain Tax					−223800
ATCF from Reversion					949219

Notes:

PAI   Passive activity income
PAL   Passive activity
PALL   Passive activity loss limit

cash flows and then determine the net present value. This will determine whether or not the project should be undertaken.

DATE	ATCF	
0	−262478	equity contribution at start of project
1	−390719	equity contribution at completion of construction
2	50949	operations
3	66386	"
4	76946	"
5	86806	"
6	1047910	operations and sale

Using a required rate of return of 13% gives a NPV of $75,300, indicating that the project's benefits exceed its costs. Therefore, the project should be undertaken. The project IRR is 15.8%.

SUMMARY

In this chapter we presented a detailed case study of how to apply the real estate investment process. We analyzed each of the various components involved in making the investment decision.

Applying the process requires analysis of various options and assumptions available to the investor. To understand the complexity of decision making, it is necessary to work all the numerical calculations. We encourage you to try your skill by working the problems at the end of this chapter.

QUESTIONS

14-1. What are the elements of developing an investment strategy?

14-2. In the case study, the first item the investor does is specify an investment objective. Why is this important?

14-3. In the case study, the analysis of the market environment is given careful consideration. In the real world, this is frequently overlooked. What are the dangers of neglecting this aspect of real estate investing?

14-4. In the case study, what other issues might be raised under the sociopolitical analysis?

14-5. In the case study, results are presented from the income and expense analysis, the financing choices, and the tax-planning decisions. Do you think the options chosen are reasonable? Why or why not?

14-6. In the case study, three scenarios are shown: most likely, optimistic, and pessimistic forecasts. What is the purpose of this presentation? How can the results help to make better investment decisions?

14-7. In the case study, the results of the rules-of-thumb calculations and appraisal methods are presented. What can you conclude from these calculations?

14-8. In the case study, the discounted cash flow models are analyzed. What do the results indicate for the investment under consideration?

14-9. Should the project be accepted as analyzed in this chapter? Why or why not?

14-10. What changes in assumptions and inputs might be interesting to improve the attractiveness of the investment?

PROBLEMS

14-1. Using Table 14-2, explain how the following were calculated:
   a. Price per apartment
   b. Price per room

    c. Price per square foot

    d. Operating expense ratio

    e. Vacancy rate

    What, in your opinion, is the best unit of comparison for this example?

14-2. What would happen to the expected equity rate of return if the investor decided to use 100 percent equity in the most likely case?

14-3. What would happen in the case study if acquisition costs were accounted for in the example?

14-4. Suppose the investor had the choice of debt financing assumed in the chapter on the following:

Mortgage amount	$375,000
Interest rate	12.5%
Maturity	25 years/monthly payments
Financing costs	2%
Prepayment penalty	None

Which is the optimal choice?

14-5. Suppose the investor's marginal tax rate is not expected to be constant over the holding period. How would this be taken into account in the example?

15

REAL ESTATE
INVESTMENT DECISION
MAKING: AN OVERVIEW

The literature on real estate investments has expanded rapidly during the past twenty years.[1] Since the publication of Wendt and Cerf's book in 1969,[2] which developed the discounted cash flow model for real estate on an after-tax basis, scores of articles and studies have been provided by academics, practitioners, and laymen. Real estate has continued to fascinate many people as an investment vehicle and has enjoyed widespread popularity as a method of achieving financial success.[3] In addition, numerous journals have come into existence as a further indication of the maturing and growing interest of real estate as a developing discipline.

In this chapter we summarize the area of real estate investment analysis by highlighting our view of "what is known" and "what is unknown" about real estate investing. Although we have restricted our list to five points in each category in the interests of brevity, it is certainly true that the study of real estate has provided more than five principles of use to investors. Similarly, there are many more unanswered questions than the representative sample provided here. In the final section of this book we discuss the future of real estate investment analysis from our perspective today.

[1] See Austin J. Jaffe and C. F. Sirmans, *Real Estate Investment Decision Making* (Englewood Cliffs, N.J.: Prentice-Hall, Inc., 1982), for a detailed review of the history of real estate investment analysis.

[2] See Paul F. Wendt and Alan B. Cerf, *Real Estate Investment Analysis and Taxation* (New York: McGraw-Hill, 1969).

[3] As a testimonial, consider the fact that several books of the how-to-get-rich genre continue to make the best-selling list each year.

THE FIVE PRINCIPLES OF REAL ESTATE
INVESTMENT DECISION MAKING

1. *Real estate investment analysis is a systematic type of economic analysis.* *Investing* has been defined as the process in which an analyst decides to forgo or sacrifice known or certain resources for expected but uncertain potential benefits. The investor has economic incentive to identify all the factors that are likely to affect the investment in the future and decide how influential these factors will be. In addition, the investor has incentive to rank each potential investment according to its attractiveness to him or her as an investment vehicle. Finally, the investor has incentive to revise original estimates of parameter values in response to changes in the investment environment or changes in his or her perspective or economic position.

Note that these required steps force the investor to carefully evaluate the relationship of the project to the environment. As a result, the investor is likely to be worse off by carelessly selecting a real estate project at random or by failing to consider the impact of a change in the institutional arrangement within which the project is located. Therefore the investor will ensure that his or her decisions are the best possible by systematically evaluating the choices available at every point in time. One elaborate paradigm to accomplish this task has been outlined in Chapter 1 and serves as the basis for this book: the *real estate investment process*. Implicit in this approach is the belief that real estate investors can benefit from a careful and critical analysis of the economic factors that affect the investment. This is consistent with the belief that high returns are more readily available to investors through economic analysis than they are by luck or an ability to "pick the winners." Those attributes would be tremendous attributes to have as real estate investors. Unfortunately, few of us can count on luck and ESP to make money.

2. *Risk and return are closely related.* Theoretically, there is little doubt about the relationship between expected risk and expected return. If these two factors were not strongly positively related, investors would act such that the market prices of competing investments would change until they were. If one investment offered higher returns and lower levels of risk than other investments, every investor would attempt to buy the high-return, low-risk investment. Since such demand for the investment would bring pressure to the price, it is likely the price of the investment would rise. In subsequent periods, the expected rate of return would fall, since a higher acquisition price would be required.

Similarly, the market prices of other investments would fall, as few investors would find these investments attractive relative to the first investment. It may be that more individuals would enter the market (if we have been talking about a subset of possible investors), but they, too, would prefer the other investment to the remaining several.

The basic principles that underscore the positive relationship between risk and return are the notion of investor risk aversion and the opportunity for economic returns through arbitrage. *Risk aversion* refers to the belief that investors will demand high returns for high levels of risk. If high returns are not expected, they will seek other investments with lower levels of risk for the same level of return, or low returns in compensation for lower levels of risk undertaken by the investor.

Risk aversion implies that an investor will insist on an added amount of return if he or she is forced to bear added risk, since the presumption is that less risk is preferred to more and that high returns are preferred to low returns. *Arbitrage* is a term that describes an economic process in markets where participants will act in the interest of wealth maximization to exploit market opportunities without risk. Such opportunities arise as a result of market inefficiencies, inside information, or for other reasons. In all cases, arbitrage opportunities imply a violation of the risk and return relationship. As a result, investors will always accept arbitrage opportunities in real estate markets because, by definition, there is no risk and some expected return.

3. *The goal of wealth maximization will ensure the optimal set of investments.* One of the most widely debated topics in the popular business literature is the question of what is the appropriate goal or objective of the investor. One of the more intuitive notions advocated by many real estate writers is that investors should adopt several investment goals, based on personal preferences, needs, and special objectives. We have argued that the basic objective of the equity investor in real estate "should" be to maximize the value of the equity position. This objective is identical with what has been called the "goal of wealth maximization" earlier in the book.

If there are conflicting investment goals, the problem the investor faces becomes one of optimization (i.e., optimize the economic returns, given the two or more conflicting goals). While this is possible, it can become unnecessarily cumbersome, since it may be difficult to specify all the objectives for a multi-goaled investor.

However, if the investor can accept the goal of wealth maximization as a desirable goal, there are likely to be several benefits. For example, the investor can then proceed to accept any real estate investment that maximizes the value of the equity claim on the investment. This means the investor can be confident that any investment chosen will be expected to increase his or her wealth as much as or more than any other project available at the time. If wealth maximization is chosen as the investment goal, the investor can be confident that all the benefits associated with the investment—such as income, leverage gains, and growth in property values—will be taken into account *if* and *only if* the method used by the analyst is robust enough to account for these factors. If not, the method is defective, not the investment goal. Finally, if the goal of wealth maximization is satisfactory, the investor can be confident with the use of a single method if the method proves to be consistent with the goal.

Fortunately, there is a well-known method that achieves these desires. The net present value method is ideal, since it gives the investor estimates of how much the equity position would increase (or decrease) by accepting the investment. If the investor ranks potential investments by this calculation and chooses those with the highest net present values, he or she can be assured that no other set of investments will provide a greater increase to his or her wealth position. In addition, the model developed in Chapter 12 was all-inclusive in that it analyzed income, vacancies and bad debts, operating expenses, financing expenses, depreciation, growth in property values, amortization, and settlement of the mortgage at the time of sale. In addition, it permitted an evaluation of the time value of money. As a result, the calculation of the net present value of equity contained all the items most investors believe are fundamental to selecting the best real estate investment projects. Finally, if the investor uses the model developed in Chapter 12 and wealth maximization is accepted as the appropriate investor goal, no other investment method, technique, or model is required. More emphatically, no other investment approach is even useful.

4. *The analysis of the institutional environment of real estate is essential.* There are two major points of departure for the financial analysis of real estate compared with the financial analysis of any other enterprise or asset. The first is that real estate values are determined not only by their physical location vis-à-vis other real estate down the block and in the same neighborhood but also in relationship to the urban area. There is no doubt that location affects the value and hence the analysis of real estate as much as or more than any other attribute. In addition, the distance from choice economic property is also an important variable. It affects the economic rent the location commands, the clientele interested in the real estate, and the likely infrastructure surrounding the asset.

The second reason for the unique characteristics of real estate investment analysis is the set of real estate institutions affecting the real estate participants. These institutions have been categorized in this book in terms of their environments: market, legal, financing, and taxation. Real estate investments have specialized environments in each category. Society has long treated land and improvements on the land differently from other assets.

Because real estate values are based on their unique locations and institutions, the analysis of real estate is fundamentally an analysis of the value of locations and institutions. In this sense, real estate investment decision making requires critical analyses of the economic relationship between specific parcels of land and their location and an understanding of the environments that have been created by forces in society to use, direct, and maintain the asset called real estate.

5. *Real estate investment analysis is risk analysis.* During the past few years, many people have learned how to "do the numbers" when analyzing real estate investments. Indeed a careful reading of this book will enable you to join the club of evaluating investment projects by systematically representing the important attributes of real estate in an organized process. The good news is that this approach is better than several others. The bad news is that investment analysis is far more difficult in real life.

If successful investing in real estate were as simple as calculating a few numbers and choosing the largest one, everyone would be rich as an investor. The difficulty comes about in deciding on which of the attractive projects is likely to pay off. In other words, the *risk* associated with investment is fundamental to an analysis of which investment is more attractive than the others. Since risk analysis is so fundamental, it follows that the investor with the most sophisticated real estate computer software is unlikely to be more successful than numerous competing investors *if* he or she fails to evaluate risk. As a result, risk analysis is what real estate investment analysis is all about. Those who are superior in identifying and measuring risk are likely to be those who make the most money as real estate investors. Those who neglect risk are likely to earn the same returns as everyone else, including those who never calculate anything but the interest earned on their passbook savings account at their local bank.

THE FIVE UNRESOLVED ISSUES OF REAL ESTATE INVESTMENT DECISION MAKING

1. *How efficient are real estate markets?* This is an important question because the answer determines the type and method of analysis for investors. If studies can show that real estate markets are relatively efficient in the sense that market prices reflect available public information about the bundle of rights for sale, then investors will be unlikely to earn superior returns in general by investing in real estate, even if the real estate is "well located" or "is expected to yield a positive cash flow" or "is expected to sell for three times what the investor would pay for it in eight to ten years." If the market prices out these expectations quickly and accurately, "news" to the investor is of little benefit in an attempt to outperform the market.

On the other hand, if valuable information is slow to affect market prices, investors may be able to identify properties for sale with positive net present values and take advantage of others in the market. In effect, if market prices are not efficient, there will be violations of the risk-return relationship and, therefore, opportunities for abnormal returns to accrue to the investor. If inefficient markets prevail, it suggests that superior returns to real estate may be likely for investors who take advantage of the mispricing.

The notion of market efficiency is well known in much of the real estate literature. However, considerable confusion exists regarding what the efficient market hypothesis (EMH) means for investors. Some have argued that the EMH suggests that all real estate investments must be efficiently priced. Others have presumed that the EMH implies that abnormally high rates of return are not possible in any real estate investment. Still others seem to believe that advocates of the EMH are unaware that many well-known and not-so-well-known individuals have made fortunes by investing in real estate.

None of these arguments imply that the EMH is incorrect or useless. In each case, there is a defect in the application of the EMH to the experience in real estate markets. For instance, the EMH suggests that in the absence of insider information, there is no reason to believe that systematically higher returns would accrue to one individual over another unless the market mechanism was precluded. If so, high returns could accrue to investors relative to risk. If not, the typical investor would probably earn a typical rate of return, the market rate of return.

The important point is that the EMH is a mere, albeit important, hypothesis. What has not been resolved is the degree of market efficiency that characterizes real estate markets. This question can only be resolved empirically (i.e., by looking at the specific numbers). At present, we know little about the degree of efficiency in real estate markets.

In the future, it seems likely that more empirical tests of the degree of efficiency in many types of real estate markets will be performed. This will be valuable for practitioners, researchers, and investors. Once the issue of market efficiency can be resolved, these parties can know how valuable fundamental analysis is, how rapidly decisions must be made in light of new information, and how useful the EMH ultimately is, not so much as a predictor of real estate investment outcomes, but as a basic approach to the real estate investment problem.

2. *Why do investors like real estate as an investment vehicle?* This question is not nearly as easy to answer as it would appear. According to most observers and social commentators, investors have traditionally favored real estate for investment purposes. The interesting question is why is this so, given well-established markets and some of the disadvantages associated with the ownership of real estate.

Some of the answers are unsatisfactory on a theoretical level. For example, such answers as "land is fixed in nature," "improvements on the land are long-lived and durable," or "individuals need space as population expands" are clearly not acceptable reasons for real estate as a favored investment vehicle. As long as competing investors are aware of these factors, including current owners of real estate and subsequent sellers of the asset, the prices charged for ownership interests are likely to reflect these characteristics. It is only when the "market" does not perceive the attribute such that only a few parties in the market are aware of a certain characteristic is it likely that real estate investments will be preferred, since the returns associated with these assets are likely to be higher for a given level of risk.

It is difficult, indeed, to determine why real estate is so highly favored. Perhaps market prices are slow to reflect information and, as a result, investors make money if they are early into the market and sell it to a later entrant. Perhaps real estate investors are confident that social policy will always favor real estate and are really in the market for government subsidies. Perhaps investors can delineate themselves into narrow tax clienteles, given the progressive nature of the federal tax system and the complex nature of tax calculations. Whatever the reason, we are at this time unable to explain why real estate is such a preferred investment form. After all, if we could, then this would truly be valuable information for all investors in all markets!

3. *What affects net operating income?* Every textbook on real estate investment analysis (including this one) as well as every textbook on market value appraising devotes a considerable amount of space to the market analysis. This area is generally recognized as essential in the modern analysis of real estate valuation. The problem is that the linkages between the microeconomic activities in the marketplace and the impact on the individual investment are simply unknown.

Some analysts devote considerable effort in trying to identify keys to effective and successful investments by examining the market environments where successful investments have been made. While this "case approach" is useful as a teaching device and is often interesting, it is not always successful in identifying what the functional relationship is between, for example, the growth in census population and the market rent of a two-bedroom apartment. It is this type of relationship that would be extremely useful when making income estimates for new investments or income projections for future years of the investment.

It has been argued that if students of markets actually knew how markets worked, such functional relationships could be designed and verified through empirical testing. It is fair to say that despite a considerable amount of interest in this area, few studies, if any, have satisfactorily provided many of the linkages we need. The linkages exist; it is up to students and researchers of the future to identify and discover them.

4. *How sensitive are investments to changes in financing and tax policy?* In other words, this question asks, If changes in financing and/or tax policies are critical to real estate investment decision making, how sensitive are investment projects to such changes? For example, if the method of calculating depreciation allowances is changed by Congress as was recently done again in 1986, what is the likely impact on the market for real estate investments?

While numerous studies have shown the direction of the change in policy as a result of new programs, the estimate of the magnitude of the change is a particularly difficult problem. However, the issue is critical for investors as well as policy makers. If the change in policy is expected to have a dramatic impact but, in actuality, the impact is minimal, the effectiveness of the policy is brought into question. On the other hand, if the change in policy is expected to have a minimal impact but the impact is dramatic, the policy may do considerable harm. Clearly, the magnitude of the change in social policy is an issue of serious consequence.

5. *Is there a future for real estate and portfolio analysis?* This question is currently of interest to corporate asset managers, pension fund managers, real estate investment trust officers, and life insurance real estate managers. The move toward portfolio approaches to real estate asset management over the past several years has been phenomenal and well documented. Institutional investors are now becoming interested in real estate in record numbers. The professional real estate investment communities are seriously looking at real estate as an institutional vehicle instead of only as a vehicle for small-equity investors.

These developments are interesting because the next few years will require continued reevaluation of real estate investment approaches and methods as a result of different types of investors and different forms of ownership. But, in addition, investors are likely to move toward the analysis of real estate returns in a portfolio context. In other words, the evaluation of real estate projects will not be a function of the valuation of the asset in isolation, but rather in how the real estate asset fits into the portfolio. In technical terms, the measurement of risk will be based not on how this asset's cash flows *vary* over time compared with other available investments, but rather how the inclusion of this asset's cash flows affects the portfolio's risk by measuring how this asset's cash flows *co-vary* with other investments' assets in the existing portfolio.

It seems that the time for real estate portfolio theory has finally arrived. Banks are building portfolio models for real estate holdings. Insurance companies are trying to develop models to evaluate portfolio risk. Pension funds are actively seeking professional advisers to build portfolio selection models. The market for real estate consultants is alive and well again, as it was during the late 1970s. However, the fundamental question remains unanswered, that is, Given the difficulty in identifying similar attributes across several types of real estate projects, how likely is it that real estate portfolio models can be operationally used to measure risk? Most of the existing models that have been developed and tested in securities markets are limited in their applicability as a result of necessary restrictive assumptions. In the case of real estate markets, the assumptions are more difficult to make.

Some researchers have reached the conclusion that real estate portfolio analysis is still far away and that it will only be feasible when data sources are much better or when markets are less localized and information is more readily available for nationwide investors. At least for the next several years, the valuation of real estate is likely to remain a single-asset analysis.

THE FUTURE OF REAL ESTATE INVESTMENT DECISION MAKING

What can we expect in the future? There are several developments currently under way that point the path of the future. First, an increasingly large number of investors are becoming interested in real estate as an investment. These typically come from the ranks of the professional investment community as opposed to the individual investors with limited or no training or experience in the area. This change is likely to result in more resources being devoted to research in real estate and more funds being allocated to real estate investments from the large corporations in the United States and Canada.

Second, it seems that the future will require an increasing amount of financial expertise in the area of real estate investment decision making. This means that not only computerized real estate investment analysis but also increasingly higher levels of financial analysis will be required for students seeking entry-level positions and for consultants seeking work with financial institutions. If the past several years have witnessed several developments of "real estate as a numbers game," the next several years are likely to witness "real estate as financial analysis."

Third, it seems unlikely that the environment in which real estate financial decisions are made will become less complex. In the areas of legal and tax policy, the relationship between real estate and the rest of the environment is becoming more and more complicated. In the area of financing, real estate has enjoyed an explosion in development and creative new instruments. As a result, the institutions that affect real estate are becoming more and more distinctive.

Finally, the prospects for the future in providing opportunities for success as an investor remain favorable. However, increased competition and higher standards of analysis are likely to transform real estate investment analysis into a much more specialized activity than it already is. For some, this is welcome news because it will enable them to try out their new sets of technologies and training. For others, it implies that making money in real estate will become that much more difficult. To be sure, the future is likely to be different from the past. In the area of real estate investing, this is almost a certainty.

SELECTED REFERENCE

JAFFE, AUSTIN J., and C. F. SIRMANS, "The Theory and Evidence on Real Estate Financial Decisions: A Review of the Issues," *American Real Estate and Urban Economics Association Journal*, 12 (Fall 1984), 378–400.

APPENDIX A: REAL ESTATE INVESTMENT TABLES

The tables presented in this appendix are used in making real estate investment decisions. There are four sets of tables:

Table 1—Present Value of $1.00 Factors (Annual)
Table 2—Mortgage Constant (Monthly Payments)
Table 3—Mortgage Constant (Annual Payments)
Table 4—Proportion Outstanding on Mortgages

Table 1 provides the factors for finding the present value of a payment to be made in the future at various rates of discount. Tables 2 and 3 provide the mortgage constant factors for monthly and annual payments, respectively. The mortgage constant, when multiplied by the amount borrowed, tells the investor the payment necessary to fully amortize the loan. Table 4 contains the proportion outstanding on mortgages at various interest rates, mortgage maturities, and holding periods.

TABLE 1   Present Value of $1 Factors (Annual)

	INTEREST RATE						
YEARS	7.00%	7.25%	7.50%	7.75%	8.00%	8.25%	YEARS
1	.93458	.93240	.93023	.92807	.92593	.92379	1
2	.87344	.86937	.86533	.86132	.85734	.85338	2
3	.81630	.81060	.80496	.79937	.79383	.78835	3
4	.76290	.75581	.74880	.74188	.73503	.72826	4
5	.71299	.70472	.69656	.68852	.68058	.67276	5
6	.66634	.65708	.64796	.63899	.63017	.62149	6
7	.62275	.61266	.60275	.59303	.58349	.57412	7
8	.58201	.57124	.56070	.55038	.54027	.53037	8
9	.54393	.53263	.52158	.51079	.50025	.48995	9
10	.50835	.49662	.48519	.47405	.46319	.45261	10
11	.47509	.46305	.45134	.43996	.42888	.41811	11
12	.44401	.43175	.41985	.40831	.39711	.38625	12
13	.41496	.40256	.39056	.37894	.36770	.35681	13
14	.38782	.37535	.36331	.35169	.34046	.32962	14
15	.36245	.34998	.33797	.32639	.31524	.30450	15
16	.33874	.32632	.31439	.30292	.29189	.28129	16
17	.31657	.30426	.29245	.28113	.27027	.25985	17
18	.29586	.28369	.27205	.26091	.25025	.24005	18
19	.27651	.26452	.23507	.24214	.23171	.22175	19
20	.25842	.24664	.23541	.22473	.21455	.20485	20
21	.24151	.22996	.21899	.20856	.19866	.18924	21
22	.22571	.21442	.20371	.19356	.18394	.17482	22
23	.21095	.19992	.18950	.17964	.17032	.16150	23
24	.19715	.18641	.17628	.16672	.15770	.14919	24
25	.18425	.17381	.16398	.15473	.14602	.13782	25
26	.17220	.16206	.15254	.14351	.13520	.12731	26
27	.16093	.15110	.14190	.13327	.12519	.11761	27
28	.15040	.14089	.13200	.12369	.11591	.10865	28
29	.14056	.13137	.12279	.11479	.10733	.10037	29
30	.13137	.12248	.11422	.10653	.09938	.09272	30
31	.12277	.11421	.10625	.09887	.09202	.08565	31
32	.11474	.10648	.09884	.09176	.08520	.07912	32
33	.10723	.09929	.09194	.08516	.07889	.07309	33
34	.10022	.09258	.08553	.07903	.07305	.06752	34
35	.09366	.08632	.07956	.07335	.06763	.06238	35
40	.06678	.06083	.05542	.05050	.04603	.04197	40
45	.04762	.04287	.03860	.03477	.03133	.02823	45
50	.03395	.03021	.02689	.02394	.02132	.01899	50

TABLE 1   Present Value of $1 Factors (Annual)

			INTEREST RATE				
YEARS	8.50%	8.75%	9.00%	9.25%	9.50%	9.75%	YEARS
1	.92166	.91954	.91743	.91533	.91324	.91116	1
2	.84946	.84555	.84168	.83783	.83401	.83022	2
3	.78291	.77752	.77218	.76690	.76165	.75646	3
4	.72157	.71496	.70843	.70196	.69557	.68926	4
5	.66505	.65744	.64993	.64253	.63523	.62803	5
6	.61295	.60454	.59627	.58813	.58012	.57223	6
7	.56493	.55590	.54703	.53833	.52979	.52140	7
8	.52067	.51117	.50187	.49275	.48382	.47508	8
9	.47988	.47004	.46043	.45103	.44185	.43287	9
10	.44229	.43222	.42241	.41284	.40351	.39442	10
11	.40764	.39745	.38753	.37789	.36851	.35938	11
12	.37570	.36547	.35553	.34589	.33654	.32745	12
13	.34627	.33606	.32618	.31661	.30734	.29836	13
14	.31914	.30902	.29925	.28980	.28067	.27186	14
15	.29414	.28416	.27454	.26526	.25632	.24770	15
16	.27110	.26130	.25187	.24281	.23409	.22570	16
17	.24986	.24027	.23107	.22225	.21378	.20565	17
18	.23028	.22094	.21199	.20343	.19523	.18738	18
19	.21224	.20316	.19449	.18621	.17829	.17073	19
20	.19562	.18682	.17843	.17044	.16282	.15556	20
21	.18029	.17179	.16370	.15601	.14870	.14174	21
22	.16617	.15796	.15018	.14280	.13580	.12915	22
23	.15315	.14525	.13778	.13071	.12402	.11768	23
24	.14115	.13357	.12640	.11964	.11326	.10722	24
25	.13009	.12282	.11597	.10951	.10343	.09770	25
26	.11990	.11294	.10639	.10024	.09446	.08902	26
27	.11051	.10385	.09761	.09175	.08626	.08111	27
28	.10185	.09550	.08955	.08399	.07878	.07391	28
29	.09387	.08781	.08215	.07687	.07194	.06734	29
30	.08652	.08075	.07537	.07037	.06570	.06136	30
31	.07974	.07425	.06915	.06441	.06000	.05591	31
32	.07349	.06828	.06344	.05895	.05480	.05094	32
33	.06774	.06278	.05820	.05396	.05004	.04641	33
34	.06243	.05773	.05339	.04939	.04570	.04229	34
35	.05754	.05309	.04899	.04521	.04174	.03853	35
40	.03827	.03490	.03184	.02905	.02651	.02420	40
45	.02545	.02295	.02069	.01867	.01684	.01520	45
50	.01692	.01509	.01345	.01199	.01070	.00955	50

TABLE 1   Present Value of $1 Factors (Annual)

| | INTEREST RATE | | | | | | |
YEARS	10.00%	10.25%	10.50%	10.75%	11.00%	11.25%	YEARS
1	.90909	.90703	.90498	.90294	.90090	.89888	1
2	.82645	.82270	.81898	.81529	.81162	.80798	2
3	.75131	.74622	.74116	.73615	.73119	.72627	3
4	.68301	.67684	.67073	.66470	.65873	.65283	4
5	.62092	.61391	.60700	.60018	.59345	.58681	5
6	.56447	.55684	.54932	.54192	.53464	.52747	6
7	.51316	.50507	.49712	.48932	.48166	.47413	7
8	.46651	.45811	.44989	.44183	.43393	.42619	8
9	.42410	.41552	.40714	.39894	.39092	.38309	9
10	.38554	.37689	.36845	.36022	.35218	.34435	10
11	.35049	.34185	.33344	.32525	.31728	.30953	11
12	.31863	.31007	.30175	.29368	.28584	.27823	12
13	.28966	.28124	.27308	.26517	.25751	.25009	13
14	.26333	.25509	.24713	.23944	.23199	.22480	14
15	.23939	.23138	.22365	.21619	.20900	.20207	15
16	.21763	.20989	.20240	.19521	.18829	.18164	16
17	.19784	.19036	.18316	.17626	.16963	.16327	17
18	.17986	.17266	.16576	.15915	.15282	.14676	18
19	.16351	.15661	.15001	.14370	.13768	.13192	19
20	.14864	.14205	.13575	.12976	.12403	.11858	20
21	.13513	.12884	.12285	.11716	.11174	.10659	21
22	.12285	.11686	.11118	.10579	.10067	.09581	22
23	.11168	.10600	.10062	.09552	.09069	.08612	23
24	.10153	.09614	.09106	.08625	.08170	.07741	24
25	.09230	.08720	.08240	.07788	.07361	.06958	25
26	.08391	.07910	.07457	.07032	.06631	.06255	26
27	.07628	.07174	.06749	.06349	.05974	.05622	27
28	.06934	.06507	.06107	.05733	.05382	.05054	28
29	.06304	.05902	.05527	.05176	.04849	.04543	29
30	.05731	.05354	.05002	.04674	.04368	.04083	30
31	.05210	.04856	.04527	.04220	.03935	.03670	31
32	.04736	.04404	.04096	.03811	.03545	.03299	32
33	.04306	.03995	.03707	.03441	.03194	.02966	33
34	.03914	.03624	.03355	.03107	.02878	.02666	34
35	.03558	.03287	.03036	.02805	.02592	.02396	35
40	.02209	.02018	.01843	.01684	.01538	.01406	40
45	.01372	.01239	.01119	.01011	.00913	.00825	45
50	.00852	.00760	.00679	.00607	.00542	.00484	50

TABLE 1   **Present Value of $1 Factors (Annual)**

	INTEREST RATE						
YEARS	11.50%	11.75%	12.00%	12.50%	13.00%	13.50%	YEARS
1	.89686	.89486	.89286	.88889	.88496	.88106	1
2	.80436	.80077	.79719	.79012	.78315	.77626	2
3	.72140	.71657	.71178	.70233	.69305	.68393	3
4	.64699	.64122	.63552	.62430	.61332	.60258	4
5	.58026	.57380	.56743	.55493	.54276	.53091	5
6	.52042	.51347	.50663	.49327	.48032	.46772	6
7	.46674	.45948	.45235	.43846	.42506	.41213	7
8	.41860	.41117	.40388	.38974	.37616	.36311	8
9	.37543	.36794	.36061	.34644	.33288	.31992	9
10	.33671	.32925	.32197	.30795	.29459	.28187	10
11	.30198	.29463	.28748	.27373	.26070	.24834	11
12	.27083	.26365	.25668	.24332	.23071	.21880	12
13	.24290	.23593	.22917	.21628	.20416	.19278	13
14	.21785	.21112	.20462	.19225	.18068	.16985	14
15	.19538	.18892	.18270	.17089	.15989	.14964	15
16	.17523	.16906	.16312	.15190	.14150	.13185	16
17	.15715	.15128	.14564	.13502	.12522	.11616	17
18	.14095	.13538	.13004	.12002	.11081	.10245	18
19	.12641	.12114	.11611	.10668	.09806	.09017	19
20	.11337	.10841	.10367	.09483	.08678	.07945	20
21	.10168	.09701	.09256	.08429	.07680	.07000	21
22	.09119	.08681	.08264	.07493	.06796	.06167	22
23	.08179	.07768	.07379	.06660	.06014	.05434	23
24	.07335	.06951	.06588	.05920	.05323	.04787	24
25	.06579	.06220	.05882	.05262	.04710	.04219	25
26	.05900	.05566	.05252	.04678	.04168	.03716	26
27	.05291	.04981	.04689	.04158	.03689	.03274	27
28	.04746	.04457	.04187	.03696	.03264	.02885	28
29	.04256	.03989	.03738	.03285	.02889	.02542	29
30	.03817	.03569	.03338	.02920	.02557	.02239	30
31	.03424	.03194	.02980	.02596	.02263	.01973	31
32	.03070	.02858	.02661	.02308	.02002	.01738	32
33	.02754	.02558	.02376	.02051	.01772	.01532	33
34	.02470	.02289	.02121	.01823	.01568	.01349	34
35	.02215	.02048	.01894	.01621	.01388	.01189	35
40	.01285	.01175	.01075	.00899	.00753	.00631	40
45	.00746	.00674	.00610	.00499	.00409	.00335	45
50	.00433	.00387	.00346	.00277	.00222	.00178	50

TABLE 1 Present Value of $1 Factors (Annual)

	INTEREST RATE						
YEARS	14.00%	14.50%	15.00%	15.50%	16.00%	16.50%	YEARS
1	.87720	.87336	.86957	.86580	.86207	.85837	1
2	.76947	.76276	.75614	.74961	.74316	.73680	2
3	.67497	.66617	.65752	.64901	.64066	.63244	3
4	.59208	.58181	.57175	.56192	.55229	.54287	4
5	.51937	.50813	.49718	.48651	.47611	.46598	5
6	.45559	.44378	.43233	.42122	.41044	.39999	6
7	.39964	.38758	.37594	.36469	.35384	.34334	7
8	.35056	.33850	.32690	.31576	.30503	.29471	8
9	.30751	.29563	.28426	.27338	.26295	.25297	9
10	.26974	.25819	.24718	.23669	.22668	.21714	10
11	.23662	.22550	.21494	.20493	.19542	.18639	11
12	.20756	.19694	.18691	.17743	.16846	.15999	12
13	.18207	.17200	.16253	.15362	.14523	.13733	13
14	.15971	.15022	.14133	.13300	.12520	.11788	14
15	.14010	.13120	.12289	.11515	.10793	.10118	15
16	.12289	.11458	.10686	.09970	.09304	.08685	16
17	.10780	.10007	.09293	.08632	.08021	.07455	17
18	.09456	.08740	.08081	.07474	.06914	.06399	18
19	.08295	.07633	.07027	.06471	.05961	.05493	19
20	.07276	.06667	.06110	.05602	.05139	.04716	20
21	.06323	.05822	.05313	.04850	.04430	.04047	21
22	.05599	.05055	.04620	.04199	.03819	.03474	22
23	.04911	.04441	.04017	.03636	.03292	.02981	23
24	.04308	.03879	.03493	.03148	.02838	.02560	24
25	.03779	.03387	.03038	.02726	.02447	.02197	25
26	.03315	.02958	.02642	.02360	.02109	.01886	26
27	.02908	.02594	.02298	.02043	.01818	.01619	27
28	.02551	.02257	.01997	.01769	.01567	.01390	28
29	.02237	.01971	.01737	.01532	.01351	.01193	29
30	.01963	.01721	.01510	.01327	.01165	.01024	30
31	.01722	.01503	.01313	.01148	.01004	.00879	31
32	.01510	.01313	.01142	.00995	.00866	.00754	32
33	.01325	.01147	.00993	.00861	.00746	.00648	33
34	.01162	.01001	.00864	.00745	.00643	.00556	34
35	.01019	.00875	.00751	.00645	.00555	.00477	35
40	.00529	.00444	.00373	.00314	.00264	.00222	40
45	.00275	.00226	.00186	.00153	.00126	.00107	45
50	.00143	.00115	.00092	.00074	.00060	.00048	50

TABLE 1   Present Value of $1 Factors (Annual)

| | INTEREST RATE | | | | | | |
YEARS	17.00%	18.00%	19.00%	20.00%	21.00%	22.00%	YEARS
1	.85470	.84746	.84034	.83333	.82645	.81967	1
2	.73051	.71818	.70616	.69444	.68301	.67186	2
3	.62437	.60863	.59342	.57874	.56447	.55071	3
4	.53365	.51579	.49867	.48225	.46651	.45140	4
5	.45611	.43711	.41905	.40188	.38554	.37000	5
6	.38984	.37043	.35214	.33490	.31863	.30328	6
7	.33320	.31393	.29592	.27908	.26333	.23859	7
8	.28478	.26604	.24868	.23257	.21763	.20376	8
9	.24340	.22546	.20897	.19381	.17986	.16702	9
10	.20804	.19106	.17560	.16151	.14864	.13690	10
11	.17782	.16192	.14757	.13459	.12285	.11221	11
12	.15197	.13722	.12400	.11216	.10153	.09198	12
13	.12989	.11629	.10421	.09346	.08391	.07539	13
14	.11102	.09854	.08757	.07789	.06934	.06180	14
15	.09489	.08352	.07359	.06491	.05731	.05065	15
16	.08110	.07078	.06184	.05409	.04736	.04152	16
17	.06932	.05998	.05196	.04507	.03914	.03403	17
18	.05925	.05083	.04367	.03756	.03235	.02789	18
19	.05064	.04308	.03670	.03130	.02673	.02286	19
20	.04328	.03651	.03084	.02608	.02209	.01874	20
21	.03699	.03094	.02591	.02174	.01826	.01536	21
22	.03162	.02622	.02178	.01811	.01509	.01259	22
23	.02702	.02222	.01829	.01509	.01247	.01032	23
24	.02310	.01883	.01538	.01258	.01031	.00846	24
25	.01974	.01596	.01292	.01048	.00852	.00693	25
26	.01687	.01352	.01086	.00874	.00704	.00568	26
27	.01442	.01146	.00912	.00728	.00582	.00466	27
28	.01233	.00971	.00767	.00607	.00481	.00382	28
29	.01053	.00823	.00644	.00506	.00397	.00313	29
30	.00900	.00697	.00541	.00421	.00328	.00257	30
31	.00770	.00591	.00455	.00351	.00271	.00210	31
32	.00658	.00501	.00382	.00293	.00224	.00172	32
33	.00562	.00425	.00321	.00244	.00185	.00141	33
34	.00480	.00360	.00270	.00203	.00153	.00116	34
35	.00411	.00305	.00227	.00169	.00127	.00095	35
40	.00187	.00133	.00095	.00068	.00049	.00035	40
45	.00085	.00058	.00040	.00027	.00019	.00013	45
50	.00039	.00025	.00017	.00011	.00007	.00005	50

TABLE 1   Present Value of $1 Factors (Annual)

			INTEREST RATE				
YEARS	23.00%	24.00%	25.00%	26.00%	28.00%	30.00%	YEARS
1	.81301	.80645	.80000	.79365	.78125	.76923	1
2	.66098	.65036	.64000	.62988	.61035	.59172	2
3	.53738	.52449	.51200	.49991	.47684	.45517	3
4	.43690	.42297	.40960	.39675	.37253	.35013	4
5	.35520	.34111	.32768	.31488	.29104	.26933	5
6	.28878	.27509	.26214	.24991	.22737	.20718	6
7	.23478	.22184	.20972	.19834	.17764	.15937	7
8	.19088	.17890	.16777	.15741	.13878	.12259	8
9	.15519	.14228	.13422	.12493	.10842	.09480	9
10	.12617	.11635	.10737	.09915	.08470	.07254	10
11	.10258	.09383	.08590	.07869	.06617	.05580	11
12	.08339	.07567	.06872	.06245	.05170	.04292	12
13	.06781	.06103	.05498	.04957	.04039	.03302	13
14	.05512	.04921	.04398	.03934	.03155	.02540	14
15	.04481	.03969	.03518	.03122	.02465	.01954	15
16	.03643	.03201	.02815	.02478	.01926	.01503	16
17	.02962	.02581	.02252	.01967	.01505	.01156	17
18	.02408	.02082	.01801	.01561	.01175	.00889	18
19	.01958	.01679	.01441	.01239	.00918	.00684	19
20	.01592	.01354	.01153	.00983	.00717	.00526	20
21	.01294	.01092	.00922	.00780	.00561	.00405	21
22	.01052	.00880	.00738	.00619	.00438	.00311	22
23	.00855	.00710	.00590	.00491	.00342	.00239	23
24	.00695	.00573	.00472	.00390	.00267	.00184	24
25	.00565	.00462	.00378	.00310	.00209	.00142	25
26	.00460	.00372	.00302	.00246	.00163	.00109	26
27	.00374	.00300	.00242	.00195	.00127	.00084	27
28	.00304	.00242	.00193	.00155	.00100	.00065	28
29	.00247	.00195	.00155	.00123	.00078	.00050	29
30	.00201	.00158	.00124	.00097	.00061	.00038	30
31	.00163	.00127	.00099	.00077	.00047	.00029	31
32	.00133	.00102	.00079	.00061	.00037	.00023	32
33	.00108	.00083	.00063	.00049	.00028	.00017	33
34	.00088	.00067	.00051	.00039	.00023	.00013	34
35	.00071	.00054	.00041	.00031	.00018	.00010	35
40	.00025	.00018	.00013	.00010	.00005	.00003	40
45	.00009	.00006	.00004	.00003	.00001	.00001	45
50	.00003	.00002	.00001	.00001	.00000	.00000	50

TABLE 2 Mortgage Constant (Monthly Payments)

			INTEREST RATE				
YEARS	7.00%	7.25%	7.50%	7.75%	8.00%	8.25%	YEARS
1	.08653	.08664	.08676	.08687	.08699	.08710	1
2	.04477	.04489	.04500	.04511	.04523	.04534	2
3	.03088	.03099	.03111	.03122	.03134	.03145	3
4	.02395	.02406	.02418	.02430	.02441	.02453	4
5	.01980	.01992	.02004	.02016	.02028	.02040	5
6	.01705	.01717	.01729	.01741	.01753	.01766	6
7	.01509	.01522	.01534	.01546	.01560	.01571	7
8	.01363	.01376	.01388	.01401	.01414	.01426	8
9	.01251	.01263	.01276	.01289	.01302	.01315	9
10	.01161	.01174	.01187	.01200	.01213	.01227	10
11	.01088	.01102	.01115	.01128	.01142	.01155	11
12	.01028	.01042	.01055	.01069	.01082	.01096	12
13	.00978	.00992	.01005	.01019	.01033	.01047	13
14	.00935	.00949	.00963	.00977	.00991	.01006	14
15	.00899	.00913	.00927	.00941	.00956	.00970	15
16	.00867	.00881	.00896	.00910	.00925	.00940	16
17	.00840	.00854	.00869	.00883	.00898	.00913	17
18	.00816	.00830	.00845	.00860	.00875	.00890	18
19	.00794	.00809	.00824	.00839	.00855	.00870	19
20	.00775	.00790	.00806	.00821	.00836	.00862	20
21	.00758	.00774	.00789	.00805	.00820	.00836	21
22	.00743	.00759	.00775	.00790	.00806	.00822	22
23	.00730	.00746	.00761	.00777	.00793	.00810	23
24	.00718	.00734	.00750	.00766	.00782	.00798	24
25	.00707	.00723	.00739	.00755	.00772	.00788	25
26	.00697	.00713	.00729	.00746	.00763	.00779	26
27	.00688	.00704	.00721	.00737	.00754	.00771	27
28	.00680	.00696	.00713	.00730	.00747	.00764	28
29	.00672	.00689	.00706	.00730	.00740	.00757	29
30	.00665	.00682	.00699	.00716	.00734	.00751	30
31	.00659	.00676	.00693	.00711	.00728	.00746	31
32	.00653	.00671	.00688	.00705	.00723	.00741	32
33	.00648	.00665	.00683	.00701	.00718	.00736	33
34	.00643	.00661	.00678	.00696	.00714	.00732	34
35	.00639	.00656	.00674	.00692	.00710	.00728	35
40	.00621	.00640	.00648	.00677	.00695	.00714	40
45	.00610	.00628	.00647	.00666	.00686	.00705	45
50	.00602	.00621	.00640	.00660	.00679	.00699	50

TABLE 2   Mortgage Constant (Monthly Payments)

| | INTEREST RATE | | | | | | |
YEARS	8.50%	8.75%	9.00%	9.25%	9.50%	9.75%	YEARS
1	.08722	.08734	.08745	.08757	.08768	.08780	1
2	.04546	.04557	.04568	.04580	.04591	.04603	2
3	.03157	.03168	.03180	.03192	.03203	.03215	3
4	.02465	.02477	.02488	.02500	.02512	.02524	4
5	.02052	.02064	.02076	.02088	.02100	.02112	5
6	.01778	.01790	.01803	.01845	.01827	.01840	6
7	.01584	.01596	.01609	.01622	.01634	.01647	7
8	.01439	.01452	.01465	.10478	.01491	.01504	8
9	.01328	.01341	.01354	.01368	.01381	.01394	9
10	.01240	.01253	.01267	.01280	.01294	.01308	10
11	.01169	.01182	.01196	.01210	.01224	.01238	11
12	.01110	.01124	.01138	.01152	.01166	.01181	12
13	.01061	.01075	.01090	.01104	.01119	.01133	13
14	.01020	.01034	.01049	.10164	.01078	.01093	14
15	.00985	.00999	.01014	.01029	.01044	.01059	15
16	.00954	.00969	.00985	.01000	.01015	.01030	16
17	.00928	.00943	.00959	.00974	.00990	.01005	17
18	.00905	.00921	.00936	.00952	.00968	.00984	18
19	.00885	.00901	.00917	.00933	.00949	.00965	19
20	.00868	.00884	.00900	.00916	.00932	.00949	20
21	.00852	.00868	.00885	.00901	.00917	.00934	21
22	.00838	.00855	.00871	.00888	.00904	.00921	22
23	.00826	.00823	.00859	.00876	.00893	.00910	23
24	.00815	.00832	.00849	.00866	.00883	.00900	24
25	.00805	.00822	.00839	.00856	.00874	.00891	25
26	.00796	.00813	.00831	.00848	.00866	.00883	26
27	.00788	.00807	.00823	.00841	.00858	.00876	27
28	.00781	.00799	.00816	.00834	.00852	.00870	28
29	.00775	.00792	.00810	.00828	.00846	.00864	29
30	.00769	.00787	.00805	.00823	.00841	.00859	30
31	.00764	.00782	.00800	.00818	.00836	.00855	31
32	.00759	.00777	.00795	.00813	.00832	.00851	32
33	.00754	.00773	.00791	.00810	.00828	.00847	33
34	.00750	.00769	.00787	.00806	.00825	.00845	34
35	.00747	.00765	.00784	.00803	.00822	.00841	35
40	.00733	.00752	.00771	.00791	.00810	.00830	40
45	.00724	.00744	.00764	.00783	.00803	.00823	45
50	.00719	.00739	.00759	.00779	.00799	.00819	50

TABLE 2 Mortgage Constant (Monthly Payments)

			INTEREST RATE				
YEARS	10.00%	10.25%	10.50%	10.75%	11.00%	11.25%	YEARS
1	.08792	.08803	.08815	.08827	.08838	.08850	1
2	.04614	.04626	.04638	.04649	.04661	.04672	2
3	.03227	.03238	.03250	.03262	.03774	.03286	3
4	.02536	.02548	.02560	.02572	.02585	.02597	4
5	.02125	.02137	.02149	.02162	.02174	.02187	5
6	.01853	.01865	.01878	.01891	.01903	.01916	6
7	.01660	.01673	.01686	.01699	.01712	.01725	7
8	.01517	.01531	.01544	.01557	.01571	.01584	8
9	.01408	.01421	.01435	.01449	.01468	.01476	9
10	.01322	.01335	.01349	.01363	.01378	.01392	10
11	.01252	.01266	.01280	.01295	.01309	.01324	11
12	.01195	.01210	.01224	.01239	.01254	.01268	12
13	.01148	.01163	.01178	.01192	.01208	.01223	13
14	.01108	.01123	.01138	.01154	.01169	.01185	14
15	.01075	.01090	.01105	.01121	.01137	.01152	15
16	.01046	.01062	.01077	.01093	.01109	.01125	16
17	.01021	.01037	.01053	.01069	.01085	.01102	17
18	.01000	.01016	.01032	.01049	.01065	.01082	18
19	.00981	.00998	.01014	.01031	.01047	.01064	19
20	.00965	.00982	.00998	.01015	.01032	.01049	20
21	.00951	.00968	.00985	.01002	.01019	.01036	21
22	.00938	.00955	.00973	.00990	.01007	.01025	22
23	.00927	.00944	.00969	.00979	.00997	.01015	23
24	.00917	.00935	.00952	.00970	.00988	.01006	24
25	.00909	.00926	.00944	.00962	.00980	.00998	25
26	.00901	.00919	.00937	.00955	.00973	.00991	26
27	.00894	.00912	.00930	.00949	.00967	.00985	27
28	.00888	.00906	.00925	.00943	.00961	.00980	28
29	.00882	.00901	.00919	.00938	.00957	.00975	29
30	.00878	.00896	.00915	.00933	.00952	.00971	30
31	.00873	.00892	.00911	.00930	.00948	.00968	31
32	.00869	.00888	.00907	.00926	.00945	.00964	32
33	.00866	.00885	.00904	.00923	.00942	.00961	33
34	.00863	.00882	.00901	.00920	.00939	.00959	34
35	.00860	.00879	.00898	.00918	.00937	.00956	35
40	.00849	.00869	.00889	.00908	.00928	.00948	40
45	.00843	.00863	.00883	.00903	.00923	.00944	45
50	.00839	.00859	.00880	.00900	.00921	.00941	50

TABLE 2 Mortgage Constant (Monthly Payments)

	INTEREST RATE						
YEARS	11.50%	11.75%	12.00%	12.50%	13.00%	13.50%	YEARS
1	.08862	.08873	.08885	.08908	.08932	.08955	1
2	.04684	.04696	.04707	.04731	.04754	.04778	2
3	.03298	.03310	.03321	.03346	.03369	.03394	3
4	.02609	.02621	.02633	.02658	.02683	.02708	4
5	.02199	.02212	.02224	.02250	.02275	.02301	5
6	.01929	.01942	.01955	.01981	.02007	.02034	6
7	.01739	.01752	.01765	.01792	.01819	.01846	7
8	.01598	.01612	.01625	.01653	.01681	.01709	8
9	.01490	.01504	.01518	.01547	.01575	.01604	9
10	.01406	.01420	.01435	.01464	.01493	.01523	10
11	.01338	.01353	.01368	.01398	.01428	.01458	11
12	.01283	.01297	.01313	.01344	.01375	.01406	12
13	.01238	.01253	.01269	.01300	.01331	.01363	13
14	.01200	.01216	.01231	.01263	.01295	.01328	14
15	.01168	.01184	.01200	.01233	.01265	.01298	15
16	.01141	.01157	.01179	.01207	.01240	.01274	16
17	.01118	.01135	.01151	.01185	.01219	.01253	17
18	.01098	.01115	.01132	.01166	.01200	.01235	18
19	.01081	.01098	.01115	.01150	.01150	.01220	19
20	.01066	.01084	.01101	.01136	.01172	.01207	20
21	.01054	.01071	.01089	.01124	.01160	.01196	21
22	.01042	.01060	.01078	.01114	.01150	.01187	22
23	.01033	.01051	.01069	.01105	.01142	.01789	23
24	.01024	.01042	.01060	.01097	.01134	.01172	24
25	.01016	.01035	.01053	.01090	.01128	.01166	25
26	.01010	.01028	.01047	.01084	.01122	.01160	26
27	.01004	.01023	.01041	.01079	.01117	.01156	27
28	.00999	.01018	.01037	.01075	.01113	.01152	28
29	.00994	.01013	.01032	.01071	.01109	.01148	29
30	.00990	.01009	.01029	.01067	.01106	.01145	30
31	.00987	.01006	.01025	.01064	.01103	.01143	31
32	.00984	.01003	.01022	.01061	.01101	.01141	32
33	.00981	.01000	.01020	.01059	.01099	.01139	33
34	.00978	.00998	.01018	.01057	.01097	.01137	34
35	.00976	.00996	.01016	.01055	.01095	.01135	35
40	.00968	.00988	.01008	.01049	.01090	.01130	40
45	.00964	.00984	.01005	.01046	.01087	.01128	45
50	.00961	.00982	.01002	.01044	.01085	.01126	50

TABLE 2   **Mortgage Constant (Monthly Payments)**

	INTEREST RATE						
YEARS	14.00%	14.50%	15.00%	15.50%	16.00%	16.50%	YEARS
1	.08979	.09002	.09026	.09049	.09073	.09097	1
2	.04801	.04825	.04849	.04872	.04896	.04920	2
3	.03418	.03442	.03467	.03491	.03516	.03540	3
4	.02733	.02758	.02783	.02808	.02834	.02860	4
5	.02327	.02353	.02379	.02405	.02432	.02458	5
6	.02061	.02087	.02115	.02142	.02169	.02197	6
7	.01874	.01902	.01930	.01958	.01986	.02015	7
8	.01737	.01766	.01795	.01824	.01853	.01883	8
9	.01633	.01663	.01692	.01722	.01753	.01783	9
10	.01553	.01583	.01613	.01644	.01675	.01706	10
11	.01489	.01520	.01551	.01582	.01614	.01646	11
12	.01437	.01469	.01501	.01533	.01566	.01599	12
13	.01395	.01428	.01460	.01493	.01527	.01560	13
14	.01360	.01394	.01427	.01461	.01495	.01529	14
15	.01332	.01366	.01400	.01434	.01469	.01504	15
16	.01308	.01342	.01377	.01412	.01447	.01483	16
17	.01287	.01322	.01358	.01394	.01429	.01465	17
18	.01270	.01306	.01342	.01378	.01414	.01451	18
19	.01256	.01292	.01328	.01365	.01402	.01439	19
20	.01244	.01280	.01317	.01354	.01391	.01429	20
21	.01233	.01270	.01307	.01345	.01382	.01420	21
22	.01224	.01261	.01299	.01337	.01375	.01413	22
23	.01216	.01254	.01292	.01330	.01369	.01407	23
24	.01210	.01248	.01286	.01325	.01363	.01403	24
25	.01204	.01242	.01281	.01320	.01359	.01398	25
26	.01199	.01238	.01276	.01316	.01355	.01395	26
27	.01195	.01234	.01273	.01312	.01352	.01392	27
28	.01191	.01230	.01270	.01309	.01349	.01389	28
29	.01188	.01227	.01267	.01307	.01347	.01387	29
30	.01185	.01225	.01264	.01305	.01345	.01385	30
31	.01182	.01222	.01262	.01302	.01343	.01384	31
32	.01180	.01220	.01261	.01301	.01342	.01382	32
33	.01179	.01219	.01259	.01300	.01340	.01381	33
34	.01177	.01217	.01258	.01299	.01339	.01381	34
35	.01176	.01216	.01257	.01298	.01338	.01379	35
40	.01171	.01212	.01253	.01294	.01336	.01377	40
45	.01169	.01210	.01252	.01293	.01334	.01376	45
50	.01168	.01209	.01251	.01292	.01334	.01375	50

TABLE 2   Mortgage Constant (Monthly Payments)

YEARS	17.00%	17.50%	18.00%	18.50%	19.00%	19.50%	YEARS
			INTEREST RATE				
1	.09120	.09144	.09168	.09192	.09216	.09240	1
2	.04944	.04968	.04992	.05017	.05041	.05065	2
3	.03565	.03590	.03615	.03640	.03666	.03691	3
4	.02886	.02911	.02937	.02964	.02990	.03016	4
5	.02485	.02512	.02539	.02567	.02594	.02622	5
6	.02225	.02253	.02280	.02309	.02338	.02366	6
7	.02044	.02073	.02102	.02131	.02161	.02191	7
8	.01912	.01942	.01972	.02003	.02033	.02064	8
9	.01814	.01845	.01876	.01907	.01939	.01971	9
10	.01738	.01770	.01802	.01834	.01867	.01900	10
11	.01679	.01711	.01744	.01778	.01811	.01845	11
12	.01632	.01665	.01699	.01733	.01767	.01802	12
13	.01594	.01629	.01663	.01698	.01733	.01768	13
14	.01564	.01599	.01634	.01669	.01705	.01741	14
15	.01539	.01575	.01610	.01647	.01683	.01719	15
16	.01519	.01555	.01591	.01628	.01665	.01702	16
17	.01502	.01539	.01576	.01613	.01650	.01688	17
18	.01488	.01525	.01563	.01600	.01638	.01677	18
19	.01476	.01514	.01552	.01590	.01629	.01667	19
20	.01467	.01505	.01543	.01582	.01621	.01660	20
21	.01459	.01497	.01536	.01575	.01614	.01653	21
22	.01452	.01491	.01530	.01569	.01609	.01648	22
23	.01446	.01486	.01525	.01565	.01604	.01644	23
24	.01442	.01481	.01521	.01561	.01601	.01641	24
25	.01438	.01478	.01517	.01557	.01598	.01638	25
26	.01434	.01474	.01515	.01555	.01595	.01636	26
27	.01432	.01472	.01512	.01553	.01593	.01634	27
28	.01429	.01470	.01510	.01551	.01691	.01632	28
29	.01427	.01468	.01508	.01549	.01590	.01631	29
30	.01426	.01466	.01507	.01548	.01589	.01630	30
31	.01424	.01465	.01506	.01547	.01588	.01629	31
32	.01423	.01464	.01505	.01546	.01587	.01628	32
33	.01422	.01463	.01504	.01545	.01586	.01628	33
34	.01421	.01462	.01503	.01545	.01586	.01627	34
35	.01421	.01462	.01503	.01544	.01585	.01627	35
40	.01418	.01460	.01501	.01543	.01584	.01626	40
45	.01417	.01459	.01500	.01542	.01584	.01625	45
50	.01417	.01459	.01500	.01542	.01583	.01625	50

TABLE 2   Mortgage Constant (Monthly Payments)

			INTEREST RATE				
YEARS	20.00%	20.50%	21.00%	21.50%	22.00%	22.50%	YEARS
1	.09263	.09287	.09311	.09335	.09359	.09384	1
2	.05090	.05114	.05139	.05163	.05188	.05213	2
3	.03716	.03742	.03768	.03793	.03819	.03845	3
4	.03043	.03070	.03097	.03124	.03151	.03178	4
5	.02649	.02677	.02705	.02734	.02762	.02790	5
6	.02395	.02424	.02454	.02483	.02513	.02542	6
7	.02221	.02251	.02281	.02312	.02343	.02374	7
8	.02095	.02127	.02158	.02190	.02222	.02254	8
9	.02003	.02035	.02067	.02100	.02133	.02166	9
10	.01933	.01966	.01999	.02033	.02067	.02101	10
11	.01879	.01913	.01947	.01982	.02017	.02052	11
12	.01837	.01872	.01907	.01942	.01978	.02014	12
13	.01804	.01839	.01875	.01911	.01948	.01984	13
14	.01778	.01814	.01850	.01887	.01924	.01962	14
15	.01756	.01793	.01831	.01868	.01906	.01944	15
16	.01739	.01777	.01815	.01853	.01891	.01930	16
17	.01726	.01764	.01802	.01841	.01880	.01918	17
18	.01715	.01754	.01792	.01831	.01870	.01910	18
19	.01706	.01745	.01784	.01823	.01863	.01903	19
20	.01699	.01738	.01778	.01817	.01857	.01897	20
21	.01693	.01733	.01772	.01812	.01852	.01893	21
22	.01688	.01728	.01768	.01808	.01849	.01889	22
23	.01684	.01724	.01765	.01805	.01846	.01886	23
24	.01681	.01721	.01762	.01802	.01843	.01884	24
25	.01678	.01719	.01760	.01800	.01841	.01882	25
26	.01676	.01717	.01758	.01799	.01840	.01881	26
27	.01675	.01715	.01756	.01797	.01838	.01880	27
28	.01673	.01714	.01755	.01796	.01837	.01879	28
29	.01672	.01713	.01754	.01795	.01837	.01878	29
30	.01671	.01712	.01753	.01795	.01836	.01877	30
31	.01670	.01721	.01753	.01794	.01835	.01877	31
32	.01670	.01711	.01752	.01794	.01835	.01876	32
33	.01669	.01710	.01752	.01793	.01835	.01876	33
34	.01669	.01710	.01751	.01793	.01834	.01876	34
35	.01668	.01710	.01751	.01793	.01834	.01876	35
40	.01667	.01709	.01750	.01792	.01834	.01875	40
45	.01667	.01709	.01750	.01792	.01833	.01875	45
50	.01667	.01708	.01750	.01792	.01833	.01875	50

TABLE 3   Mortgage Constant (Annual Payments)

			INTEREST RATE				
YEARS	7.00%	7.25%	7.50%	7.75%	8.00%	8.25%	YEARS
1	1.07000	1.07250	1.07500	1.07750	1.08000	1.08250	1
2	.55309	.55501	.55693	.55885	.56077	.56269	2
3	.38105	.38279	.38454	.38628	.38803	.38979	3
4	.29523	.29690	.29857	.30024	.30192	.30360	4
5	.24389	.24553	.24716	.24881	.25046	.25211	5
6	.20980	.21142	.21304	.21468	.21632	.21796	6
7	.18555	.18717	.18880	.19043	.19207	.19372	7
8	.16747	.16909	.17073	.17237	.17401	.17567	8
9	.15349	.15512	.15677	.15842	.16008	.16175	9
10	.14238	.14403	.14569	.14735	.14903	.15071	10
11	.13336	.13502	.13670	.13838	.14008	.14178	11
12	.12590	.12759	.12928	.13098	.13270	.13442	12
13	.11965	.12135	.12306	.12479	.12652	.12827	13
14	.11434	.11607	.11780	.11954	.12130	.12306	14
15	.10979	.11154	.11329	.11505	.11683	.11862	15
16	.10586	.10762	.10939	.11118	.11298	.11479	16
17	.10243	.10421	.10600	.10781	.10963	.11146	17
18	.09941	.10121	.10303	.10486	.10670	.10856	18
19	.09675	.09857	.10041	.10226	.10413	.10601	19
20	.09439	.09624	.09809	.09997	.10185	.10275	20
21	.09229	.09415	.09603	.09792	.09983	.10176	21
22	.09041	.09229	.09419	.09610	.09803	.09998	22
23	.08871	.09062	.09254	.09447	.09642	.09839	23
24	.08719	.08911	.09105	.09301	.09498	.09697	24
25	.08581	.08775	.08971	.09169	.08368	.09569	25
26	.08456	.08652	.08850	.09050	.09251	.09454	26
27	.08343	.08541	.08740	.08942	.09145	.09350	27
28	.08239	.08439	.08641	.08844	.09049	.09256	28
29	.08145	.08346	.08550	.08755	.08962	.09170	29
30	.08059	.08262	.08467	.08674	.08883	.09093	30
31	.07980	.08185	.08392	.08600	.08811	.09023	31
32	.07907	.08114	.08323	.08533	.08745	.08959	32
33	.07841	.08049	.08259	.08471	.08635	.08901	33
34	.07780	.07990	.08201	.08415	.08630	.08847	34
35	.07723	.07935	.08148	.08364	.08580	.08799	35
40	.07501	.07720	.07940	.08162	.08386	.08611	40
45	.07350	.07575	.07801	.08129	.08259	.08490	45
50	.08246	.07476	.07707	.07940	.08174	.08410	50

TABLE 3   Mortgage Constant (Annual Payments)

	INTEREST RATE						
YEARS	8.50%	8.75%	9.00%	9.25%	9.50%	9.75%	YEARS
1	1.08500	1.08750	1.09000	1.09250	1.09500	1.09750	1
2	.56462	.56654	.56847	.57040	.57233	.57426	2
3	.39154	.39330	.39505	.39682	.39858	.40035	3
4	.30529	.30698	.30867	.31036	.31206	.31377	4
5	.25377	.25542	.25709	.25876	.26044	.26212	5
6	.21961	.22126	.22292	.22458	.22625	.22793	6
7	.19537	.19703	.19869	.20036	.20204	.20372	7
8	.17733	.17900	.18067	.18236	.18405	.18574	8
9	.16342	.16511	.16680	.16850	.17020	.17192	9
10	.15241	.15411	.15582	.15754	.15927	.16100	10
11	.14349	.14522	.14695	.14869	.15044	.15220	11
12	.13615	.13790	.13965	.14141	.14319	.14497	12
13	.13002	.13179	.13357	.13535	.13715	.13896	13
14	.12484	.12663	.12843	.13025	.13207	.13390	14
15	.12042	.12223	.12406	.12590	.12774	.12960	15
16	.11661	.11845	.12030	.12216	.12403	.12592	16
17	.11331	.11517	.11705	.11893	.12083	.12274	17
18	.11043	.11232	.11421	.11612	.11805	.11998	18
19	.10790	.10981	.11173	.11367	.11561	.11757	19
20	.10567	.10760	.10955	.11151	.11348	.11546	20
21	.10370	.10565	.10762	.10960	.11159	.11360	21
22	.10194	.10392	.10590	.10791	.10993	.11196	22
23	.10037	.10237	.10438	.10641	.10845	.11050	23
24	.09897	.10099	.10302	.10507	.10713	.10921	24
25	.09771	.09975	.10181	.10388	.10596	.10806	25
26	.09658	.09864	.10072	.10281	.10491	.10703	26
27	.09556	.09764	.09973	.10185	.10397	.10611	27
28	.09464	.09674	.09885	.10098	.10312	.10528	28
29	.09381	.09592	.09806	.10020	.10236	.10454	29
30	.09305	.09519	.09734	.09950	.10168	.10387	30
31	.09237	.09452	.09669	.09887	.10106	.10327	31
32	.09174	.09391	.09610	.09830	.10051	.10275	32
33	.09118	.09336	.09556	.09778	.10000	.10225	33
34	.09066	.09286	.09508	.09731	.09955	.10181	34
35	.09019	.09241	.09464	.09688	.09914	.10141	35
40	.08838	.09056	.09296	.09527	.09759	.09992	40
45	.08722	.08956	.09190	.09426	.09663	.09901	45
50	.08646	.08884	.09123	.09362	.09603	.09844	50

TABLE 3   Mortgage Constant (Annual Payments)

| YEARS | INTEREST RATE | | | | | | YEARS |
	10.00%	10.25%	10.50%	10.75%	11.00%	11.25%	
1	1.10000	1.10250	1.10500	1.10750	1.11000	1.11250	1
2	.57619	.57812	.58006	.58200	.58393	.58587	2
3	.40211	.40389	.40566	.40744	.40921	.41099	3
4	.31547	.31718	.31889	.32061	.32234	.32405	4
5	.26380	.26548	.26718	.26887	.27057	.27227	5
6	.22961	.23129	.23298	.23468	.23638	.23808	6
7	.20541	.20710	.20880	.21050	.21222	.21393	7
8	.18744	.18915	.19087	.19259	.19432	.19606	8
9	.17364	.17537	.17711	.17885	.18060	.18236	9
10	.16275	.16450	.16626	.16803	.16980	.17159	10
11	.15396	.15574	.15752	.15932	.16112	.16293	11
12	.14676	.14857	.15038	.15220	.15403	.15587	12
13	.14078	.14261	.14445	.14629	.14815	.15002	13
14	.13575	.13760	.13947	.14134	.14323	.14512	14
15	.13147	.13336	.13525	.13715	.13907	.14099	15
16	.12782	.12973	.13164	.13358	.13552	.13747	16
17	.12466	.12960	.12854	.13050	.13547	.13445	17
18	.12193	.12389	.12586	.12785	.12984	.13185	18
19	.11955	.12153	.12353	.12554	.12756	.12960	19
20	.11746	.11947	.12149	.12353	.12558	.12763	20
21	.11562	.11766	.11971	.12171	.12384	.12592	21
22	.11401	.11606	.11813	.12022	.12231	.12442	22
23	.11257	.11465	.11675	.11885	.12097	.12310	23
24	.11130	.11340	.11552	.11765	.11979	.12194	24
25	.11017	.11229	.11443	.11658	.11874	.12091	25
26	.10916	.11130	.11346	.11563	.11781	.12001	26
27	.10826	.11042	.11260	.11479	.11699	.11920	27
28	.10745	.10963	.11183	.11404	.11626	.11849	28
29	.10673	.10893	.11114	.11337	.11561	.11785	29
30	.10608	.10830	.11053	.11277	.11502	.11729	30
31	.10550	.10773	.10998	.11224	.11451	.11679	31
32	.10497	.10722	.10948	.11176	.11404	.11634	32
33	.10450	.10677	.10904	.11133	.11363	.11594	33
34	.10407	.10635	.10864	.11095	.11326	.11558	34
35	.10369	.10598	.10829	.11060	.11293	.11526	35
40	.10226	.10461	.10697	.10943	.11172	.11410	40
45	.10139	.10379	.10619	.10860	.11101	.11344	45
50	.10086	.10329	.10572	.10816	.11060	.11305	50

TABLE 3   Mortgage Constant (Annual Payments)

	INTEREST RATE						
YEARS	*11.50%*	*11.75%*	*12.00%*	*12.50%*	*13.00%*	*13.50%*	*YEARS*
1	1.11500	1.11750	1.12000	1.12500	1.13000	1.13500	1
2	.58781	.58976	.59170	.59559	.59948	.60338	2
3	.41278	.41456	.41635	.41993	.42352	.42712	3
4	.32577	.32750	.32923	.33271	.33619	.33969	4
5	.27398	.27569	.27741	.28085	.28431	.28779	5
6	.23979	.24151	.24323	.24668	.25015	.25365	6
7	.21566	.21738	.21912	.22260	.22611	.22964	7
8	.19780	.19955	.20130	.20483	.20838	.21197	8
9	.18413	.18590	.18768	.19126	.19487	.19851	9
10	.17338	.17518	.17698	.18062	.18425	.18799	10
11	.16475	.16658	.16842	.17211	.17584	.17960	11
12	.15771	.15957	.16144	.16519	.16899	.17281	12
13	.15190	.15378	.15568	.15950	.16335	.16724	13
14	.14703	.14895	.15087	.15475	.14413	.16262	14
15	.14292	.14487	.14682	.15076	.15474	.15876	15
16	.13943	.14141	.14339	.14739	.15143	.15550	16
17	.13644	.13844	.14046	.14451	.14861	.15274	17
18	.13387	.13590	.13794	.14205	.14620	.15039	18
19	.13164	.13370	.13576	.13993	.14413	.14838	19
20	.12970	.13179	.13388	.13810	.14235	.14665	20
21	.12802	.13012	.13224	.13651	.14081	.14516	21
22	.12654	.12867	.13081	.13513	.13948	.14387	22
23	.12524	.12740	.12956	.13392	.13832	.14275	23
24	.12410	.12628	.12846	.13287	.13731	.14179	24
25	.12310	.12529	.12750	.13194	.13643	.14095	25
26	.12221	.12443	.12665	.13113	.13565	.14021	26
27	.12143	.12366	.12590	.13042	.13498	.13957	27
28	.12073	.12298	.12524	.12980	.13439	.13901	28
29	.12011	.12238	.12466	.12925	.13387	.13852	29
30	.11956	.12185	.12414	.12876	.13341	.13809	30
31	.11908	.12138	.12369	.12833	.13301	.13772	31
32	.11864	.12096	.12328	.12795	.13266	.13739	32
33	.11826	.12058	.12292	.12762	.13234	.13710	33
34	.11791	.12025	.12260	.12732	.13207	.13685	34
35	.11760	.11996	.12232	.12706	.13185	.13662	35
40	.11650	.11890	.12130	.12535	.13099	.13586	40
45	.11586	.11830	.12074	.12519	.13053	.13545	45
50	.11550	.11796	.12042	.12511	.13024	.13524	50

TABLE 3 **Mortgage Constant (Annual Payments)**

	INTEREST RATE						
YEARS	14.00%	14.50%	15.00%	15.50%	16.00%	16.50%	YEARS
1	1.14000	1.14500	1.15000	1.15500	1.16000	1.16500	1
2	.60729	.61120	.61512	.61904	.62296	.62689	2
3	.43073	.43435	.43798	.44161	.44526	.44891	3
4	.34320	.34673	.35027	.35381	.35738	.36095	4
5	.29128	.29479	.29842	.30185	.30541	.30898	5
6	.25716	.26069	.26424	.26780	.27138	.27499	6
7	.23319	.23677	.24036	.24398	.24761	.25128	7
8	.21557	.21920	.22285	.22653	.23022	.23395	8
9	.20217	.20586	.20957	.21332	.21708	.22087	9
10	.19171	.19547	.19925	.20306	.20690	.21077	10
11	.18339	.18722	.19107	.19495	.19886	.20280	11
12	.17667	.18056	.18448	.18844	.19241	.19648	12
13	.17116	.17512	.17911	.18313	.18718	.19127	13
14	.16661	.17063	.17469	.17878	.18290	.18705	14
15	.16281	.16690	.17102	.17517	.17936	.18357	15
16	.15962	.16376	.16795	.17216	.17641	.18069	16
17	.15692	.16112	.16537	.16964	.17395	.17829	17
18	.15462	.15889	.16319	.16752	.17188	.17628	18
19	.15266	.15698	.16134	.16572	.17014	.17459	19
20	.15099	.15536	.15976	.16420	.16867	.17316	20
21	.14954	.15396	.15842	.16290	.16742	.17196	21
22	.14830	.15277	.15727	.16179	.16636	.17094	22
23	.14723	.15174	.15628	.16085	.16545	.17007	23
24	.14630	.15085	.15543	.16004	.16467	.16933	24
25	.14550	.15008	.15470	.15934	.16401	.16871	25
26	.14480	.14942	.15407	.15875	.16345	.16817	26
27	.14419	.14885	.15353	.15823	.16296	.16772	27
28	.14366	.14834	.15306	.15779	.16255	.16733	28
29	.14320	.14792	.15265	.15741	.16219	.16699	29
30	.14280	.14754	.15230	.15708	.16189	.16671	30
31	.14245	.14721	.15200	.15680	.16162	.16646	31
32	.14215	.14693	.15173	.15656	.16140	.16625	32
33	.14188	.14668	.15150	.15635	.16120	.16608	33
34	.13165	.14647	.15131	.15616	.16104	.16592	34
35	.14144	.14628	.15113	.15601	.16089	.16579	35
40	.14075	.14565	.15056	.15549	.16042	.16537	40
45	.14039	.14533	.15028	.15524	.16020	.16517	45
50	.14020	.14517	.15014	.15512	.16010	.16508	50

TABLE 3   **Mortgage Constant (Annual Payments)**

	INTEREST RATE						
YEARS	*17.00%*	*18.00%*	*19.00%*	*20.00%*	*21.00%*	*22.00%*	*YEARS*
1	1.17000	1.18000	1.19000	1.20000	1.21000	1.22000	1
2	.63083	.63872	.64662	.65455	.66249	.67045	2
3	.45257	.45992	.46731	.47473	.48218	.48966	3
4	.36453	.37174	.37899	.38629	.39363	.40102	4
5	.31256	.31978	.32705	.33438	.34177	.34921	5
6	.27861	.28591	.29327	.30071	.30820	.31576	6
7	.25495	.26236	.26985	.27742	.28507	.29278	7
8	.23769	.24524	.25289	.26061	.26841	.27630	8
9	.22469	.23239	.24019	.24808	.25605	.26411	9
10	.21466	.22251	.23047	.23852	.24667	.25489	10
11	.20676	.21478	.22289	.23110	.23941	.24781	11
12	.20047	.20863	.21690	.22526	.23372	.24228	12
13	.19538	.20369	.21210	.22062	.22923	.23794	13
14	.19123	.19968	.20823	.21689	.22565	.23449	14
15	.18782	.19640	.20509	.21388	.22277	.23174	15
16	.18500	.19371	.20252	.21144	.22044	.22953	16
17	.18266	.19149	.20041	.20944	.21855	.22775	17
18	.18071	.18964	.19868	.20781	.21702	.22631	18
19	.17907	.18810	.19724	.20646	.21577	.22515	19
20	.17769	.18682	.19605	.20536	.21474	.22420	20
21	.17653	.18575	.19505	.20444	.21391	.22343	21
22	.17555	.18485	.19423	.20369	.21322	.22281	22
23	.17472	.18409	.19354	.20307	.21265	.22229	23
24	.17402	.18345	.19297	.20255	.21219	.22188	24
25	.17342	.18292	.19249	.20212	.21180	.22154	25
26	.17292	.18247	.19209	.20176	.21149	.22126	26
27	.17249	.18209	.19175	.20147	.21123	.22103	27
28	.17212	.18177	.19147	.20122	.21101	.22084	28
29	.17180	.18150	.19123	.20102	.21084	.22069	29
30	.17154	.18126	.19103	.20085	.21069	.22057	30
31	.17132	.18107	.19087	.20070	.21057	.22046	31
32	.17113	.18091	.19073	.20059	.21047	.22038	32
33	.17096	.18077	.19061	.20049	.21039	.22031	33
34	.17082	.18065	.19051	.20041	.21032	.22026	34
35	.17070	.18055	.19043	.20034	.21027	.22021	35
40	.17032	.18024	.19018	.20014	.21010	.22008	40
45	.17015	.18010	.19008	.20005	.21004	.22003	45
50	.17007	.18005	.19003	.20002	.21002	.22001	50

TABLE 3 Mortgage Constant (Annual Payments)

	INTEREST RATE						
YEARS	23.00%	24.00%	25.00%	26.00%	28.00%	30.00%	YEARS
1	1.23000	1.24000	1.25000	1.26000	1.28000	1.30000	1
2	.67843	.68643	.69444	.70248	.71860	.73478	2
3	.49717	.50472	.51230	.51990	.53521	.55063	3
4	.40845	.41593	.42344	.43100	.44624	.46163	4
5	.35670	.36425	.37185	.37950	.39495	.41058	5
6	.32339	.33107	.33882	.34662	.36240	.37839	6
7	.30057	.30842	.31634	.32433	.34048	.35688	7
8	.28426	.29229	.30040	.30857	.32512	.34192	8
9	.27225	.28047	.28876	.29712	.31405	.33124	9
10	.26321	.26150	.28007	.28862	.30591	.32346	10
11	.25629	.26485	.27349	.28221	.29984	.31773	11
12	.25093	.25965	.26845	.27732	.29526	.31345	12
13	.24673	.25560	.26454	.27356	.29179	.31024	13
14	.24342	.25243	.26150	.27065	.28912	.30782	14
15	.24079	.24992	.25912	.26848	.28708	.30598	15
16	.23870	.24794	.25724	.26661	.28550	.30458	16
17	.23702	.24636	.25576	.26522	.28428	.30351	17
18	.23568	.24510	.25459	.26412	.28333	.30269	18
19	.23459	.24410	.25366	.26326	.28260	.30207	19
20	.23372	.24329	.25292	.26258	.28202	.30159	20
21	.23302	.24265	.25233	.26204	.28158	.30122	21
22	.23245	.24213	.25186	.26162	.28123	.30094	22
23	.23198	.24172	.25148	.26128	.28096	.30072	23
24	.23161	.24138	.25119	.26102	.28075	.30055	24
25	.23131	.24111	.25095	.26081	.28059	.30043	25
26	.23106	.24090	.25076	.26064	.28046	.30033	26
27	.23086	.24072	.25061	.26051	.28037	.30025	27
28	.23070	.24058	.25048	.26040	.28028	.30019	28
29	.23057	.24047	.25039	.26032	.28032	.30015	29
30	.23046	.24038	.25031	.26025	.28017	.30011	30
31	.23038	.24031	.25025	.26020	.28013	.30009	31
32	.23031	.24025	.25020	.26016	.28010	.30007	32
33	.23025	.24020	.25016	.26013	.28008	.30005	33
34	.23020	.24016	.25013	.26010	.28006	.30004	34
35	.23016	.24013	.25010	.26008	.28005	.30003	35
40	.23006	.24004	.25003	.26003	.28001	.30001	40
45	.23002	.24002	.25001	.26001	.28000	.30000	45
50	.27001	.24001	.25000	.26000	.28000	.30000	50

TABLE 3 Proportion Outstanding on Mortgages with Monthly Compounding: Various Interest Rates, Mortgage Maturities, and Holding Periods

MORTGAGE MATURITY	HOLDING PERIOD	INTEREST RATE						
		8%	8.25%	8.5%	8.75%	9%	9.25%	9.5%
	1 year	.97886	.97949	.98010	.98069	.98127	.98184	.98239
	2	.95597	.95722	.95844	.95963	.96079	.96192	.96303
	3	.93118	.93304	.93486	.93664	.93838	.94009	.94176
	4	.90433	.90679	.90920	.91156	.91388	.91614	.91837
	5	.87526	.87829	.88127	.88420	.88707	.88989	.89265
20 Years (240 Months)	6	.84377	.84735	.85088	.85434	.85775	.86110	.86439
	7	.80966	.81376	.81779	.82177	.82568	.82953	.83332
	8	.77273	.77729	.78178	.78622	.79060	.79492	.79917
	9	.73273	.73769	.74259	.74744	.75223	.75696	.76163
	10	.68941	.69470	.69994	.70513	.71026	.71534	.72036
	1	.98691	.98742	.98791	.98838	.98884	.98929	.98972
	2	.97293	.97376	.97475	.97571	.97664	.97754	.97841
	3	.95738	.95892	.96043	.96188	.96329	.96466	.96599
	4	.94075	.94282	.94484	.94679	.94869	.95054	.95233
	5	.92274	.92534	.92787	.93033	.93272	.93505	.93731
25 Years (300 Months)	6	.90324	.90636	.90940	.91237	.91526	.91807	.92081
	7	.88211	.88575	.88930	.89277	.89615	.89945	.90266
	8	.85924	.86338	.86743	.87139	.87525	.87903	.88272
	9	.83446	.83909	.84362	.84805	.85239	.85664	.86079
	10	.80763	.81272	.81771	.82260	.82739	.83209	.83669
	1	.99165	.99205	.99244	.99281	.99317	.99351	.99383
	2	.98260	.98342	.98421	.98497	.98570	.98639	.98706
	3	.97280	.97405	.97526	.97641	.97752	.97858	.97960
	4	.96219	.96388	.96551	.96708	.96858	.97003	.97141
	5	.95070	.95284	.95490	.95689	.95880	.96064	.96241
30 Years (360 Months)	6	.93825	.94085	.94336	.94577	.94810	.95035	.95251
	7	.92477	.92783	.93079	.93365	.93640	.93907	.94163
	8	.91018	.91370	.91711	.92041	.92361	.92669	.92967
	9	.89437	.89836	.90223	.90598	.90961	.91313	.91653
	10	.87725	.88170	.88603	.89022	.89430	.89825	.90208

INTEREST RATE (*continued*)								
9.75%	10%	10.25%	10.5%	10.75%	11%	11.25%	11.50%	11.75%
.98293	.98345	.98396	.98446	.98495	.98542	.98558	.98632	.98676
.96412	.96517	.96620	.96721	.96819	.96915	.97008	.97099	.97187
.94339	.94498	.94653	.94806	.94954	.95099	.95241	.95379	.95514
.92054	.92267	.92475	.92679	.92879	.93074	.93265	.93451	.93633
.89537	.89802	.90063	.90319	.90569	.90814	.91054	.91289	.91519
.86762	.87080	.87392	.87698	.87998	.88293	.88582	.88865	.89143
.83705	.84072	.84433	.84788	.85137	.85480	.85816	.86147	.86472
.80336	.80750	.81157	.81558	.81952	.82341	.82723	.83099	.83470
.76624	.77079	.77528	.77971	.78408	.78839	.79264	.79682	.80095
.72533	.73024	.73510	.73990	.74464	.74932	.75394	.75851	.76302
.99013	.99053	.99092	.99129	.99165	.99199	.99232	.99264	.99295
.97925	.98007	.98085	.98161	.98235	.98305	.98374	.98440	.98503
.96727	.96851	.96971	.97087	.97200	.97308	.97413	.97515	.97613
.95406	.95574	.95737	.95895	.96048	.96196	.96339	.96478	.96612
.93951	.94164	.94371	.94571	.94766	.94955	.95138	.95315	.95487
.92347	.92606	.92857	.93102	.93339	.93570	.93794	.94011	.94222
.90579	.90884	.91181	.91470	.91752	.92025	.92291	.92550	.92801
.88632	.88983	.89325	.89659	.89984	.90301	.90610	.90911	.91203
.86485	.86882	.87270	.87648	.88017	.88378	.88730	.89073	.89407
.84120	.84561	.84993	.85415	.85828	.86232	.86627	.87012	.87389
.99414	.99444	.99472	.99499	.99525	.99550	.99573	.99596	.99617
.98769	.98830	.98888	.98944	.98997	.99048	.99096	.99142	.99186
.98058	.98152	.98241	.98327	.98409	.98487	.98562	.98634	.98702
.97274	.97402	.97525	.97642	.97754	.97862	.97965	.98064	.98158
.96411	.96574	.96731	.96822	.97026	.97165	.97297	.97425	.97547
.95459	.95660	.95852	.96038	.96215	.96386	.96551	.96708	.96859
.94411	.94649	.94879	.95100	.95313	.95518	.95715	.95904	.96086
.93255	.93533	.93801	.94060	.94309	.94549	.94781	.95003	.95218
.91982	.92300	.92608	.92905	.93192	.93468	.93736	.93993	.94242
.90579	.90938	.91286	.91622	.91948	.92263	.92567	.92860	.93144

TABLE 3 Proportion Outstanding on Mortgages with Monthly Compounding: Various Interest Rates, Mortgage Maturities, and Holding Periods

MORTGAGE MATURITY	HOLDING PERIOD	INTEREST RATE						
		12%	12.25%	12.5%	12.75%	13%	13.25%	13.5%
	1 year	.98718	.98759	.98799	.98838	.98876	.98912	.98948
	2	.97273	.97357	.97439	.97519	.97596	.97672	.97745
	3	.95646	.95774	.95899	.96021	.96140	.96256	.96369
	4	.93811	.93985	.94155	.94321	.94483	.94641	.94795
	5	.91744	.91965	.92180	.92391	.92597	.92798	.92995
20 Years (240 Months)	6	.89415	.89682	.89944	.90200	.90451	.90696	.90937
	7	.86791	.87104	.87411	.87713	.88008	.88298	.88583
	8	.83834	.84191	.84543	.84889	.85229	.85562	.85890
	9	.80501	.80901	.81296	.81684	.82065	.82441	.82811
	10	.76746	.77185	.77618	.78045	.78466	.78881	.79289
	1	.99325	.99354	.99381	.99408	.99433	.99457	.99481
	2	.98564	.98623	.98680	.98735	.98788	.98838	.98887
	3	.97707	.97799	.97887	.97971	.98053	.98132	.98208
	4	.96741	.96867	.96988	.97105	.97218	.97327	.97432
	5	.95653	.95814	.95970	.96121	.96267	.96407	.96544
25 Years (300 Months)	6	.94427	.94625	.94817	.95004	.95184	.95359	.95528
	7	.93045	.93282	.93512	.93736	.93952	.94163	.94367
	8	.91488	.91765	.92034	.92296	.92551	.92798	.93038
	9	.89733	.90051	.90361	.90662	.90955	.91241	.91519
	10	.87756	.88115	.88465	.88807	.89140	.89465	.89781
	1	.99637	.99656	.99675	.99692	.99709	.99724	.99739
	2	.99228	.99268	.99306	.99343	.99377	.99410	.99441
	3	.98767	.98830	.98889	.98946	.99000	.99051	.99100
	4	.98248	.98334	.98417	.98495	.98570	.98642	.98710
	5	.97663	.97775	.97882	.97984	.98082	.98175	.98264
30 Years (360 Months)	6	.97004	.97143	.97276	.97403	.97526	.97642	.97754
	7	.96261	.96429	.96590	.96744	.96893	.97035	.97171
	8	.95424	.95622	.95813	.95996	.96172	.96341	.96504
	9	.94481	.94711	.94933	.95147	.95353	.95550	.95741
	10	.93418	.93682	.93937	.94183	.94420	.94648	.94868

INTEREST RATE (*continued*)

13.75%	14%	14.25%	14.5%	14.75%	15%	15.25%	15.5%	15.75%	16%
.98983	.99016	.99049	.99081	.99111	.99141	.99170	.99198	.99225	.99252
.97816	.97885	.97953	.98018	.98082	.98144	.98204	.98263	.98319	.98374
.96479	.96586	.96690	.96792	.96891	.96987	.97080	.97171	.97260	.97646
.94946	.95092	.95235	.95375	.95511	.95643	.95773	.95898	.96021	.96140
.93188	.93376	.93559	.93738	.93913	.94084	.94251	.94414	.93572	.94727
.91172	.91402	.91628	.91848	.92064	.92274	.92480	.92681	.92878	.93070
.88861	.89135	.89402	.89665	.89922	.90173	.90420	.90661	.90897	.91128
.86212	.86528	.86838	.87143	.87442	.87735	.88022	.88304	.88580	.88851
.83175	.83533	.83884	.84230	.84570	.84904	.85232	.85555	.83871	.86182
.79692	.80089	.80481	.80866	.81245	.81618	.81986	.82348	.82703	.83054
.99503	.99525	.99546	.99566	.99585	.99604	.99621	.99638	.99654	.99670
.98934	.98979	.99023	.99065	.99105	.99143	.99180	.99216	.99250	.99283
.98282	.98352	.98420	.98486	.98548	.98609	.98667	.98723	.98777	.98829
.97533	.97631	.97726	.97817	.97904	.97989	.98070	.98149	.98224	.98297
.96675	.96803	.96926	.97044	.97159	.97269	.97376	.97479	.97578	.97674
.95692	.95850	.96004	.96152	.96295	.96434	.96568	.96697	.96822	.96943
.94564	.94756	.94941	.95121	.95295	.95464	.95627	.95785	.95938	.96086
.93271	.93498	.93717	.93931	.94138	.94338	.94533	.94721	.94904	.95081
.91789	.92052	.92307	.92556	.92797	.93032	.93259	.93480	.93695	.93904
.90090	.90390	.90683	.90968	.91245	.91515	.91778	.92033	.92282	.92523
.99753	.99767	.99780	.99792	.99803	.99814	.99825	.99834	.99844	.99852
.99471	.99499	.99526	.99551	.99576	.99599	.99620	.99641	.99661	.99679
.99147	.99191	.99234	.99274	.99312	.99348	.99383	.99416	.99447	.99477
.98775	.98837	.98897	.98953	.99007	.99058	.99107	.99153	.99197	.99239
.98349	.98431	.98508	.98583	.98653	.98721	.98785	.98846	.98904	.98960
.97861	.97963	.98061	.98155	.98244	.98329	.98411	.98488	.98563	.98633
.97301	.97426	.97546	.97660	.97770	.97875	.97975	.98071	.98163	.98250
.96659	.96809	.96952	.97090	.97221	.97347	.97468	.97584	.97695	.97801
.95923	.96099	.96268	.96430	.96586	.96735	.96879	.97016	.97148	.97275
.95080	.95284	.95480	.95669	.95850	.96525	.96193	.96354	.96509	.96658

APPENDIX B: USING SPREADSHEETS FOR REAL ESTATE INVESTMENT ANALYSIS

Real estate investment analysis has enjoyed a long history of computerized financial analysis. As long ago as 1974, Dasso noted that there were at least 112 articles written about computerized real estate analysis in actual practice using mainframes and canned software.[1] Now, with the development of microcomputers, a new generation of real estate computer users has arrived. In particular, it was the development of the computerized spreadsheet in the late 1970s that has had a major impact on real estate investment analysis.

There are several advantages of spreadsheets over hand-calculated analyses for real estate investors. These include the ability to perform long sets of mathematical calculations, the rapid speed of computers, accuracy and reliability, extensive storage capabilities, and the very inexpensive cost of processing.[2] Also, spreadsheets are considerably easier to learn and use than any of the other computer software that proceeded them. In effect, once an investor understands the benefits and power of spreadsheets, it is unlikely that the investor will revert to hand calculations again.

This real estate investment book contains numerous calculations. A set of templates has been developed that can be used with Lotus 1-2-3, the best-selling and most widely used spreadsheet program. With the use of this specially

---

[1] See Jerome Dasso, "Computer Applications in Real Estate," *CREUES Real Estate Report*, No. 13. (Storrs, CT: Center for Real Estate and Urban Economic Studies, June 1974).

[2] For more discussion, see Austin J. Jaffe, "Computer Technology and Real Estate Education: Some Observations," *Proceedings of the Real Estate Educators Association Annual Conference* (August 1985), pp. 15–31.

prepared diskette and Lotus 1-2-3, the reader can calculate all of the important analyses found in this book. In fact, use of the diskette may simplify some of the concepts taught in the book, and the investor may be able to concentrate on the investment choices rather than on performing the calculations. If so, this is the real value of computerized real estate investment analysis!

DESCRIPTION OF COMPUTER SOFTWARE

The real estate software that accompanies this book consists of a single diskette. This IBM or 100 percent compatible diskette contains a special file which will automatically welcome you when initially called by Lotus 1-2-3. The introductory file will provide an overview of all of the computerized applications and provide instructions for access and usage. (Written instructions are also provided.)

Each application will have its own menu so that usage, even for computer novices, will be quite easy. It will also be easy to print or graph your results if you have the proper hardware.

There are five applications included in the software. Each is briefly described here:

1. *Present Value* (pv.wk1). This template calculates a detailed table of present value factors for up to several discount rates and for scores of years. The template is automated to provide as large a table as the user indicates based upon only a few required inputs.

2. *Effective Cost of Borrowing* (effcost.wk1). The effective cost of borrowing is calculated for any loan from the borrower's point of view. This template evaluates the impact of several types of mortgage or other loan provisions on the borrower's cost of borrowing, including closing costs, early repayment with and without penalties, prepaid interest, discount points, and mortgage insurance.

3. *After-Tax Financial Analysis* (cashflow.wk1). A complete discounted cash flow analysis is provided for either simple or complex real estate investments. The user can input up to five rental types, three mortgages with prepayment penalties and amortized financing costs, various growth rates, and depreciation and capital gains tax treatment for holding periods up to ten years. This template uses the current tax law following The Tax Reform Act of 1986. Various criteria are also reported, including financial ratios, net present value, and the internal rate of return.

4. *Risk Analysis* (risk.wk1). This template calculates the expected rate of return, the variance, and the standard deviation of return for up to ten

investments. The user is permitted to compare both the expected return for any investment with the expected level of risk. Both risk and return are merged into an analysis that, in most cases, can evaluate which investment is preferred for the wealth-maximizing investor.

5. *Comparable Sales Analysis* (comp.wk1). This template calculates several units of comparison for up to twenty market comparables. It also provides several rules of thumb and uses regression analysis to provide an indicated value for the subject property.

INSTRUCTIONS FOR OBTAINING DISKETTE

The diskette containing the real estate templates is available for $29.95 plus $2 shipping from JS & Associates, Calder Square, P.O. Box 10096, State College, PA 16805. Pennsylvania residents: please add 6 percent sales tax. You will need an IBM or 100 percent compatible computer and Lotus 1-2-3, Release 2.0 or later. Please allow three-to-four weeks for delivery.

INDEX